WOMEN AND SLAVES
IN GRECO-ROMAN CULTURE:
DIFFERENTIAL EQUATIONS

Women and Slaves in Greco-Roman Culture is the first book to critally explore how slaveholding and the subordination of women shaped ancient societies and reveals how women and slaves intersected with one another in both the cultural representations and the social realities of classical antiquity.

The contributors consider a broad range of evidence including the mythical constructions of epic and drama: the love poems of Ovid; the Greek medical writers; Augustine's autobiography; the brief record of an unnamed Roman slave and the archaelogical remains of a slave mining camp near Athens to argue that the distinctions between male and female, servile and free were inextricably connected.

This erudite and well-documented book provokes questions about how we can hope to recapture the experience, and subjectivity, of ancient women and slaves, and addresses the ways in which femaleness and servility interacted with other forms of difference, such as class, gender and status. *Women and Slaves in Greco-Roman Culture* offers stimulating and frequently controversial insight into the complexities of gender and status in the ancient world.

Sandra R. Joshel teaches at the New England Conservatory of Music in Boston. Her previous publications include *Work, Identity, and Legal Status in Rome*. **Sheila Murnaghan** is Associate Professor of Classical Studies, at the University of Pennsylvania. She is the author of *Disguise and Recognition in the Odyssey*, and articles on ancient Greek epic, and drama and gender in classical culture. Her current work is on twentieth century women writers and the classics.

WOMEN AND SLAVES IN GRECO-ROMAN CULTURE

Differential Equations

Edited by
Sandra R. Joshel and
Sheila Murnaghan

London and New York

First published 1998
by Routledge
11 New Fetter Lane, London EC4P 4EE

Simultaneously published in the USA and Canada
by Routledge
29 West 35th Street, New York, NY 10001

First published in paperback 2001

Routledge is an imprint of the Taylor & Francis Group

Typeset in Baskerville by Florence Production Ltd, Stoodleigh, Devon
Printed and bound in Great Britain by
T.J. International Ltd, Padstow, Cornwall

British Library Cataloguing in Publication Data
A catalogue record for this book is available from the British Library

Library of Congress Cataloging in Publication Data
Women and slaves in Greco-Roman culture / edited by
Sandra R. Joshel and Sheila Murnaghan.
Includes bibliographical references and index.
1. Women – Greece – History – To 500. 2. Women – Rome
– History – To 500. 3. Slaves – Greece – History. 4. Slaves –
Rome – History. 5. Women and literature – Greece –
History. 6. Women and literature – Rome – History.
7. Slavery in literature – History. 8. Civilization, Classical.
I. Joshel, Sandra R.
II. Murnaghan, Sheila.
HQ1134.W623 1998
305.4′0938—dc21   97–35631

ISBN 0–415–16229–7 (hbk)
ISBN 0–415–26159–7 (pbk)

To
Amy Richlin
and
Deborah H. Roberts

CONTENTS

CONTENTS

ACKNOWLEDGMENTS

This volume originated in a panel organized by the Women's Classical Caucus at the Annual Meeting of the American Philological Association in Atlanta in December 1994. We want to thank the steering committee of the WCC for its sponsorship of the project, and especially Judith Hallett for suggesting that the two of us should work on it together. In putting the manuscript in final form, we have benefited from the editorial and computer skills of Adam Breindel and from funds supplied by the University of Pennsylvania. We are indebted to Catherine Connors and James A. Klein for their support and advice and to Carlin Barton, Hugh Gordon, Holly Haynes, Amy Richlin, and Brent Shaw for insightful comments on various drafts of our Introduction. We are especially grateful to our contributors for their patience, their openness to discussion, and their intellectual energy. In honor of our rewarding experience as co-editors, we have chosen each to dedicate the book to a friend and scholar with whom we have enjoyed the pleasures of collaboration on other projects.

S.R.J. and S.H.M.

NOTES ON CONTRIBUTORS

Shane Butler is currently a fellow at the American Academy in Rome, where he is completing a dissertation on the written word in the Roman Empire. He is a graduate student at Columbia University.

Patricia A. Clark teaches in the Department of Greek and Roman Studies at the University of Victoria (British Columbia, Canada) and works primarily in the areas of family history, mental illness in antiquity, and ancient medicine.

Joy Connolly is Assistant Professor of Classics at the University of Washington with research interests in feminist theory, ancient education, and Greco-Roman literature of the imperial period. She has recently completed a dissertation on problems of gender, performance, and identity in Roman rhetoric and is currently writing on Roman elegy and Petronius' *Satyricon*.

Nancy Demand is a professor in the Department of History at Indiana University, Bloomington. Her fields of interest are history of medicine, social history, and urban history. In the field of women and medicine she has published *Birth, Death and Motherhood in Classical Greece* (Baltimore 1994); "Monuments, Midwives and Gynaecology," in *Ancient Medicine in its Socio-Cultural Context*, Vol. 1 (1996); and "Medicine and Philosophy: the Attic Orators," in *Proceedings, Xth International Hippocratic Colloquium* (Erlangen 1996). She held an NEH Fellowship for 1990–91.

Steven Johnstone is a social and cultural historian whose work focuses on the fourth century BCE. He is the author of *Disputes and Democracy: The Consequences of Litigation in Ancient Athens*, a study of the social and political effects of litigation in Athens, which will be published by the University of Texas Press in 1999. He teaches Greek History at the University of Arizona.

Sandra R. Joshel teaches at the New England Conservatory of Music. Her research interests focus on women, gender, and slavery in ancient Rome. Her publications include *Work, Identity, and Legal Status at Rome* (Norman, Oklahoma 1992); "The Body Female and the Body Politic: Livy's Lucretia and

Virginia," in *Pornography and Representation in Greece and Rome*, ed. Amy Richlin (New York 1992); "Nurturing the Master's Child: the Roman Child-Nurse," *Signs* 12 (Autumn, 1986). She is currently working on a book on the construction of gendered subjects in imperial narratives.

Kathleen McCarthy is an assistant professor of Classics and Comparative Literature at the University of California at Berkeley. She is currently completing a book on the relations of authority in Plautine comedy.

Denise Eileen McCoskey is an assistant professor of Classics and an affiliate of Black World Studies at Miami University (Ohio). She is working on several projects reflecting her interest in applying contemporary theory about difference, race, and ethnicity to the classical world, including a study of the intersection of femininity and foreignness in the rhetoric of Augustan Rome and an essay entitled "Reading Cleopatra When Race Matters." She was awarded the John J. Winkler Memorial Prize in 1992.

Ian Morris is Professor of Classics and History and Chair of the Classics Department at Stanford University. He has excavated in Greece and Britain, and is currently publishing the Iron Age remains from Lerna. He is the author of *Burial and Ancient Society: The Rise of the Greek City-State* (Cambridge 1987) and *Death-Ritual and Social Structure in Classical Antiquity* (Cambridge 1992). He edited *Classical Greece: Ancient Histories and Modern Archaeologies* (Cambridge 1994), and co-edited *A New Companion to Homer* (Leiden 1997) with Barry Powell and *Democracy 2500?* (Dubuque 1997) with Kurt Raaflaub.

Sheila Murnaghan teaches in the Department of Classical Studies at the University of Pennsylvania. She is the author of *Disguise and Recognition in the Odyssey* (Princeton 1987) and of articles on Greek epic and drama and gender in classical culture. Her current work is on twentieth-century women writers and the classics.

Holt Parker received his Ph.D. from Yale University. He is Associate Professor of Classics at the University of Cincinnati and a fellow of the American Academy in Rome. He has written articles on various topics, including sex, slavery, Sappho, and Sulpicia. He is currently preparing an edition, translation, and commentary on the *Gynecology* by Metrodora, the oldest surviving work by a woman doctor.

Nancy Sorkin Rabinowitz, best known for *Anxiety Veiled: Euripides and the Traffic in Women* (Ithaca 1993) and *Feminist Theory and the Classics* (co-edited with Amy Richlin, New York 1993), has written on a wide variety of topics from Aeschylus to Margaret Drabble. She is currently working on women's relationships to women in Greek vase painting. Professor Rabinowitz teaches Comparative Literature at Hamilton College, Clinton, NY.

Annalisa Rei has been a visiting assistant professor in the Department of Classics at the University of Virginia. She is currently working on a book on female characters in the comedies of Plautus.

Richard Saller is Professor of History and Classics at the University of Chicago with a special interest in Roman social history. His books include *Personal Patronage under the Early Empire* (Cambridge 1982); *Patriarchy, Property and Death in the Roman Family* (Cambridge 1994); and *The Roman Empire: Economy, Society and Culture* (with Peter Garnsey, Berkeley 1987).

William G. Thalmann is Professor of Classics at the University of Southern California. His publications include *Conventions of Form and Thought in Early Greek Epic Poety* (Baltimore 1984); *The Odyssey: An Epic of Return* (New York 1993); and *The Swineherd and the Bow: Representations of Class in the Odyssey* (Ithaca 1998).

1

INTRODUCTION
Differential equations

Sandra R. Joshel and Sheila Murnaghan

Now the female is distinguished by nature from the slave. For nature makes nothing in an economizing spirit . . . but one thing with a view to one thing; and each instrument would perform most finely if it served one task rather than many. The barbarians, though, have the same arrangement for female and slave. The reason for this is that they have no naturally ruling element: with them, the partnership [of man and woman] is that of female slave and male slave. This is why the poets say "it is fitting for Greeks to rule barbarians" – the assumption being that barbarian and slave are the same thing.
Aristotle, Politics 1252b1–9 (Carnes Lord, trans.)

When [Sextus Tarquinius] found [Lucretia] obdurate and not to be moved even by fear of death, he went farther and threatened her with disgrace, saying that when she was dead he would kill his slave and lay him naked by her side, that she might be said to have been put to death in adultery with a man of base condition. At this dreadful prospect her resolute modesty was overcome, as if with force, by his victorious lust; and Tarquinius departed, exulting in his conquest of a woman's honor.
Livy, History of Rome 1.58.4–5 (B.O. Foster, trans.)

In two prominent statements of cultural identity, Aristotle and Livy juxtapose women and slaves to express what it means to be a Greek or a Roman. For Aristotle, society at its most fully evolved is marked by a purposeful differentiation between the female and the slave as two distinct and specialized types of human beings, each falling short of the full virtue of the free man in its own way. The inferiority of barbarians is reflected in their failure to manifest this refinement. Barbarians are all by nature slavish and thus subject to tyrants. Among them, there are no men who are not slaves, and slaves, in their subordination and dependence, are indistinguishable from women. In the absence of freedom, there is also no

1

meaningful distinction between male and female. The categories that articulate the more advanced social structure of the Greeks are blunted, so that a barbarian marriage is simply a union of two slavish beings whose division into male and female is an unimportant detail, rather than the complex dynamic of partnership, specialization, and hierarchy that Aristotle elsewhere describes. One senses that there is something bizarre, even distasteful, to Aristotle's Greek audience about the leveling effect that Aristotle attributes to barbarian marriage.

In Livy's account of the rape of Lucretia, the leveling of female and slave appears, not as a given of barbarian life, but as the condition that the tyrannical king seeks to impose on his Roman subjects. While the tyrant Tarquin enslaves Roman men by forcing their labor, his son Sextus asserts his power by reducing a free woman to the status of a slave. He does this both through the false scenario with which he threatens her – a union that evokes and intensifies the shock value of Aristotle's slavish marriage – and through the real action that he desires and carries out: his use of Lucretia's body for his own pleasure. And yet Lucretia's virtuous identity as a free Roman is not obliterated; her honor remains central to the workings of the narrative. Lucretia's honor is what makes her desirable to Sextus; Livy tells us that he is as much aroused by her evident chastity as by her beauty (*cum forma tum spectata castitas incitat*). Lucretia herself accepts the ordeal of rape so that she can escape the dishonor of appearing to have slept with a slave, and so that she can live long enough to proclaim her violation, providing Roman men with an occasion for overthrowing the tyrant. By rallying to the defense of Lucretia's honor, Brutus and his confederates reassert their own liberty, founding the Roman republic and defining themselves as free citizens rather than Tarquin's slavish subjects. Acting out the terms of Aristotle's analysis, these Roman heroes realize their superiority over their oppressors by defending the distinction between a woman and a slave. At the same time, neither the overthrow of the tyrant nor Lucretia's suicide can undo the fact of her rape, which lives on in Roman memory as evidence that free men and women can be subjected to tyrannical power. The idea of the free person reduced to the status of the slave – so powerful that Sextus can use it to have his way "as if with force" – continually haunts the Roman imagination.

For the Greek philosopher reflecting on contemporary social arrangements and the Roman historian constructing a national past, slaves and women are, in Lévi-Strauss' famous formulation, "good to think with." To define the proper order of society, Aristotle and Livy bring women and slaves together and yet insist on their distinction. In creating images of social dysfunction, they each evoke the specter of a sexual union in which a woman and a slave are undifferentiated and then assert that, among true Greeks or true Romans, this cannot happen. The process illustrated in these passages was repeated throughout the cultures of ancient Greece and Rome, which regularly exploited the similarities and differences of women and slaves to articulate individual and national identities. Classical scholarship, especially of the last three decades, has extensively documented the ways in which the societies of Greco-Roman antiquity were at once slave societies, dependent for their economic and political functioning on various forms of forced labor, and patriarchies, founded on the subordination of women to men (for slavery, see Garlan 1988; Bradley 1984; Finley 1980; for women Pomeroy 1975; Blundell 1995; Gardner 1986; Fantham *et al.* 1994). Building on that scholarship, this volume explicates the symbiosis, both actual and conceptual, between these two constitutive features of ancient society.

Whatever their particular forms, ancient Greek and Roman societies always combined slaveholding and patriarchy, and this combination promoted a constant process of comparison and differentiation. Women and slaves were similarly distinguished from free men by their social subordination and their imagined otherness. Both were excluded from full participation in political life; both occupied an ambiguous position in the patrilocal family as indispensable outsiders; and both were viewed as morally deficient and potentially dangerous. On the other hand, slavery and femaleness – although they could intersect in the person of the female slave – were very different kinds of liability. Unlike femaleness, slavery was not based on anatomical difference (although people could be viewed as naturally servile, most famously by Aristotle at *Politics* 1255a1–3), nor was it necessarily a permanent condition: there was constant mobility from freedom to slavery and slavery to freedom. Unlike slaves, free women were never themselves property; even when their autonomy was highly constrained, they could still enjoy the honor and prerogatives of free status.

The essays in this volume trace this pervasive process of simultaneous assimilation and distinction throughout the Greco-Roman world, encompassing the entire time-span of classical antiquity and drawing on a wide range of evidence – textual and material, high cultural and popular. They show the operation of this process in the mutually reinforcing realms of social practice and cultural representation. They raise questions about whether we can recapture the experience and subjectivity of women and slaves, or whether we can hope to see them only through the screen of their use by free men, whether as human instruments or as representatives of convenient conceptual categories. The essays also address the ways in which femaleness and servility are implicated in and informed by such other categories of difference as age, ethnicity, and class.

Taken together, these essays show how thoroughly the ancient Greeks and Romans relied on the polarities of male/female and free/slave in order to understand themselves and to organize their societies, and they make it clear that these categories achieved their signifying power, not in tandem, but in combination with each other. Gender and slavery are not independent phenomena that operate in parallel ways, but intersecting variables in a process that we have labeled "differential equations" whereby women and slaves are assimilated only to be distinguished, compared but never quite identified. A full understanding of ancient culture requires an awareness that gender and slavery – to borrow the words that Anne McClintock applies to race, class, and gender in the British Empire – "come into existence *in and through* relation to each other" (McClintock 1995, 5). Throughout Greco-Roman culture, the most urgent issues are addressed through the permutations that result when gender and slavery are crossed with one another: the free woman, the female slave, the male slave, the free man.

The essays in this volume show how persistently the analogy of slavery was used to define the position of the free woman in her presumed inferiority and subordination to the free man. Several take as their starting point the shared situation of free wives and slaves as outsiders whose incorporation into the patri-local household was essential to its success (William Thalmann writing on the *Odyssey*; Holt Parker writing on Roman popular tales of loyal subordinates. Introducing her discussion of women and slaves in the Greek medical writers, Nancy Demand points out that, in classical Athens, the shared liminality of women and slaves was reflected in ritual: the same ceremony welcomed new brides and slaves to the household (p. 69). The householder's need to rely on these two types of outsider generated similar anxieties and prejudices: women and slaves were similarly viewed as duplicitous and given to excess in ways that might endanger the person and property of free male citizens. As Patricia Clark demonstrates, Augustine portrays his mother Monnica as herself adopting the comparison: she uses slavery as a model for marriage and servile modes of placating as a paradigm for the appropriate wifely response to male violence (pp. 114–15).

At the same time, as the rape of Lucretia makes clear, the free woman is crucially distinguished from the slave by the honor that comes with her status. Her honor is bound up especially with her chastity, which assures the legitimacy of the next generation and reinforces the honor and authority of her father and husband. Richard Saller's essay on the distinctions that structured the Roman household lays stress on the honor of the free wife, which he locates in Roman naming practice, in the reverence owed by children to their mothers, in the laws of property, and in religious rituals. In Roman ritual, as in Aristotle's philosophy, gender itself distinguishes the freeborn from the slave: in the annual festival of the Compitalia, male and female woolen dolls were hung in the cross-roads for each free member of the household, for each slave an undifferentiated woolen ball, thus distinguishing visually between "those symbolically humanized and gendered, and those dehumanized in form" (p. 88). In the realm of law, Steven Johnstone points out that in classical Athens the legal interests of a citizen woman were acknowledged in limited ways but those of a slave were not (p. 230).

The honor of the free woman was frequently established and fortified through her pointed differentiation from the female slave. The very existence of women who were not free gave meaning to the status of those who were, and the foundation of the free woman's honor on the dishonor of the slave was dramatized in rituals and narratives. The Roman festival of the Matralia honored citizen mothers through the ritual exclusion of slave women from the observances (Saller, 89). In her analysis of the conventions of Roman comedy, Annalisa Rei notes that respectable matrons, unlike female slaves, are never depicted as participating in the deception, role-playing, and rule-breaking that drive comedy's plots (Rei, 94–5). In Homer's *Odyssey*, anxiety about female chastity is displaced from Odysseus' wife Penelope to the female slaves of the household. Penelope remains faithful, while the slave women sleep with Penelope's suitors, thus expressing, as she does not, the female's capacity to undermine the legitimate head of the household (Thalmann, 30–1). The aetiological myth attached to a Roman festival for slave women makes that displacement even plainer (and a source of glory rather than of reproach for the slave women). In the myth, slave women's bodies are actually substituted for those of free women, whose honor is thereby preserved. At a time of military weakness for the Romans, their enemies, the Latins, demand freeborn Roman virgins and widows for wives: acting in a manner reminiscent of Plautus' female slave tricksters, a group of slave women dress up in the clothes of free women and are sent instead; once in the Latin camp, they signal the Romans to attack (Saller, 88–9).

In contexts like comedy and ritual that offer a carnivalesque celebration of slave agency, the relationship between free and slave women is inverted in a way that reveals how much free women were constrained as well as elevated by their honor. These constraints remind us that the social asset of honor may have had different meanings, both positive and negative, for women than for their male relatives. The restrictions on the role of the matron in Plautine drama meant that she was left out of the holiday fun and high spirits of comedy. The slave women who recalled their glorious predecessors at their own festival imitated male heroes by participating in a mock battle: "they strike and throw stones at one another in token that on that earlier day they assisted the Romans and shared with them in their battle" (Plutarch, *Romulus* 29.6, Bernadotte Perrin trans.). A further scenario involving the substitution of the slave woman's body for the free woman's – one in which the female slave protects the free woman from sexual contamination by her own husband – offers unintended testimony of another kind to the possible costs of female honor. Giving advice to a newly married couple, the second-century CE moralist Plutarch charges the bride to accept her husband's sexual relations with a slave woman because he is visiting his "debauchery, licentiousness, and wantonness" on the slave as a mark of "respect" for his legitimate, freeborn wife (Plutarch, *Moralia* 140B; Saller, 89). More grimly, we recall that Lucretia's loss of chastity, even under the circumstances of her coercion by Tarquin, demands her suicide (Livy 1.58.7–12; Joshel 1992b, 124–5).

Male-authored texts often depict free women as defining themselves against female slaves (even as these texts also link free and slave women through their shared inferiority to men). In a speech delivered during a fourth-century BCE Athenian trial, in which a woman is charged with holding herself out as a respectable free citizen when she is actually an ex-slave and former prostitute, the accuser asks the jurors to make their judgment with the responses of their wives and daughters in mind: he conjures up the outrage those women would feel if the defendant should get away with obliterating the distinction between herself and them (Demosthenes 59.114; Johnstone, 233–4). In another such speech, Euphiletus, a husband defending himself against the charge of murdering his wife's lover, claims that his adulterous wife has cleverly exploited the respectable women's antipathy to the slave, slyly accusing her husband of playing around with their female slave. In this account, a woman masquerades as a respectable wife by either inventing or emphasizing a rivalry between herself and her slave; in reality, according to the husband, the wife's respectability is compromised and the slave is her ally, making the baby cry so the wife can escape to meet her lover (Johnstone, 226–7, 229–30).

In her analysis of Aeschylus' *Agamemnon*, Denise McCoskey shows how the powerful queen Clytemnestra goes out of her way to define the captive Trojan priestess Cassandra as a slave, a conquered and powerless barbarian. Clytemnestra shores up her own position by constructing Cassandra as sharply different from herself, ignoring Cassandra's previous condition and denying the similarities between the slave's disempowerment and her own as a woman in her husband's household. When she murders Cassandra along with Agamemnon, Clytemnestra enacts the free woman's distinction from the slave in blood. Yet, as McCoskey also shows, the male playwright ultimately limits the force of Clytemnestra's discriminations; in his own project of portraying her as inferior and subordinate to the male, he endows Clytemnestra, however free and legitimate she may be, with the very qualities that she attributes to Cassandra.

The same positioning of the free woman as superior to the slave but rightly subordinate to the free man can be seen in Roman accounts of matrons who beat their slaves. Like Clytemnestra, these women perform their difference on the bodies of their slaves. As Saller points out, "the application of the whip generally marked slave from free." The numerous known instances of women administering corporal punishment to slaves and children suggest that the "categories of free and slave were more important than hierarchies of gender or generation in determining who whipped whom" (Saller, 90). At the same time, the figure of the savage mistress who whips slaves for trivial reasons or to take out the frustration caused by her husband's dissatisfaction with her is a stereotype of Greek and Roman literature. The role of the woman as the one who does the beating confirms her privileged status and affirms the integrity of her body in contrast to that of the slave; at the same time, the depiction of the free woman's violence against slaves as frequently arbitrary, excessive, and depraved, and as particularly feminine, also operates to distinguish the free woman from the free man and justifies the control of the household by its male head. Doubts about women's ability to punish slaves support the authority of free males to command both women and slaves, serving a slippage between wifely obedience and servitude. Good wives placate their husbands as slaves placate their masters; at the same time, the honor accorded the legitimate wife offers compensation for her subordination and sharply distinguishes the free woman from the slave (Clark, 118–19)

For the female slave, there was no honor to compensate for her subordination to the interests of the master. Unable to reproduce him through the children she bore, she could only add to the master's property. In a single person, the female slave embodied the "double exclusion" (Vidal-Naquet 1986, 188) of women and slaves from the institutions of ancient society and took on a more than double burden of ideological functions. Not only did she guarantee the honor of the free woman through her own dishonor, but she served as a focal point for tensions throughout the hierarchies of both gender and status. As Thalmann points out, the unfaithful slave women of the *Odyssey* figure the potential disloyalty of both women and slaves to their adopted households. In Plautus' *Casina*, a female slave becomes the focus of rivalry between free and unfree as the master and his male slave both attempt to rape the same slave woman. In the story of betrayal and antagonism between husband and wife evoked in Euphiletus' defense speech, a female slave is variously used by both parties. The wife employs the slave woman as her accomplice and as her alleged rival – the supposed source of her own grievance against her husband; the husband turns the slave into his accomplice, using the threat of torture to make her tell him what is happening and then to aid in his revenge. These examples bespeak a constant project of redefining the extreme powerlessness of the female slave in ways that obscure her suffering and make her vulnerability a vehicle for addressing others' concerns. Her sexual vulnerability becomes the occasion for playful comic competition or a source of disruption within the household or a manifestation of female treachery and seductiveness; her liability to physical punishment serves the revelation of truth (in particular the revelation – at once shocking and predictable – of a wife's infidelity).

The complex instrumentality of the female slave is explored in Nancy Rabinowitz's discussion of Euripides' Trojan plays. The doubling of slavery and femaleness in the enslaved figures of those plays allays for the male spectators a "double anxiety around slavery – that Greek men might be enslaved, that they might be attacked by slaves." The femaleness of those characters, along with their foreignness, safely distinguishes them from Greek males, who were themselves at risk of enslavement through war. Furthermore, the dealings of these female slaves with their masters are portrayed through their interactions with free women, with the result that class tensions between slave and free are displaced onto relations that occur exclusively between women and, in the process, neutralized. Thus antagonism between slave and free is recast as sexual competition between free women and and slave women. Conversely, slave women and free women are portrayed as making alliances on the basis of their shared femaleness, which shows that "Greek men have nothing to fear from slaves because they identify along gender lines with not against their owners" (Rabinowitz, 59). This move also exploits the intermediate position of the free woman, who is at once able to represent the interests of the master and to identify with the sorrows of the slave.

Female slaves were also often the focus of tensions between free men or between free women. A number of Athenian lawcourt speeches describe situations in which competition between two citizen males took the form of a dispute over the possession of a slave woman. In Augustine's account of the early married life of his mother Monnica, dissension between Monnica and her mother-in-law is blamed on "malicious" female slaves, who are punished by Monnica's husband. "In effect," comments Patricia Clark, "the potential animosity between a mother-in-law and her new daughter-in-law is denied. Rather, any ill-feeling is projected onto the slave women, who are then beaten. These beatings are the cost of concord between the two free women" (Clark, 116).

The story of Monnica also highlights one of the few roles in which slave women could be seen as legitimately having power – the children's nurse, whose lower status is countered by her relative age. An "aged servant" charged with the care of the master's children instills in the free girl the self-control and submissiveness to her husband appropriate to her future role as a respectable wife. Here the assumption of this important role by a slave is tempered by her advanced age, which removes the possible complications of sexuality and fertility, and by her espousal of the master's values. In describing the old slave's intervention, Augustine draws on the language of statecraft and military command to make her a metaphorical representative of the masculine world she supports (Clark, 111). As Joy Connolly points out, in other texts, such as the first century CE *Rural Life* of Columella, in which the master's reliance on a slave-woman is described, she is similarly converted into an approximation of a good man. The freedom with which these male authors can redescribe slave women as free men is itself a mark of the slave woman's subordination, her availability for use by others, whether actual or symbolic (Connolly, 138–40).

Monnica's story also includes a more disturbing instance of a slave woman's influence. After her marriage, Monnica becomes a closet drinker until she is brought to her senses by the taunting comments of a young slave woman. That she should stand to benefit from such instruction shows how dangerously low she has sunk; this threatened leveling is echoed in the relative closeness in age of mistress and slave (Clark, 112–13). The anxieties about the loss of distinction between mistress and slave that lurk in this episode despite its happy ending are registered in the many Roman texts of the imperial period that develop the stereotype of the bad slave nurse. Her very existence reflects the "decadence of an imperial society that has abandoned the virtues of their ancestors who reared their own children": the men who are supposed to rule foreigners are exposed as ineffective at home, unable to compel free women to fulfill their proper (and male-defined) role. Not surprisingly, the slave nurse manifests the vices of which the freeborn matron is suspected: intemperance, bibulousness, and unchastity (Joshel 1986, 197–9). And, once again, the slave woman is evoked as a means of defining the free woman rather than for herself.

As herself, the slave woman is at once indispensable, an overdetermined representative of the exploitable human being, and impossible, a mixture of two categories that must be kept distinct. Her femaleness is perpetually in conflict with her servility. As a woman, she may spark male concerns about resistance to control, in which case she is disqualified as an instrument, as in the *Odyssey* or in tales of evil nurses. Alternatively, her sexual attractiveness may create situations in which she gains a measure of honor that clashes with her status. As Steven Johnstone shows, in classical Athens, a female slave could aquire gender through her sexual relations with a free man, and this status shift from slave to woman could provoke conflict and even litigation (Johnstone, 231–2). Strikingly, the Roman ritual that recalls slave women's impersonation of free women suppresses their femaleness, preferring to rewrite the original myth by having them play male soldiers.

Like the free woman, the male slave occupies an ambiguous, intermediate position in the social hierarchy. He shares the subordination and social inferiority of the female slave, yet his biological sex differentiates him from all women, free and enslaved. From the point of view of the free man, the male slave's anatomical similarity to his male master makes him an especially troubling figure whose existence challenges the supposedly natural distinction between free and slave. As a consequence, ancient laws, social practices, and popular attitudes worked in various ways to deny the masculinity of the male slave, effacing his confusing distinction from the clearly inferior female. This denial took place within a sex/gender system characterized by the contradictory assumptions that masculinity was at once a fact of nature and "a duty and a hard-won achievement" (Winkler 1990, 50), "grounded in 'nature,' yet . . . fluid and incomplete until firmly anchored by the discipline of an acculturative process" (Gleason 1990, 412). Writing of the widespread practice of using subtle physiognomic traits to identify effeminate men, one scholar notes, "there exist masculine and feminine 'types' that do not necessarily correspond to the anatomical sex of the person in question" (Gleason 1990, 390).

Male slaves were often treated as incapable of realizing the masculinity towards which free men strove and were attributed the supposedly feminine traits of deceitfulness, moral depravity, emotional excess, and addiction to bodily pleasures. Joy Connolly shows how the characteristics of women and slaves were conflated as they were set against the qualities that the elite Roman man sought to develop through oratorical training. For Quintilian in particular, this conflation was expressed by the figure who most fully embodied oratorical vice, the eunuch – at once servile and, physiologically, not completely male. The discursive emasculation of the male slave has a haunting echo in the historical record, in the brief reference to a slave in Rome who in 101 BCE castrated himself in an act of devotion to the goddess Cybele, discussed in this volume by Shane Butler. But, as Butler movingly demonstrates, we are in no position to assess the meaning of this action for the slave himself and must forgo deciding whether the slave was enacting his own disempowerment or not.

While the figure of the eunuch offers physiological substantiation of the male slave's imperfect masculinity, the sexual economy of Greco-Roman culture performed the same function more routinely for male slaves who were not anatomically different from their masters. As a number of recent studies have shown, ancient sexuality was organized around the polarization of penetrater/penetrated (Dover 1989; Winkler 1990; Halperin 1990; Richlin 1992). The role of penetrater was assigned to the free man, for whom it was the only appropriate and honorable role, while the role of penetrated was properly that of women, free and slave, and male slaves. The free boy, the incomplete free male, was understood to be, like the woman, a legitimate object of free male desire, but his future status as an adult member of the free elite required complex regulations and behavioral norms to safeguard his chastity. Among these regulations were some designed to forestall the particularly compromising situation of a boy being used sexually by a male slave. Thus the Athenian lawgiver Solon is said to have made up laws governing the activities of male slaves in dangerous positions as teachers and especially as instructors in gymnasia (Aeschines, *Against Timarchus* 9–12).

The fact that the male slave could be a legitimate sexual object for another man even as an adult meant that he was both like a woman and like a perpetual boy – a status that was pointedly evoked in the Latin designation of male slaves of all ages as *puer*, "boy" (Richlin 1993, 536). Conversely, a free man who allowed himself to be sexually penetrated in adulthood put his free status in jeopardy, as is seen in the notorious case of the Athenian Timarchus. Through his alleged activities as a prostitute for other men, Timarchus became subject to legal disenfranchisement, through the loss of his right to speak in certain public settings, and to social stigmatization. In the hostile speech by the orator Aeschines through which we know Timarchus' story, Timarchus is denigrated with metaphors of femaleness and of enslavement, enslavement both to the desires of the other men to whom he has submitted himself and to his own uncontrolled appetites (Just 1985). The routine sexual exploitation of male slaves by their masters receives temporary, symbolic redress through the comic reversals of Plautus' *Casina*. There, two male slaves in opposite camps use different strategies to avenge their sexual use by their master: one makes freedom from further advances the precondition for helping his master to try to rape a free woman; the other has the opportunity to beat his master as punishment for that attempt (Rei, 102–3). The sexual subordination of the male slave could be summed up by the formulation that he possessed a penis but not a phallus – the phallus being the penis as signifier of "the sexual and political domination exercised by adult male [Greek and] Roman citizens" (Butler, 248).

Even in sexual situations in which the male slave could legitimately assert himself, that is in his relations with other slaves, especially female slaves, his role was circumscribed by various restrictions. In Rome, one such restriction was the denial of slave fatherhood. While Roman law acknowledged slave motherhood, at least for the sake of determining the ownership of slave children, socially and legally no slave father could claim children and no slave children a father, a stricture that always left the freed slave vulnerable (Joshel 1992a, 29, 32, 45). When the male slave fathered children with female slaves, his role in reproduction lacked phallic significance because the issue of his body became the property of the slave mother's owner. Large-scale slave owners often policed the sexual activities of their slaves. Thus Plutarch, describing the activities of the elder Cato during the formative period of large-scale slavery at Rome, tells how Cato segregated male and female slaves and charged male slaves a fee to enter the women's quarters; the master thus provided sexual release for his male slaves at a profit to himself – an instance of the double vulnerability of female slaves (Plutarch, *Cato* 21.1; Plautus, *Mostellaria* 156, 758, 908; Bradley 1987, 146–7; cf. Xenophon, *Oeconomicus* 9.5). Later agricultural manuals assume "spontaneous sexual relationships among slaves" but also attest to forms of control by the master that used sexual access to the bodies of female slaves to assure better performance of assigned tasks (Bradley 1987, 50–1).

Alternatively, the inherent ambiguity of the male slave could be dealt with through his empowerment rather than his emasculation. In many of our sources, especially fictional ones such as epic, drama, and the popular tale, male slaves are granted abilities and virtues to match their maleness, above all the virtue of unwavering loyalty to the master. Several texts discussed in this volume present male slaves as going to great lengths to uphold their masters' interests in fictional scenarios that also evoke the possibility that the energetic male slave might displace his master – a possibility constantly raised by the capacity for agency and autonomy implicit in his maleness. In Plautus' *Casina* the male slave Chalinus dresses up as the female slave his master Lysidamus plans to rape, then emerges from his disguise to beat and humiliate Lysidamus. The motif of female disguise here points up both the way in which Chalinus' act is an assertion of masculinity and the lack of agency of the female slave who cannot take revenge herself (Rei, 102–3). Chalinus attacks his master, however, not on his own behalf, but as the agent of his mistress in a plot designed to correct Lysidamus' errors and to restore him to his rightful place as the moral as well as the legal head of the household. Holt Parker identifies a subgenre of Roman popular tales in which male slaves dress up as their master and take their master's place, but only in order to preserve the master's life or honor (Parker, 162). Such plots suspend the usual equation of virtue with free status and, in doing so, gloss over the problems presented by the male slave's agency. In contrast, Homer's *Odyssey* maintains that equation by presenting the loyal slave Eumaeus, the swineherd who protects Odysseus' interests during his long absence, as essentially free: his origins are aristocratic – he is the kidnapped son of a king – and his loyalty is rewarded through his designation by Odysseus as a companion of his son Telemachus, thus higher than a household slave, but not quite Odysseus' social equal and certainly not his rival for power (Thalmann, 31–3; Murnaghan, 1987: 39–42).

The chief authors and the chief beneficiaries of these constructs were, of course, the free men who depended not only on the labor and services of real women and real slaves but also on the categories of female and slave to establish their own identities. In a range of discourses and cultural practices, the free man bolstered his privileged status by externalizing what he did not want to be and projecting it onto women, slaves, and other marginalized people. The essays in this volume instance James Clifford's generalization that "every version of an 'other,' wherever found, is also the construction of a 'self'" (Clifford 1986, 23). Patricia Clark quotes Galen's self-conscious account of how he formed his character by identifying with his "father's noble deeds" and rejecting the passionate irrationality of his mother who "was so very prone to anger that sometimes she bit her handmaids" (Clark, 122–3). The male construction of self through female and slave was particularly evident in the realm of oratory, one of the principal fields in which masculine identity was fashioned and performed. In classical Athenian lawcourts, citizen men competed with one another by delivering speeches in which complex situations were reduced to disputes over their interests, in which slaves had no interests of their own and women's subjectivity was acknowledged only for its bearing on the fortunes of men (Johnstone 224–6, 228–9). In the Roman oratorical schools, young men were prepared for their adult roles by arguing different sides of hypothetical cases whose narratives featured the shared vices of women and slaves and celebrated the relations between free men (Connolly).

The expediency of these categories is evident from their fluidity, the ease with which they could be configured and reconfigured in whatever way best served the "male project of selfhood" (Zeitlin 1996, 347). Thus Quintilian, instructing the young orator to find himself by avoiding what is slavish, characterizes slaves as overly refined and effeminate at one point and as overly rustic and boorish at another (Connolly, 141–2). Deceit and disguise are denigrated in rhetorical handbooks as distastefully servile and feminine, but in Roman popular narratives of slave loyalty, the deployment of those strategies on behalf of the master makes the slave a "resourceful" possessor of the "characteristics of the ideal Roman citizen-soldier" (Parker, 162). In Euripides' Trojan War plays, free male anxiety about free/slave conflict is sometimes allayed by making free and slave women rivals, sometimes by making them allies (Rabinowitz 64–5).

Even the most seemingly natural qualities are subject to manipulation. In Greek medical texts male slaves, whose bodies are anatomically indistinguishable from the bodies of free men, are not presented as having a distinctive set of pathologies, as are women, whose anatomical difference is magnified by the tendency to view all women's maladies as malfunctionings of the reproductive organs. And yet, Nancy Demand concludes in her analysis of these texts, "in the end the difference [between the treatment of female and slave bodies] is overridden because, although used differently, the bodies of both women and slaves were instruments . . . with a single purpose – work in the case of slaves and reproduction in the case of women." (Demand, 83). The social condition of one man's use by another outweighs their biological similarity: a body that is owned by another man becomes effectively different from a free man's body and thus comparable to the biologically different body of a woman. The woman's biological difference makes her useful to men, who cannot reproduce themselves without her; the male slave's availability for use itself creates a difference between him and the free man that might as well be biological.

And yet, despite their malleability, these categories also implicated the men who exploited them in logical contradictions, always threatening to evade their control. Reliance on women and slaves, whether as individuals or as types, meant a constant and intimate involvement with the very figures from whom the master or husband was striving to distinguish himself. Once again, oratory provides a particularly clear illustration for, as Joy Connolly demonstrates, successful public speech required the role-playing and artful speaking that were viewed as feminine and servile practices; moreover, in Rome, the teachers of rhetoric, like most of the people who nurtured and instructed the upper-class child, were usually slaves. In their vision of the educational process through which free male identity was formed, the Romans transformed the slaves and women who did the teaching and the arts that they taught, refining them as well as the young man himself. Quintilian recommends a "course of supervised exploitation" to convert women, slaves, and freedmen into "models of elite Roman manliness, despite the realities of their status as social inferiors" and thus obscures the free man's reliance on slave and female labor (Connolly, 138–9).

Just as the elite man mastered those on whom he depended, at least in fantasy, so he created a proper male body by mastering the servile and feminine within himself, "obliterating any trace of bodily or vocal practices associated with women and slaves." The young man could then learn an eloquence that was dissociated from the dangerously persuasive speech acts of women and slaves by "a persistent re-naming of the 'tricks' of deceit and ornament on which women were commonly believed to rely, transforming them into codified 'techniques' of professionalized manly speech." As the free male masked his material dependence on real slaves and women, so he masked his intangible dependence on the categories slave and woman by "the demonization of feminine and slavish speech" and by "the sanitization of oratory for manly use" (Connolly, 135–6).

Yet the very constructedness of a male and masterly identity haunts this "demonization" and "sanitization," for the program itself works on the implicit assumption "that identity is not ineffable, that virtue is the natural possession of no single class or gender, and that authority is not the manifestation of the natural superiority of free men" (Connolly, 136). The notion that free male identity is something acquired through the use of theatrical techniques suggests the fragility of that identity and the dangerous foundations on which it rests. The theatricality of status is acknowledged only in the most protected contexts, such as tales of loyal slaves who impersonate their masters only to save them, or comedies in which free men experience temporarily both the licentiousness and the humiliation of slaves, or rituals like the one in which Roman slave women recall their predecessors' impersonation of free women by themselves acting like men.

These stories attest to a transferability of identity and status between the free man and his wife or slaves that constantly complicated his use of them as instruments of his own purposes. The master's reliance on others implied a loss of independence that compromised his authority. In the case of his wife, a limitation to his control was essential to her role: while he might attempt to confine her

13

sexuality and appropriate her fertility, he could not own her like a slave, because she had to be free in order to bear free children. In the case of slaves, legal ownership could not guarantee an effective instrument or a satisfactory relation of subjection. Mastery was, as Kathleen McCarthy puts it, a "delicate project" requiring ideological work, and the male imagination constantly wrestled with the problem of the human instrument (McCarthy, 181) . In the realm of scientific classification, Aristotle struggles to pin down the character of the slave by calling him "a sort of animate property" (*Politics* 1253b, 33); this philosophical abstraction is embodied in Homeric epic through the mechanical maid-servants who act as crutches for the limping god Hephaestus – "a utopian projection of male wishes about women" and slaves (Thalmann, 25–6).

In these fantasies, the complete obedience of the ideal instrument is made possible by a lack of independent volition; yet in anxious thoughts about actual situations "the lack of real volition in turn produced what was viewed as duplicity" (Thalmann, 25–6; Joshel 1992a, 64). Kathleen McCarthy observes the doubt raised by the "cheerfully obedient slave" whose seeming acceptance of his "master's absolute authority" might only be a manipulative façade. The "inscrutability" of the slave is especially problematic because, as the executor of his master's desires, the slave is effectively the master's surrogate:

> the logic of surrogacy requires instruments that are as efficacious as possible; yet, especially when the power of these instruments consists in going where the principal cannot go and doing what s/he cannot do, the more powerful these instruments become, the more obviously they threaten either to escape control or to supplant the principal.
>
> (McCarthy, 180–1)

McCarthy's discussion includes a close analysis of a pair of Ovid's love elegies in which the figure of the poet/lover is presented as failing in an attempt to win his female beloved. On the one hand, his failure confirms that his relationship to his beloved is like that of a slave; on the other hand, it reassuringly exposes the failed surrogacy of the slave woman he has used as his messenger (McCarthy, 182–4). Here the male author solves his ideological dilemmas by exploiting the divisibility of women into free and slave: he elevates the free woman while he denigrates the female slave.

While the elegiac poet might be willing to portray the poet/lover as the quasi-slave of a free mistress, the thought of Roman men as effectively subject to their slaves was deeply troubling. Roman moralists, such as the first-century CE Stoic philosopher Seneca, address the compromising dependence of masters on their slaves by portraying it as the limited condition of a decadent few who are caricatured as needing a slave to meet their every whim and as the unwitting dupes of their powerful slaves. This isolation of a few extreme cases masks the pervasive dependence of the entire elite class on slave labor. Most men are presumed to be sufficently in control of their appetites to escape this demeaning stereotype; one example used by Seneca provides further protection through the portrayal of a man whose slavish overdependence on slaves can be traced to his literally servile ancestry (McCarthy, 181).

One common response to the problem that women and slaves cannot be counted on to share the volition of their husbands and masters is the identification of laziness as an intrinsic flaw of both groups. Trying to read behind the stereotype, we might find a resistance to subjection or an assertion of control over the pace of work (Bradley 1987, 32–3; Genovese 1976, 285–309). Yet the masking function of the stereotype provides a particular assurance, for it "inscribes as legitimate – even natural – the master's claim to his slave's labor and eclipses the power relations that uphold it" (Joshel 1992a, 7; cf. Carby 1987). A lack of shared interests is construed as a personal flaw that requires masterly control and guidance.

Another common response involves an inverse procedure, the portrayal of the wife or the slave as a kind of flawless second self, whose interests naturally coincide with those of the husband or master. The figuring of the wife or the slave as a second self depends on the formulation of a "differential equation" in which the master himself is a variable. The wife or slave is equated with the master through an identical outlook and virtuous fidelity, usually stemming from qualities that each may share with the master – freedom in the case of the wife, maleness in the case of the slave. Yet both are still differentiated by the fact of their femaleness and/or servility, which justifies their continued domination despite their moral parity. Penelope in the *Odyssey* and the unnamed wife in Xenophon's *Oeconomicus* are two examples from the Greek literary tradition of wives who are portrayed as closely identical with their husbands in both their interests and their attributes and as capable of filling in when their husbands are away from home, yet both are firmly subordinated to their husbands as well (Thalmann; Murnaghan 1987, 118–47; 1988). Some of the Roman tales of loyalty analyzed by Holt Parker show how the interchangeability of terms in this equation can work to the master's advantage. Under the pressures of political crises, often brought about by oppressive state power, the loyal wife enacts the role of husband so that the husband will not be reduced to the role of a wife, just as the "slave enacts the role of master so that the master can escape the role of slave." In the same group of stories, the celebrated suicides of loyal slaves and wives confirm their status as mere instruments of the husband/master's will: once the wielder of the instrument is gone, the instrument is meaningless and willingly enacts his or her own meaninglessness by choosing death (Parker, 161–2, 166–7).

Generating solution after solution to the dilemmas of mastery, the male citizen constructed himself as free according to a definition of freedom that was produced by slavery (O. Patterson 1991) and that combined control over others with control over oneself. Freedom demanded mastery of others and self-mastery, the overcoming of unacceptable fears and desires and the management of bodily appetites, the "care of the self" that Foucault and his followers have recently publicized (often, in the process, idealizing it and themselves replicating the suppression of women and slaves on which it was based: cf. Richlin 1993, 1997a). As the previous discussion has shown, this link between mastery and self-mastery was reinforced – and complicated – through the identification of the qualities to be mastered in oneself with those of the other people who had to be mastered too: women and slaves. A further, and equally important, element in this definition of freedom was political liberty – freedom from domination by other citizens, by internal tyrants, or by foreign powers. "Freedom was control of oneself by oneself – and by nothing other than oneself" (Just 1985, 178). Participation in public life and the relations among cities, peoples, and nations were experienced through the same paradigms of free/unfree and male/female as were domestic relations and the individual psyche. The historical narratives of nations were shaped by the same "differential equations" as were more personal stories, and political freedom for the male citizen was constantly linked, both in actuality and in fantasy, to the existence of women and slaves who were properly subordinated and properly distinguished.

In M. I. Finley's succinct formulation, "one aspect of Greek history . . . is the advance, hand in hand, of freedom *and* slavery" (Finley 1968, 72). For classical Athens, a definitive chapter in this advance occurred in the early sixth century when Athenian society was reformed by the lawgiver Solon. Solon's reforms included the abolition of debt slavery, which established the liberty of Athenian citizens by freeing them from the peril of enslavement to each other. The Athenians' increased liberty – and increased sense of their own liberty – required the enslavement of more and more non-Athenians. The concept of liberty "reduced the potential for exploitation within the civic community and thus increased both the number and the demands of the privileged. Meanwhile this process was accompanied by an increase in chattel slavery, that is, by a massive recourse to a foreign labor force entirely subject to the will of its master" (Garlan 1988, 39). Ancient Greek notions of what it meant to exercise the prerogatives of citizenship presupposed a degree of leisure that would have been impossible without the labor of slaves. The creation of this leisure is dramatized in Xenophon's account in the *Oeconomicus* of the ideal citizen landowner Ischomachus, who is free to participate in public affairs because his household is maintained in excellent order by his dependents.

Ischomachus' account of how he turned himself into someone with the free time necessary for business and politics illustrates both the way mastery registered itself simultaneously in several overlapping spheres of experience and the intimate link between issues of freedom and issues of gender. The key to Ischomachus' success is his training of his wife, through which she gains manly self-control and becomes a trustworthy surrogate who secures the order of his household. This training is figured in the text as a demonstration of Ischomachus' own self-control and – as his household is transformed through her new skills into a place of order on the model of a well-run city – of his political virtue (Murnaghan 1988). The *Oeconomicus* is only one of many texts – the two with which we began this discussion are also prime examples – in which political liberty for men is guaranteed by the honorable status of the free woman, which is maintained by her careful differentiation from both free men and slaves. Thus a central narrative of Athenian political liberty, the story of the Tyrannicides, hinges on a free woman's honor. When, during the late sixth century BCE, the Athenians had become subject to the extra-constitutional rule of a tyrant, the tyrant's oppression was manifested through the activities of his brother Hipparchus, who wished to detach a young man, Harmodius, from his lover, Aristogiton. When Harmodius asserted his freedom by repulsing Hipparchus' advances, Hipparchus took revenge by publicly impugning the honor of Harmodius' sister, at which point Aristogiton organized a revolt against Hipparchus and his brother. Even though this revolt was unsuccessful and the tyrant was not expelled for several more years, Harmodius' and Aristogiton's defense of a free woman's honor came to be celebrated as the founding moment of Athenian freedom (Herodotus, *Histories* 5.55–65; Thucydides, *Peloponnesian War* 6.53–9).

For the Greeks, and especially for the Athenians, the repulsion of two foreign invasions by the Persians in 490 and 480 BCE added a cultural dimension to this political identity: Greek freedom came to mean freedom from domination by foreigners and notions of freedom spawned in domestic contexts colored Greek perceptions of international relations. Depictions of the conflict with Persia made the Persian king a Greek tyrant in barbarian clothing and the wars a struggle between freedom and servitude. The obverse of this freedom was Greek domination over non-Greeks and, as we have seen, Aristotle saw that domination as justified by the backwardness of foreigners, manifested in their lack of significant distinctions between male and female and between slave and free. For the Athenians, freedom from foreign rule also came to be identified with rule over other Greeks as they turned a league formed in opposition to Persia into an empire – an empire characterized by the historian Thucydides as a tyranny that could not be relinquished without incurring the danger of servitude (Thucydides, *Peloponnesian War* 2.63.2).

As we have seen from Livy's account of the rape of Lucretia (a story that was modeled on the Athenian legend of the Tyrannicides and even dated to the same year), Roman historical memory also identified the establishment of political liberty with the defense of a free woman's honor. In general, Roman citizen identity rested on a similar nexus of the freedom of citizens from enslavement to each other; the importation of foreign slaves; and, eventually, rule over foreigners. At Rome, the incompatibility of citizenship and bondage was expressed in a provision, dating from as early as the fifth century BCE, that those enslaved because of debt had to be sold "beyond the Tiber [River]," that is, outside the community. Livy's account of the conditions leading up to the law abolishing debt slavery in 326 BCE recalls the story of Lucretia, only in this case the violated body is a man's, not a woman's and the obstacle to freedom is not the oppressive power of a tyrant but the institution of debt-slavery, which permitted the enslavement of one citizen to another. Lucius Papirius made sexual advances to Gaius Publilius, his debt-bondsman of citizen status; when the young man proved to be as obdurate as Lucretia, more mindful of his free birth than his present condition, Papirius had him stripped and beaten. His outraged virtue, like Lucretia's, stirred the crowd to act and debt-slavery was abolished: "a new beginning of liberty," Livy comments (8.28). This story helps to show why, in the Athenian legend of Harmodius and Aristogiton, the tyrant's power is figured through his brother's unwanted sexual designs on a male citizen. The bodily integrity of the male citizen was the definitive expression of free status because it was available to even the very poorest (even, in the case of Publilius, the completely dispossessed) – a criterion of freedom that glossed over distinctions of wealth and united all citizens, rich and poor, in their distinction from slaves (cf. Halperin 1990).

The bond of freedom shared by male Roman citizens at all levels of wealth was also shored up by the enslavement of foreigners. "The presence of a substantial number of slaves in Roman society defined free citizens, even if they were poor, as superior" (Hopkins 1978, 112). And the importation of foreign slaves went hand-in-hand with the conquest of foreign nations, whose leaders were often cast as would-be Tarquins, tyrannical rulers with designs on the liberty of Roman citizens. Rule over foreigners was justified by the Romans' supposed aptitude for self-control, instilled through a long tradition of discipline and self-sacrifice, and by the contruction of foreigners as naturally servile – whether effete and decadent like the Greeks (Edwards 1993, 92–7) or boorish and disorderly like the Gauls (Livy 5.33.2, 36.1–4; Tacitus, *Annals* 3.56, *Agricola* 2.3). With the establishment of the principate and the development of the empire, these formulations became both more urgent and more challenging to maintain. For elite male citizens, rule by any emperor, good or bad, meant potentially demeaning restrictions on political achievement and on the free speech that signaled political autonomy. The romanization of the provinces undermined the presumed superiority of all native Italians; the extension of citizenship to provincials gradually effaced the republican distinction between Italian and foreigner.

Our attempt to graph the patterns that consistently emerge when gender and status are plotted onto one another has produced a discussion that is synchronic and generalizing, in which the specificity of particular historical moments, social settings, and modes of representation is inevitably elided. At the same time, our examination of these variables in combination with each other is an attempt to restore one form of specificity that often gets lost as scholars of antiquity overlook gender when talking about status or overlook status when talking about gender. As Valerie Smith warns, in the context of modern American racial difference: "when historical specificity is denied or remains implicit, all the women are presumed white, all the blacks male" (1989, p. 44). Further specificity is to be found in the essays themselves, with their close attention to the conditions of particular social settings, to the conventions of different genres, and to variables other than status and gender, such as age, ethnicity, and class. Patricia Clark, for example, shows how age alters the relations of women, free and slave, in Roman households in North Africa in the fourth century CE.

Aeschylus' Clytemnestra, analyzed by Denise McCoskey, and Plautus' Cleostrata, analyzed by Annalisa Rei, are two wives, in different genres, at different cultural moments, who exemplify the complex variations within the larger process of differential equations: in fifth-century BCE Athenian tragedy, the wife who usurps her husband's position treats the female slave as other and a rival, insisting on a fatal difference between herself and the slave; in Roman comedy of the second century BCE, the wife whose honor limits her comedic agency makes common cause with her slaves to circumvent a husband who abuses his position at the head of the household. Ian Morris confronts the difficulty of recovering slave experience through the evidence for imported Thracian and Phrygian slaves who worked in large groups in silver mines near Athens in the fifth century BCE; Shane Butler takes on the same issue by considering an individual slave, possibly belonging to the temple of Cybele at Rome, and placing him in the context of slave revolts in Sicily in the second century BCE.

In tracing the permutations of gender and status we have also focused on the experiences of slaves and women as constructed and classified by free men, thus eliding the most particular and elusive form of historical specificity: individual subjectivity. In doing so, we have, of course, been reproducing the restricted perspective of our sources. We have very little direct testimony from the women and slaves of the ancient world and no voices raised in unmistakeable opposition to the dominant order. We have no slave or female witnesses to consult: no Frederick Douglass, Harriet Jacobs, or Mary Chesnut. The oppression of the marginalized produced in antiquity no surviving literature of protest. We observe the intersection of gender and status in a world without a women's movement: no Mary Wollstonecraft or Elizabeth de Gouges argued for women's rights. Slave revolts in classical antiquity did not produce a Toussaint L'Ouverture or a rhetoric of rights and a constitution as in eighteenth- and nineteenth-century Haiti. The few texts authored by women and slaves that do survive are in highly conventional forms, such as epitaphs on tombstones, in which the dominant language of the culture tends to obscure individual testimony (Joshel 1992a; cf. Bloomer 1997, chapter 3). Meanwhile, the works of free men are deceptively full of details about women and slaves but, as we have seen, these details tell a story of men and masters. In doing so, they not only suppress "full accounts of the agency, experience, interests and subjectivity of women and slaves" (Johnstone, 222) but constitute a process of active disinformation where those subjectivities are concerned. The danger, notes Johnstone, is "that all they do say about these groups will obscure their fundamental omissions, and that we will unwittingly adopt their narrative constraints as our own in writing history" (Johnstone, 222; cf. Clifford 1986, 10).

Sadly, the material evidence studied by archaeologists offers no ready corrective to the skewed perspective of our textual sources. In his contribution, Ian Morris sets out the considerable difficulties involved in treating the material record as a neutral mirror to external, non-discursive realities. Rather, he suggests, the archaeological record in classical Athens was shaped by the same power relations that determined the textual record. In effect, citizen males controlled words and things in similar ways. Material culture had a role in structuring the relations of men and women, masters and slaves, and functioned to uphold citizen discourses of gender and social status. Analyzing the architecture and pottery of the slave camps at the silver mines near Athens and the use of domestic space by free men and women, Morris finds that Athenian material culture reifies the primacy of masters and free men. The ethnic identities of foreign slaves are obliterated as they are turned into instruments of their Athenian masters. Even the most painstakingly attentive examination of their everyday objects reveals no sign of retained native traditions or an alternative culture. Female space is not the site of an independent style or developed subculture, but functions like the female character as a ground against which the particularities of male culture are developed. Much as women were frequently thought of as imperfect men, "space was conceived as having varying degrees of maleness, lying along a gender spectrum rather than falling into one of two distinct categories" (Morris, 217). Rejecting suggestions that the blankness of the material culture of ancient women and slaves reflects our own inability to access it, Morris concludes "Women and slaves remain invisible not because of the inevitable methodological problems with attributing gender and legal status to excavated remains, but because Athenian male citizens wanted it that way" (Morris, 220).

The nature of ancient evidence thus forces us to deal with a profound silence that lies behind all the noise generated by our sources. In attending to the silenced people of antiquity, we are always in danger of ourselves generating more noise, obscuring them further through our own projections (cf. Spivak 1988). Two of our essays take complementary approaches to this challenge. Shane Butler offers a negative reminder of what we cannot reach through our discourses of knowledge; Steven Johnstone takes a more positive view in suggesting new ways of knowing. While Butler insists on preserving and honoring that silence, Johnstone uses it to talk about the construction of the subject.

At the center of Butler's essay is a notice in Roman prodigy literature of an unnamed slave who castrated himself in honor of the Magna Mater in 101 BCE. For late twentieth-century readers, concerned with subjectivity and experience, the moment when the slave takes action – to us an extreme and violent action on his own body – raises urgent questions: was the slave ratifying his servility by making his body conform to his disenfranchisement, or was he challenging the authority of a slave society by asserting his own control over his body? Butler mines the regimes of knowledge about the past for answers, but our understanding of history, prosopography, religion, the body, and gender brings us no nearer the slave whose "act seems to be itself a kind of writing" (Butler, 239). The gap between the slave's act and the place where it is recorded for us to read seems insurmountable. The pursuit of history only unfolds questions of reading and projection, even where the dominant historical narrative includes slaves – in this case, the slave revolts in Sicily in the late second century

BCE. Every attempt to learn about the slave's experience sends us back to Roman cultural anxieties about slaves and gender. For the act itself, our knowledge relies on the invasive phallic sexual economy, outlined above, but this knowledge, Butler argues, only allows a reading "in which [the slave] *traces* an already implied text of his own subordination" (248). If we assume that the slave authors his own castration, "then we must allow his body to mean in unexpected, even poetic ways" (249). Butler's insistence on silence is not an insistence on total invisibility or absence, for in the notice of this unnamed slave's action he observes a moment of "*presence*," however resistant to our desire to tell a story.

For Johnstone, the silences in Athenian legal orations, like those in other ancient sources, certainly occlude the experiences of women and slaves. Yet, at the same time, they can be understood as themselves a form of experience. Representation is not simply a reflection of social structures but "part of the complex process of reproducing them. . . . Silences, then, are not (or not only) the result of hierarchy and oppression, but also one of the means through which these were reproduced" (222). In this way, they belong to "the historical processes that, through discourse, positions subjects and produce their experiences" (Scott 1991: 779). Silences contribute to an understanding of "what [marginalized subjects] experienced [and] how they were constituted as experiencing subjects" (Johnstone, 223). By taking the gaps in the ancient sources as "facts to be understood and incorporated into historical accounts," Johnstone attempts "to link ideology with lived experience" (223).

There might seem to be an unbridgeable contradiction between Johnstone's use of silence to reconstruct subject positions and Butler's insistence on silence as a bar to any conclusive reconstruction of experience. Our task is perhaps to keep both positions in view at once. Work like Johnstone's responds to our desire to tell a story about women and slaves and acknowledges that they had stories to tell. Yet we must remember that the stories we tell remain provisional and are, like all historical narratives, what James Clifford calls "fictions" (1986, 6–7) – not invention as opposed to fact or lies as opposed to truth, but rather something made and made up. Butler's often ironic and ever frustrated pursuit of a story through the means to truth at our disposal highlights the potential pitfalls of our "fictions"; eschewing "epistemological certainty," he asserts an epistemological integrity for an unnamed slave. And while we will always have special trouble recovering the subjectivities of ancient women and slaves, the differential equations of slavery and gender can teach us to relinquish the pseudo-subjectivities constructed in ancient male and masterly texts and practices. At the very least, we can resist the totalizing visions of Greek and Roman law and literature and avoid making them our own.

2

FEMALE SLAVES IN THE
ODYSSEY

William G. Thalmann

Charles Dickens's *Pickwick Papers* contains an anecdote about a man who gathered material for a work on Chinese metaphysics from the *Encyclopaedia Britannica*. It was no obstacle that, as Mr. Pickwick reasonably points out, the *Encyclopaedia Britannica* had no article on the subject. " 'He read, sir,' rejoined Pott, laying his hand on Mr. Pickwick's knee, and looking round with a smile of intellectual superiority, 'he read for metaphysics under the letter M, and for China under the letter C, and combined his information, sir.' "

If we ask why this story is funny, and why the method of research strikes us as bizarre, we might want to say that what is preposterous is the procedure's additive nature, as though a combination were simply the sum of its parts, and as though the parts were not somehow altered in synthesis. What would Chinese metaphysics, after such an operation, look like? But there is such a thing as Chinese metaphysics, and if we cannot understand it this way, how can we? How do we bring together things that belong together without doing violence to them or to the specificity of their combination? What is "Chinese" about Chinese metaphysics, and what is recognizably metaphysical about a portion of Chinese thought? Conversely, it is perhaps possible to know about both China and metaphysics without knowing about Chinese metaphysics, but would our understanding of either be complete?

For "China" and "metaphysics," substitute "women" and "slaves," and we can see how Dickens's epistemological joke encapsulates the problem of understanding how gender and class organize social practice in some relation to each other. For one thing, his literary hack tried to synthesize, unlike the *Encyclopaedia Britannica*; in classical studies, at least, it has been customary to study class and gender in isolation from each other, or to emphasize one over the other. It is natural to do so, for analytical clarity, and because there is so much to say about each that often it seems impossible to consider both together within a single argument (I write from experience here). Enormous progress has been made recently in the study of class and gender in ancient societies, but disconnecting them imposes limits and risks distortion. Perhaps we have never been in so good

22

a position to overcome this compartmentalization and consider both at once. How to bring them together is the problem.

Class and gender would seem to converge in the lives of female slaves, and although I shall discuss this group as the *Odyssey* portrays them, this topic has important implications for the class and gender position of elite women also, as I hope will emerge. When one uses an adjective/noun phrase like "female slaves" or "slave women" that specifies a certain kind of slave or woman, the question is already begged of the relation between categories – as it is with "Chinese metaphysics." As Dickens's anecdote warns us, we need to avoid simply combining disparate bits of information. It would, for example, be tempting to say that in societies marked, like Greece and Rome, by sex and status asymmetries, female slaves were "doubly disadvantaged" by their class and gender. So no doubt they were in many respects, but not in all. In some ways, women slaves might be better treated than male slaves, and they were free of some of the restrictions placed on the behavior of elite women. But the main problem with such a statement is that it falls squarely into the additive fallacy that Dickens makes amusing. It obscures the crucial point made by some feminist scholars that class and gender operate inextricably to determine the social experience of individuals and groups, the forms of privilege and oppression, in hierarchical societies (Spelman 1988; McClintock 1995, Chapters 1 and 3). The challenge is to understand class and gender in their reciprocal influence on one another and so as parts of a system that is not static but is constantly being recreated, without ignoring the distinctions between them.

The *Odyssey* presents an interesting example for thinking about this relation. As an ideological product it played a role in the processes surrounding the formation of the polis (or "city-state") in the late eighth century BCE (evidently the period of the text's main formative phase), and such was its cultural prestige that it helped shape one of the dominant discourses in Greek society for many centuries after – and therefore in our own. In this role, it transmitted certain attitudes about the "right" form of society and its proper structures of inequality that were the more compelling for being embedded in narrative rather than explicitly articulated. After a twenty-year absence, Odysseus returns to Ithaca in the guise of a dispossessed beggar to find his home in disarray. His wife's suitors are in possession of his house, consuming its wealth with their constant banquets, with his son Telemachus helpless against them. Some of his dependents are now the suitors' minions, and the loyal ones are exploited for their labor. Odysseus gains the upper hand and kills the suitors with the aid of Telemachus and the faithful servants Eumaeus and Philoetius, and Telemachus puts to death the disloyal slaves: the brother and sister Melanthius and Melantho and eleven other women who have slept with the suitors. With Athena's help, Odysseus is reconciled with the suitors' kinsmen and by implication restored to authority over not only his own household but also all of Ithaca. The hierarchical order thus reinstated is presented as all the more right for its near overthrow, so powerfully that we need to remind ourselves that it is founded on systematic inequality

23

between men and women, aristocrats and slaves. The persuasive force – or in the poem's own term for it, the enchantment – of the *Odyssey*'s representations, in fact, may be measured by the generations of readers who have accepted as self-evident the subjugation of those on whose work the opulence of Odysseus's household is founded and his dominance over wife and son. Even feminist critics, who have shed such valuable light on the poem's representations of gender, have paid insufficient attention to what Odysseus's wife Penelope and their maid-servant Eurycleia, for example, have in common and what separates them.

The relation between high and low in this society is not clear in all details, but it certainly is one of domination. Although many would agree that the characters I am about to discuss are slaves (for example, Finley 1978, 54, 58–9; Ramming 1973; Gschnitzer 1976), not all would (Wickert-Micknat 1983, 117; Beringer 1982; on the difficulties in inferring their status from terms used for them, see Garlan 1988, 35–6). That there can be any debate evidently arises from the *Odyssey*'s tendency to represent historical conditions in simplified and mystified form rather than to reproduce them. There is no use, however, getting mired in questions of status. Much more important than the fact that some of these characters are bought and sold is their dominated and exploited position *vis-à-vis* their "superiors" – the head of the household to which they are attached and his family. This relation has been seen as the essence of slavery by one cross-cultural study (O. Patterson 1982). I believe, therefore, that the term "slavery" is justified in relation to Homer, and that what the epics depict has much in common with later Greek and Roman chattel slavery, but my argument does not hinge on this point. Any reader uneasy with my use of the term should consider it shorthand for the underlying relation of domination, which is surely present despite the text's attempts in some cases to disguise it as benevolent and reciprocal.

To judge from the *Odyssey*, thinking about and justifying this relation in the eighth century BCE entailed the same problems as slavery always has wherever it existed. In fact, I would like to approach slavery in Homer, and eventually its intersection with gender asymmetry, through Aristotle's *Politics*, a text written four centuries later which codified and rationalized attitudes toward slavery that had been deeply ingrained in Greek culture and long taken for granted. There, just after his famous definition of the slave as "a sort of animate property," Aristotle says,

> Every subordinate is, as it were, an instrument prior to [other] instruments. For if every instrument were able to accomplish its work on command or by anticipating a command, and if shuttles wove and *plêktra* struck the lyre by themselves, just as they say the statues of Daedalus [moved themselves] or the tripods of Hephaestus, which the poet [Homer] says "enter the divine assembly of their own accord," master craftsmen would need no workers, and masters no slaves.
>
> (*Politics* 1253b33–54a1)

He then makes a distinction between instruments, which serve the purpose of production, and property, including slaves, which serves the purpose of action and whose value is wholly one of use – and thereby muddles his argument. The confusion is interesting because it reflects contradictions inherent in customary attitudes to slaves, which themselves lie behind Aristotle's definition of them as "animate property." The main difficulty, for him as for popular thought, is in categorizing as property beings who, insofar as human qualities beyond mere animation must be conceded to them (as Aristotle himself cannot avoid doing), resist assimilation to other forms of property.

As Elizabeth Spelman has shown, the *Politics* projects a gender as well as a class attitude, through both its silences and what it does say. In the well-ordered polis as Aristotle conceives it, only free men and women have gender, in the sense of a socially constructed set of roles and expectations based on, but distinct from, biological sex. Slaves do not (Spelman 1988, 14, 41–3, 52–4). Free women are inferior to male citizens, their husbands, differently from the ways slaves are, and – although Aristotle himself does not discuss this – male slaves would be inferior to free women. "Masculinity" and "femininity," therefore, are not simply gender concepts but are importantly functions of class as well (ibid. 55). This denial of gender to slaves would seem a striking case of a "structured silence" that leaves only "traces or symptoms" in the text (Macherey 1978; Rose 1992, 36). It is consistent, however, with conventional attitudes toward slaves, according to which they are "socially dead" (O. Patterson, 1982). And yet, given that slaves are *animate* property to whom even Aristotle has to concede some human characteristics, this view inevitably entails contradictions.

Aristotle's fantasy of perfectly responsive instruments and his suppression of slaves' gender are an attempt to cope with just these contradictions. This strategy has a counterpart in Homer in the form of *ecphrasis* or icon. Aristotle himself indicates as much in the above quotation when he alludes to the self-moving tripods that Hephaestus, the divine smith, is making when the sea-nymph Thetis visits him to seek armor for her son Achilles (*Iliad* 18.373–7). Very soon afterward another description occurs that illustrates Aristotle more richly, when Hephaestus leaves his forge to greet Thetis:

> He [Hephaestus] went outside
> limping, and two maidservants bustled beneath their lord,
> golden ones, like living girls.
> There is thought in their hearts, in them is speech
> and strength, and they know skills from the immortal gods.
> (*Iliad* 18.416–20)

Here on Olympus, where life is easy, are the perfect embodiments of Aristotle's "animate property," which cannot be realized among mortals. Hephaestus is lame, but nowhere else does he need crutches, human-shaped or otherwise. His golden maid-servants are an ideological emblem: slaves as their masters want to think of them and would like them to be, objectified and mechanically obedient. They have just enough qualities to make them serviceable, possessing strength, voice, and mind but surely not independent subjectivity.

The Aristotelian passage is in the rhetorical form of the *adynaton* or impossibility; the Homeric image projects the same wish onto the gods. Both connect with Greek visions of slaveless utopias, where objects do move themselves to serve their owners, visions which are motivated by the ambivalence common in slave-holding societies to the institution itself (Garlan 1988, 126–38). For the slave, though an indispensable source of labor, was human property with some irreducible subjectivity, who reacted to his or her situation in ways ranging from acceptance and internalization of dominant values through sullen resistance (the slave's proverbial shiftlessness: see *Odyssey* 17.322–3) to theft, flight, and occasionally murder of the master. The slave was an alien presence in the house who had to be relied on but could never be trusted.

The description of Hephaestus' automata also entails a glaring departure from narrative convention that makes them iconic for gender simultaneously with class. Everywhere else in Homer, not the master but the *mistress* of the house, when she appears before visitors, is attended by a pair of maid-servants, in an attitude that signifies female chastity (Nagler 1974, 65–86). When similar figures accompany a male god, the incongruity makes their gender stand out. They are a utopian projection of male wishes about women, as we can appreciate by contrasting the too-independent Pandora, who brings utopian conditions to an end by releasing miseries into the world from the jar in which they had been confined. A projection of male anxieties about women, she is, according to Hesiod, a "manufactured woman" (πλαστὴν γυναῖκα, *Theogony* 513), and he credits her with a "bitchy mind" and a "thievish nature" (*Works and Days* 67): that is, excessive autonomy.

These Aristotelian and Homeric fantasies, then, represent parallel attempts to negotiate and control anxieties surrounding class and gender in a hierarchized, androcentric culture. In its use of female slaves, the *Odyssey* represents a more naturalized and complicated version of the same phenomenon. It does not attempt to reduce them wholly to instruments but gives them some attributes of gender and recognizes their sexuality. It does so, however, in very circumscribed ways, as these things impinge on their masters' interests. There is no question of recognizing in them a genuinely autonomous subjectivity. The female slaves who remain faithful to Odysseus and Penelope despite the suitors offer a positive example that manages the possibility of betrayal by turning it into its opposite. The "bad" ones, on the other hand, figure through their sexuality the potential disloyalty of both slaves and women, and are savagely punished in the end. These two modes of representation contradict one another but are connected by the common purpose they serve.

Before discussing particular characters in the *Odyssey*, we must set female slaves within the context of the narrative's representation of slaves in general. The portrayal of slaves is simplified along the lines of their masters' interests; a sign of this is that in the whole poem male and female slaves never talk to one another or otherwise interact (except for a brief speech by the swineherd Eumaeus to Eurycleia, *Odyssey* 21.381–5; there are also Dolius, who serves Laertes, and the mother of his children – 24.389–90 – but even they are never shown speaking together). If their gender matters, it is not in relation to one another. It is rare enough that male slaves talk to other male slaves, and female slaves among themselves. Generally, slaves interact with a superior of the same sex; the few exceptions confirm the general pattern (*Odyssey* 20.149–56, 22.431–4, 17.240–53, 178–99). Slaves in the *Odyssey* are portrayed for their masters' sake, not for themselves, and everything they do or say serves that purpose – as Aristotle will later say that the common interest served by master and slave is the master's (*Politics* 1278b32–7).

And it is according to their compliance with or betrayal of their masters' interests that the text divides slaves into "good" and "bad." As in virtually all slave-holding societies, this polarity corresponds to two modes of representing the relation of slavery, which reflect its ambivalence but try in opposite ways to naturalize it. There is the "suspicious" view that sees slaves as inferior and unreliable, and therefore as naturally subordinate but in need of coercion and control. The persuasive model, by contrast, depicts slavery as a mutual exchange of benefits and disguises an exploitative relation as reciprocal, often invoking the model of kinship. We shall see presently how "good" and "bad" behavior in slaves is specifically modeled on socially constructed expectations for men and women respectively among the elite.

A crucial division of social space in Homeric society is that between the inside and the outside of the house, and part of its significance is to articulate the distinction in non-servile gender roles. Men work outside and compete for honor with the male heads of other households in public spaces. Women stay in the house and maintain their families' honor by carefully avoiding any behavior that might be construed as unchastity (cf. Pitt-Rivers 1977, 20–3, 116–18). Slaves are excluded from these categories, but by their labor they reflect this division. Male slaves do the agricultural and pastoral work on the land. Female slaves do housework indoors and, typically, weave. In the latter task, they are supervised and often joined by their mistress. But whereas for her weaving is emblematic of sexual virtue and therefore honor, for them it is practically-directed labor, signifying at most their subjugation (see *Iliad* 1.29–31). The elite man, however, also dominates inside the house, and male slaves are active there as well (in the *Odyssey*, particularly in scenes of feasting). By the nature of virilocal marriage, in which the wife comes as an outsider to her husband's home, there is a tension between male and female interests within the household (Vernant 1965, 105–7, 112–15), and from their subordinate position one prominent pair of female slaves reflects it.

Eurycleia is associated with the males of the master family (Scott 1918). She was bought by Laertes (*Odyssey* 1.430) and was nurse of Odysseus and then Telemachus. She appears in the narrative mainly in connection with male spaces in the house, for example the "storeroom of the father" to which Telemachus goes to get provisions for his journey (*Odyssey* 2.337). She abets Telemachus by keeping his departure for Pylos secret from Penelope, as she hides the beggar's identity from her in Book 19, and she helps Odysseus at least passively in his struggle against the suitors. Her doublet Eurynome, on the other hand, enters the poem in Book 17 (495) emphatically associated with Penelope, whose sudden, inexplicable wish to appear among the suitors she seconds and helps rationalize in the next book (*Odyssey* 18.158–76). She may be the Actoris who alone shares with Penelope the secret of the marriage bed and who was a gift from Penelope's father on the latter's marriage, in strong contrast to Eurycleia's history (*Odyssey* 23.228–9; the name Actoris would in that case be a patronymic). This is disputed, but it is clear that Eurynome enjoys an intimacy with Penelope and belongs in her company as Eurycleia never does; one of the few times Eurycleia appears in a similar context she has to admit to helping Telemachus deceive Penelope and invites her mistress to kill her (*Odyssey* 4.742–57). The moment when Eurynome and Eurycleia together prepare the richly symbolic bed for the reunion of Odysseus and Penelope (*Odyssey* 23. 289–90) offers an ideal resolution to the opposition between male and female latent in the household by presenting marriage as an equal and fully reciprocal relation. The text itself, however, marks this resolution as provisional; Odysseus leaves the house the next morning, having ordered Penelope to stay in the house and upstairs, to face the public problem of the suitors' relatives, as he will later leave Ithaca to placate Poseidon on a journey that further defers his resuming a settled relationship with Penelope.

To say that slaves configure a contradiction between gender roles among their social superiors is not of course to say that they themselves have gender. But in certain ways the gender and sexuality of female slaves matters in the *Odyssey*'s narrative as it does not in Aristotle, even if it is regularly to the slaves' disadvantage. In the first place, there are limits to Eurycleia's identification with the male side of the master family, evidently because she is female (cf. Doherty 1995, 153–4, with different emphases). At two critical moments, Odysseus silences her when she is on the point of utterance (*Odyssey* 19.476–90, 22.407–10). The first time, when she recognizes him by his scar and turns to tell Penelope, he grabs her by the throat and threatens her with death if she betrays him. However violently, the male maintains control over speech and over the plot of the poem. Eurycleia's intimate knowledge of Odysseus's body and his history makes him vulnerable to her – an instance of the dilemma slavery always poses to the master. In this case, however, Eurycleia possesses this knowledge because she performed the feminine subordinate role of children's nurse. And it seems to be as female, and not just as slave, that Odysseus does not fully trust her, for in the same way he does not confide in Penelope either. Among slaves, his affective relations, and his trust, are reserved for the males: Eumaeus, with whom he exchanges stories, and Philoetius.

In the second place, and more generally, just as the *Odyssey* polarizes nonslave women into the virtuous (chaste) and the evil (unchaste) from the point of

view of male interests – Penelope as opposed to Helen or Clytemnestra, cata-
strophically adulterous elite wives – so the moral quality of female slaves is
measured by their sexual behavior, whereas the standard for male slaves is their
action for or against their master. Melanthius, the "bad" male slave, kicks the
beggar Odysseus, for example, and the loyal Eumaeus and Philoetius fight alongside him against the suitors. The narrative of the *Odyssey* thus takes account of
the gender of slaves, in two ways. It distinguishes among them, as we have just
seen; we might say "discriminates," for it is the loyalty of male slaves, the
treachery of female slaves, that is emphasized. For female slaves, furthermore,
as for elite women, betrayal typically takes a sexual form. The reasons differ
importantly, but it is true that the sexuality of both categories of women is
acknowledged in the text, and considered a threat.

The sexuality of even a "good" slave is seen as potentially disruptive to the
family she serves, but in keeping with the benevolent paradigm of slavery this
threat is averted. So it is with Eurycleia, who represents a sort of limiting case
in this aspect of female slaves. When she is first introduced, we are told her
history, and among the essential facts about her is that

> Laertes bought her with his own possessions
> when she was still in earliest youth, and he paid twenty cattle's worth.
> He honored her equally in his hall with his dear wife,
> but he never mingled with her in bed, for he shunned his wife's wrath.
>
> (*Odyssey* 1.430–3)

The natural inference (it has been disputed, on flimsy grounds: see Beringer
1961, 273–83) is that, as certainly was the case in later Greece, in Rome, and
in most slave-owning societies, a master might sleep with a female slave without
violating social norms. That is, control of her person extended to, and was most
dramatically demonstrated by, sexual enjoyment of her body. Laertes' abstinence
is treated as remarkable. His motive, however – fear of his wife's anger – momentarily evokes, even as it suppresses, horrific family situations such as that explored
by Phoenix's story in the *Iliad* (9.447–57), where, at the jealous wife's instigation,
the son vies with his father in a classic Oedipal conflict over the father's concubine
and is punished with sterility. The disaster in Sophocles' *Women of Trachis* similarly springs from Deianeira's inability to accept a triangular relationship with
her husband Heracles and his captive Iole. "So now the two of us," she says
scornfully, "wait beneath one blanket, a single armful" (539–40). Even in the
case of the "good" slave Eurycleia, then, we can see the inconvenience, even
the danger, posed by the presence of an alien in the house, inserted as an excess
into the nuclear family, even as her story valorizes that family and ideally resolves
this problem of incorporation. The slave is not, cannot be, just "animate property." She possesses sexuality, though she is not meant to control it; and the
master finds the control he exerts, like all other aspects of slavery, an ambivalent
possession.

The twelve maidservants who sleep with the suitors do seem, from one point of view, to exercise control over their sexuality. They are therefore seen as treacherous – outrageously so. Odysseus is furious when he sees them trooping to the suitors' beds (*Odyssey* 20.5–30), and, with the suitors dead, Telemachus exceeds his father's orders and kills them ferociously in revenge (*Odyssey* 22.457–73). Clearly their liaisons overturn the hierarchical order of the household by calling into question the authority of its male head. But it is important to go farther and to ask why betrayal by the female typically is expressed as sexual wrongdoing.

We can answer this question by considering the maidservants' behavior, and all women's violations of codes of expected behavior, as (to use a linguistic metaphor) particular utterances (or *parole*) of the language (*langue*) of honor that so pervasively structured both the practice and the conceptual world of ancient Greek and Roman, as well as modern Mediterranean, culture (on honor and its implications for slave and free women in the Roman family, see Saller, this volume). The negative way of expressing women's role in this system is that a man's and his family's honor is "vulnerable through the sexual behavior" of the female (Pitt-Rivers 1977, 161; cf. 77–80). The surest way to dishonor a man is to seduce his wife or daughter. Here, however, we have to make a class distinction. These standards of honor and shame apply to elite women in Homer. In the *Odyssey*, Helen vilifies herself (4.145–46), and the Trojan War has been fought to vindicate Menelaus' honor, which her adultery has crippled. Agamemnon's honor is permanently damaged by Clytemnestra's adultery and her murder of him; because he never has a chance to avenge himself, he is worse off than his brother Menelaus.

Slaves, on the other hand, being "socially dead," are by definition outside this system of honor. By their sexual misconduct the maidservants can neither shame themselves nor threaten Odysseus' honor directly. Aside from the spectacle of subjugated people appearing to act independently, the challenge to Odysseus' honor should instead be seen from the point of view of male competition, so that here too whatever a slave does is significant as it affects the master's interests. The suitors' sexual appropriation of these slaves is an assault on his property (or more precisely, on his family's, since they think he is dead). Because it is on this property that his household's standing on Ithaca is based, the threat to Odysseus' social being is grave and is met with a correspondingly fierce reaction. We are not, after all, very far from the situation of the quarrel between Agamemnon and Achilles in the first book of the *Iliad*, in which their honor was implicated in the dispute over possession (clearly to be expressed sexually) of the subjugated captive woman Briseis.

The injury to Odysseus' honor that results from the maidservants' relations with the suitors ends up looking like the one that would occur if Penelope were to marry one of the suitors while her husband still lived (this would not be adultery, but is evidently considered the next thing to it). Both are the objects of a generalized male suspicion of women, and to that extent slaves do participate in the dominant gender system; but the class distinction is crucial. That suspicion, for one thing, is much more bluntly expressed in the case of female slaves: they actually do what Penelope *might* do – but if so only through marriage. Even the stress on these slaves' sexuality in itself has a class aspect, in that it serves the bias toward elite interests in the poem's representation of both class and gender. Marilyn Katz interestingly comments that the abuse of Odysseus in Book 19 (65–9) by Melantho, an individual representative of the treacherous maid-servants, "displaces the question of sexual misconduct from Penelope onto her faithless serving-woman and thus functions to absolve Penelope from the suspicion of wrongdoing" (Katz 1991, 132). Melantho's liaison with the suitor Eurymachus surely does the same, even more clearly (Doherty 1995, 144). So in order for Penelope to be perceived as innocent, a slave must be guilty. This fact clearly shows how misleading it is to speak of women in the *Odyssey* without considering their class.

For her part, Penelope herself is well-versed in class differences and their dynamics. "Wanton! Shameless bitch," she snaps at Melantho, "you don't fool me at all with your outrageous behavior, which you will wipe off with your head" (*Odyssey* 19.91–2). She does not physically punish Melantho herself, although her prophecy will be fulfilled by Telemachus. But she understands that slaves are physically at their masters' mercy, and uses this fact when provoked (for similar complicity by free women in the slave system of the American south, see McCoskey, this volume). Similarly, she assures the suitors that the beggar can have no thought of marrying her even if he does string the bow, "for it absolutely is not fitting" (*Odyssey* 21.314–19).

In one aspect, it is true, the female slave's exclusion from the system of honor is liberating, Penelope's implication in it confining. The "bad" slave is free to satisfy her desires, and so controls her sexuality as "good" slaves and aristocratic women cannot. One might want to push this possibility if we were dealing with actual slaves, but let us observe how the *Odyssey*'s representational system discourages any such thoughts and endows their sexual behavior with a signification arising from the attitudes of the superordinate culture. According to an ideology that seeks to naturalize socially constructed class divisions, the slave, seen as inherently inferior, is easily corrupted, and that is how the narrative depicts the maidservants' relations with the suitors. From that point of view, slaves can only assume one of two predetermined roles. Either they remain loyal to the good master or they allow themselves to be corrupted by his evil adversaries. If the latter, they have not made a moral choice at all, since they act just the way slaves can be expected to behave. Penelope, by contrast, does seem to be a moral agent (Foley 1995). Conversely, an aristocratic woman is seen as naturally good, though still, as woman, open to suspicion. A Helen or a Clytemnestra in that case betrays the standards of her class and challenges this fundamental class distinction. Melantho merely confirms it; but still, like them, she is blamed, and she must be punished to vindicate Odysseus' honor.

The story of his life that Eumaeus tells the disguised Odysseus (*Odyssey* 15.403–84) embodies perhaps better than any other passage the important themes in the poem's representation of class and gender. With the detailed portrayal of the "good" slave in the person of Eumaeus, loyal and affectionate to his master, the text has run into a problem, even though it reaps from his character the advantage of portraying hierarchical relations as benevolent. The problem is that he contradicts the grounding of class distinctions in nature. Eumaeus is a slave, but he is not slavish. The text attempts to deal with this difficulty by appropriating him into the elite. In Book 15, after he has furnished a positive paradigm of slavery for several books, we find, in his account of his origins, that he is really the son of an aristocrat (a *basileus*). His goodness comes from his innate nobility (his counterpart Eurycleia seems similarly high-born, to judge from her father's aristocratic-sounding patronymic, son of Peisênor, at *Odyssey* 1.429). The paradox of the good slave can at least be controlled in this way, and if we still wonder why Eumaeus should be a slave he is at least portrayed as content with his lot.

This strategy is, however, undercut by the counter-example of Eumaeus' nurse, whose story is enfolded within his. Like him, she came of a wealthy family, was stolen (by Taphian pirates), and was sold as slave to a rich master. But she betrays her master, steals his son Eumaeus and some possessions, and sets sail for home with traders from her homeland, one of whom has seduced her. In her case, nobility does not automatically accompany high birth; she poses the same difficulty for that key ideological theme as the noble but lowly Philoetius does, but for the opposite reason. Her death at sea – she drops dead in the bilge like a marine bird – leaves no doubt of the ethical judgment to be passed. But her example, no doubt meant to point up Eumaeus' loyalty by contrast, shows more than seems intended. Someone torn from country, position, and the relations that define her social being, someone "natally alienated" (O. Patterson 1982) or "brutally deracinated" (Finley 1980, 104) might plausibly feel a primary loyalty to the land and family of her birth. She reveals what Eumaeus' example seeks to enchant and disguise: slavery's arbitrary nature that results in the incorporation of a subjugated alien into the house, makes the bond between master and slave tenuous, and leaves betrayal a constant possibility.

There is, then, a contradiction between the two versions of slavery represented by Eumaeus and his nurse. The narrative cannot cancel it but seeks to control it by presenting the nurse as easily corrupted by nature, as both woman and slave. It is no accident that the loyal slave in this story is male and his evil foil female. And once again, her treachery initially takes sexual form:

> Crafty Phoenicians deceived her.
> As she washed the clothes, one first had intercourse with her by the
> $\qquad$ hollow ship
> with bedding and sex, which always [τε] deceive the minds
> in women, even those who are upright.
>
> $\qquad$ (*Odyssey* 15.419–22)

Women's weakness for sex is not an idea that could be so baldly expressed in connection with any other aristocratic woman, except Clytemnestra, Helen, and their ilk (and even Clytemnestra held out for a time against Aegisthus' seduction, "for she had good instincts": *Odyssey* 3.265–6). The sexual suspicion to which Penelope is subjected is handled with subtlety. But another figure offers a more direct contrast with the nurse that shows the refined rules governing sexuality among the elite. When she was seduced, the nurse was doing laundry by the seashore. So, we recall, was the aristocratic Nausicaa when Odysseus appeared before her, naked but for that important olive branch. There the possibility of marriage (*not* a casual liaison) was much in the air, but neither said or did anything to breach aristocratic decorum. With the nurse, we get a simple coupling on the beach.

In its representation of two dominated groups, slaves and women, the *Odyssey* has much to tell us about how class and gender operate as social categories, and about the relation between them. On the one hand, they are distinct in important respects; gender relations do not function quite the way those of class do. We have seen differences in the portrayal of elite and servile women in the poem. The constraints on them differ significantly, especially in regard to sexual behavior and its social meaning, although for both that meaning is imposed by an androcentric value-system. Penelope's class position is carefully distinguished from that of the women who attend and serve her. For better or worse, elite women are more fully integrated into the gender system; female slaves are granted gender within only narrow limits, when it is convenient for rational-izing their subjection. At the same time, there are convergences in the ways both groups are viewed as women, as opposed to men. Conversely, male and female slaves are represented differently, even though they belong to the same class and can be contrasted, as slaves, with the elite. The habits of conceiving gender differences among non-slaves seem to guide the way this text, with the class perspective it mainly incorporates, views slaves from the outside and from above. On the other hand, to make these statements is to show already how intimately connected class and gender are in determining the social experience of any individual (cf. Doherty 1995, 159).

I have been speaking throughout of a mode of *representation* exemplified by the *Odyssey* and persisting through later centuries, as the example of Aristotle's *Politics* shows. We cannot, of course, infer actual *practice* from it, the undoubtedly more complex experience of lived social relations. But this representation is historically interesting because, as an instance of class and gender discourse, it reproduces a set of attitudes that legitimated and perpetuated practice. From this perspective, what women and slaves crucially have in common is that they are constituted as groups, in analogous ways, by one of the dominant discourses of their society, publicly performed epic poetry; that they are endowed by it with an exterior, and viewed in typifying and essentializing ways that naturalize their social inequality. This is the differential and relational dynamic of class division that Fredric Jameson eloquently describes (Jameson 1971, 300–3, 380–2). Thus whatever else one wishes to say about them, it remains true that the *Odyssey* represents women and slaves in similar ways that serve the interests and flatter the self-image of the male elite.

When we look at *female slaves*, we should be careful not to think of class and gender as simply added to one another (Spelman 1988, 80–113). That would be to superimpose two categories upon one another without getting at their underlying connection, like the man who wrote the article on Chinese meta-physics in Dickens's anecdote, and it tempts one to emphasize either class or gender at the expense of the other in a process of abstraction that is ultimately misleading. The representation of female slaves in the *Odyssey* is determined at once, and inseparably, by their sex and their status. In them the discourses of class and gender are intertwined – a combination for which Hephaestus' golden maid-servants provide an icon.[1]

Note

1   I would like to express my gratitude to the editors, Sheila Murnaghan and Sandra Joshel, for organizing the APA panel in which this paper originated and for their excellent comments and suggestions on an earlier draft. One could not hope for more tactful or discerning editors. Thanks also to my USC colleague John Wills for information about Chinese metaphysics.

3

"I, WHOM SHE DETESTED SO BITTERLY"

Slavery and the violent division of women in Aeschylus' *Oresteia*

Denise Eileen McCoskey

Yet I, whom she detested so bitterly, had far more pity for her than [her husband] had, whose duty it was to make her life happy. I never wronged her, or wished to wrong her; and one word of kindness from her would have brought me to her feet.

(Jacobs 1987, 365)

suddenly a woman threw herself at our feet! She had heavy irons bound around her ankles, a workman's hoe in her hands, her head was shaved, her body was all grimy, her miserable clothing was hitched up for work, and she cried out: "Have mercy on me, m'lady, as one woman to another. I am free by birth, though now a slave as Fortune chooses."

(Achilles Tatius, *Leucippe and Clitophon*, 5.17, trans. J. Winkler)

Harriet Jacobs' statement about her feelings for her "perversely vindictive mistress," Mrs Flint (Gwin 1985b, 41), attests to the complexity of identifications that women, both slave and free, experienced in the American south during the period of slavery. Jacobs records with some degree of irony the pity she, as a slave, has felt for her free mistress, who has suffered from her husband's indifference. The possible unity between the women, however, was seemingly never acknowledged by Mrs Flint, who continued to detest Harriet bitterly and to take out that hatred on the slave woman's body. The potential for solidarity between slave and free women is represented very differently in Achilles Tatius' novel *Leucippe and Clitophon*, written during the second century CE. In *Leucippe and Clitophon*, feelings of sympathy and pity unite a free woman with the abused slave woman who seeks assistance from her "as one woman to another." Thus, for Melite (the free woman) and Lacaena (the female slave) the unity of gender proves to outweigh any class distinctions and Melite ultimately intervenes to secure Lacaena's manumission.

Taken together, the two scenes present inverse responses to an appeal for a common bond between women occupying differential positions of power in slave societies. In the first, Mrs Flint violently denies any similarity to Harriet, a denial that privileges the "free" over the "woman" in Mrs. Flint's process of self-identification. Melite, on the other hand, responds to Lacaena's appeals for sympathy based on their shared gender – preferring to recognize that unity, rather than emphasize their differences. The purpose of this paper is to explore the intricate ways in which such women of different status and ethnic positions articulated their identities through, alongside, or against one another in ancient Greece. Specifically, I explore the link of "women and slaves" by positing the category "woman" in both terms, examining the particular, often troubling, relationships between slave women and their mistresses.

My analysis, although grounded in the general social and historical realities of ancient Greek slavery, focuses not on historical evidence for slavery, but on the violent encounter between Clytemnestra and Cassandra in Aeschylus' play, *Agamemnon*, a literary text which must be understood in relation to its author's context and "designs." Despite the fictional nature of this evidence (and the caveat implied by its fictionality when applying any conclusions to "historical" women), I nonetheless use Aeschylus' scene because, in its depiction of violent conflict between a free woman and a slave, it powerfully represents the multiple structural tensions created by the system of ancient Greek slavery. Such a complex articulation of the relationship between slave and free women is difficult to find in historical evidence from ancient Greece (a condition hampered by the lack of extant writing by women and slaves). Therefore, after discussing Aeschylus' scene in detail, I turn to comparative historical narratives written by women in the American south in order to further broaden our perspective on the positions of both women – slave and free – and on the construction of those positions by the interlocking systems of gender and slavery. Finally, I consider ways in which the scene highlights tensions in modern feminism, which has yet to resolve the struggle between the insistence on a common identity (the unity of "all" women) and the appreciation of differences between women (differences, for example, of race, ethnicity, sexual orientation, cultural practice or class) (for example, Roman 1993 and Spelman 1988).

Studies of slavery in ancient Greece and Rome have often focused on its economic aspects as scholars situate themselves generally around Marxist theories of production.[1] Greek and Roman philosophies of slavery (particularly those of Aristotle), the ethnic origins of slaves and the dynamics of the slave market, forms of abuse directed against slaves, and modes of slave resistance have also figured prominently (for example, Bradley 1992; Bradley 1987; Finley 1980; Garlan 1988). Acknowledging the deep political and ethical questions that the institution of slavery raises, scholarship on ancient slavery has also been used to reflect on contemporary systems of slavery, as when Henri Wallon wrote in his preface to *Histoire de l'esclavage dans l'antiquité* (published in 1847):

> Slavery among the ancients! It may seem strange that one should seek so far away, when slavery still exists among us. In taking this path, I do not at all divert minds from the colonial question; on the contrary, I wish to bring them back to it and concentrate them on a solution.
>
> (quoted in Finley 1980, 12)

Nineteenth- and twentieth-century scholarship on slavery has often relied (both explicitly and implicitly) on the comparison of Greek and Roman slavery to that practiced in the American south, a trend which caused William Linn Westermann to assert that "Western scholars bring with them fixations upon the subject which derive from Negro slavery" and to argue instead that when seeking to understand ancient systems "we must first discard all the paraphernalia of modern slavery" (1968, 25). Westermann's work provides an important challenge to the frequent parallels drawn between ancient and American slavery – in particular he makes the important point that ancient slavery had "no color line" (31).

Given such warnings about the need for historical specificity, my use of material from the nineteenth century in this context requires a brief defense. First of all, I believe that both periods can be compared on a broad level because they each exhibit a specific form of slavery (chattel slavery) "dominated by the idea that slaves are *par excellence* foreigners who are bought and sold as though they were simply objects" – a practice Yvon Garlan distinguishes from other forms of "communal servitude" that often existed alongside chattel slavery in antiquity (Garlan 1988, 24 and 85ff.). And although ancient slavery is not marked by race in precisely the same way as the American system (that is, as a consequence of skin color), the emphatically foreign origin of slaves in chattel slavery nonetheless separates the female slave of antiquity from the wives and daughters of citizens. The arrangement of ancient Greek society and economy around the *oikos*, or extended household, also provides a compelling corollary to the southern plantation, since both systems initiate complex power relationships among the members of the household, relationships dominated by the patriarchal "head of the household" – whether the Athenian male citizen or the southern plantation owner.[2] Finally, I agree with Keith Bradley, who acknowledges that ancient slaves "have left no records of their views of life in slavery that will allow their mental world to be fully penetrated ..." (1992, 129) and attempts to get closer to their experiences by analyzing slave narratives from other periods, narratives which record personal reactions to the objectification and exploitation that lie at the heart of slavery.

While such accounts underline the importance of coming to terms with the conditions and structures that shaped slaves' "every-day" lives – factors such as "the slave's property status, the totality of the power over him, and his kinlessness"

(Finley 1980, 77), in focusing on the production of women's identities in the Greek slavery system, I rely more heavily on Garlan's theoretical description of the slave's position in "'a rhetoric of otherness' founded upon certain textual constraints and a certain shared knowledge, which as a general rule turns the slave into the reverse of a free man – that is, a subversive incarnation of incompleteness and disorder" (1988, 19).

This conceptual framework applied to slavery, with its insistence on the definition against the free man, has often encouraged scholars to link the position of slaves with that of women in classical Athens, a practice seemingly encouraged by ancient writers such as Aristotle. Pierre Vidal-Naquet, for example, cites the passages in Aristotle which argue for similarities between women and slaves, suggesting that although Aristotle insisted on their natural difference, both hold parallel positions of disempowerment (1986, 189). Vidal-Naquet's defense of his own analysis, which considers the two groups together (even if only to prove eventually that in Athens they are somehow distinguished) lies in the exclusion of both from positions of power:

> The justification for examining the place of slaves together with that of women is this. The Greek city in its classical form was marked by a double exclusion: the exclusion of women, which made it a "men's club"; and the exclusion of slaves, which made it a "citizen's club . . ."
>
> (188)

In her own reading of Aristotle, Eve Browning Cole similarly argues that the status of free women and slaves "carries with it a static marginality, an ontologically fixed residence on the fringes of (male) human concerns" (1994, 130).

In defining the categories of women and slaves, however, most writers, like Cole, Vidal-Naquet and even Aristotle, fail to consider an important position at the intersection of both groups: the female slave.[3] For with the female slave, the "double exclusion" practiced by Athenian citizens becomes embodied in a single individual. The invisibility of the slave woman in such analyses, since she is potentially a member of both categories but never quite accounted for by either, seems poignantly to parallel the position defined by Black Feminists, who critique the assumption in contemporary scholarship that "all women (are) . . . white, all the blacks male."[4] In the rest of my paper, I strive to make the slave woman once again visible. By focusing on her "doubly excluded" status, as both a woman and a slave, I hope to demonstrate the ways in which her difference (of both ethnicity and status) complicates, and often obstructs, relationships with other women, particularly those with free Greek women.

The interaction of these two positions, female slave and free woman, is a complicated process, especially when that free woman is situated in a direct power relationship over the slave woman. As Harriet Jacobs' opening quotation suggests, mistresses, even as they held power over their slaves, often shared a certain subordinate status with slave women, as they too were subjected to the inherent structural misogynies of the social and political systems under which they lived. Thus, when mistresses like Mrs Flint insisted on their *complete* difference from their slave women (a separation often demonstrated by violent acts against their slaves), they refused to recognize any potential for identification with these women. Such a strategy often attempted to obscure or deny their own disenfranchisement from power in the family and in the state during this period, as they sought to displace their own disempowerment onto the body of the female slave.

The dynamics of such a relationship in an ancient text can be witnessed perhaps most violently in the encounter between Aeschylus' Clytemnestra and the slave Cassandra, whom Clytemnestra butchers alongside her husband, Agamemnon. As we shall see, Clytemnestra, in trying to retain the power she has seized in her husband's absence, chooses to construct Cassandra as the disempowered other, a barbarian. Clytemnestra uses Cassandra's foreignness and her enslavement to "justify" this distinction, and in doing so, she implicitly denies any connection to the priestess's structural disempowerment. Clytemnestra's violent insistence on their difference culminates in her murder of the priestess. Yet, in slaughtering Cassandra, Clytemnestra pointedly ignores the many similarities that she shares with her, an "oversight" that ironically is reproduced in the final play of the trilogy when Athena in turn insists on her own difference from Clytemnestra, a forced difference that will allow Athena to justify the death of Clytemnestra herself.

I begin, then, with an analysis of Aeschylus' *Agamemnon*, focusing particularly on the one-sided exchange between Clytemnestra and Cassandra that seals the young priestess's fate (1035–71). In this scene, as we shall see, Aeschylus makes use of crucial elements of Greek slavery, including its foundations in the distinction between foreigners and Greeks and the strain it places on the *oikos*. Yet, even as Aeschylus alludes to the general structures of slavery, it is important to note that his discourse on slavery is articulated entirely around the figures of two women. Thus, although Agamemnon is the one who enslaves Cassandra, an event that occurs off-stage, Clytemnestra emphasizes her role as Cassandra's new master and it is against Clytemnestra that Cassandra directs her most bitter hatred.

The *Agamemnon*, first produced in 458 BCE, depicts the violent events surrounding the return of the hero Agamemnon from the Trojan War. Unlike his comrade, Odysseus, whose arduous voyage home is finally completed when his wife Penelope accepts him back into her bed, Agamemnon never reassumes his role as head of his household; instead he is butchered violently in his bath by his wife Clytemnestra, who has been long planning such revenge against her husband for his sacrifice of their daughter Iphigenia at the beginning of the war. The power struggle between Agamemnon and Clytemnestra is thus already determined by the events preceding the play, by the king's decision to kill his daughter, and by the hatred Clytemnestra nurses toward him because of it.

Agamemnon, however, is not the only one whom Clytemnestra executes. Alongside her husband, Clytemnestra murders the priestess Cassandra, whom

Agamemnon has taken as a slave from the eastern city and brought to the household. It is this second murder, that of Cassandra, that interests me here – Cassandra's death, after all, has not been anticipated by Clytemnestra in her long years of planning. The murder of Cassandra depends entirely on the way in which a relationship between the two women is produced within the play.

Since Clytemnestra has long awaited the return of her husband, it is perhaps not surprising that she concentrates primarily on her husband when he first enters with Cassandra. This is the moment, after all, which secures Clytemnestra's domination over Agamemnon, as she pressures him into a series of hubristic actions that prefigure his downfall.[5] Although Agamemnon urges Clytemnestra to be kind to the enslaved Cassandra during this scene, claiming that no one willing accepts the yoke of slavery (950ff.), Clytemnestra herself addresses the young priestess only after she has returned from leading Agamemnon into the house. At that point, Clytemnestra encourages Cassandra, too, to enter the house and to prepare to engage in sacrifice with "all the other slaves" (1035–8).[6] Ordering Cassandra to come down from the chariot, Clytemnestra tells her not be ashamed of her servile status, arguing first that even Heracles served as a slave, then that she should be grateful for the wealth of her master's house (1040–6). Cassandra, however, does not respond; the Chorus prompts her, urging her to obey if she can (1047–9). Clytemnestra, angered, suggests that the foreign woman must have understood and should obey her – unless, she suggests, the priestess speaks only a "barbarian tongue" (1050–2). Again the Chorus encourages Cassandra to obey (1053–4).

The choice is given: understand Greek and obey or be labeled a barbarian with a wild, uncivilized language. When still no response is given, Clytemnestra, becoming impatient, repeats her order, again emphasizing Cassandra's supposed recourse to savage communication by making the paradoxical command that if Cassandra does not understand her words she should wave her "barbarian" hand (1059–61).[7] The Chorus replies on Cassandra's behalf, saying they do not think Cassandra has understood, but needs an interpreter, concluding with a comparison of her to a captured animal (1062–3). Unconvinced, Clytemnestra remarks that Cassandra has come from her captured city ill-prepared to endure the yoke, a subordination she will learn only when her blood has been shed. Clytemnestra then exits, refusing to take the priestess's contempt any longer (1064–8).

Since Clytemnestra chooses ultimately not to identify with the disempowered status of Cassandra, who has been enslaved by the Greek forces, but rather emphasizes her barbarity, a trait demonstrated by Cassandra's presumed inability to speak Greek, it is significant that upon Clytemnestra's exit, Cassandra dissolves the image of foreignness that Clytemnestra constructs, for she does speak and in Greek. Mirroring Clytemnestra's threats, she eventually predicts first Agamemnon's death (1100–4, 1107–11, 1114–18, and 1125–9) then her own (1136–9).[8] When the Chorus fails to understand Cassandra's prophecies, she promises a clearer vision, but its language and mode of expression, too, elude the Chorus's comprehension. After she attempts to demonstrate the roots of her prophetic powers to the Chorus (1202–14), Cassandra's language becomes "more and more violent" (Denniston and Page 1972, 166). She sees first the past atrocities of the House of Atreus, then the murder of Agamemnon (1123ff.). In tracing the forthcoming violence, Cassandra first attacks Aegisthus (a "cowardly lion"), who occupies his master's bed (1224–5) – her own master, too, she quickly amends, since she now bears his yoke of slavery as well (1226). She scornfully pronounces that Agamemnon has been fooled by the flattery of the "detestable bitch" (1227–30). In her building rage against Clytemnestra, Cassandra struggles to find an appropriately monstrous image to describe her (1232–6). She then assures the Chorus that whether they understand her or not, she will eventually be proclaimed a true prophet (1239–41).

Since the Chorus still does not understand her prophecy, Cassandra finally predicts Agamemnon's death explicitly in a single line (1246).[9] Yet their comprehension of this event proves to be only partial, as they ask specifically what man will attempt the deed. Cassandra finally wonders why she has been misunderstood, claiming, "Yet I know Greek; I think I know it far too well" (1254). To which the Chorus responds that oracles, too, are difficult to understand, even though they are uttered in Greek (1255). Cassandra then bemoans her fate more, claiming that the "woman-lioness" will strike her down, a punishment for having been brought by Agamemnon. She further laments Apollo's abandonment of her, then predicts that an avenger will come from another land to exact revenge. She ultimately agrees to submit to her death (1264–94) and enters the house, asking only that her death, that of a simple slave, be avenged (1322ff.).

Critics have interpreted this important scene in a variety of ways, many focusing particularly on the self-conscious attention to language and persuasion in the speeches, a theme that has become prominent in scholarship on the entire trilogy (for example, Harriott 1982; Elata-Alster 1985; Thalmann 1985a; Thalmann 1985b). Simon Goldhill relates the scene to "the complex set of interrelations between the role of language and the discourse of sexuality which so dominates the text of the trilogy" (1986, 23). The breakdown of communication here (as, for example, when the Chorus fails time and time again to understand Cassandra's prophecy) parallels the breakdown of sexual roles in the play overall, both of which symbolize the larger disorder that the play evokes.

> The orderings of language, the orderings of sexuality – mutually implicative – are seen as breaking down in adultery, female dominance, "misuse" of language. It is this misuse of signs, the corruption of the process of exchange, that constitutes the threat to the *oikos* and society.
>
> (Goldhill 1984, 98)

Just as Clytemnestra, in refusing to return the reins of the state to her husband, embodies the greatest threat to both the *oikos* and society,[10] so, too, she retains

the greatest potential to control and corrupt language and meaning in the play.
William G. Thalmann writes that "it is Clytemnestra who is most in command
of language and uses it as an instrument to accomplish her purposes. Her
manipulation of words to exploit their imprecision is splendid and terrifying"
(1985b, 226). Clytemnestra succeeds, for example, in convincing Agamemnon
to walk on the purple cloth by the pure force and persuasiveness of her arguments.[11] Thus, language remains Clytemnestra's strongest weapon of attack and
her most public one – unlike the knife, which she uses off-stage when striking
Agamemnon and Cassandra down in the bath.[12] Clytemnestra herself understands well the power of language – her very first speech as she enters after
the double murder, after all, acknowledges openly that she used deceptive speech
to carry out her revenge (1372ff.).

In turning her attention from Agamemnon to Cassandra, Clytemnestra hopes
to gain the same verbal domination. She is reduced to a one-sided exchange
with the priestess, however, one which becomes self-reflexive of the process of
communication itself as both Clytemnestra and the Chorus attempt to determine
whether Cassandra has understood her mistress's orders. Goldhill believes
that Cassandra's silence in response to Clytemnestra demonstrates a breakdown
of communication (1986, 25). This disruption seems to reach its climax in
Clytemnestra's frustrated request for a non-verbal response, a "sign without
language" (Goldhill 1986, 25) as she asks Cassandra to wave her hand (cf.
Denniston and Page 1972, 163).

Other scholars, however, have read Cassandra's silence not as indicative of
the failure of language, but rather as a symbol of her resistance. Thalmann
argues:

> [O]nly one character in the play can resist Clytemnestra, and that is
> Cassandra. Lines 1035–1071 represent a failed persuasion-scene which
> contrasts with the successful one with Agamemnon. Cassandra meets
> Clytemnestra's attempts to persuade her to enter the house . . . and
> characteristic verbal ironies . . . with silence. Whatever Cassandra's
> motives – contempt, indifference, preoccupation with her suffering –
> this silence is a brilliantly effective response. To try to resist Clytemnestra
> on her own terms would be dangerous and probably futile; but silence,
> the apparent absence of any response at all, is the one attitude that
> renders Clytemnestra's skill with language impotent. . . . Cassandra uses
> silence voluntarily and in order to prevail, to claim the only freedom
> left open to her: to enter the palace to her death at the time and in
> the way she chooses – unlike Agamemnon.
>
> (1985b, 228–9)

And indeed we can contextualize such activity within the forms of individual
non-violent resistance to slavery that are not always attested in sources about
slavery. David Barry Gaspar argues that for slave women in Antigua

the typical style of resistance ... was unquestionably of the day-to-day variety that nibbled away most insidiously at the efficiency of the slave system. ... A whole range of behavior was crowded into this category of resistance, the intensity and meaning of which might vary: displays such as gestures, attitudes, posture, facial expression, gait, or verbal play.

(1996, 229)

Yet, despite her resistance to Clytemnestra's orders, Cassandra is paradoxically united with her mistress through this very exchange – for she is the only character in the play who understands clearly the implications of Clytemnestra's speech, a comprehension that is threaded throughout her subsequent prophecy, uttered only after Clytemnestra has exited.

Similarly, when Cassandra herself does speak, her own communication is marked by an ambiguity, a failure to be understood, which ironically mirrors Clytemnestra's. Goldhill writes of the transition from Clytemnestra to Cassandra:

The strong emphasis on the process of communication and language as a prelude to Cassandra's prophecies is particularly important. After the scenes dominated by Clytemnestra, in which we have considered the queen's manipulation of speech, where language was both the means and the matter of transgression, after the chorus' and others' repeatedly expressed hopes for a true and accurate language, now the stage will be dominated by Cassandra, the inspired princess, possessed of complete insight, an absolutely true language. But ironically enough, this is language which is incapable of being understood, incapable of being received.

(1984, 26)

We can see, then, the complex alignments of similarity and difference between the two women in this scene, since although Cassandra in some respects "represents the inverse of Clytemnestra" (Thalmann 1985b, 229), the two women are linked both by a cryptic style of communication (the one conscious and the other perhaps unconscious) and by Cassandra's singular ability to comprehend Clytemnestra's speech.

Clytemnestra, however, is not on stage to hear Cassandra speak and reveal her understanding of the fatal plans. Even more important, Clytemnestra does not hear Cassandra speak *Greek* – an aspect of Clytemnestra's self-consciousness about language and communication in the scene that often goes unnoticed. Clytemnestra's insistence on the importance of Greek to successful communication, after all, fundamentally affects her strategy in the scene. This emphasis on the Greek language here is crucial; I am aware of no other scene in tragedy in which Greek becomes so explicitly problematized – that is, any scene in which characters reflect on one anothers' knowledge of Greek so openly.[13]

After all, for all her "strangeness" in Jason's eyes, perfect Greek still flows from Medea's mouth.

Clytemnestra's focus on Greek specific..y allows her to underline the distinction between Greeks and barbarians, one that she will use forcefully against the foreign priestess. And in framing Cassandra as her other, Clytemnestra has chosen her weapon well, since linguistic difference, as Edith Hall argues, remained a primary criterion for Greeks in distinguishing same (Greek) from other (barbarian) (1989, 5 and 179ff.).[14] Clytemnestra's interest in forcing this distinction can be located in the larger social context of the fifth century, in which, as Hall (1989) and others demonstrate (for example, Schlaifer 1968), the Greeks began progressively to formulate a "national" identity in opposition to the external threats of "barbarians." Garlan writes specifically of Aeschylus' participation in this "project" following the Persian Wars

> which gave the Greeks an acute sense of their own superiority over the Asiatic hordes ruled by the Great King. As early as 472, in *The Persians*, Aeschylus represented the battle of Salamis as a confrontation between the very principles of liberty and slavery.
>
> (1988, 120)

As Garlan suggests, the link of a Greek "nationalism" to ideologies of slavery in the fifth century is a close one (cf. Schlaifer 1968) – and one that Aeschylus presumably exploits in the initial image of speechless Cassandra.

Thus, Clytemnestra seeks to emphasize Cassandra's role as the foreign other by labeling her silence not resistance (a form of power), but ignorance of Greek (a type of disempowerment and "evidence" of her barbarity). Similarly, Clytemnestra's attempt to force Cassandra to resort to a physical response (a wave of the hand) can be read not only as the replacement of "a sign without language" for "a sign in language" (Goldhill 1986, 25), but also as a derogatory characterization of Cassandra's presumed foreign tongue. Here Carol Dougherty's analysis of the language of Aeschylus' *Women of Aetna* is crucial, particularly in her general conclusions about the relationship between language and colonialism, where colonialism might provide a model for understanding symbolically Clytemnestra's attempts to dominate the enslaved priestess.[15]

> Colonization is not limited to transplanting populations and building cities on foreign land; it includes supplanting native speech as well. For language, i.e., the language of the colonist, is the sign of culture and civilization. Confrontation with foreign peoples speaking a different tongue demands strategies for dealing with such linguistic and cultural conflict. One approach denies the very existence of the native language – wild and savage natives cannot communicate at all.
>
> (Dougherty 1991, 120)

44

In their forced confrontation, then, Clytemnestra adopts particular "strategies for dealing with linguistic and cultural conflict." First emphasizing Cassandra's ignorance of Greek, "the sign of culture and civilization," Clytemnestra then negates Cassandra's "native" language by reducing her communicative potential to non-verbal means – to a waving of her "barbarian hand." This elaborate construction of Cassandra's foreignness, dependent upon her ignorance of Greek, will, of course, reveal its erroneous foundation when Cassandra shortly after opens her mouth – as Cassandra acknowledges, she speaks Greek only too well.

Since we have seen now the way in which Clytemnestra sets the stage for Cassandra's murder, finding "justification" for it ahead of time in Cassandra's presumed otherness, we might ask why Clytemnestra even includes the priestess in her revenge against Agamemnon. Clytemnestra, after all, has not been plotting Cassandra's death these long years as she has Agamemnon's. Indeed, there is no difficulty in finding motivations for Clytemnestra's murder of her husband. She herself credits Agamemnon's slaughter of Iphigenia (1417–18, 1432ff., 1525–9) and the necessity of bringing the bloodshed that has plagued the House of Atreus to an end (1497–1504, 1567–77). So, too, Clytemnestra acknowledges jealousy over Cassandra (1438–47),[16] a sexual jealousy that is demonstrated graphically by her use of a pointed obscenity in characterizing Cassandra's sexual activity with a term that Wm Blake Tyrrell takes to mean "rubbing Agamemnon's erection (while) on the ship's benches" (1980, 45; cf. Koniaris 1980). As we have seen above, Cassandra, too, credits her looming death to the fact she has been brought home by Agamemnon. Although we will see that jealousy and sexual competition, aspects both women importantly acknowledge, underlie such a system of slavery in which (male) masters have unrestricted sexual access to their slaves, this motivation in itself seems insufficient, since Clytemnestra has herself taken a new lover.

Aeschylus despicts Clytemnestra's murder of Cassandra as a means of violently denying any structural similarity between the two women. As Gail Pheterson suggests, "maintaining a posture of dominance is often tenuously balanced upon denying inferior status; the individual suppresses and conceals characteristics which reveal social powerlessness" (1986, 159). Or, as Clytemnestra contrives here, inferior status and social powerlessness are displaced onto the Other. Thus, although the enslaved woman offers no "real" threat to Clytemnestra's power or rule (her status as the disempowered slave is emphasized by Agamemnon, Clytemnestra, and Cassandra herself in turn), if Clytemnestra is to assert power in her society, power as it is defined by men, she must prove her right to that power by destroying any conceptual links between herself and the enslaved foreign priestess. Such a distinction between women and slaves seems especially important for Clytemnestra, who is attempting to retain her political power in the play, since, as we have seen above, ancient writers often equated the two groups according to their disenfranchisement from the state. Winnington-Ingram captures Clytemnestra's dilemma by expanding the conception of jealousy in the play, arguing that Clytemnestra envies Agamemnon's position of power as a man within Greek society; he writes that "she hated Agamemnon, not simply because he had killed her child, not because she loved Aegisthus, but out of a jealousy that was not jealousy of Chryseis or Cassandra, but of Agamemnon himself and his status as a man" (1948, 132). So, too, the Chorus, although acknowledging Clytemnestra's power, nonetheless makes it clear to her that she rules only in Agamemnon's absence (259).

Ironically, many of the ways in which Clytemnestra tries to symbolize Cassandra's difference are the exact ones that the play uses to characterize Clytemnestra herself. Clytemnestra, for example, emphasizes Cassandra's foreignness, yet foreignness is a characteristic Clytemnestra herself paradoxically represents throughout the trilogy, perhaps most obviously when she reaches for an axe in murdering Orestes. Even more, Clytemnestra seems to adopt a foreign style of expression in the play. Helen Bacon writes:

> Wilamowitz apparently was the first to observe that Clytemnestra's greeting to Agamemnon . . . and parts of her last speech in that scene . . . imitate, and even echo, an Egyptian hymn of praise. As Kranz pointed out, to Agamemnon her words as well as her actions have a foreign flavor. . . . It intensifies the irony of the scene to know that Clytemnestra consciously uses a foreign style of speech, as she urges on Agamemnon a foreign style of behavior.
>
> (1961, 40–1)

Edith Hall writes of Clytemnestra's general characterization: "a brilliant device is shown to have been deployed . . . the 'vocabulary of barbarism' has been transferred to illuminate the psychology and motivation of a *Greek*" (1989, 203). Thus, although she ostensibly despises Cassandra for her foreignness, Clytemnestra is portrayed by Aeschylus as equally susceptible to accusations of "foreignness" – it remains a quality that paradoxically unites the women in a position of marginalization from the play's normative Greek center.

So, too, Cassandra's disempowerment parallels Clytemnestra's own position at her husband's court, where she faces replacement by the returning hero. As Winnington-Ingram argues, Clytemnestra's conflict with her husband involves more than revenge for her daughter; it expands to include a fight for the autonomy she has assumed in his absence, since "the dominance of a man is abhorrent to her" (1948, 132). Thus, "when [Clytemnestra] kills her husband, it is not only an act of vengeance, but also a blow struck for personal liberty" (ibid.). And " personal liberty" is a strong term here since the loss of it is even more directly reflected in Cassandra's position. Thus, the more tenuous the dividing line between the women, the more Clytemnestra forces a distinction.[17] And the positions they occupy can be imagined in even closer terms, as Euripides did later in his *Iphigenia at Aulis*, making Clytemnestra claim that she herself was once Agamemnon's captive, as she bitterly charges that she married him against her will after he murdered her first husband and child (1147–53).

In sum, Clytemnestra attempts first to dominate the priestess outright (force her into the house) or, when that fails, to insist on their difference from one another – a forced difference that will prove fatal to the priestess, but one which is nonetheless illusory. The women are indeed closer than Clytemnestra allows: Cassandra, after all, speaks Greek only too well.

In his novel *Absalom, Absalom!*, William Faulkner restages a similar conflict in the American south of the nineteenth century, also acknowledging the complex web of emotions and identifications involved in such a relationship between a slave woman and her mistress. In the novel, he even alludes to Aeschylus' text by suggesting that one of the women, Rosa Coldfield, had in her youth "an air Cassandralike and humorless and profoundly and sternly prophetic out of all proportion to the actual years of a child who had never been young" (1986, 15).[18] Faulkner completes the allusion by naming one of Rosa's main foils in the text Clytemnestra (Clytie). And in recasting Cassandra and Clytemnestra, Faulkner pointedly highlights the similarities between the positions of the two by inverting them – for in this text Clytie is the (black) female slave and Rosa the free (white) woman (although not directly Clytie's mistress). Their relationship is explored through a series of tense interactions, one of which involves Rosa's violent response to Clytie's attempt to acknowledge their mutual bond (Gwin 1985a, 111–29). Faulkner provocatively draws the link even closer through the white master's "confusion" of the ancient names alone, having one of his narrators claim:

> Yes. He [Sutpen] named Clytie as he named them all. . . . Only I have always liked to believe that he intended to name her Cassandra, prompted by some pure dramatic economy not only to beget her but to designate the presiding augur of his own disaster, and that he just got the name wrong through a mistake natural in a man who must have almost taught himself to read.
>
> (48)

Thus, in Faulkner's text the figures of Cassandra and Clytemnestra are so intertwined that one gets "mistaken" for another. And the power that Sutpen (the southern male) maintains over the entire system, symbolized by both the naming and the "begetting" he controls here, provides perhaps the most fundamental connection between the two.[19]

Faulkner's symbolic transference of the ancient confrontation between mistress and slave to the American south illustrates very powerfully the parallel gender dynamics that marked both slavery systems.[20] Even though, as we have seen previously, the systems of, and philosophies behind, slavery in ancient Greece and the American south differed in many ways, writings from the American experience can still expand our understanding of relationships between mistresses and female slaves – perhaps most importantly by recording these women's voices directly.

Scholarship on slavery in the American south, like scholarship on classical slavery, has been criticized for approaches which too often left the role of the slave women subsumed under broader, insufficient categories, such as the family (Stetson 1982, 62ff.). A more sophisticated approach to the study of gender and race in slavery of the American south suggests that the position of the American slave woman echoes the "double exclusion" of the ancient slave woman. Joan Rezner Gundersen points out that for slave women in colonial Virginia "the bonds of a female slave were twofold, linking her both to an interracial community of women and setting her apart as a slave in ways that make evident the special burden of being black and female in white, patriarchal society" (1989, 353). Narratives written by female slaves from this period focus particularly on this interracial community of women, giving greater attention in their text to the characterization of women, both slave and free. Brenda Stevenson argues, for example, that although men tend to be represented as "stock figures" in female slave narratives (for example, "the sadistic, sexually depraved slave masters; the vicious, deceptive slave traders; and the fun-loving, emasculated black male youths"), "slave women . . . conspicuously constructed not only their own identities in their recollections but also the identities of their mistresses" (1996, 181). Thus, in their narratives, slave women constructed their own identities in part by situating themselves in relation to the free white women – at times expressing their common bonds, while at other times emphasizing the oppositional forces that separated them.

Mary Prince, in her account of life as a slave, records great affection and sympathy for her mistress, who remained subordinate to her selfish husband. Importantly, even as she identifies with her mistress, Prince still recognizes the power that the system gives to Mrs Williams. She says of their relationship:

> I was truly attached to her, and, next to my own mother, loved her better than any creature in the world. My obedience to her commands was cheerfully given; it sprung solely from the affection I felt for her, and not from fear of the power which the white people's law had given her over me.
>
> (1987, 188)

Slave mistresses, too, at times identified with their female slaves, often treating them with compassion or acknowledging their own disempowerment in the plantation's hierarchy. Yet, at times their insistence on this similarity obscured the real power differences between the two groups that Prince's narrative refuses to forget (this parallels Jacobs' assertion that she would be at Mrs Flint's *feet* with a kind word – my emphasis). Erlene Stetson points out, for example, that some white women drew parallels between their position in society and that of the slaves. Mary Chestnut wrote that 'There is no slave, after all, like a wife. . . . Poor women, poor slaves. . . . All married women, all children and girls who live in their fathers' houses are slaves.

(1982, 76)

In making such erasures of the power differential between black and white women, Chestnut's sentiments have dangerous implications. As Minrose Gwin writes:

Chestnut views the black woman as the embodiment of her own fears and disappointments. She equates white womanhood with slavery. In the black woman she sees sexual freedom and maternal joy. What she does not see is that the black woman's sexuality and fertility often led to her greatest indignities and deepest pain.[21]

(1985a, 108)

It is this type of inability to come to terms with the structures of patriarchy and slavery, to comprehend the different experiences of women within it, that kept white and black women most divided – especially since the systems themselves demanded a separation of women, both in ideology and practice, encouraging, on the one hand, sexual jealousy from slave mistresses and, on the other, moral condemnation from slave women.

As the American slavery system granted slavemasters complete freedom to exploit their slaves sexually, writings from the period suggest that slave mistresses often felt a sense of competition with their female slaves, a feeling frequently accompanied by sexual jealousy.[22] According to Harriet Jacobs, her jealous mistress Mrs Flint

felt that her marriage vows were desecrated, her dignity insulted; but she had no compassion for the poor victim of her husband's perfidy. She pitied herself as a martyr; but she was incapable of feeling for the condition of shame and misery in which her unfortunate, helpless slave was placed.

(1987, 366)[23]

Once again, Mrs Flint, like many white women, chose to act as if Harriet had complete freedom over her sexuality. The perspective of the slaves was, of course, very different: "where white women saw sexual competition – with connotations of equality – black men and women saw rank exploitation that stemmed from grossly disparate levels of power" (Painter 1994, 207).

While white women often felt sexual jealousy of their slave women, the slaves in turn felt anger at their mistresses for too often becoming willing participants in the system of exploitation. Harriet Jacobs shows how Mrs Flint enacted the simultaneous positions of power/disempowerment:

> Mrs. Flint, like many southern women, was totally deficient in energy. She had not strength to superintend her household affairs; but her nerves were so strong, that she could sit in her chair and see a woman whipped, till the blood trickled from every stroke of the lash.
>
> (1987, 347)

This combination of passivity (a refusal to resist the system) and aggression (directed against a more victimized member of the system) is sharply criticized time and time again in the writings of slave women, for whom resistance was a daily strategy.

Yet, it would be wrong to categorize the conflicts in entirely personal terms, since all these texts allude to the ways in which the larger systems of patriarchy and slavery encouraged (and even depended on) this division of women. Ideologically, for example, women were divided into "two classes: ladies, always white and chaste; and whores, comprising all black women (except for the saintly Mammy) and any woman who defied the established constraints on her sexual behavior" (Clinton 1982, 204). And these divisive categories functioned alongside a social structure that brought the two groups into close contact. Thus, the codes of the slavocracy "demanded moral superiority from white women and sexual availability from black, yet simultaneously expected mistress and slave woman to live and work in intimate physical proximity" (Gwin 1985b, 39). The tension underlying the presence of both groups of women in a single household, even as the system set them up in competition, poignantly highlights some of the ambiguities of Agamemnon's request that Clytemnestra accept Cassandra kindly into her house.

It is this paradox that forced women to identify through and against one another. According to Gwin,

> there is no doubt that there was a powerful connection built upon a shared sense of societal demands that placed them in opposite but deeply interdependent roles. In terms of a wholeness of female identity, each had only half. Their struggles, often subconscious, to obtain the missing piece of self as it is displayed in the Other make their lives and their writings about the relationships studies in the female struggle to attain wholeness and the terrible price to be paid in that struggle.
>
> (1985a, 51)

The contradictory claims of similarity and difference between slave women and their mistresses, especially when coupled with their varying opportunities to exert power and control, often yielded violent results. As Gwin further explains: "It is this sense of 'two-ness' coupled with the complete power of the white woman over the black, which imbues the writings of these women with a tension, a straining toward the Other, and an underlying violence born of repression, frustration, and fear" (1985a, 51).

In all, such writings demonstrate graphically the implications of a slavery system that bound women in patterns of mutual identification and differentiation and they provide a means for understanding the complex motivations, including sexual jealousy and the fear of acknowledging a similar position of disempowerment, that drive Clytemnestra to construct Cassandra as a barbarian, "as sexual competition," as a dark side of her own sexual self – her other (paraphrased from Gwin 1985a, 5) rather than recognizing the common bonds the two women share. Importantly, even though Clytemnestra, unlike the white women discussed above, manages to transgress certain sexual codes of Aeschylus' text by taking Aegisthus as her lover, she does not smash the system entirely. Instead, she ignores the abusive constraints of slavery controlling Cassandra when she holds her responsible for the presumed sexual activity with Agamemnon – casting Cassandra in one line graphically as Agamemnon's whore. And this refusal of any identification with the enslaved princess becomes violently played out on the body of Cassandra, as Clytemnestra's distinction from the princess is finalized with her murder.

Ironically, Clytemnestra's denial of solidarity with Cassandra is paralleled by Athena's own denial of Clytemnestra, a process Winnington-Ingram locates with Athena's vote (1948).[24] For, when Orestes, Clytemnestra's son, murders her in revenge for the death of his father, Athena acquits him, judging Clytemnestra's death a lesser threat to the social order than that of her husband. In siding with Orestes, Athena makes her infamous denial of allegiance with all women, claiming "No mother bore me. The male I commend in all things – except for marriage – with all my heart, and am strongly on my father's side" (Winnington-Ingram 1948, 144). Thus the goddess differentiates herself from Clytemnestra, who stands here as both mother and wife, two roles that Athena pointedly repudiates. And even though Clytemnestra is made to serve these feminine roles here, the tragedy results from her attempts to do precisely what Athena has done – align herself with masculine power (144–5).

Thus, the *Oresteia* places its female characters on three levels: slave, citizen wife, and goddess. And although the three positions might parallel each other in important ways, such similarity is denied throughout the play and violent differences are insisted upon, as first Clytemnestra then Athena attempt to secure their power in a "man's world" over the corpses of their female counterparts. It is finally our conception of the "man's world" that brings us back to the figure of Aeschylus as the trilogy's author and to the broader fifth-century social context of the play. For, by making Cassandra, Clytemnestra, and Athena participants in a violent structure that keeps women divided from each other – a structure that leaves two of the three dead at the trilogy's conclusion and which allows for no identification or compassion between them – the play ultimately reaffirms its placement in an Athenian patriarchal slavocracy, which structurally forces competition between women, even as it locates them in close proximity, both spatially and ideologically.

Finally, I wish to use the murder of Cassandra to comment more broadly on feminist theory – and the flawed perspective of any feminism that leaves Cassandra invisible. I apply this warning specifically to feminist appropriations of Clytemnestra. Sally MacEwen, for example, in the introduction to her volume *Views of Clytemnestra, Ancient and Modern* writes generally, "Our sympathies, in the end, usually end up with Clytemnestra" (1990, 14). Later, in her essay within the volume, MacEwen examines whether Clytemnestra is the "victim" or the "villain" more fully, but does not bring the murder of Cassandra into the equation (31).[25] As feminists, however, I believe that we should be wary of any uncritical valorization of Clytemnestra's transgressions and power, since she becomes in many ways a prototypical "Superwoman," who attempts not to tear down the system of patriarchy, but to become its sole exception. As Audre Lorde so poignantly asserted, "(t)he master's tools will never dismantle the master's house. They may allow us temporarily to beat him at his own game, but they will never enable us to bring genuine change" (1984, 112).

More broadly, the image of Clytemnestra murdering Cassandra seems to me to evoke a powerful symbol of the consequences of asserting a feminism that produces, then subsequently destroys or ignores traces of difference. While feminism is currently trying to broaden its perspectives beyond that of a single race or class, even now it has not completely internalized the essential nature of understanding difference, as Vron Ware argues:

> many feminists are interested in notions of difference from choice rather than necessity. It is too easy for women occupying privileged positions in race and class hierarchies to assume that it is for them to invite others to join them in feminist politics, and that parity can be achieved merely by acknowledging that they are somehow 'different.'
>
> (1994, 221)

Black Feminist criticism, however, recommended by Ware as a "model" for feminist historians (222), provides one means for understanding the complexity of identity and the intricate webs with which power and dominance operate.[26] Such a framework can be used to formulate a more complex reading of the relationship between Clytemnestra and Cassandra, one which acknowledges both the similarities between the two women and Cassandra's particular positioning at the intersection of two excluded groups: women and slaves.

And once again we can turn to the context of the American south in understanding the specific legacy of power and oppression which too often has divided American feminists, since the relationships between white mistresses and slaves in many ways "help explain the thorniness of women's contacts across the color line well into the twentieth century" (Painter 1994, 212), particularly because of the ways in which white women, although themselves oppressed, nevertheless often became complicit in the system.[27] From the examples of Clytemnestra and her American counterparts, then, we, as feminists, can realize fully that the decision to exercise power (either by consciously seizing new forms or subconsciously making use of "advantages" conferred by class, race, or ethnicity) always has grave consequences for any formation of unity among women.[28]

Notes

1 See particularly the work of Finley (1980) and Garlan (1988), the second of whom presents a historiography of Marxist approaches to ancient slavery in his introduction.

2 Saller (1987) provides an excellent analysis of the impact of slavery on Roman family organization, focusing not only on structural arrangements, but also on emotional patterns, etc. He, too, draws comparisons/contrasts with the American plantation.

3 In particular, Vidal-Naquet's mythical evidence concentrates on the conjunction of the rule of slaves with the rule of women — an association represented symbolically by sexual union predicated on heterosexual sex with the presumption that all slaves are men (1986). Similarly, while Eve Browning Cole acknowledges that Aristotle's "three-level moral typology corresponding to men, women, and slaves" treats slaves as "genderless," (1994, 129), she does not acknowledge the specific position of the female slave in her own arguments.

4 This is a paraphrase of Valerie Smith, who critiques modern critical approaches that too often reproduce a singular historically dominant perspective. She writes: "the move away from historical specificity . . . resembles all too closely the totalizing tendency commonly associated with androcentric criticism. In other words, when historical specificity is denied or remains implicit, all the women are presumed white, all the blacks male" (1989, 44). Black Feminist criticism, in general, has sustained a powerful critique of the biases in much feminist scholarship. Recently, Shelley P. Haley has applied the critique specifically to classics (1993).

5 Critics have debated the exact reasons for Agamemnon's yielding. See for example Konishi (1989). Interestingly, Meridor argues that Agamemnon gives in to Clytemnestra's demands so that Clytemnestra will in turn treat Cassandra with kindness, a request he makes in lines 950–5. Meridor argues somewhat unconvincingly that "[f]rom this perspective, it is Cassandra, not Clytemnestra, to whom Agamemnon is subjugated" (1987, 42).

6 Denniston and Page see the latter claim as an insult – a means of letting "Cassandra understand that she is now just one among a herd of slaves" (1972, 160).

7 Denniston and Page discuss the rare word *karbanoi* which seems to mean "barbarian" (1972, 164).

8 Cassandra's prophecy, especially in its mode of expression, has been analyzed extensively (for example, Goldhill 1984, 85 ff. and 1986, 26ff.).

9 Significantly this is the first time that she names Agamemnon (Denniston and Page 1972, 183).

10 For a discussion of this aspect of Clytemnestra's actions, see MacEwen, who writes: "The crime of Clytemnestra is above all political, which is to say, it is an assault on the institutions of civilization. Even her disruption of the *oikos* is a crime because it disrupts her proper role in the state" (1990b, 29).

11 Konishi (1989) discusses this victory in great detail. The Chorus repeats forms of the word "persuasion" three times in their first attempt to make Cassandra obey Clytemnestra (1049) – an allusion, Goldhill points out, to the earlier verbal dominance Clytemnestra achieves over Agamemnon (1986, 25).

12 See Prag (1991) and Sommerstein (1989) for a description of the debate over Clytemnestra's weapon.

13 See Bacon (1961) for a discussion of the use of foreign languages in the three tragedians, 15–24 (on Aeschylus), 64–73 (on Sophocles), and 115–20 (on Euripides). Of

particular interest is her claim that: "[o]nly one reference to the fact that a character speaks a foreign language exists in the extant plays of Sophocles (Ajax 1263). ... Tecmessa's foreignness might, like Cassandra's in *Agamemnon*, have been developed by drawing attention to her speech, but Sophocles does not raise the point" (64). Also her later claim that Tecmessa "has more in common with the Greek-mannered Trojans of Euripides than with Aeschylus' foreign princess, Cassandra" (101–2). Her overall conclusions about Aeschylus' use of "foreignness" suggest that "in general Aeschylus did not concern himself with foreign material, but tried to represent foreigners accurately and completely in the plays in which they occur. It is an accident that three of the seven surviving plays are so rich in foreign material that we have come to think of Aeschylus as a poet greatly preoccupied with barbarians" (61).

14 Importantly, the Greek/barbarian distinction is later undermined by the Chorus – outside of Clytemnestra's hearing – when they respond that oracles, too, are difficult to understand, even though they are uttered in Greek (1255).

15 For a broader understanding of Clytemnestra's use of colonial power here, see the work of McClintock, who draws distinctions between men's and women's experiences of colonialism (1995, 6).

16 Lawrence Richardson, jr, in private conversation, suggested a link between Clytemnestra's anger over Iphigenia and her jealousy of Cassandra, arguing that Cassandra is meant to symbolize a replacement for the dead Iphigenia – presuming the two are approximately the same age and that Cassandra's clothing as a priestess would resemble Iphigenia's final appearance.

17 Jonathan Smith's descriptions of the varying positions of difference help explain the intensity of Clytemnestra's feelings toward Cassandra. He writes: "The radically other is merely other; the proximate other is problematic, and hence, of supreme interest" (1985, 5).

18 Similarly, Faulkner later calls Rosa's childhood "that aged and ancient and timeless absence of youth which consisted of a Cassandralike listening behind closed doors" (1986, 47).

19 I am endebted to Sheila Murnaghan for the clearer articulation of Sutpen's role in this turbulent identification between the two women.

20 I am grateful to Hubert Martin for pointing out a similar staging decision in Robert Schenkkan's series of plays entitled *The Kentucky Cycle* (1993), in which Cassandra's counterpart is a black slave. For an expanded treatment of interracial relationships between women in American fiction, see Schultz 1985.

21 See also Ware (1994, 228–9) and Stetson, who claims that "Black female slave narratives provide a theoretical frame of reference for working out the close analogy between the oppression of Black woman and that of white women. ... It seems that Black female slave narratives written (edited) by white women are expressions of white women's covert protest against their subordination, and of their hostility toward men as well as toward the Victorian home" (1982, 71).

22 See, for example, Painter (1994, 197) and Angela Davis (1971). We should recognize that although scholars of both the ancient and American periods often emphasize sexual abuse as a form of exploitation, each system operates under a different conception of sexual identity and power, so that while work on American slavery emphasizes female slaves primarily as victims of such abuse, ancient sources attest the violation of both male and female slaves (for example, Garlan 1988, 152–3).

23 Importantly, despite her suffering, Jacobs nevertheless offers some compassion for her mistress's situation, claiming: "I knew I could not expect kindness or confidence from her under the circumstances in which I was placed. I could not blame her. Slaveholders' wives feel as other women would under similar circumstances" (1987, 366).

24 See also Gagarin (1975) and Hester (1981) for a discussion of Athena's vote.

25 Since I have defended Clytemnestra's position in the *Iphigenia at Aulis* in an unpublished paper, I find a critical examination of her role at times wrenching. It is the same dread that I felt upon reading Gayatri Spivak's critique of *Jane Eyre* (1989). In the essay, Spivak exposes the explicit imperialism of Brontë's text by comparing it to Jean Rhys's re-working of the "earlier" story, in which Rochester first meets and marries the foreign woman, who will later become the exoticized, demonized, madwoman in the attic. While it may be painful to challenge literary women such as Clytemnestra or Jane Eyre, who have been important to feminist critics and readers, the politics that produce these women, especially in setting them against other women, must nevertheless be exposed. See also Sharpe (1993) for a treatment of gender politics in colonial texts.

26 See for example, Collins, who argues for the replacement of "additive models" with "interlocking" ones (1991, 225 and passim).

27 Michelle Wright argues similarly that "the two opposing characteristics (i.e., of sexual promiscuity of black women, purity of white women), despite the fact that they were myths, were partly responsible for the never-mended rift that exists between European American feminists and African American feminists (or womanists). Coming from two different perspectives, these stereotypes become a mountain that has yet to be surmounted" (1991, 36).

28 A version of this paper was delivered at the Kentucky Foreign Language Conference, April 18–20, 1996. I am very grateful to the organizers (particularly Ross Scaife) and to the participants in the Classics section for their encouragement of the piece and for their many helpful suggestions. I would also like to thank Lisa Vollendorf for allowing me to accompany her to a rainy Pittsburgh at a critical moment in the article's formulation. The essay itself is dedicated with greatest affection and gratitude to Ann Wood and Jane Bullock who each, at critical times, demonstrated with great courage the true strength in forming coalitions among all groups of women.

4

SLAVES WITH SLAVES

Women and class in Euripidean tragedy

Nancy Sorkin Rabinowitz

Beginning with Henri Wallon in 1847, modern scholars have generally taken up the question of slavery and its relationship to ancient Greek political and cultural achievements in a partisan manner (Garlan 1988, 1–14; Vogt 1975, 172; cf. Wood 1988, chapter 1). In the nineteenth century, there was significant resistance to seeing Greek culture as a "slave society": the abolitionist movement left nineteenth-century Europeans troubled about the inconsistency between the Greeks, revered "Fathers of democracy," and the Greeks as slaveholders. There is considerably more agreement about and emphasis on slavery now; scholars face the old "contradiction," but they handle it in different ways. While Moses Finley argues that the enslavement of some was the prerequisite for Greek democracy (1968, 72; cf. Garlan 1988, 39; Austin and Vidal-Naquet 1977, 19), Joseph Vogt rationalizes the contradiction in this way: "Slavery and its attendant loss of humanity were part of the sacrifice which had to be paid for this achievement" (1975, 25).

If the abolitionist debate provided the context for nineteenth-century discussions of Greek slavery, the Cold War did so for more recent discussions. East European classicists took up the question, addressing it through Marxist theories of class struggle (Finley 1968, 68–9). Given the anti-Communist bias of the US post-war academy, the conversation until recently was highly politicized and difficult to engage in at all without being accused of communism.[1] Although it remains open to debate whether Greek slaves and slave owners were classes according to a strict Marxist definition, it makes sense to use the concept of class in discussing them because to be owned implies a radically different position than does owning.[2]

In these terms, the class origins of classical literature, with which this essay is concerned, seem inescapable. As G. E. M. de Ste Croix points out, members of the propertied class "liberated from toil, are the people who produced virtually all Greek art and literature and science and philosophy . . . what we know as Greek civilisation expressed itself in and through them above all, and it is they who will normally occupy the centre of our picture" (1981, 115). Certainly the propertied class is the focus of interest in tragedy, the genre on which my discussion centers. Literary evidence is nonetheless useful in the study of class consciousness; as David Konstan notes (1994a, 67) "Class antagonisms were a fact of life in ancient Athens ... palpably present in classical literature"; as his discussion of individual texts reveals, though, "they appear only in an altered register" (50). Konstan holds that the critic's task is "to tease out the dimension of class conflict that is latent or implicit in the drama" (50).

Konstan's approach directs attention to the tensions between free and slave in a work of literature, but what about women and gender conflict? When it comes to women, scholars working on class have shared the blind spot of classics in general. For instance, Konstan's article has a footnote alluding to feminist studies of gender roles, but gender is not a factor in his analysis of *Antigone* and *Electra* (1994a, 48 n. 1). Ste Croix ignores gender when he lays out the basis for his work on class struggle; he adds a section on women (1981, 93–111, with an apologetic note to feminists at the end) because he holds that women constituted a class, but he seems to think only of women of the citizen class. In this essay, I approach gender and class as interconnected categories by analyzing the representation of enslaved Trojan women and their relationship to more ordinary enslaved women in Euripides' Trojan War plays.

The tendency to make class a monolith, not varied by gender, or gender a monolith, not varied by class, has a long tradition going back to antiquity. According to Herodotus (*Histories* 6.137), before there were slaves, Athenian girls fetched water from a spring outside the city. They stopped doing so after they were raped by Pelasgians settled at the foot of Mount Hymettus. "Slavery" was made necessary then because "women" were perceived to be sexually vulnerable. Although slaves and women appear to be interchangeable as workers in this story, only a certain construction of women, as "to be raped" and "to be protected from rape," is at issue. But which women had to be protected from rape? That question is not typically asked, nor do scholars question the gender of the slaves who did the work. If they were also women, then we must understand that their possible rape was not significant, or did not count as rape.[3] The raped women must have been elite women, for the story depends on the importance of female chastity in that class; the protection/seclusion of Athenian women of the citizen class, however, was made possible only by the availability of servants to do the work.

The most often cited ancient authority on slavery is Aristotle. According to Aristotle, there are "some who are by nature free, so others are by nature slaves, and for these latter the condition of slavery is both beneficial and just" (*Politics* 1255a1–3). He acknowledges that there is a debate; some hold that slavery is not justified, since some slaves are taken by force in war, his "slaves by convention" (1253b20–3). He gives some support to this position by acknowledging that "some slaves ... have the bodies of freemen – as there are others who have a freeman's soul" (1254b32–4). But he notes that the Greeks *like* to maintain the distinction between free and slave, even though they are aware of the contradiction presented by the existence of prisoners of war as slaves: "Greeks do not like to call such persons slaves, but prefer to confine the term to barbarians" (1255a28–9). Even if individuals were enslaved as a result of a war or raid, they would not necessarily be called slaves because to do so would mean acknowledging that men of the highest rank could be sold into slavery (1255a27–8). The concept of natural slavery is thus useful to men of the ruling classes because it denies the possibility of their own enslavement.

The concept is useful in another way as well, for it erases the possibility of class strife; thus Aristotle concludes the section by asserting a community of interest between master and slave "when both of them naturally merit the position in which they stand. But the reverse is true when matters are otherwise and slavery rests merely on legal sanction and superior power" (1255b12–16). When masters are natural owners, and slaves naturally owned, there is a mutual benefit that overrides any reason for slave uprising.

Emphasizing the slave/free opposition underlying the notion of a natural slavery, Aristotle is led to overlook gender; he talks about slaves in general, as if they were all men even though there were many female slaves, and even though it would seem that slave labor as well as free followed a division along sexual lines (cf. Biezunska-Malowist and Malowist 1989, 18–19). According to Elizabeth Spelman, Aristotle assumes that "when a people are a slave people, it doesn't matter – for the purpose of their function in a well-ordered political community – whether they are male or female" (Spelman 1988, 42; *Politics* 1252b1–9).[4]

The Aristotelean opposition of free/slave, supported by the concept of natural slavery, correlates to another binary, that of Greek/Barbarian, and to Aristotle, Asians seem particularly well suited to slavery (1252b5–9; 1255a28–9; 1327b27–30; Lévy 1989). Modern authors have followed his lead and identified Greek slaves as outsiders or barbarians. Moses Finley writes

> The impression one gets is clearly that the majority of the slaves were foreigners. In a sense, they were all foreigners. That is to say, it was the rule . . . that Athenians were never kept as slaves in Athens, or Corinthians in Corinth. . . . No wonder some Greeks came to identify slaves and barbarians.
>
> (Finley 1968, 61; 1980, 118–19; cf. Just 1985, 188)

But as all slaves were not slaves by nature, so all slaves might not have been noticeably foreign (Garlan 1988, 19, 41). Resident aliens could become slaves, and even Athenian citizens could become slaves in another city. If, as it appears from Plutarch's *Life of Solon* (13.3, 23.1), any daughter found to be unchaste could have been sold into slavery (Schlaifer 1968, 179; Garlan 1988, 45; Harrison 1968, I.73), the possibility of slavery within an otherwise free family would always have existed. We must recognize that the slave was constructed as foreign or barbarian in order to protect the Greek sense of self as free and independent; the line was not fixed or natural.[5]

Aristotle delineates two visions of slavery – as a natural and as a conventional state – and then focuses on the former; for various reasons, and with interesting consequences, tragedy develops the latter. Aristotle was writing philosophy, which theorizes and may thus tend to abstraction; Greek drama, on the other hand, of necessity realized its vision through a particular situation enacted in front of an audience (cf. Just 1985, 176, 178). "A slave" could not be put on stage; it had to become a character with a gender and an ethnicity, whether marked or not. To make this somewhat abstract discussion more specific, I will look at two plays of Euripides on the Trojan War theme where the question of slavery is dealt with at length.

The Trojan War afforded the fifth-century tragedians a legendary paradigm for the hegemony of democracy over the slavish East (cf. Euripides, *Hecuba* 479ff., *Electra* 315f., *Helen* 274ff., *Iphigenia at Aulis* 1400f.), and for the kind of overturn in fortune so important for a good Aristotelean tragedy; at the same time, the fall of Troy was staged as the fall from freedom into slavery. In this way, tragedy enacted what Aristotle labeled "conventional slavery," slavery as a result of war. Plays on the Trojan War theme that were produced during the Peloponnesian War would have gained additional meaning from the contemporary context. In *heroic* times men were killed and the women taken captive, but, in the fifth century, inter-city warfare and piracy made slavery – arguably a fate worse than death for an epic aristocrat (as we will see when we look at Polyxena in Euripides' *Hecuba*) – a live issue for Athenian citizen men. As we know from Thucydides' *History of the Peloponnesian War*, they would have been in a position to be enslaved or to enslave others.[6]

Because the plays refer to and challenge the barbarian slave/Greek free antinomy, they cannot use the defensive strategies to which Aristotle resorts in the *Politics*; instead they deploy strategies of their own to deal with the double anxiety around slavery – that Greek men might themselves be enslaved, that they might be attacked by the slaves they own. In the *Hecuba* and the *Andromache*, Euripides mitigates the first cultural fear in two ways. Most notably, he emphasizes the femininity of the slave women. Because women were enslaved at Troy, these plays could not entirely ignore gender; but Euripides goes further and *highlights* the effects of gender on class and ethnicity. Secondarily, through the highborn Trojan characters, the plays emphasize the possibility that the slave might remain noble in character (cf. Vogt 1975, 21). The second fear, the possibility of slave resistance, is addressed by creating an alliance of women across class lines, particularly in the *Andromache*. In short, the plays raise two different kinds of fears around slavery and offer some consolation for each. On the one hand, men will not become slaves, because they are not women, but even if they fall into slavery, they may retain their nobility; on the other hand, Greek men have nothing to fear from slaves because they identify along gender lines with, not against, their owners.

The *Hecuba* (written around 425) and the *Trojan Women* (written around 415) both take place after the fall of Troy; in the *Hecuba* the enslaved Trojan women are with the Greek army in Thrace, stymied by contrary winds that prevent them from completing their return to Greece. Hecuba, Queen of Troy, that day loses two of her remaining children, Polyxena – who will be demanded as a sacrifice to honor Achilles – and Polydorus – killed by his host Polymestor. The first part of the play enacts the sacrifice; the second shows the working out of Hecuba's vengeance against Polymestor for having killed Polydorus. The *Trojan Women* focuses on the mourning of the women who survive the war, having as its two events the murder of Astyanax, son of Andromache and Hector, and the "trial" of Helen.

As others have noted, concepts of freedom and slavery seem to organize the *Hecuba* (Daitz 1971, 217), but instead of opposing them in a stable binary, the play complicates the categories, first by exposing and undercutting the opposition between free Greek and slave barbarian, second, by stressing the femaleness of the enslaved Trojan women, and, third, by stressing the ways in which these women are still free.

On one level, this play appears to confirm the notion that barbarians are slaves, slaves barbarians by stressing the women's foreignness.[7] The Trojan survivors grieve not just for themselves but for their city, lamenting the Asia that they have left behind, the Europe they have come to (479–83). Moreover, the Greek/barbarian opposition is emphasized and credited with the Greek victory. Odysseus distinguishes the Hellenes from the non-Hellenes on the basis of the honor they give to their heroes, living and dead (328–31), and attributes the Greeks' good fortune to this practice. At the same time, the text stresses Hecuba's slavery from the first (*douleion* 56, *homodoulon* 60). Her discourse assumes her slavery; for example, she contrasts slave and free (234), asking if it is permissible for a slave to speak. She makes claims based on what Greeks owe to slaves, depending on the Greek custom of treating slave and free equally in the case of murder (291–2). More broadly, when she confronts Agamemnon, Hecuba bases her argument on universal right, the gods' order which applies to slave and free alike.

This conflation of Asian and slave does not, however, support the ideal of natural slavery, for Polyxena and Hecuba exemplify slavery as an accident of fate (Schlaifer 1968, 97). Obviously, Hecuba's slavery itself plays a central role in her misery, but from Polydorus' prologue on, that enslavement also signifies a fall from good fortune. He says:

> O Mother,
> poor majesty, old fallen queen,
> shorn of greatness, pride, and everything but life,
> which leaves you slavery and bitterness
> and lonely age.
> Some god destroys you now,
> exacting in your suffering the cost
> for having once been happy in this life.
> (Arrowsmith 1959, lines 55–8; cf. 156–61, 284–5)

And Talthybius continues the theme, specifically recognizing that as an old man he might end up like Hecuba; he wishes her fate away from himself (484–500). The prologue to the *Trojan Women* also stresses the changeability of fortune: Athena has formerly aided the Greeks, but now in anger at their treatment of her temples, she urges Poseidon to turn the sea against them and to make their return voyage difficult. The fall of Troy will give way to the fall of the Greek warriors; glorious deeds are not permanent.

Euripides allays some of the cultural anxieties of the citizen man, however, by rendering the newly created slaves very specifically female; in this way the play grants the distance Talthybius desires. Both Agamemnon and Polymestor categorize Hecuba as woman, generalizing (falsely, to her way of thinking) about women's weakness (883) or wickedness (1095, 1178–82) respectively. Hecuba's femaleness is underscored by her defining role as mother. If her gender determines that she will be a slave, not killed, her age determines the form of her slavery. As an old woman, she is past desirability, so she can look forward to performing non-sexual women's work such as that described by Polyxena: "kneading the bread and scrubbing the floors" (362–4, cf. *Trojan Women* 193–5). In contrast, the young women are made sexual partners of their conquerors. This play, as well as *Andromache* and the *Trojan Women*, bears out Gerda Lerner's point that "For women, sexual exploitation marked the very definition of enslavement" (1986, 89).[8] The slavery of the women of the Chorus is explicitly sexualized: each woman is depicted as coming out of the tent of the man to whom she has been allotted (99–101); they mention that they were taken from their bed chambers (482) after the deaths of their husbands; that scene is rendered intimate in detail (914–42). In *Trojan Women* the pressing question is "whose slave shall I be" (185, cf. 203, 240ff.).

Polyxena provides the best example of the gendered and eroticized nature of the young women's slavery. Like the rest, she is enslaved because she is a woman; because she is a slave and a woman, she is to be sacrificed. The text emphasizes gender from the first – when Polydorus tells the audience that "some woman" was demanded as a sacrifice – and status later, when we hear that Achilles should not be stinted of his honor for a slave (135). Thus, Polyxena's slavery and her flowering youth (her mother is not an acceptable substitute) make her a suitable offering; her slavery is predicated on her femaleness, and even in death her body is not safe (Hecuba fears what the army will do to it 605–8). In her long speech, Polyxena explicitly contrasts her slavery to the marriage she could have expected:

> I had a father once,
> king of Phrygia. And so I started life,
> a princess of the blood, nourished on lovely hopes
> to be a bride for kings. And suitors came
> competing for the honor of my hand, while over the girls
> and women of Troy, I stood acknowledged mistress
> courted and envied by all, all but a goddess
> though bound by death.

And now I am a slave.
It is that name of slave, so ugly, so strange,
that makes me want to die. Or should I live
to be knocked down to a bidder, sold to a master
for cash? Sister of Hector, sister of princes,
doing the work of a drudge, kneading the bread
and scrubbing the floors, compelled to drag out
endless weary days? And the bride of kings
forced by some low slave from god knows where
to share his filthy bed?

(Arrowsmith 1959, lines 351–66)

In this passage Polyxena anticipates either auction or cohabitation with some lowly man, while Hecuba views her daughter's death as a marriage to Hades (611–15). The act of sacrifice replaces sexual slavery; Polyxena is given to Achilles in the same way that Cassandra is given to Agamemnon. In the *Trojan Women*, Cassandra explicitly reveals the eroticism of female slavery in her mad celebration of her "nuptials" to Agamemnon (310ff.).

Having undermined the notion of natural slavery by emphasizing the war, Euripides further stresses the femininity of the slaves. But he complicates the issue by also underlining the nobility of the royal Trojan slave women; these Asian women do not behave in a slavish fashion but instead retain their personal greatness, as if royalty were inborn. Polyxena shows her nobility by opting for death with freedom (367, 550) instead of an ignoble life. Although Hecuba "ignobly" seeks life at any cost for her daughter, she too is represented as possessing the kind of freedom that Odysseus and Agamemnon lack, although they are literally free. Odysseus panders to the army (254–7) and is afraid of Polyxena (345). Hecuba looks at Agamemnon in shock because he cannot do what he wants because he fears the wishes of the mob. Is any man free if he has something he fears to lose? It would appear not (864–7). Therefore, although the Trojans are slaves, the Greeks are not inherently free.

The *Hecuba* is a very complex text, destabilizing fundamental categories by having characters shift back and forth between them. Barbarian and Greek are not naturally slave and free; therefore the play does not offer the consolation inherent in the concept of natural slavery. Instead it suggests, on the one reading, that only women are slaves, or on the other, that a slave may nonetheless be noble. The *Andromache* gives a similarly complex account of the relationships among the shifting categories of conventional/natural slave, Greek/barbarian, male/female. The play tracks the trajectory of a noble foreign slave who has been enslaved not only because she is Trojan but because she is a woman; her fate seems to reinforce the naturalness of the hierarchy of gender at the same time that it undercuts the naturalness of the enslavement of "barbarians." Unlike the *Hecuba*, however, this play includes other more "realistic" slave figures. Subjectivity and individual identity (reflected in the possession of a name) are reserved for the high status slave. The slave who serves her has no name, and there is no hint that she is enslaved for any reason. Her class constitutes her entire identity. Thus, the "slave by convention," although Asian, is constructed as a woman and a wife, whereas the "natural slave" is constructed as servant, similar only to other servants. Yet, crucially, the low status servants are represented as identifying with the high status slave or the owner.

As the play opens, Andromache, widow of Hector, the great Trojan hero, and slave/mistress of Neoptolemus, sits at the altar of Thetis. She seeks protection from attack by Neoptolemus' wife, Hermione, and Hermione's father, Menelaus, who are jealous of her position as the mother of Neoptolemus' only son. Her faithful servant arrives to inform her of a new plot against her son, but this danger is averted when Thetis' husband, Peleus, rescues them. Now Hermione fears that Neoptolemus will kill or enslave *her*, but she is rescued in turn by the unexpected arrival of her cousin Orestes, who has just killed Neoptolemus. They exit, and Thetis appears as *deus ex machina* to solve all the text's problems.

Andromache is characterized strongly as a slave and as an Asian; thus she seemingly supports the association of those two categories. The opening scene contrasts freedom and slavery: Andromache has gone from being a member of the category "most free" (*eleutherōtatōn*) to being a slave (*doulē*, 12). Her first lines recall her past: "Thebé my city, Asia's pride, remember/ The glory and the gold of that procession/ When I arrived at Priam's royal home?" (Nims 1959, 1–3). Andromache literally looks back to a golden age; once she was wealthy and noble; she was enviable (*zēlōtos en ge tōi prin Andromachē chronōi*, 5). That only makes her current situation more poignant for her; in the present, she repeatedly refers to herself and is referred to as a slave (64, 89–90, 99, 110, 114). As if to underline her status, she addresses her servant as "fellow slave" (*sundoula*, 64; cf. *Hecuba* 60).

Andromache's slavery is not, however, presented as simply a natural consequence of her Asianness. First, Andromache takes her experience as evidence about the human condition: "call no mortal blessed before he is dead, until you see how he will finish the last day, crossing below" (100–2, my translation). The woman fallen into slavery as a result of war stands for human frailty in general (cf. *Ajax* 487, 488). Second, Andromache is a slave *because* she is a woman, and her slavery is inflected by her gender. Like Iole in *Women of Trachis* or Cassandra in the *Oresteia*, she is construed as a sexual rival to Hermione, a construction which reaffirms the centrality of men.

In the conflict between the two women, Hermione tries to assert her superiority by naturalizing slavery, which would make the slave Andromache a lesser human being. For instance, she tells Andromache to leave the temple, since she is only a slave in a foreign land (137–8). She believes that Andromache has wooed Neoptolemus away with drugs that she knows as a *slave* woman (155, 157). Her insults are based on xenophobia: the foreigners (*barbaron genos*) are incestuous and kin murdering (174–6); Andromache uses similar commonplaces, agreeing that in wild Thrace it is the custom for men to have many wives

(215–18). But Hermione's attempt to deny her similarity to the barbarian "other" fails, for her stereotype of the barbarian resembles the Greeks of myth, especially members of her own family who are kin murderers *par excellence.*

Instead, gender similarity is stressed over ethnic/class difference; the conflict between the two women is figured as sexual rivalry rather than as class struggle. Although the Chorus thinks that Andromache's opposition to upper-class Spartans makes things worse for herself (127–30), she does not threaten the political system through her position as a slave but through her sexuality, which might displace the King's lawfully wedded wife, Hermione. The two are represented as rivals for the same man, and their similarity as women overrides their class difference. For instance, Andromache does not hesitate to speak her mind to Hermione (186); although Hermione claims to have good sense on her side because she is Greek, Andromache implies that she is wiser because she is older.[9] Because the role of women as women is perceived to go beyond national and class boundaries, Andromache can attempt to advise Hermione about what makes a good woman or wife. In her view, a woman should treat her husband with respect and not struggle with him (213–14). So the wife's freedom is not so different from the slave's slavery. As in Aristotle's theoretical formulation, both are subservient to the master. In short, the fact that Hermione vehemently attacks Andromache as both slave and barbarian does not demonstrate what she so desires: Andromache's natural slavery and difference from her. On the contrary, Hermione knows all too well that if her husband were to discover her plan, she would be enslaved herself (927); her precious freedom is fragile because she is a woman, and women are vulnerable either to rape and capture, or to dismissal.[10]

The main plot then denies the claim that barbarians are natural slaves by alluding to the potentially general significance of Andromache's experience and to the potential slavery of Hermione. By stressing the women's similarities – on the basis of their gender and the status they formerly shared – over their current differences in class, by basing their rivalry in sexuality rather than class, the play mutes the note that Andromache initially sounds ("This could happen to you") or transmutes it into "This could happen to any woman."

The theme of gender similarity is used to short-circuit any potential threat of slave resistance as well. The two women who are not royal slaves, the servant and the nurse, are each affiliated with one of the major figures. Different strategies are used to represent these women – unindividualized, they are identified only by their work – but that difference does not provide the basis for a class ideology. Andromache's nameless servant feels that Andromache is still her mistress even though she is now a slave. From her point of view, they are not equals nor does she resent the inequality she perceives; as she says, "Mistress, I will never abandon this name for you, since I always thought it fitting" (56–8). When Andromache asks for her help, she calls on her as a woman, saying "Surely you can find some device; for you are a woman" (85). The servant replies: "It is dangerous" (86). After Andromache scolds her for abandoning friends in trouble, the servant changes her mind because she does not want that reputation. She is willing to prove her loyalty to Andromache then at some risk to herself; she believes that as a slave she is unimportant: "the life of a slave woman is not very significant, even if I suffer evil" (89–90). Similarly, Hermione's nurse, also identified only by her position, shares her mistress's misery (802–3); "I have worn myself out keeping my mistress from the noose" (815–16). This nurse presumably was Hermione's caretaker as a child, since she has no children of her own; she nurtures her in the present as she did in the past. In short, as if to further alleviate male owning class anxieties, both of the stereotypical servants are represented as loyal to their mistresses, and both act on their behalf.[11]

This alliance of women can be threatening to men, as it is for instance in the *Hecuba*, but it is not here: these women of the *Andromache* express a hegemonic ideology and remain within the discourse set out by the owning class, and thus do not challenge male dominance. For example, Andromache and her fellow servant share common assumptions about women's nature, both invoking the category of woman as an explanatory device. Andromache expects her servant to find a solution, because women are associated with devices (*mēchanē*, 85, cf. 181–82), and she herself will moan and groan for "it is natural for women to take pleasure in speech when trouble is pressing" (93–5). Here she has recourse to what is inborn (*empephuke*) in women as an explanation for her behavior, even though she mourns events that have turned her from one sort of woman into another, from a freeborn princess into a slave.

Hermione also reinforces this set of beliefs. She tries to excuse or explain her behavior by blaming the words of the bad women who taunted her for sharing the marriage bed with the slave Andromache (930–5). She then tells us what she has learned, which is that her position should have satisfied her; after all, she ruled the house (940). And she has this piece of advice for men who have wives: don't let them have women friends visit, for they are the teachers of evil (*didaskaloi kakōn*, 946). So women should be kept within and safe from other women (950–1). Only that way will they be healthy (953); the Chorus agrees (956) speaking in general terms about women's illnesses and the need for order. And the nurse supports the dominant order's view of women's place by telling Hermione to cover herself up (832) and "go within lest appearing outside you incur shame" (876–7).[12] Clearly the servant repeats beliefs about women that can only be maintained by women of property. She herself comes and goes, as she must in order to do her job. These generalizations claim to speak of women, but they overlook the women outside the elite and ignore the differences between women that the text itself has recognized.

The *Andromache* simultaneously privileges the "contingent" conception of slavery and limits it to women, who are shown to be vulnerable to it, thus glossing over the possibility that Greek men might experience a similar tragedy. This displacement reinforces owning class male authority. Second, as in the *Hecuba* the essential status of the royal slave, Andromache, is seen to be untouched. At the same time, there is no class struggle; the only rivalry occurs between women for the sake of a man. "Real" slaves are represented as remaining loyal to their mistresses on the basis of gender, instead of opposing them on the basis of class.

Euripides, then, unlike Herodotus and Aristotle, is mindful of the impact of gender on class and of class on gender. But what difference does that awareness make? Having pointed out the political grounding of earlier work on slavery in antiquity, I feel honor bound to acknowledge that my work is also grounded in an ideological struggle. In the wake of post-modern and anti-racist challenges to early and unproblematized calls to sisterhood, feminist theorizing has been increasingly attentive to differences between women. I began this project hoping to find evidence, if not of class warfare, then at least of class consciousness. Basing my thinking on feminist reconceptions of Marxist standpoint theory, I hypothesized that the characters or Chorus members who were servants would express a different standpoint from that of the rulers (Hartsock 1983, 283–4). As I turned my attention to tragedy, however, my hypothesis was disconfirmed; instead, I found that the class affiliation of the playwright and the form effectively controlled the construction of the subjectivity of the female servants (Austin and Vidal-Naquet 1977, 15). The slaves in tragedy do not represent a real class but rather respond to the desires and anxieties of the author and *his* audience. At the same time, I have had to confront the extent to which I have been drawn into the interests of the original author and audience as my attention has been deflected from ordinary slave women by the aristocratic Trojan women with their glamor and mythic centrality and their ability to reflect on their experience as slaves precisely because it is new to them. The "natural" slaves thus have gotten short shrift in my analysis as well as in the plays I have examined. Of course in order to study real slaves, we need to look outside of tragedy. In so doing, however, we should not assume that we are getting at some factual reality without any mediation: grave epigraphs and terracottas are more material than texts in one sense, but they are nonetheless shaped by ideological constraints.

Undertaking this work, conscious of the ideological nature of the construction of knowledge, I have to wonder what are the blind spots that I cannot yet recognize. If Greek tragedy in its own day constructed a normative male subject on stage and a normative male viewer in the audience, and humanist traditions posited a universal (male) student, what has our charting out of "women in antiquity" as a subfield accomplished? We have established a subject position (albeit a marginalized one) for ourselves as women and feminists, but how much else has changed? Are we not then dependent on the maintenance of gender because it gives us status? It remains all too easy to content ourselves with discussing white women in the field, or gender, much harder to discuss gender in conjunction with race, class, or sexuality. This essay attempts to study the representation of class differences between women in order to move our discourse beyond gender alone. Deconstructionist post-colonial theory warns against simplistic searching for an authentic native; like the subaltern in Gayatri Spivak's formulation (1988), the ancient slave cannot speak to us. I hope that my work here on the figure of the woman slave can be part of an effort to do different cultural work, and that is to reveal our own assumptions about antiquity. In looking at the past, we must simultaneously try to uncover the lived reality as best we can, and at the same time acknowledge our own investment in the project.[13]

Notes

1 Chester Starr's tone makes it clear that the topic was problematic because of anti-slavery feelings and suspicions of Marxism (1977, 68, 90).

2 Moses Finley and Pierre Vidal-Naquet, adhering to strict Marxist definitions, argue that slaves did not constitute a class because they did not have a clear relationship to the means of production, performed no task exclusively, and thus had no basis for class struggle (summarized in de Ste Croix 1981, 63–7; Finley 1973, 49, 67–8; Austin and Vidal-Naquet 1977, 21–3; Vidal-Naquet 1986, 163). G. E. M. de Ste Croix (1981, 91) holds that slaves and slave holders constituted clearly distinguished classes. Vogt (1975, 103–4), discusses the overschematization of the Marxist analysis and foregrounds the relationship that developed between classes.

3 Vidal-Naquet (1986, 172) indicates that the story's effect is to link boys, women and slaves as "others *excluded from the Greek city*."

4 All slaves are analogous to powerless women; Aristotle draws a parallel between the master/slave and the husband/wife dichotomies (1252a25–610, 1253b5–12, 1260a4–b20). Slaves and women were both welcomed into the household with the same ritual shower of fruits and nuts (Garlan 1988, 41); they were united under the rubric of outsider to the *oikos* that must nevertheless depend on them. Roger Just argues that "the Athenian conception of women can be fully understood only by reference to the broader context of freedom and slavery" (1985, 172). Similarly, however, slaves and children were analogous, both called *pais*; boys at least, unlike girls or slaves, would grow up to become adults themselves. Thus they had to be marked off from the slaves with whom they were in other ways so closely associated (Golden 1984, especially 163).

5 Ernest Barker (1962, 16 n.1) points out that the Athenian statesman Lycurgus attempted to pass a law forbidding the purchase of formerly free men as slaves. Schlaifer notes that Greek theories of slavery were related to Hellenism, a campaign to divide barbarian and Greek, slave and free (1968, 93); he maintains that "there is little difference in theory between the free foreigner and the slave; the only real difference is that the one is in point of fact under the physical control of a master" (110). Suzanne Saïd (1984) analyzes the lack of a clear "frontier" in Euripides' representation of the barbarian (cf. Hall 1989). Biezunska-Malowist and Malowist (1989, 27) emphasize the racial similarity: "nul ne peut distinguer l'esclave de l'homme libre dans les rues d'Athènes ou de Rome."

6 The Athenians enslaved the whole people of Hykkara (Thucydides 6. 62. 2–4), men and women. In the disastrous expedition against Sicily, the Athenians lost, and Thucydides remarks: "this was by far the greatest reverse that ever befell an Hellenic army. They had come to enslave others, and were departing in fear of being enslaved themselves" (7.7.75). In inter-city warfare citizen men might have been enslaved and were in twenty-five percent of the cases mentioned by historians (Garlan 1988, 48; see also 47 with n. 35). Greeks could be enslaved for debt; the practice did not disappear simply because Solon abolished the practice in Athens (Harrison 1968, 164–5). Consequently, Athenian men of the fifth century could have looked around them and seen men more or less like themselves in slavery. For women as slaves and the connection between female slavery and rape, see Lerner 1986, 83–7.

7 The difference could have been underlined by staging. For instance, did the Trojan women wear elaborate costumes easily distinguished from those worn by the Greeks? We know that Polydorus' dress was not Greek (734). The dominant paradigm slave/free would have been visibly aligned with outsider/Greek, depending on how Polymestor was dressed.

8 While I would agree with Lerner that slavery was not sexually marked for men, nonetheless, in the classical period, male slaves were available as sexual partners for free Athenian men (see for instance Halperin 1990, 88–112; Golden 1990, 145).

9 This age differential is highlighted by a preponderance of words with *ne* (a prefix signifying youth); see 184, 192, 196.

10 Andromache may have dropped from wealth and luxury to poverty, but the rupture with her former life is not total, for, as she was given as the childbearing wife of Hector (*dotheisa paidopoios*, 4), so is she now given to Neoptolemus. As if to underline the similarity, the poet uses the same word (*dotheisa*) to describe both relationships (15); in Andromache's case her slavery and sexual status are linked (*doulon lechos*, 30). She has borne a son to each man; each son is threatened by the enemy.

11 For an analysis of the opposite situation, see Lerner (1986, 98) on the *Odyssey*.

12 The echo here of the values stated by Hippolytus in Euripides' *Hippolytus* are clear: he thinks women are counterfeit coin, should be kept inside and given no servants to take messages out. His loathing infects Phaedra with anxiety and leads to her violence against him.

13 Portions of this paper were presented at the Berkshire Women's History Conference in 1994, as well as at the American Philological Association Meeting in 1994. I wish to give special thanks to the FWC at Hamilton College, to Patricia Francis Cholakian, the commentator on the Berkshire Conference panel, and to the editors of this volume for their sage advice. Errors that remain are, of course, my own.

5

WOMEN AND SLAVES AS HIPPOCRATIC PATIENTS

Nancy Demand

In Greek culture slaves and free women, despite significant differences, shared certain marginalizing characteristics. Neither was allowed full development of potential beyond the limited roles they were to play, and both were inducted into these roles as soon as they were capable of performing them. Thus slaves were put to work as children, and females of citizen status were married at, or perhaps even before, puberty. (In contrast, free male citizens were not fully incorporated into their social and political roles until about 30.) And while both women and slaves left childhood behind very early, neither could ever achieve full legal maturity. Moreover, this incapacity was marked by similar nomenclature: both were commonly identified by the possessive of their *kyrios*, or master, as were free male children. Both slaves and free women as wives were necessary members of the *oikos* (household), but they were also both outsiders, and the ceremony welcoming them into the household was the same for both – a showering of fruits and nuts to symbolize the abundance their arrival promised to the household (Theopompus, Kock 1880, frag. 14; Aristophanes, *Wealth* 768).

In this paper I will examine these two marginalized groups from the perspective of medical treatment. As background, I will review briefly the general Greek attitudes toward women and slaves, including the evidence of Plato and Aristotle, who express opposite poles of Greek "common sense," and the professional components of the Greek medical system (the doctors and the texts of the Hippocratic Corpus).[1] Then I will focus on the Hippocratic medical texts, comparing the doctors' medical concern with, and treatment of, women and slaves, and asking to what extent their authors were in accordance with the opinions of the wider community concerning these two marginal groups. In discussing Hippocratic treatment, I will rely mostly on the case histories recorded in the *Epidemics*, seven books containing doctors' reports on the course of their patients' illnesses, since here we find doctors treating all of our categories – slaves, women, and free men.[2]

The "natural" inferiority of women and slaves

Much study has recently been devoted to the role and status of women in Greek society.[3] There seems to be no question that Greek "common sense" (male) accorded women an inferior status and role as members of the *oikos* and of the *polis* (city-state). There are some hints in the speeches of the Attic orators that this may have been ameliorated to some extent within individual households, and that in some families women, especially older women, may have been able to exercise a degree of indirect influence even when they had no direct imput into decision-making.[4] A number of tragedies and comedies – Aristophanes' *Lysistrata*, *Thesmophoriazusae*, and *Ecclesiazusae*, and Euripides' *Medea* – can be read as reflections of dissatisfaction with the *status quo*.

It was the philosophers Aristotle and Plato who put these two tendencies into explicit form, providing the two poles of "common sense." At the conservative pole, Aristotle's discussion of the nature of women was intended to justify the *status quo*. He stated quite bluntly that women were inferior to men: "The male is by nature superior, the female inferior; and the one rules, the other is ruled." (*Politics* 1254b12–15)

Aristotle drew on a sharp and value-laden distinction between mere matter and the form that organizes it to justify his claims of female inferiority (Aristotle, *Physics* 194b16–195a5). Thus, in the creation of a human being, matter was supplied by the female in the form of menses; the male seed acted as the formal and efficient causes of conception, supplying the bodily shape and rational facility; and the final cause was the continuation of the species (Aristotle, *Generation of Animals* 729a38–730b32). Aristotle's explanation of the menses embodied two other evaluatory concepts that also helped to explain female inferiority: concoction and temperature. For Aristotle, menses were an imperfect residue created when female coldness made it impossible for concoction (a sort of cooking) to take place. In males, warmth allowed concoction to occur, producing efficient seed. Thus females were imperfect males. These same concepts of temperature and concoction underlay Aristotle's explanation of the separation of the sexes into male and female during embryonic development. The embryo that grew in the warmest part of the womb developed more fully and quickly, and thus became a male. The embryo that developed in the colder part of the womb lacked the heat to concoct fully and thus became an imperfect female.

For Aristotle, the inferiority of the female was not limited to the body but extended to the soul as well. He conceived of the soul as having two parts, the rational and the emotional (Aristotle, *Politics* 1252b 1; Fortenbaugh 1977). In free adult males both the emotional and the rational parts of the soul were fully developed and the rational was naturally in control. The souls of women, however, had less well-developed rational parts, although their emotional souls were fully formed. As a result, women were ruled by emotion.

For Aristotle, male slaves were also inferior to free men, but their inferiority rested upon a different basis than the inferiority of females. Aristotle located the core of the slave nature in differences in degrees and types of rational ability:

> For that which can foresee by the exercise of mind is by nature intended to be lord and master, and that which can with its body give effect to such foresight is a subject, and by nature a slave. . . . For he who can be, and therefore is, another's, and he who participates in rational principle enough to apprehend, but not to have, such a principle, is a slave by nature.
>
> (*Politics* 1252a32–1254b22)

This view in which bodily strength marks a slave and rational ability marks a free man must have had some empirical basis in a society in which slaves were drawn mostly from *barbaroi*. Linguistic and cultural differences, and differences of perspective and self-interest, would have made it likely that the slave often failed to share the master's foresight. Intelligence in slaves would more likely have appeared, from the master's point of view, as cunning acting at cross purposes to his own foresight. But sometimes things did not work out as nature planned:

> Nature would like to distinguish between the bodies of freemen and slaves, making the one strong for servile labour, the other upright, and although useless for such services, useful for political life in the arts both of war and peace. But the opposite often happens – that some have the souls and others have the bodies of freemen. . . . It is clear, then, that some men are by nature free, and others slaves, and that for these latter slavery is both expedient and right.
>
> (*Politics* 1255a3).

Although male slaves by nature lacked a rational soul, they had a capacity to understand reason, and thus to obey. Women, in contrast, had rational souls, but these were not authoritative – the female rational soul was unable to over-rule the emotional soul. This explanation both accounted for the difference between the two inferior groups, and justified the subordination of free women. Female slaves suffered the twofold inferiority of femaleness and slavishness.

Plato represented the radical opposite pole from Aristotle on gender differences and evaluation: he reflected the uneasiness about the subordination of women that is found in some of the dramatic literature. While Plato did not deny that there was a difference between men and women, and that in fact women were inferior, at least in strength, to men, he argued that the difference was not relevant to their ability to serve the political community:

> Socrates is asked: "Can it be denied then that there is by nature a great difference between men and women? Is it not fitting, then, that

71

a different function should be appointed for each corresponding to this difference of nature?"

Socrates replies: "But if it appears that they differ only in just this respect that the female bears and the male begets, we shall say that no proof has yet been produced that the woman differs from the man for our purposes [to serve as Guardians]. . . . Then there is no pursuit of the administrators of a state that belongs to a woman because she is a woman or to a man because he is a man. But the natural capacities are distributed alike among both creatures, and women naturally share in all pursuits and men in all – yet for all the woman is weaker than the man. . . . The women and the men, then, have the same nature in respect to the guardianship of the state, save in so far as the one is weaker, the other stronger.

(*Republic* 454de, 455d, 456a)

Plato's argument was revolutionary – in fact, utopian. Some women could think and reason as well as the brightest men and were therefore as able to contribute to the administration of the state. But even he did not claim that females were equal to males in every respect.

Plato took a somewhat similar position on the inferiority of slaves. Despite the widespread opinion that they were all inferior and not to be trusted (*Laws* 776b–778a), he recognized that, in practice, some proved to be far better men than free brothers or sons. But Plato did not recommend a revolutionary change in the situation of slaves similar to that which he advocated for women in the *Republic*. Assuming that the use of slaves was unavoidable, he made only practical recommendations for their management: that a household's slaves should be of different stocks and languages so that they would be less likely to unite against their master; and that the master should not treat them violently, but rather wrong them with more reluctance than an equal, this being the real test of a master's character and also less likely to produce undesirable behavior in the slave.

Hippocratic medicine: doctors and texts

Most of the evidence for doctors and medical treatment in ancient Greece consists in the Hippocratic collection of medical texts. These texts date from about 410 to the second century BCE, although most of the treatises fall within the classical period (410–350 BCE). Most seem to be written by doctors (a few, however, may be sophistic pieces by non-physicians, and some may be collections of folklore remedies simply recorded by physicians). The doctors were itinerant, as can be seen by the many references to the location of their patients in the *Epidemics*, but they appear to have stayed for extended periods in a location, perhaps traveling on a local circuit.[5] The principal locale of practice of the doctor-authors of the *Epidemics* was the northern Aegean – Thrace, Thessaly, and Thasos – although some did visit Athens. They thus offer a useful non-

Attic perspective to our otherwise mostly Athenian sources on attitudes to, and treatment of, women and slaves.

No one today attributes the entire Hippocratic Corpus to an historical Hippocrates, and even the debate over which treatises can be considered to be genuine works of Hippocrates is not currently fashionable. To a great extent this is because the treatises vary considerably in content, ranging from empirical "textbooks" that describe procedures (surgical texts such as the *Fractures*), to various theoretical explanations of illness. Some are formal speeches in defense of medicine in general or of some particular medical theory. A few discuss the proper conduct of the physician. There are collections of aphorisms, and a large number of gynecological books describe various problems and give lists of remedies. Finally, there are the seven books called the *Epidemics*, which contain many case histories of the illnesses of patients, mingled with other types of material such as aphorisms and descriptions of medical conditions in a given area over a period of time, usually a year (the *Constitutions*). Some of the texts give fairly specific treatment suggestions, but many completely ignore treatment.

Although the treatises espouse various medical theories, and even contradict each other, they share an essential core of "Hippocratic" medical thinking (Lain Entralgo 1970, 141). They agree in attributing illness to natural rather than supernatural causes and in firmly rejecting the Homeric and Hesiodic idea that gods, *daimons*, or any other sort of supernatural beings cause illness. When they depart from strict empiricism, it is by interpreting illness in terms of the philosophical concepts of the day. Thus many describe illness as an imbalance in the basic elements that make up the body, an idea akin to the philosophers' attempts to identify the basic elements of the cosmos.[6] The gynecological treatises, however, make comparatively little use of such philosophical constructs, attributing many difficulties to mechanical causes such as blockages of menstrual or lochial bleeding or displacements of the uterus (a condition called the Wandering Womb, in which the womb was believed to be a sentient creature that could move about the body, impinging on other organs and causing symptoms such as suffocation) (Dean-Jones 1994). This difference in reliance on philosophical constructs may reflect the basic distinction seen by the doctors between male and female. While, as we shall see, many of the Hippocratic doctors practiced "general" medicine, in that they treated both men and women, the treatises tend to follow traditional views of women's physiology. The gynecological treatises in particular contain many recipes and treatments that appear to have originated in midwives' lore, and many diagnoses and treatments of women patients focus on the reproductive faculties (Riddle 1992).

The seven books of the *Epidemics* date from the end of the fifth century to mid-fourth century and record the observations of several physicians as they cared for the sick at various sites. All known physicians were male, although shadowy female figures operated in the background – assistants and midwives. The social status of doctors at that time is unclear and probably varied considerably. For example, Plato portrayed a doctor, Eryximachus, as an important participant in the symposium of the *Symposium*, which might suggest a very high status indeed, at least for this doctor. However, we also note the presence of Socrates, a poor but free philosophizing stoneworker, at Plato's symposium. Plato's main concern was with philosophical issues, not with presenting a correct historical account, and he often took liberties with historical details. Status boundaries in fifth-century Athens may have been as fluid as Plato portrays them in the *Symposium*, but his work is not alone sufficient evidence to confirm this conclusion.

An especially important question concerning status and also involving Plato's accuracy in the matter of historical fact is raised by a passage in Plato's *Laws* in which Plato suggests that slaves were treated mainly by slave-doctors and in a more cursory manner than free persons.[7]

> Athenian: ... There are physicians, and again there are physicians' assistants, whom we also speak of as physicians. ... All bear the name, whether free men or slaves who gain their professional knowledge by watching their masters and obeying their directions in empirical fashion, not in the scientific way in which free men learn their art and teach it to their pupils. You agree that there are those two types of so-called physicians?
> Clinias: Certainly I do.
> Athenian: Now have you further observed that, as there are slaves as well as free men among the patients of our communities, the slaves, to speak generally, are treated by slaves, who pay them a hurried visit, or receive them in dispensaries? A physician of this kind never gives a servant any account of his complaint, nor asks him for any; he gives him some empirical injunction with an air of finished knowledge, in the brusque fashion of a dictator, and then is off in hot haste to the next ailing servant – that is how he lightens his master's medical labors for him. The free practitioner, who, for the most part, attends free men, treats their diseases by going into things thoroughly from the beginning in a scientific way, and takes the patient and his family into his confidence. Thus he learns something from the sufferers, and at the same time instructs the invalid to the best of his powers. He does not give his prescriptions until he has won the patient's support, and when he has done so, he steadily aims at producing complete restoration to health by persuading the sufferer into compliance. Now which of the two methods is that of the better physician or director of bodily regimen? That which effects the same result by a twofold process or that which employs a single process, the worse of the two, and exasperates its subject?
>
> (*Laws* 720a–e, trans. A.E. Taylor)

Kudlien (1968, 26–38), in discussing this passage, stressed the fact that Plato was speaking metaphorically. The subject was not medicine but legislation: the philosopher argued that, just as the effort of the "free doctor" to explain to the patient is superior to the brusque order of the "slave doctor," so too the legislator should adopt a persuasive approach, enacting laws double in form, accompanying every prescription with a persuasive preamble. The fact that there is no evidence in the Hippocratic texts for actual slave doctors acting on their own in the treatment of patients supports Kudlien's conclusion that the passage cannot be taken literally.

Other scholars have also taken Kudlien's position in rejecting Plato's slave physicians (Temkin 1953, 14–15; Cohn-Haft 1956, 14–15). Assistants were used, and there is evidence that helpers were sometimes employed to watch the patient. In fact, some of the observations in the *Epidemics* seem to have been made by someone other than the physician himself. But one doctor admonishes his colleagues not to leave a layperson in charge of a patient, but to choose an apprentice:

> Let one of your pupils be left in charge, to carry out instructions without unpleasantness and to administer the treatment. Choose one of those who have already been admitted into the mysteries of the art, in order that he can add anything necessary and give the treatment with safety. He is also to prevent those things escaping notice that happen in the intervals between your visits.
>
> (*Decorum* 17, trans. P. Potter)

There are a few specific references to women helpers with female patients, and to midwives, and it seems reasonable to assume that the doctors employed slaves for cleaning and for heavy tasks, but there is no evidence whatsoever that slaves in the role of assistants ever practiced medicine themselves, concentrating their attentions on slave patients, as Plato says. On the contrary, slave and free patients (to the extent that these can be differentiated) received the same type of attention, and the course of their illnesses is recorded in the same way by the same doctors.

Hippocratic distinctions between patients

The Hippocratic doctors recognized that the general pattern of illness was affected by many individual factors in each patient: climate, season, bodily type (even color and type of hair), previous state of health, age, and sex. For example:

> Among persons that have these and similar diseases, a man differs from a woman in the ease or difficulty with which he recovers, a younger man differs from an older man, and a younger woman differs from an older woman; additional factors are the season in which they have fallen ill, and whether or not their disease has followed from another disease. Besides, one affection differs from another, being either greater or less, one body from another, and one treatment from another.
>
> (Hippocrates, *Diseases* I. 22, trans. P. Potter)

At least among the Hippocratic doctor-authors, most recognized that women were different from men in ways that were relevant to their illnesses. However, some doctors did not share this view, for the author of *Diseases of Women* I complained that many women were mistreated due to a failure to understand that the treatment of women's diseases differs greatly from that of men's diseases (Hippocrates, *Diseases of Women* I.62 [VIII.126.14–19 Littré]).

The Hippocratic treatises portrayed the distinctiveness of the woman as innate, based on the natural constitution of the female body as such, and they judged that this constitution was inferior to that of the male.[8] The doctor-authors of the treatises had various physical explanations for the inferiority of females. Some, like Aristotle, attributed it to the "fact" that they were colder (but some claimed warmer) and moister than males, and that their flesh was spongy rather than firm. These female conditions, which were favorable to parturition and nursing, were attributed by some to fetal environment (Hippocrates, *Epidemics* VI.2.25; compare Hippocrates, *Nature of the Child*, chs 18, 21; and Lonie 1981, 190ff.):

> Because [the male fetus is] in the warmest spot, the most firm part, on the right, males are dark, and have prominent veins. They are formed and firmed more quickly, are sooner moved, then subside and grow more slowly and for more time. They are firmer, more bilious, and have more blood, because this is the warmest place in living beings.
>
> (*Epidemics* VI.2.25)

Other doctors traced sex differences back to the nature of the female seed, for, unlike Aristotle, some doctors took the position that women as well as men produced complete and efficacious seed. Thus in some medical texts an explanation of the results of conception is given in terms of the quality of the seed contributed respectively by the father and the mother: if the male seed predominated, a strong male would be born; if, on the other hand, the female seed predominated, the result would be a female.[9] Other authors carried this further. According to the author of *On Regimen* 27–8, both parents have both male and female seed; if both contributed male seed to a conception, the result would be a strong male; if both contributed female seed, the result would be a feminine female. But other, less desirable combinations were possible as well, depending upon which parent contributed which seed, and which seed was dominant – effeminate males, manly females, hermaphrodites. Thus, even though some Hippocratics allowed women a contribution to the embryo in the form of seed, female seed was considered to be inherently weaker than male seed, and its predominance to lead to less favorable results.

The various theories of Greek doctors on sex determination all incorporated and supported the general cultural belief in the inferiority of the female. In contrast, in the matter of slavery, while doctors seem to have shared the common belief that slaves were inferior to free men, this was not considered a relevant factor in their practice. They attributed the inferiority of slaves not to innate differences in the body or mind, as did Aristotle, but to the same environmental factors and customary practices that shaped the lives of free men. Thus the author of *Airs, Waters, Places* related the differences between individuals and nations to their postnatal environment:

> For where the land is rich, soft, and well-watered, and the water is very near the surface, so as to be hot in summer and cold in winter, and if the situation be favourable as regards the seasons, there the inhabitants are fleshy, ill-articulated, moist, lazy, and generally cowardly in character. Slackness and sleepiness can be observed in them, and as far as the arts are concerned they are thickwitted, and neither subtle nor sharp. But where the land is bare, waterless, rough, oppressed by winter's storms and burnt by the sun, there you will see men who are hard, lean, well-articulated, well-braced, and hairy; such natures will be found energetic, vigilant, stubborn and independent in character and in temper, wild rather than tame, of more than average sharpness and intelligence in the arts, and in war of more than average courage.
>
> (Hippocrates, *Airs, Waters, Places* 24, trans. W.H.S. Jones)

Since most slaves were foreigners, they naturally expressed the environmental influences of their homeland and were different from Greeks. Significant individual differences also arose from the exigencies of a slave's life. For example, an individual's constitution was significantly affected by customary activities. The author of *Epidemics* II.1.8 says that "long heads and long necks [come] from bending. The breadth of the blood vessels and their thickness come from the same causes, and their narrowness, shortness, thinness from the opposite ones."

Habits of personal hygiene that might be affected by the life of slavery also had a bearing on treatment. One of them was the number of meals a person was accustomed to eat in a day; a slave used to one meal a day might be harmed by frequent feedings during illness. Another variable factor was the frequency of the use of purges. It was assumed everyone would use purges in some form and on some schedule for the sake of their health (Hippocrates, *Regimen in Health* 5), but slaves may have been less able to attend individually to such hygenic regimes, being subjected to mass purges of the household's slaves, and they may also have been more liable to receive strong purges that would be quickly effective. (The subject is interesting, considering our medicalizing of purge behavior as an illness, bulimia.)

As we saw above, in the lists of things that the physician should observe in diagnosis, sex occurs frequently, as does age, followed by various individualizing characteristics. It is significant, however, that status (slave or free) is never mentioned among the things to be considered. A good example of specific medical reasoning in a situation involving both sex and status as variables can be seen in the following passage:

In an outbreak of illness, which modern scholars have labeled the "Cough of Perinthus," women are said to have suffered less than men, they had little fever, and few had peripneumonia and these were older and all survived – the doctor comments that this may have been because they did not go out of the house to the same extent that men did. He comments that only two free women suffered from angina and it was mild; in contrast, slave women were much more affected, and in violent cases they died very quickly.

(*Epidemics* VI.7)

Here the doctor observed a difference between the outcome of an illness in slave and in free female patients. However, he did not suggest that the difference resulted from any innate inferiority of the slaves. Rather, he attributed the difference to the different environmental conditions of their lives: slave women went out of the house, as did men, while free women stayed home (an interesting hint of a recognition of contagion).[10] There is no suggestion that the slaves were given different medical treatment or that the doctor was less concerned with them.

Hippocratic practice: female patients

The patients whose cases were recorded in the *Epidemics* included women and slaves of both sexes as well as free males. Women as a proportion of patients mentioned range from a high of 55 percent in Book II to a low of 25 percent in Books V and VII.[11] Book I has 29 percent female patients, Book III 43 percent, Book IV 36 percent, and Book VI 32 percent. Obstetrical and abortion cases make up the majority of female patients only in Book II (68 percent). While these numbers do not reflect exact patient loads, since doctors did not report all cases, the general picture is probably fairly accurate: with the exception of Book II, doctors mention fewer female than male patients, but they do treat women both in complications of pregnancy and in non-pregnancy-related illnesses.

Given the Hippocratic belief in an innate difference between the sexes, it was quite consistent for them to be on the lookout for sex differences in the effects of illness:

In an epidemic of causus fever at Perinthus, the doctor observes that some women had a rash but none of these died, and no men had a rash.

(*Epidemics* II.3.1)

The sister of Diopeithes had violent pains in the heart in a semi-tertian fever; other women suffered similarly, except at the sinking of the Pleiades, but few men.

(*Epidemics* V.89)

In most such cases of differential suffering, doctors were able to find a cause in women's "nature" or to see specifically female aspects of an illness. As has been amply documented by a number of recent studies focusing especially on the gynecological treatises (Lloyd 1983; Hanson 1975, 1987, 1989, 1990, 1991; Dean-Jones 1987, 1991), this "cause" often involved the menses, menarche, or the womb. Thus in *Epidemics* II.3.1, the doctor relates symptoms in women to female characteristics: after remarking that women with fever, nausea, and chills also have red faces, fatigue, pains in the eyes, heaviness of the head, and paralyses, he advises the reader to observe the patient's menses: if they appear, especially for the first time, or at long intervals, or not in the accustomed time, then the patient will become very pale.

There are many examples of the doctors' focus on women's reproductive lives and their view of female symptoms as arising from a hidden if not an overt connection with their sex. Suppressed menses were especially feared:

> Two fatal cases of virilism are noted in women with suppressed menses. "At Abdera, Phaethousa, the wife of Pytheas, in charge of the *oikos*, had had children in the past; her husband ran away [both were apparently slaves] and her menses were suppressed for a long time. After that, pains and reddening of the joints. These things happening, the body was masculinized: she became hairy all over; she grew a beard and her voice became rough. Despite everything being done to recall the menses, they did not come, and she died, having lived not a long time after this occurred. And the same thing happnened to Nanno, [wife?] of Gorgippus, in Thasos. It seemed to all the doctors whom I have met that there was only one hope of restoring femaleness, if the menses should come in accordance with nature. But in this case, despite doing everything, they could not be restored, and she soon died."
>
> (*Epidemics* VI.8.32)

> a servant is ill whose menses had not come for seven years.
>
> (*Epidemics* IV.38)

> suppression of menses in a patient with arthritis caused a violent pain in the hip with loss of voice, although she could hear and understand.
>
> (*Epidemics* V.91)

Since suppressed menses were considered dangerous, it is not surprising that menses themselves were thought to be curative. This is in line with a general belief that bleeding is beneficial (in any patient, male or female, a nosebleed was generally taken as a good sign, as was the bleeding of hemorrhoids).

> Abundant menses after suppression coincided with the crisis (the turning point in an illness) in a quartan (malarial) fever that had lasted a year.
>
> (*Epidemics* II.3.13)

an asthmatic servant, who had hemorrhage (beneficial) at time of menses.

(Epidemics IV.32)

Menarche, or the first menstrual period, was considered to be especially significant:

> Onset of menses coincided with improvement in paralysis that occurred with a slight cough; the doctor remarked that it was perhaps menarche, for the patient was a *parthenos* (young girl).

(Epidemics II.2.8)

Delayed menarche was of special concern since it could be caused by blocked menses, a condition often accompanied by a whole syndrome of potentially fatal symptoms to which an entire small treatise was devoted, *Diseases of Maidens.*[12] The doctor's recommended cure was marriage. Similarly, at *Epidemics* V.12, a woman with severe headaches that were temporarily relieved by menses was cured by pregnancy.

Failure to bear children had life-long effects:

> Indistinct breathing in consumptives, and also in those who have not borne children, is bad.

(Epidemics VI.7.8)

We can thus see that in practice doctors pursued a womb-centered approach in dealing with women, attributing many ailments of the body in general to the womb and failure of reproduction. Reproductive functions were at the forefront of female diagnosis, and the doctor carefully noted the timing, amount, and character of menstrual flow. Treatment often involved fumigating the womb or mechanically straightening the cervix. Abundant menstruation, intercourse, and pregnancy were deemed necessary for female health.

Hippocratic medical theories of female physiology, and especially the fear of suppressed menses in young girls, did much to bolster traditional Greek (Athenian) practices of early marriage for girls and continued childbearing for married women. Unfortunately, early childbearing is more dangerous for both mother and child; Aristotle called attention to this (*Politics* 1335a13–23), and the Spartans were also aware and avoided the problems by later female marriage (Plutarch, *Lycurgus* 15.3). The focus on reproduction, with frequent use of fertility tests and treatments, also sometimes provided a risk to female health:

> A woman who was healthy and stout was gripped by pain in the belly from a medication taken for the sake of conception; twisting in the intestines; she swelled up; breathing prominent, difficult, with pain. She did not vomit much. She was on the verge of dying for five days, so that she seemed to be dead. Vomiting cold water did not relieve either the pain coming upon her or the breathing. They poured about thirty

amphorae of cold water over her body, and this alone seemed to help. Later she passed much bile from below, but when the pain gripped her, she was not able to. She lived.

(Hippocrates, *Epidemics* V.42 [5.232.9–16 Littré], trans. W. Smith)

Hippocratic practice: slave patients

The proportion of slaves among the doctors' patients is more difficult to determine than that of female patients since in many cases we cannot decisively distinguish slave from free in the case histories. In an intensive study of the terminology used by the Hippocratics, Kudlien found only a few secure indicators of slave status: the use of explicit words denoting slaves (*doulos* or *doule*, which are used of individual patients only twice);[13] the term *paidiske* (the female diminutive of *pais*); indications of servile employment, as a *pais* who served as a *hippokomos* (horse groom), or one working in the vineyards; persons to whom various "servant" words were applied (*oiketis, amphipolos, therapon*); persons designated by a preposition as from a particular household (*para* + gen.); and one person who is specifically said to have been marked with the stigmata of slavery. But many of the more common ways of designating slaves were ambiguous. For example, the word *pais* often denoted a slave, but it was also commonly used to identify a son or daughter. Similarly, the genitive of possession was used both to indicate slaves and to refer to free sons/daughters or to wives. Some earlier translators assumed that all women indicated by the genitive case with a named man were wives, but that this is not a safe assumption is shown by *Epidemics* IV.49: there, a patient who is first called "the female one of Istaeus," which we might translate "wife of Istaeus," is later called a *paidiske*, and thus identified as a slave. The extent of the problem is shown by the fact that in Book II there are two certain slaves (both female) and six uncertain cases, while in Book IV fifteen patients are of certain slave status, twenty-four are uncertain, and four are certainly family members and not slaves (specifically called *gyne*, wife, or *thygater*, daughter). Nevertheless, there are sufficient cases to show that the doctors of the *Epidemics* regularly treated slaves as well as free patients and that slaves made up a significant portion of their clientele, even if this is not numerically determinable. In his prosopographical study of Hippocratic patients, Deichgräber concluded that most were seen by doctors because they were members of large households whose masters engaged a doctor for all the needs of their *oikoi* (Deichgräber 1982, 15, 35.).

As we saw above, in contrast to Hippocratic reports of female illnesses that focused on sex difference, in discussing cases of illness in slaves, the Hippocratic authors never hint that their illnesses might be caused by natural servile traits, despite the evidence for a general and philosophical Greek belief in natural slavery and the existence of a servile nature.[14]

Nevertheless, the conditions of work and slave life in general made slaves especially susceptible to certain ailments, as is shown by the numerous cases of

81

workers' injuries. Thus our experience of repetitive-movement injuries such as carple-tunnel syndrome would have been very familiar to a Hippocratic doctor; in fact, there are two cases that seem to document a similar injury in vineyard workers who twist vines. In *Epidemics* VI.50 workers with coughs suffer paralysis in parts of the body most used in working:

> Of people with coughs, those who work with their hands, like the slave who tied up the grape vines and the son (*pais*) of Amynteus, they were both paralyzed in the right hand only. It went away and then they developed that affection along with the coughing. People who rode horses or walked got it in the lower back or hams.
>
> (trans. W. E. Smith)

A similar case involving a woman is described in *Epidemics* VI.4.4: "the woman who suffered while working with right hand (she was also pregnant)." Another occupational hazard is reported in a young slave: "an eleven-year old groom, injured by a horse" (*Epidemics* V.16).

Many other symptoms followed general overwork and fatigue. For example, in *Epidemics* VI.7.1, which describes the "Cough of Perinthus," patients (apparently predominantly workers) were affected in parts of the body that they especially used: those who worked the voice excessively were struck with severe sore throat; those who worked with the hands were paralyzed in the hands; those who rode horses or were fatigued by journeying, or in any other way fatigued the legs suffered paralysis in the lower back or legs. Numerous other cases related to fatigue or overwork:

> a man suffered weakness and heaviness after being fatigued by a journey.
>
> (*Epidemics* VI.6.4)

> weakness in the legs, such as of those walking too much just before an illness, or just after, perhaps because [something] from the *kopon* (pains, suffering, weariness) is carried to the joints, wherefore the legs are become weak.
>
> (*Epidemics* VI.1.9)

Compare:

> women who after childbirth take up burdens too much for their nature – winnowing, splitting wood, running – will suffer the next day with regard to this especially.
>
> (*Diseases of Women* II [VIII.328 Littré]

A doctor reflected on this effect in *Epidemics* VI.27:

The slave (*pais*) who belonged to the woman who was Apemantus' sister: enlarged hypochondria and spleen, breathing problems. Slimy bilious feces mixed with normal. Easily tired from labor. On the twentieth day it went to the feet and there was a crisis. In fatigued people does it go to the joints and not the eye?[15]

In their interest in the effects of heavy or dangerous physical effort, the doctors supported a common Greek belief that physical labor was servile because it caused bodily deformity.[16] But the therapeutic focus of their interest is suggested by a passage in which the doctor discussed positions that relieve pain:

The positions that relieve more, as the one weaving or twisting with the hand, in excessive pain, finds relief lying down and grasping the end of a peg fixed above.

(*Epidemics* VI.3.8)

Conclusion

The cases in the *Epidemics* show the doctors following the general attitude of Greek culture in their theory and treatment of women. In fact, they reinforced the popular belief in the innate inferiority of women by their physiological speculations. In contrast, they looked on differences between slaves and free not as a result of a lack of rational capacity on the part of the slaves, as did Aristotle, but as a result of an inferior barbarian environment or the harsh or hazardous conditions of their working lives.

In their practical approach, however, the distinction between doctors' views of women's bodies and slaves' bodies proves to be superficial. In practice slaves' bodies were treated for problems related to their labor, and women's bodies for problems related to reproduction. The diverse purposes only seem to spell a difference: the slave's instrumentality is diffused throughout his/her entire body, whereas a woman's instrumentality is focused on one set of organs. Yet, in the end the difference is overridden because, although used differently, the bodies of both women and slaves were instruments. The bodies of both groups were treated as instruments with a single purpose – work in the case of slaves and reproduction in the case of women.

Kudlien concluded his discussion of slaves as patients by optimistically arguing that the treatment of slaves by the Hippocratic doctors demonstrates that they followed the principle of the "equality of all human beings" (Kudlien 1968, 25, citing Edelstein 1942). While in one sense this is true, in that they saw no natural distinction between slave and free, such an idealistic conclusion ignores the abundant evidence for occupational injuries and illnesses and the probable treatment of slaves as instruments of the *oikos*, and the focus on successful reproduction in women, which also relegated them to the instrumental category. Doctors reflected the larger society and its values when they saw, and treated, slaves and women as uni-dimensional beings.

Notes

1 This "professional" component forms only part of the medical system, according to the widely employed analysis of Kleinman 1980, see especially p. 50; the other components are the popular sector (the advice of family, neighbors, and commonly accepted community practices), and the folk sector (religious and alternative healers). In this paper, I will concentrate on the professional sector, which is defined by the Hippocratic texts.

2 A good introduction to Hippocratic medicine is G.E.R. Lloyd, *Hippocratic Writings*, 1978. I have examined the childbirth cases in detail with English translations (Demand 1994). These, as well as the abundant gynecological material in the other Hippocratic treatises, are less useful than female non-obstetrical cases in a comparative study that includes men.

3 There is an immense and growing bibliography on women in ancient Greece; a good place to start is Sue Blundell, *Women in Ancient Greece*, 1995.

4 For instance, the orator and speech writer Lysias managed to insert into a speech given before the public courts a speech given by a woman in a private family council (Lysias 32.12–17), thus circumventing to an extent the ban on women speaking in the courts; see Walters 1993; also Hunter 1989.

5 The public physicians hired by various Greek city-states were also itinerant; they probably held a higher status than most free-lancers. See Cohn-Haft 1956.

6 On Presocratic philosophy, see Kirk, Raven, and Schofield 1983. To a great extent these philosophical theories were themselves probably derived from earlier folk notions of the body as a balance, whether of humors (fluids), or of qualities (hot/cold, moist/dry).

7 See also *Laws* 857c–d. The idea is reinforced by the later slave-status of many Greek doctors in Rome.

8 Numerous recent works concentrate on the Hippocratic conception of the female body; see, for example, Hanson 1990, 1992; Dean-Jones 1994, esp. 112–19. The fact that some doctors do insist that women are intrinsically different suggests, however, that there was a minority who believed otherwise.

9 Hippocrates, *On the Seed*. Lloyd 1983, 91, n.124, suggests that the aspect of inferiority is a popular idea taken over by the author.

10 Holladay and Poole 1979, argue that Thucydides was the first to recognize contagion in his description of the plague in Athens in 430; while this is disputed by Solomon 1985, the Thucydidean passage contains various usages and conceptions of illness that suggest that the historian was writing within the same intellectual circle as the Hippocratic writers; for recent discussion, see Parry 1969; Hornblower 1987, 110–35.

11 These figures differ somewhat from those in Lloyd, 1983, 67–8; I have counted the women used as examples as well as those whose cases are recounted, since the doctor had apparently previously seen those cases he cites as similar.

12 Hippocrates, *Illness of Maidens*; numerous cases in the *Epidemics* III case 12 (second series), diagnosed by Hanson 1989; IV.30; V.12; VI.1.1; VI.8.32; VII.64 (cf. V.67); VII.96; VII.123. Generally interpreted as "hysteria," but see discussion and references in Demand 1994, 103–7.

13 Both occurences are in the same passage, *Epidemics* VI.7.1 (V.230.1 and 232.6 Littré).

14 Aristotle, *Politics* 1254a17–1255a2; that not all agree with him is shown by his argument against those of a contrary opinion, *Politics* 1255a3–1255b15.

15 Trans. W. D. Smith, who suggests that the *pais* may have been a child; the mention of fatigue, however, seems to point to slave status.

16 On servile work that incapacitates a man for the citizen life, see Aristotle, *Politics* 1258b35–8; 1278a15–21.

6

SYMBOLS OF GENDER AND STATUS HIERARCHIES IN THE ROMAN HOUSEHOLD

Richard P. Saller

Under the influence of classical literary critics, social historians have increasingly come to appreciate the contribution of literary works to the construction of Roman categories and hierarchies of status and gender. It should be remembered, however, that literature and rhetoric constituted only two among the many spheres of symbolic discourse that contributed to this cultural system. The task of social historians is to explore the other, non-literary, spheres, both verbal and non-verbal, and to ask how they reinforced or stood in tension with the literature written by elite men. For insights into how social and gender categories were marked and ordered, the household is the crucial site to examine, because the power of the social and gender hierarchies must have depended on children being socialized to accept them as natural by their earliest experiences. Through an analysis of the ways in which freeborn women and slaves were differentiated or assimilated in habits of address, law, and ritual, I wish to highlight an important dimension of the hierarchy: that of honor, which is related to, but not identical with, that of power. While freeborn women and slaves were assimilated in some respects in their subordination, other forms of symbolic behavior sharply distinguished the honorless slave from the honorable matron in ways that should not be trivialized. The jurist Ulpian focused precisely on honor in his definition of the *mater familias* as a woman "who has not lived dishonorably (*inhoneste*)" (*Digest* 50.16.46.1).

Since the linguistic sphere is too complex to be treated satisfactorily in a page or two, a few salient points will have to suffice. Like slaves and children, the *mater* (mother) was categorized as a member of the *familia* (family) and *domus* (household) along with slaves and children under the authority of the *pater* (father) in archaic Rome. In this sense the *mater* could be said to have been grouped with other subordinates in the household. But it is important to notice differences of usage in different spheres of discourse: *familia* in the sense including mother, children, and slaves was confined mainly to legal discourse (Saller 1994, 75–80). In ordinary social discourse, *familia* usually meant only the slaves of a house, as distinct from freeborn mother and children, or sometimes a lineage sharing a *nomen* or clan name. By the classical era, the typical form of marriage, labeled *sine manu*, left the wife outside her husband's *familia* and beyond his legal authority (Treggiari 1991, 32–6). Whereas Roman assumptions about gender did not allow an adult woman to be recognized as head of a *familia*, Roman property law did permit women to own a *domus* encompassing the physical building and the human residents.

Within the elite Roman household, terms of address would conventionally have marked off the free family from the slaves. In public the *tria nomina* ("three names," such as Gaius Julius Caesar) were the honorable prerogative of the male citizen, in contrast to slaves who had one name, often foreign or mocking (for example, Felix meaning "Lucky"). Within the household only one of the *tria nomina* was used for a freeborn male, but that name would have clearly distinguished the bearer from the surrounding slaves. The wife/mother would also have carried an honorable Roman *nomen* taken from her father; her name would thus have marked her as different from the slaves on the basis of citizenship and from her husband and children in being from another family.

In another mode of address the wife/mother would have been associated with her husband in contrast to their slaves, in so far as she was called *domina*, the feminine form of "lord" and a term of deference. Not only did slaves address their female owner as *domina* (as in Petronius, *Satyricon* 105, 7), but husbands also addressed their wives with this term which connoted mutual respect (*Digest* 32.41.pr; 33.1.19.1). On the other side, slaves were summoned by the degrading term *puer* or "boy," which relentlessly pointed to their lack of adult dignity and independent judgment (Finley 1980, 96). In early Rome, *puer* had been incorporated into slaves' names such as Lucipor and Marcipor (slave of Lucius or Marcus). Various linguistic habits of the household, then, marked the *matrona*, in contrast to slaves, as an honored member to whom deference was owed.

In legal terms the Roman family and household are often characterized by *patria potestas*, which left slaves, children, and, in archaic Rome the wife, subordinated to the male head of house. This characterization is not wholly false, but is oversimplified to the point of being misleading. In law, *reverentia* (reverence) and *obsequium* (obedience) were owed by children not only to their father but also to their mother, who in turn had a duty to look after the interests of her children (Dixon 1988, 61–5). If a Roman abused with insults either his mother or father, the urban prefect was to treat it as a public offense (Ulpian, *Digest*, 37.15.1.2).

In law the rights of a wife and a slave to own property were quite different. The typical form of marriage from the late Republic, *sine manu*, left the wife under the authority of her father rather than her husband. The husband's lack of authority had important consequences for the property regime of the household.

Legitimate marriage was conventionally accompanied by a dowry from the wife or her father to the husband in order to underwrite the expenses of the household. The dowry came under the ownership of the husband (or his *paterfamilias*) for the duration of the marriage, but had to be returned if the marriage was dissolved by divorce or death of the husband (Saller 1994, 204–24). Any non-dotal property which the woman inherited or otherwise received after the death of her father – and it could be considerable among the elite – remained under her ownership. She had a completely independent right to dispose of it, and the jurists went to considerable lengths to protect it from her husband: no major gifts could be legally transferred between husband and wife. This wealth gave the wife power and authority in the household and an incentive for her husband and children to cultivate her with respect. The jurist Papinian implied that it was a commonplace that a husband would go some way to keep his wife happy in order to benefit from her testamentary discretion; he noted that a husband was not to be construed as exerting undue, illegal influence over the formulation of his wife's will when he tried to soothe her anger "by the usual husband's talk" (*ut fieri solet . . . maritali sermone*) in order to avoid being cut out of her will (*Digest* 29.6.3). Cicero recognized the importance of his son Marcus cultivating his mother, Cicero's divorced wife Terentia, in order to benefit from her considerable wealth (*Letters to Atticus* 13.38, 29, 41, 42). Slaves' lack of property rights precluded the exercise of this sort of influence within the family.

With regard to approval of children's marriages, there was a sharp gender distinction in the law, which required the *pater*'s and child's consent but not the mother's. In practice that sharp distinction was muted: mothers participated in the choice of a spouse while their husbands were living, and mothers were more likely than fathers to be living at the time of a child's marriage (Treggiari 1991, 125–38). The mother's part in arranging marriages gave some women the opportunity to influence political alliances between elite families in ways that violated the neat dichotomy between the public male and the domestic female spheres (Dixon 1985a).

Finally, the power to apply physical coercion is often associated with *patria potestas*, but in fact texts suggest that the Romans did not think of corporal punishment as primarily a legal issue, and mothers and maternal grandfathers are occasionally reported to have disciplined children with beatings (Saller 1994, 147).

Religious ritual was surely important in sanctifying gender and social hierarchies, but little is known about the daily practice of household cult (Orr 1978, Harmon 1978). Certainly, the father was the ritual head of the household, and his *genius* was celebrated in the household cult. But it does not follow that his wife, children, and slaves were undifferentiated subordinates; rather, the contrary is the case. For instance, according to Latin antiquarian writers, during the Compitalia held in January woollen balls and male and female woollen dolls were hung in the cross-roads – one ball for each slave in the household, and one doll for each free member (Festus 272L). According to these writers, the aim of the rite was to direct the attention of the Lares, underworld gods, to the balls and dolls, so that they would leave unharmed the living members of the house (Scullard 1981, 58–60). The ritual gave crude, stark expression to a model of the household in which all members, free and slave, gained protection through this rite, but in a fashion that distinguished visually between those symbolically humanized and gendered, and those dehumanized in form. Unfortunately, the social historian's analysis of this festival must remain at the level of formal distinctions and cannot penetrate to the subjective experience of household members to discover, for example, whether the slaves felt more secure from the threatening Lares by being represented, or more dehumanized on account of being represented by genderless woollen balls.

The Romans celebrated in early May a festival for the goddess Maiestas, a divine embodiment of the quality of dignity. Ovid tells us that Maiestas watched over Jupiter to protect his dignity; among humans the goddess ensured that mothers as well as fathers were held "in devoted honor" (*in pio honore*), and she was a "companion to boys and unwed girls" (*comes pueris virginibusque*) (*Fasti* 5.43–52). In the belief in a divinity of dignity protecting the free family members, both parents and children, male and female, lies an implicit but fundamental contrast with the unfree members, who had no dignity to protect.

The festival calendar held a few holidays for the benefit of slaves, the rituals of which involved an interplay of gender and status distinctions. The Saturnalia in December is the most familiar, but there were also the festival of slave girls on July 7 and the *servorum dies festus*, the slaves' holiday on August 13. The aetiology of the *ancillarum feriae* (festival of the slave girls), given by Plutarch (*Camillus* 33, *Romulus* 29; Scullard 1981, 161–2), is very interesting for an understanding of gendered hierarchies implicit in festive rituals. After the Gallic sack of Rome in 390 BCE, an army of Latin allies tried to take advantage of Rome's weakness by challenging the city. According to Plutarch, the Latin allies demanded, as a symbol of submission, Rome's virgins and widows to take as their wives. Unable to repel the Latin army, the Roman magistrate was uncertain about what to do, until a slave woman suggested that, instead of freeborn women, she and other slave girls of freeborn appearance be sent in freeborn dress. At night, when the Latins were asleep, these *ancillae* were to signal the Romans to attack. The ruse worked, and thereafter the Romans celebrated a holiday in which slave women ran out of the city to engage in a mock battle.

As with other aetiologies, the historical authenticity of this one is dubious. Nevertheless, the festival instantiated Roman assumptions about the distinction between free and slave women by transgressing it. The trick appealed to the Romans because they could send their honorless slave women in place of their chaste daughters, whose sexual honor would be violated by a single night with strange men. The trick worked only because in general slave women were assumed to have a different appearance from free women. But it was recognized that some slave women looked sufficiently similar to their free counterparts that, with a change of dress, they could pass as free and fool the Latin soldiers, who apparently did not have the wit to think of the possibility of slave women in free dress. The legend hinges on distinctive dress marking off honorable free women from slave women. This distinction in clothing was taken for granted in the real world, where the jurists used it as a basis for their discussion of legal actions for insult (the insult being decreasingly significant depending on whether its victim was dressed as a matron, a slave woman, or a prostitute, *Digest* 47.10.15.15). In this legend, as in the real world, the slave woman's lack of honor removed moral inhibitions to give her space for independent action, at the same time as it denied her certain protections.

The Matralia on June 11 honored the goddess Mater Matuta and citizen mothers to the pointed exclusion of slave women (Scullard 1981, 150–1). Slaves were either kept away from the temple or ritually beaten if they entered, because matrons were jealous of slave girls who attracted their husbands. This rationale was surely grounded in the experiences of the household. Musonius Rufus (Fragment 12) and Seneca (*Letters* 94.26; 95.37; 123.10) pointedly criticized the conventional double standard which allowed husbands a slave mistress but condemned reputable women who had sexual relations with slaves. For a husband to keep such a mistress (*paelex*) was an insult (*iniuria*) to the honor of his wife in Seneca's view (*Letters* 95.37). However, Plutarch advised a new bride not to be jealous of her husband's slave girl, because "it is respect for her [the wife] which leads him to share his debauchery, licentiousness, and wantonness with another woman" (*Moralia* 140B). We may strongly suspect that this advice represents only the ancient male point of view, but that may be a modern failure to appreciate the force of arguments based on honor. In any case, it is indicative of the slave's lack of honor that none of these elite moralists condemned the practice of taking a slave mistress on the grounds that it exploited and abused slave women.

The Matralia and the *ancillarum feriae* in their different ways marked off slave women as different from freeborn women, and their aetiologies reveal the assumptions and tensions resulting from the difference. Slave women stood outside the value system of honor and chastity that regulated the lives of citizen women and also protected them (Cohen 1991a). In the symbolic system of the Roman male, slaves and women were assimilated in the subordinate category of the passive. But within the passive category, there was a considerable difference between the legitimate wife in an honorable marriage, who had the power to initiate divorce and walk away from an abusive husband, and the powerless slave, female or male.

The slaves' holiday (*servorum dies festus*) on August 13 was said to be held in honor of King Servius Tullus, who in legend was borne of a slave woman in the sixth century before Christ (Scullard 1981, 173–4). In the ritual celebrating the holiday, according to Plutarch (*Roman Questions* 100), the matron of the household washed her slaves' heads as well as her own. Plutarch was unable to explain the strange practice, which is difficult to interpret, but its festive quality probably lay in the reversal of the usual roles of *domina* and servant. Similarly, the legend of Servius

Tullus' servile birth recognized the permeability of the boundary between master and slave status in the household, but only as the exception that confirmed the boundary.

In addition to sexual exploitation, slaves' bodies were vulnerable to another symbolically potent form of abuse, the whip. In Roman political thought, the whip symbolized servitude in contrast to the freedom of the citizen. *Provocatio*, the citizen's right of appeal against arbitrary beating or execution by the magistrate, was celebrated as a victory of *libertas*. Within the household, the application of the whip generally marked slave from free. The master–slave relationship was recognized as inherently exploitative, and slaves were believed to be naturally recalcitrant; consequently, as Cicero noted, the exercise of authority over slaves required "breaking" them. Cicero explicitly contrasted this coercive authority with paternal authority, which was considered beneficent and therefore readily obeyed (*Republic* 3.25). Precisely because whipping was thought to instill a servile character, Quintilian's *Oratorical Training* (1.3.14) and *The Education of Children* ascribed to Plutarch strongly recommended against it in rearing and educating freeborn children.

> Children ought to be led to honorable practices by means of encouragement and reasoning, and most certainly not by blows nor by ill treatment; for it is surely agreed that these are fitting rather for slaves than for the freeborn; for so they grow numb and shudder at their tasks, partly from the pain of blows, partly also on account of the hybris.
>
> (*The Education of Children* 12)

Altogether, Roman texts provide a lot of evidence for the whipping of honorless male and female slaves, which was a topos in comedy and later (for example, Terence, *Phormio* 220–1); and they provide some evidence for the corporal punishment of freeborn children, though much less than most historians suppose; the classical texts provide virtually no evidence for the beating of honorable wives. We have more evidence for women themselves applying corporal punishment to slaves and children. Thus, Roman authors suggest that among elite families of the classical era categories of free and slave were more important than hierarchies of gender or generation in determining who whipped whom (Saller 1994, 133–53). As early as the second century before Christ, the elder Cato, a senatorial advocate of traditional values, is supposed to have beaten his slaves cruelly but said that only a fool would lay hands on what was most precious and sacred to him, his wife and children (Plutarch, *Cato the Elder* 20.2).

In sum, gender and social categories in Roman society were complex and represented in differing ways in various symbolic spheres. In certain respects, law and religious rites gave the *paterfamilias* a power and authority that subordinated children, slaves and women, who in Roman male ideology all lacked full powers of judgment. But a nuanced analysis of law, language, religion, and other behavior reveals a major symbolic divide, acted out in the household every day, between the shame of slavery and the honor which privileged male citizens but also protected female citizens.

Note

I have discussed in more detail the status hierarchy of the household in "The hierarchical household in Roman society: a study of domestic slavery," in Michael Bush, ed., *Serfdom and Slavery* (1996): 112–29, but that essay gives less attention to issues of gender. My thanks to the editors for their valuable suggestions.

7

VILLAINS, WIVES, AND SLAVES IN THE COMEDIES OF PLAUTUS

Annalisa Rei

Roman comedy offers a fruitful field for the exploration of the hierarchies of
Roman society because its characters behave in ways that reverse the norms of
ordinary life. The Roman comic playwright Plautus (*c.* 254–180 BCE) freely
adapted Greek plays written about a century earlier to suit the expectations of
a Roman audience of the late third and early second centuries BCE.[1] In this
paper I shall be especially concerned with how social expectations inform the
dramatic functions and characterizations of women and slaves. In particular, I
shall examine two roles which Plautus greatly expanded with respect to his
Greek models: the clever slave and the dowered wife. With the expansion of
these two roles, the playwright addresses the social tensions of a period marked
by the Roman conquest of the Mediterranean, the advent of large-scale slavery,
and the emergence of new rules governing women's relation to property.

Plautus' expansion of the role of the clever slave with respect to his Greek
models has long been acknowledged. Following the groundbreaking studies of
Plautus' originality by Friedrich Leo (1912) and Eduard Fraenkel (1922), this
role has received much critical attention.[2] However, the implications of gender
in Plautus' comic inversions have not yet been fully explored.[3] This study
addresses the question of how free and unfree female characters were distinguished from one another in the comedies. My principal example is Plautus'
Casina, a play whose plot hinges on an alliance between a highborn wife and
a clever slave in female disguise, and which is therefore particularly revealing
with respect to the intersection of gender and status in Roman comedy.

In the plays of Plautus, the discourse of the body is linked to the discourse
of social status: those who cannot control their physical impulses end up having
their bodies subjected to the will of others. This condition is associated on the
one hand with the vulnerability of slaves to physical and sexual abuse by their
masters, and on the other hand with the expected role of the sexually passive
and socially submissive woman. The wealthy wife, however, occupies an

92

ambiguous position in Roman society because she is "high" in status but "low" in gender. In Plautus' comedies, she often appears in situations which reverse the hierarchy between husbands and wives and invite comparison to the comically inverted relationship between the master and the slave.

In the comedies, slaves and women share certain dramatic functions which derive from their social inferiority with respect to high-class men. But free, upper-class women are also sharply differentiated from unfree women. For example, the function of the trickster, male or female, is reserved for characters of the lower classes. The rogue's trickery is in fact motivated by his or her lack of social and economic power. Typically, the trickster's ruse humiliates a powerful obstacle figure and thus reverses normal social hierarchies. The principal means by which this comic humiliation is achieved are role-play and disguise. This is well illustrated in the *Casina*, where a male slave is disguised as a bride and participates in a traditional wedding ceremony of a kind that in real life was restricted to free citizens.

The prominence of slave tricksters in Roman comedy reflects the large-scale influx of foreign slaves into Rome during Plautus' lifetime. Plautus' plays were first produced in the later third and early second centuries BCE, during the early stages of Rome's conquest of the Mediterranean. At this time Rome was no longer a small, agriculture-based city-state but had become the center of a vast empire. Rome's expansion throughout the Mediterranean brought with it an increase in agricultural resources and control over important trade routes, together with the manpower of captive slaves.[4] At the same time, Rome's expansion to the East also resulted in intensified contact with Greek culture. As is well known, highly educated Greek slaves contributed to the spread of Greek culture in Rome, often as tutors of the Roman nobility.[5]

Plautus' adaptations of Greek comedies are themselves products of the intense Hellenization of Rome during this period. It was a formal convention of this genre of comedy that all characters wore Greek costumes and had Greek names. The genre was called *fabula palliata* ("comedy in Greek dress") as opposed to the *fabula togata* ("comedy in Roman dress"), which had Italian settings and characters. *Fabula palliata* is said to have been introduced to Rome a generation before Plautus, in 240 BCE, by Livius Andronicus, a Greek from Tarentum who was brought to Rome as a captive. Plautus himself came to Rome from Umbria, and like other theater professionals of his time, he belonged to the lower rank of society.[6] The Greek settings and costumes of these plays allowed a disguised representation of Roman weaknesses. Their clever Greek slaves reflect both the Romans' contempt for the captive foreigners and their admiration for Greek education.

Rome's expansion in the late third and early second centuries BCE also affected the status of women. The influx of foreign wealth meant that property no longer consisted primarily of land, and there was a need for new ways to transfer property among the elite. Women were central to this process, since dowries were important vehicles for such transfers, and marriage was a means of forging the political and commercial alliances that allowed members of the elite to control and increase their wealth.[7] The portrayal of upper-class women in Plautus' comedies reflects tensions associated with ongoing changes in the regulations concerning marriage and divorce. Anxiety about the possible economic empowerment of women runs parallel to anxiety concerning the empowerment of slaves. In these plays, wealthy wives dominate their husbands just as tricky slaves control their masters. But, as the subsequent discussion will show, the empowerment of elite women was a more real possibility than the empowerment of slaves.

Plautus' plays involve a marked difference in the dramatic functions of free and unfree women based on notions of morality as tied to rank. As William Anderson (1993, 88–92) has pointed out, the quintessential "virtue" of the trickster in the reversed value system of comedy is *malitia* ("badness"). Female tricksters in particular are referred to and proudly refer to themselves as *malae* ("bad") in this context.[8] It is important, however, to qualify Anderson's observation by pointing out that the trickster's *malitia* sidesteps ethical evaluation: the term is always used in reference to his or her theatrical skill at circumventing power through disguise and role-play. Unlike unfree women, upper-class women are never *malae* in this sense, even though they may be characterized as unpleasant by their husbands, who resent their economic superiority.

Unlike upper-class men in comedy, who lose their dignity by indulging in lust or greed, female characters of the same rank never behave in morally transgressive ways. They appear as moral foils to their transgressive husbands, yet, unlike slaves and prostitutes, they are generally not sympathetic characters but are presented as anti-comic agents. The high moral standards of the ideal upper-class wife restrict comedy's freedom to represent inversions in the social hierarchy. The moral qualities that defined an ideal Roman *matrona* were *pudicitia* (chastity) and *fides* (loyalty), which comprised her sexual fidelity to her husband and her overall loyalty to the interests of the common household (Treggiari 1991, 229–61). In the comedies, this ideal is reflected in the wife's dramatic function as guardian of the economic and moral integrity of the household.

Characteristically, a wife takes action to avenge not a husband's infidelity, but his violation of the property which the couple shares or which even belongs to the wife entirely.[9] The pursuit of courtesans, both by married and by unmarried men, was not considered immoral in Roman society.[10] The audience's sympathies might even be explicitly steered towards the unfaithful husband, as in the *Menaechmi*, where the husband appeals to the adulterers in the audience for sympathy (128) while the wife receives a negative characterization even from her own father (766–7). The woman's father condones his son-in-law's extramarital affairs and only comes to the rescue of his daughter when he realizes that the husband is stealing from her to finance his affairs. When husbands in comedy compete with their own sons for the same courtesan and steal from their wives to finance their affairs, their fault lies in a failure to respect the economic interests of their family. By contrast, the honor of wives and daughters is never compromised in comedy, either by the women themselves or by others. The serious transgression of pursuing the wife or daughter of a citizen is never represented.[11] And the rape of a virgin, which is a frequent theme in the Greek plays adapted by Plautus, rarely figures in his plays.[12]

This correlation between female morality and status is well illustrated by the type of the *pseudomeretrix*, a character who appears in several of Plautus' plays (*Cistellaria*, *Curculio*, *Rudens*, *Poenulus*). The *pseudomeretrix* is a woman of free status who has been enslaved in a brothel by some fantastic accident of fate, such as being kidnapped by pirates. These women are always portrayed as especially virtuous, even when this characterization contrasts with their apparent role as prostitutes. The *pseudomeretrix* Adelphasium in the *Poenulus*, for instance, delivers a moralizing tirade against women's luxury (210–32) and against cheap whores (300–7; 323), and asserts her moral and social superiority throughout the play (cf. 1201f.). The exaggerated virtue of the *pseudomeretrix* anticipates the recognition of her real status – by tokens or by a reunion with the father – which enables her to marry her high-born lover. Significantly, all *pseudomeretrices* also actively reject the typical behaviors of tricksters, such as disguise and role-play.

While the sexual restraint of wives and daughters in comedy can be explained by the strict requirements of chastity for free women in Roman society, it is perhaps more surprising that upper-class female characters are also excluded from such non-sexual activities as role-play and disguise. In the *Persa* (3.1), for example, a free daughter objects to impersonating a prostitute in a ruse orchestrated by the clever slave. All she would have to do is wear a costume and make conversation, but she argues that her appearance in the clothes of a prostitute might make her neighbors believe that she actually *is* one. Similarly, in the *Casina*, where a wife plots a ruse against her husband, Plautus is careful to assign the actual performance of the role-play in disguise to slaves and thus to differentiate the wife from the low-class tricktsters. For a wife to engage in role-play and disguise would have put her on the same low level as actors, who were marginalized in Roman society, and whose social condition was considered shameful. In Rome, unlike Greece, actors were despised. As foreigners and slaves, they were considered licentious and effeminate, thus comparable to prostitutes. Acting, like pandering and stealing, brought the stigma of *infamia*, the diminution of a person's social and legal status.[13]

At the same time, the social status that inhibited the freeborn woman's participation in role-play and disguise did give her a particular role in the comic plot. The wife's economic power often leads to an inversion of the conventional conjugal roles of dominant husband and submissive wife. In these comic situations, wives actively oppose their husbands, and assert a dominance over them that is explicitly likened to a slave's dominance over his master in comedy.[14] In the words of the wife's father in the *Menaechmi* (766–7), women rely on their dowries to force their husbands into submission.[15] In another play, a husband complains that he has sold his power (*imperium*) for a dowry and that the slave who manages his wife's dowry handles more money than he does (*Asinaria* 85–7).

Not only are subservient husbands compared to slaves, but their humiliation is intensified by comparison to the lowest in the social hierarchy, those who are not only unfree but also female. Thus, in the *Menaechmi* (795–7), the husband is pictured as sitting at home spinning like a maid. While the subservient husband is seen as emasculated by his position of inferiority, as a series of castration jokes makes clear (for example, *Mercator* 275), the wife is seen as defeminized by her empowerment. Accordingly, she is typically described by the husband as unattractive, domineering, and both verbally and physically abusive.[16]

These prominent negative portraits of powerful wives reflect the social tensions of Plautus' own cultural moment. The domineering wife is one of the features that distinguish the Roman comic world from its Greek models.[17] As Eduard Fraenkel (1922/1960, 131–4) pointed out, Plautus' frequent attacks on the Roman dowry system constitute some of his most obvious innovations.[18] While complaints about wealthy wives were not a Roman invention,[19] Plautus exploited the potential conflict between a husband and a wealthy wife to a larger extent than the Attic playwrights of the fourth century had done. His expansion of the wife's function as an obstacle figure goes along with his interest in plots which involve married men pursuing prostitutes, a theme that is absent from the extant plays of Attic New Comedy. The Attic playwrights presented domestic conflicts between men and their concubines, but not between men and their legitimate wives (Konstan 1993); upper-class wives in Attic New Comedy never have significant speaking roles and do not actively intervene as obstacle figures.[20]

With the character of the dowered wife, Plautus brings his adaptations of Greek plays closer to the experience of his Roman audience. Roman women of the upper classes were greatly empowered by their dowries and, unlike their Athenian counterparts, they could own and transfer property, even if they were nominally supervised by a guardian for certain transactions.[21] Roman matrons could also make public donations and dedications from their dowries and other properties.[22] And they could rally against policies that affected them, as they did in 195 BCE, when a group of matrons appeared before the senate to demand the repeal of the Oppian Law, a sumptuary law that restricted the amount of wealth that a woman could display in public.[23]

The prominence in Plautine comedy of husbands who would rather put up with an unpleasant wife than give up the money she has brought into the household illustrate the real importance of the wife's dowry in the lives of upper-class men of the period. A woman's wealth enhanced the social status and prestige of her husband but also imposed responsibilities on him.[24] In particular, the dowry had an ambiguous legal status, since it typically became part of the husband's property but had to be returned to the wife if the marriage ended through divorce or the death of the husband.[25] Husbands were responsible for maintaining their wives at a standard commensurate with their dowries and with the status of the family.[26] They were expected to keep the dowry intact during the marriage, and the wife could demand its return if it was handled negligently.[27] The requirement that the dowry be returned in the event of a divorce gave married women some protection against mistreatment by their husbands. Cato the Elder (234–149 BCE), a contemporary of Plautus, provides evidence of the real power that could be exercised by wealthy wives over their husbands. In a speech delivered in support of the Voconian Law (169 BCE),[28] a law intended to limit the amount that women from the wealthiest families could inherit, Cato (*Orations* 40; *Oratorum Romanorum Fragmenta* 156–60, esp. 158) cites the case of a woman who had lent a part of her property to her husband and, in a fit of anger, demanded its immediate repayment. To make matters worse, the husband had to suffer the humiliation of being harassed by his wife's servant, a slave who formed part of her dowry (cf. Plautus' *Asinaria* (85), where the slave who manages the woman's property is called *servus dotalis* "a slave who belongs to the dowry").[29]

A woman's wealth could put further pressure on her husband through the way in which its public display reflected on the honor and prestige of her male relatives. Polybius (*Histories* 31.26–7) illustrates the noble character of his patron Scipio Aemilianus (185–129 BCE) by recounting how he passed on the possessions he had inherited from his grandmother, Aemilia, to his mother, Papiria, who was divorced and impoverished, thus allowing her to make such a display. He comments that Papiria's means had been well below what was fitting for a woman who had been married to the great Scipio Africanus (235–183 BCE), so that she had long been forced to stay home on ceremonial occasions, when other women of her rank paraded their wealth in the streets of Rome. When Papiria finally appeared in public with her wealth visibly restored, the crowd cheered Scipio for his generosity. At the same time, however, Scipio's family owed huge sums to the husbands of his sisters for their dowries, which were supposed to be paid in installments (Polybius 31.26).[30] Dowries, therefore, were means to assert one's rank in society, while at the same time they could represent a significant financial burden.

Plautus' emphasis on the figure of the domineering wife coincided historically with a shift in marriage patterns that gave even greater financial power and autonomy to wives.[31] Roman jurists clearly distinguished two forms of marriage. In early Rome, the norm among the elite was marriage *cum manu*.[32] In marriage *cum manu*, the bride left her native family and came under the *potestas*, or authority, of her husband (or of his father, if he was still alive). Any property she owned or acquired in addition to her dowry became her husband's. If he died, she shared equally with her children in any inheritance, so that her legal status was comparable to that of a daughter.[33] During the late third and second centuries BCE, another form of marriage, marriage *sine manu*, became increasingly common, and by the time of Cicero in the first century BCE it had almost completely replaced marriage *cum manu*.[34] In marriage *sine manu* the bride remained under the *potestas* of her father, or, if he was dead, she was legally independent and could own property which by law was entirely separate from that of her husband.[35] In this form of marriage, the woman had no claim to her husband's estate but retained her claim to a share of her father's patrimony as part of her inheritance.[36] Her dowry still became part of the husband's property for the duration of the marriage but had to be returned in the case of a divorce.[37]

Modern scholars generally attribute the increasing predominance of marriage *sine manu* to the changes in economic conditions that came about as a result of Rome's expansion during the third and second centuries BCE.[38] The earlier form of marriage *cum manu* was more appropriate to a land-based economy in which a woman's marriage meant her physical departure from her father's estate and her dowry took the form of household goods or a plot of land. With the growth of fortunes based on other forms of wealth, marriage *sine manu* became more appealing because it enabled both families to prevent the dispersal of their property through marriage.

A woman's dowry gained even more importance when divorce practices began to be liberalized in the late third century BCE, partly as a response to the increased use of marriage to create political alliances.[39] As divorce became more common, strategies were developed to avoid dispersing a family's holdings through dowries. Down to the middle of the third century BCE, in a traditional marriage *cum manu*, Roman women could not initiate a divorce at all, and men themselves could only repudiate their wives under specific circumstances, such as adultery, "poisoning of children" (infanticide or, possibly, abortion) and negligence in guarding the family property.[40] A husband who repudiated his wife under any other circumstances forfeited his property, so that a woman was to some extent protected from capricious repudiations.[41] Around 230 BCE Spurius Carvilius Ruga set a precedent that changed not only the divorce laws but also the handling of dowries.[42] He divorced his sterile wife without penalty because he convinced the censors that his marriage was not valid under a definition of marriage as existing for the procreation of legitimate heirs.[43] In response to more relaxed divorce laws, the Romans established the *actio rei uxoriae*, the legal recourse by which a wife could reclaim her dowry in the case of a divorce. This kind of legal action is mentioned as a routine transaction in Plautus' *Stichus* (204), a play first performed in 200 BCE.[44]

Furthermore, in a marriage *sine manu*, the form that was becoming more popular as the divorce laws were liberalized, the wife could herself initiate a divorce, as she could not in a marriage *cum manu*. At the time when Plautus wrote, both forms of marriage were practiced, and both are depicted in his works. The wives in Plautus' plays often threaten their husbands with a divorce, initiated either by them or by their fathers.[45] As we shall see, the distinction between the two types of marriage becomes important in the *Casina* (2.2), where the wife discusses the conditions of both with her neighbor and expresses frustration that her own marriage contract does not allow her to initiate a divorce.

The anxiety about women's wealth that are expressed in Plautus' comedies is also reflected in legal measures and other elite male actions of the second century. The Voconian Law, passed in 169 BCE to limit the amount that women of the first census class could inherit, was only one in a series of laws designed to restrict women's ability to own and move property.[46] Cato the Elder, a supporter of the Voconian Law, had already proposed in 184 BCE that women's possessions in the form of clothes, jewelry, and other luxury items be catalogued at ten times their value and then taxed at three times the prevailing rate.[47] He had also objected to the repeal in 195 BCE of the Oppian Law, a sumptuary measure that restricted the amount of wealth that could be displayed in public by women during the Second Punic War (Livy 34.4.1ff.). As for his own marriage, Cato is said to have married a woman with a modest dowry because he was convinced that a financially dependent wife would be more obedient (Plutarch, *Cato the Elder* 20.2), a view echoed by the wealthy Megadorus in Plautus' *Aulularia* (534).

But economics alone did not govern the relations between husbands and wives, nor was property the only defining criterion in the self-presentation of the Roman elite. Upper-class men and women recognized each other as members of the same class not only by their property but also, ideally, by their acceptance of a common value system and of a shared code of honor. Even if marriage could be a temporary economic transaction, it was still conceived of as a partnership in which the wife shared authority over the household with her husband, while at the same time being subordinate to him by virtue of her gender.[48] Although the legal texts paint a grim picture of Roman family life under a husband's and father's *patria potestas*, his absolute power over his wife and children,[49] the relations between family members were in fact governed by a code of honor, and the law was invoked only when the traditional mechanisms of problem-solving within the family failed. As Richard Saller (1994, 102–32) has shown, a strictly legalistic approach to the Roman family fails to uncover its dynamics and organization precisely because it ignores the unwritten rules of the honor code, which were enforced by peer pressure. Saller identifies the positive force of this honor code as *pietas*, a set of mutual obligations that applied not only to the relations of inferior to superior but also of superior to inferior.[50] The violation of this ideal of shared property and mutual respect between husbands and wives and between parents and children is often the starting point for Roman comedy. Typically, the abandonment of his responsibilities by a figure of authority, a father or husband, sets in motion a series of plot mechanisms that leads to his corrective humiliation by his subordinates. With its characteristic parody of legal terms and procedures,[51] Plautine comedy reinforces the notion that, in reality, domestic conflicts are not to be solved by law, but by the assertion of a commonly accepted code of honor.

This pattern is well illustrated in the *Casina*, where a husband forfeits his authority over his household because he blatantly disregards the interests of his wife and son. There the *paterfamilias*, Lysidamus, is pursuing Casina, a servant who has come into his household as a foundling.[52] His wife, Cleostrata, has raised Casina, in her own words, "like her own daughter" (45f.) and, being well aware of the foundling's free status, she supports her son's wish to marry the young woman. But Lysidamus has other plans for Casina: in order to retain the privilege of raping her with impunity, he plans to keep her enslaved by arranging a "slave-marriage" between Casina and his bailiff Olympio while his son is out of town. Cleostrata tries to thwart her husband's plans by plotting a counter-marriage between Casina and her own faithful servant Chalinus. The two slaves draw lots and Casina is assigned in marriage to Lysidamus' candidate Olympio. But Cleostrata does not give up and devises a new strategy with the help of her servants: in the wedding ceremony, Casina is replaced by the slave Chalinus in disguise. After the ceremony, when both Olympio and Lysidamus approach the bride for sex, Chalinus beats them and threatens to rape them. Chalinus' revenge is not staged but when Olympio reports the incident, Lysidamus becomes the laughing-stock of the entire household. Finally, he apologizes to his wife, and the play ends with the formal reinstatement of Lysidamus as the head of the household.

Lysidamus is temporarily deprived of his status because he fails to uphold the moral responsibilities associated with his position. While the law is undoubtedly on the side of his *patria potestas*, or masterly prerogative, Lysidamus blatantly violates the code of honor through his lack of *pietas*. Thus, while he insists that his son is under his absolute authority (263–5), Cleostrata points out that he is expected by moral convention (*officium*) to share important decisions about the household with her (259–61). In fact, Lysidamus is abusing his paternal power by pursuing the young man's bride. His behavior goes beyond the stock rivalry of a father and son who pursue the same courtesan found in other plays. Lysidamus must know that Casina is really freeborn, since she is eligible for marriage, and in Rome, as in Athens, only free citizens could contract a legal marriage.[53] The slave wedding he is plotting is presented in the prologue as a legal incongruity (68–72).

More seriously, Lysidamus is himself attempting to commit *stuprum*, defined in the legal texts as "sex with the daughter or the wife of a citizen," a serious transgression that is not usually dealt with in comedy.[54] Casina's position could be considered ambiguous since, legally, freeborn foundlings remained free, but the absence of parents made their status difficult to prove.[55] Lysidamus' insistence on keeping Casina in a servile condition and therefore exposed to sexual exploitation has a parallel in the well-known story of Verginia, reported by Livy (*History of Rome* 3.44–50). There the powerful magistrate Appius Claudius, in order to rape Verginia, the daughter of a free Roman citizen, Verginius, claims that she is not really the daughter of Verginius but a slave who was stolen in infancy from the household of one of his friends and then presented to Verginius as his own child. That story ends in tragedy: rather than see his daughter humiliated, Verginius kills her in the Roman Forum in a sacrificial act that sparks a revolt against the tyrannical Appius Claudius.

Comedy proposes more peaceful solutions to such abuses. In the *Casina* a massacre is only threatened in a tongue-in-cheek report that Casina has gone mad and intends to kill her unwanted groom(s) with two swords (3.5). The supposed slave woman is avenged through the humiliation of Lysidamus during the wedding scene, in which he is deprived of both his authority and his male identity. The wedding scene (4.4) includes a parody of a significant moment in the traditional Roman ceremony at which the bride received advice from a respected matron, the *pronuba*.[56] In the *Casina*, this role is played by the clever servant Pardalisca, who advises the bride to dominate and financially ruin her future husband (814–24) – just what a defeminized *uxor dotata* is expected to do in comedy.

Lysidamus' comic humiliation is represented not only as emasculation but also as enslavement. When he returns on stage after the attack by Chalinus, he compares himself to a fugitive slave and even anticipates a slave beating from his own wife (953–59; 1003). In Rome, corporal punishment was normally associated with the inherently shameful condition of slaves and represented extreme humiliation for a free citizen.[57] While allusions to slave beatings are common in Plautus,[58] the role reversal involved in a free man being subjected to physical violence by his slave was evidently beyond what the free members of the audience would have found acceptable.[59] Thus we do not see the attack on Lysidamus by Chalinus on stage but only hear about it in a displaced form in Olympio's narrative in Act 5, scene 2. Olympio reports on his own experience at length and then concludes with a brief indication that Lysidamus has suffered a similar attack (932–3). Like the exclusion of honorable matrons from ludic agency, this avoidance of representing the corporal punishment of free citizens illustrates the limits of comic inversion.

While the humiliation of Lysidamus results from an appropriation of power by his wife, Cleostrata does not act on her own behalf but rather through the agency of two slaves: Chalinus, who disguises himself as the bride, and the maid Pardalisca, who plays the *pronuba* in the wedding scene (4.4) and delivers a fictional messenger's speech about Casina's murderous madness (3.5) in order to terrify Lysidamus. By using her servants as surrogates, Cleostrata preserves the hierarchical order of the household and maintains the dignity that is expected of her. As they join forces, the slave Chalinus and the matron Cleostrata present two complementary versions of the comic avenger: Cleostrata is socially high by virtue of her status but low in the hierarchy of gender, while Chalinus is low in status but high in gender.

Cleostrata's reliance on Chalinus and Pardalisca to achieve her ends constitutes an interesting variation on the more typical avenging wife plots represented by Plautus' *Asinaria* and *Mercator*. In those plays, wives use their dowries to oppose their husbands, but Cleostrata does not have this option and is therefore obliged to team up with her servants. The playwright motivates her alliance with these powerless and marginalized figures by demonstrating early in the play (2.2) that she cannot rely on her property as leverage because she is married *cum manu* and thus cannot threaten to initiate a divorce.[60]

Plautus makes an elaborate business out of the revelation of Cleostrata's marital status, first playing with the audience's expectations to suggest that it is something different. Cleostrata first appears in Act 2, scene 1, when she is locking her husband out of the house. This action identifies her as a typical angry wife (144–61) engaged in gender reversal as she locks her husband out of the house. In particular, it puts her in a position that recalls the behavior of a man repudiating his wife according to the ancient legal formula codified in the Twelve Tables, the most ancient legal text of the Romans. In that situation, the husband would tell the wife to gather her belongings, then take away her keys and send her away.[61] Furthermore, careless handling of the household's keys was cited in the Twelve Tables as one of the three causes that justified a wife's repudiation.[62] The next scene (2.2), however, reveals Cleostrata's true situation as she admits that she has no legal recourse against her husband (189–90). In her legalistic arguing about property, Cleostrata here conforms to the figure of the powerful comic wife as she appears in the *Asinaria, Menaechmi*, and *Mercator*. But it turns out that, unlike the angry wives in those plays,[63] she cannot rely on a dowry as leverage against her husband. She complains that Lysidamus is stealing from her by trying to impose his will on a slave who, she claims, was brought up with her money and is therefore part of her property (194).[64] Cleostrata's neighbor, Myrrhina, refutes her claim with a legal argument of her own. She states that during her marriage a wife was not allowed to own property independently, including a slave, since whatever she acquired became the property of her husband (198–202), making it clear that Cleostrata's is a marriage *cum manu*. Cleostrata's situation, Myrrhina continues (204–7), not only precludes her from initiating divorce, but on the contrary makes her vulnerable to her husband's repudiation (210–12). Thus Cleostrata is shown to be hampered by a lack of legal avenues that justifies her recourse to a slave's ruse.

Because Chalinus masquerades as the bride in a supposed slave marriage, Lysidamus is, in effect, reduced to sexual and social submission by the figure most associated with those conditions, the powerless slave woman. The double vulnerability of the female slave is underscored in the alliance between the slave Olympio and his master Lysidamus. In their scheme, the female slave would be exploited by a fellow slave on account of her gender and by her master on account of her unfree status. Thus Cleostrata's use of both substitution and disguise in her plot results in the most thorough possible reversal of the violence and domination reflected in Lysidamus' abusive behavior against both his wife and his slaves. Yet it is notable that, like the matron Cleostrata, Casina can only gain revenge through the male Chalinus, who acts as a surrogate for both of them.

As female agency is ruled out and displaced onto the male slave, the revenge on Lysidamus becomes a transaction between men, free and servile. By making Chalinus the one who imposes a moment of fictive enslavement and emasculation on Lysidamus, the play emphasizes a weak point in the Roman slave system, namely the lack of a clear natural distinction between male master and male slave. In the course of the play, both of Lysidamus' male slaves – his accomplice Olympio as well as his punisher Chalinus – challenge his domination. Both have experienced that domination in the form of unwanted sexual advances by their master (451ff.; 515ff., 811). As a consequence, Olympio, although he is his master's accomplice in the planned rape of Casina, is not as willing a participant as Lysidamus had hoped for. In exchange for his cooperation, he demands to be treated like a free man who has the right to reject Lysidamus' sexual exploitation (723–47).[65]

Olympio's rejection of the submissive role expected from slaves is paralleled by Chalinus' attack on Lysidamus, in which what has appeared to be a docile bride turns out to be a valiant soldier instead. Chalinus is not, in fact, a simple household servant, but the military attendant (*armiger*) of the absent son (257, 277, 769).[66] This association with weapons promotes the recurring use of phallic props to express Lysidamus' humiliation. Chalinus' sword is stressed in Olympio's report in Act 5, scene 2,[67] where it becomes the object of much obscene wordplay. In the inserted narrative through which Pardalisca attempts to confuse Lysidamus in Act 3, scene 5, "Casina" is raging inside the house brandishing *two* swords with which she intends to kill her groom(s). This emphasizes Chalinus as an avenger who possesses the phallus and thus the feature that distinguishes him from Casina, but not from Lysidamus.

Correspondingly, Lysidamus' humiliation is underscored by the loss of his staff and his cloak, the symbols of his social and gender status. Both of these props carry multiple meanings. The hooked stick is the identifying feature of the old man in comedy,[68] and Lysidamus has in fact given up his conventional role of *senex* to behave more like the typical *adulescens amans*, the irresponsible young man in love. At the same time, his loss of his staff expresses that temporary loss of social power to Chalinus that is also expressed in Chalinus' brandishing of a sword. The wrinkled state of Lysidamus' cloak is an indication of his debauchery from the very beginning of the play (246). After the struggle with Chalinus, Lysidamus returns on stage without it, wearing a slave's short *chiton*.[69] Appearing without his cloak, Lysidamus is like an adulterous matron who, as a result of her shame, would lose the right to wear her distinctive cloak, the *palla*.[70] Furthermore, the "uncloaking" of Lysidamus also plays with the dramatic conventions of the *fabula palliata*, a comic genre that disguised universal human weakness behind the mask of despised "Greeklings." When Lysidamus realizes that he has lost his cloak, he exclaims that he has been *expalliatus* (945), "un-cloaked," and thus exposed to the audience as one of them, a flawed human rather than a Greek caricature.[71]

Lysidamus has a ready excuse for the disappearance of the cloak, blaming it on a sudden attack by raging Bacchants. This excuse is dismissed by Myrrhina, who counters that there are no Bacchic rites at the time in Rome (978–81). In fact, Dionysiac rites were banned in the city in 186 BCE by a famous decree of the senate following a scandal involving the participants in these mystery cults, among whom were distinguished matrons.[72] Lysidamus' reference to Bacchants works against him, however, because it evokes mythical gender reversals. In Euripides' *Bacchae*, Pentheus is torn apart by Bacchants when he tries to overstep gender boundaries by watching an all-female ritual. This myth must have been well known in Rome at the time, since Plautus uses it again in another play.[73] Further, the reference to the Bacchants incongruously elevates the gender reversal of Chalinus' attack to mythological heights, one of Plautus' favorite comic techniques.[74] Cleostrata, however, is not about to turn into a murderous Bacchant. Unlike the avenging wives in the *Asinaria* and the *Mercator*, she cheerfully accepts Lysidamus' apologies (1004) and the two reconcile.

The family conflict of the *Casina* is not resolved by law, as initially proposed by the angry Cleostrata in Act 2, scene 2, nor by a perversion of the law, as Lysidamus attempts in the "slave marriage," but by an entertaining *ludus* that brings the head of the household back to his senses and restores order. Like the author himself, Cleostrata manipulates events behind the scenes. Her cleverly contrived reinstatement of Lysidamus as the head of the household also reaffirms her status as ideal *matrona* – respectful of her husband's authority and at the same time in control of the servants. As Cleostrata forgives Lysidamus, she both reasserts her own virtue and rescues her husband from the threatening implications of his humiliation. Husband and wife are reunited in order to affirm domestic stability and, at the same time, to re-establish solidarity among the free, both men and women. Within the now properly functioning household the distinctions between free and unfree are again clear. The questions raised in the course of the action about the upper-class male's control over his subordinates have been resolved in his favor.

As the ending of the *Casina* demonstrates, Plautine comedy ultimately validates existing social arrangements. Comedy reinforces an ideal in which economic and social superiority is legitimized by adherence to a shared moral code. At the end of the play, everyone knows his or her place once again. Social stability is restored after chaos and reversals, and the spectators are sent home with the satisfying notion that, at least in the world of happy endings, stability among the orders and within the family is not only desirable but also feasible.

Notes

1 Recent studies have shown that Plautus was working within an established tradition of Roman playwrights adapting Greek plays, a tradition that had already generated its own aesthetic and dramatic conventions (Wright 1974, 15–32).

2 On Plautus' slaves see also Spranger 1984; Slater 1985; Segal 1987 [1968], 99–170.

3 On women and the family in Plautus, cf. Schuhmann 1977; Konstan 1977, 1978, 1983, 47–56; Wiles 1989; Stärk 1990.

4 The enslavement of the vanquished enemy was one of the principal sources of slave-supply during the central period of Roman history. For a brief introduction to the Roman slave system, see Bradley 1994a, with sources and bibliography.

5 See, for example, Bonner 1977.

6 Our information about Plautus' life is sparse and unreliable. Aulus Gellius (*Attic Nights* 3.3.14), who quotes Varro (116–27 BCE), the most important ancient editor of Plautus, states that Plautus earned his living in theatrical work. He is said to have made a fortune and to have lost it in a trade venture, so that he was forced to hire out his services in a mill for some time. See Leo 1912, 63–86; Duckworth 1952, 49–51; Gratwick 1982, 181–2.

7 See Corbier 1991; 1992.

8 Cf. *Truculentus* 448–79; *Miles Gloriosus* 188–94; 355f., 879–95, *Casina* 826. Unless indicated otherwise, the plays are all cited from W. M. Lindsay's edition in Oxford Classical Texts (1904–5). Passages from the *Casina* are cited from MacCary and Willcock (1976). Translations are mine where no author is indicated.

9 See, for example, *Mercator* 700–4.

10 Cf. Cicero *In Defense of Caelius* 42; Plautus *Curculio* 37–8; Griffin 1985, 1–31; Saller 1987, 78–9; Treggiari 1991, 299–309. On the double standard in marriage, see *Mercator* 817–29, where a female servant imagines a topsy-turvy world in which married men are held accountable for marital infidelity in the same way as women are.

11 Fantham 1991; Paul, *Sententiae* 2.26.16 *(Fontes Iuris Romani AnteIustiniani (FIRA)* 2.352).

12 Plautus differs here from Terence, whose adaptations remain closer to the Greek originals. On rape plots see Fantham 1975.

13 Cicero, *Philippics* 2.8.26; *In Defense of Plancio* 30; *On Divination* 2.66; *The Republic* 4.10; Cornelius Nepos, *On Famous Men*, preface 5; Livy 7.2; Valerius Maximus 2.4.4; Ulpian, *Digest* 3.2.1 [6 *ad edictum*]. See Baltrusch 1988, 128–9; Leppin 1992, 71; Edwards 1993, 98–172.

14 *Asinaria* (5.2), *Amphitruo* (2.2, 3.2), *Casina* (2.3), *Mercator* (4.3–4), and *Menaechmi* (4.1). Cf. Konstan 1978; 1983, 47–56. Even Alcumena, the wife who is seduced by Jupiter disguised as her husband in Plautus' mythological travesty, *Amphitruo*, behaves like a conventional virtuous wife.

15 *Ita esse solent quae uiros supseruire/sibi postulant, dote fretae feroces.* – "That's the way they are, those women: just because they have a fat dowry they are mean and expect their husbands to be subservient to them." Similarly, see *Aulularia* 158–69, 474–535. Outside of comedy, too, the wife's dowry is regarded as an element that reverses the roles of men and women in the household. For instance, Tacitus (*Germania* 18.2) relates that in Germany the groom brings a dowry to the bride; cf. Horace, *Odes* 3.24.19–20 on the Scythians. Columella (12.3.5) regards separate property in the household as a source of imbalance in marriage, as he describes the dowered wife's constant demands with the same *topoi* found in comedy. The gender reversal in Plautus' comedies is paralleled by Martial (8.12.1–2), who plays with the gendered terms for marriage in Latin when he has a man say that he does not want to be the "wife" of a wealthy woman (*uxorem quare locupletem ducere nolim / quaeritis? uxori nubere nolo meae.* "You ask why I don't want to marry a rich woman? Because I'd rather not be the bride of my wife.").

16 Cf. *Asinaria* 4, 743, 894–5, 937, 942, 946. The nagging wife is repeatedly compared to a yapping dog, as in *Miles Gloriosus* 681, *Menaechmi* 716–18, 837; *Casina* 319–20. Husbands always pursue their affairs with *meretrices* in fear of retaliation by their wives and in anticipation of corporal punishment, as in *Asinaria* 897–8; 946; *Casina* 451, 1003; *Mercator* 275, 545, 798, 819, 827, 1002; *Menaechmi* 161, 1138.

17 The Romans themselves were aware of the differences in the social conditions of Greek and Roman women. Cornelius Nepos (*On Famous Men*, preface 6) observes that while Roman women accompanied their husbands to social occasions such as the banquet, Greek women lived segregated in a separate part of the house and did not attend the symposium.

18 Attacks on the dowered wife are scattered throughout Plautine comedy but are most prominent in the tirades delivered in the *Aulularia* (475–535), *Epidicus* (221–35), and *Miles Gloriosus* (672–700).

19 Cf. Alexis frag. 146 K; Anaxandrides frag. 52 K; Antiphanes frag. 320 K; Menander, frags 333, 334 K–T; Menander, *Plokion* (Sandbach 1990, 311–12); Plato, *Laws* 774c; Aristotle, *Nicomachean Ethics* 8.1161a.

20 In the comedies of Menander, for example, married women hardly ever speak and, when they do, they are reserved, kind, and submissive. In the *Epitrepontes*, for instance,

Pamphile refuses to leave her husband despite the rift between them and the pressure of her father (134–5; 1065–7). In the *Heros* Myrrhina is treated with respect by her husband (65ff.) when she tells him that she was raped in her youth. See Stärk 1990, 70.

21 Evans 1991, 51, with sources. On women and property in Athens see Schaps 1979.

22 According to Livy (5.23.8–11; 5.25.4–10; 5.50.7), in 395 BCE Roman women deposited sufficient gold in the state treasury to redeem Camillus' vow of a one-tenth part of the Veiientine spoils to Apollo. These matrons earned the right to be eulogized in funeral orations (Plutarch, *Camillus* 8). Similarly, in 207 BCE, the temple of Juno on the Aventine was rebuilt with money donated by matrons from their dowries (Livy 27.27.1–15).

23 Livy 34.4.1 ff.; cf. Johnston 1980; Culham 1982; Hemelrijk 1987.

24 Evans 1991, 53ff. with sources and extensive bibliography on the subject of the Roman dowry.

25 Cicero, *Topics* 66; Tryphonius, *Digest* 23.3.75 [6 *Disputationes*]; Ulpian, *Titles* 6.3–5; cf. Treggiari 1991, 323–5; Watson 1965; Dixon 1992, 51.

26 Corbett 1930, 147, 152–4; Dixon 1992, 50; Saller 1994, 210–11; Treggiari 1991, 332. Until the marriage legislation of Augustus, a dowry was not legally required as a condition for marriage but it was socially expected. The jurists recognize the importance of dowries to enable women to marry and preserve the institution of marriage, cf. Paul, *Digest* 23.3.2 [60 *ad edictum*]; Pomponius, *Digest* 24.3.1 [15 *ad Sabinum*].

27 Dixon 1992, 50; Gardner 1986, 108–9; Ulpian, *Titles* 6.8; Ulpian, *Digest* 24.3.24 pr. [33 ad edictum].

28 An excerpt of this speech is quoted by the antiquarian Aulus Gellius (17.6.1).

29 Cf. Festus 356 (Lindsay); Nonius 54 M.

30 Dixon 1985b; Evans 1991, 64; Fantham *et al.* 1994, 262.

31 See Schulmann 1977,65.

32 Watson 1971, 17; Treggiari 1991, 324–6; Cantarella 1996, 56–67.

33 Gaius, *Institutes* 1.111.

34 We are much better informed about marriage and divorce in the late Republican period than we are about the period of Plautus; cf., for example, Bradley 1991, 156–204; Corbier 1991, 47–78.

35 Gaius, *Institutes* 1.136l; Cf. Corbett 1930, 90–4.

36 Hallett 1984, 90–1.

37 Watson 1967, 66–76; Gardner 1986, 105–6.

38 Saller 1994, 207; Dixon 1992, 41; Frank 1933, 109–214.

39 Pomeroy 1976, 222; Gratwick 1984, 46–9; Corbier 1991; 1992.

40 *Digest* 24.2.1; Corbett 1930, 222, 242; Yaron 1962.

41 Plutarch, *Romulus* 22; Cicero, *Philippics* 2.28.69; cf. Dixon 1992, 68.

42 Gellius 4.3.1–2; 17.21.44. Gellius took the story from the late republican jurist Servius Sulpicius, who had noted it for the regular *actio* for recovery of dowry by widows or divorced women and their fathers. Gellius terms it "the first divorce in Rome" to illustrate a deterioration of the moral climate. Cf. Evans 1991, 54; Saller 1994, 208; Treggiari 1991, 492; Dixon 1992, 68.

43 The censors regularly asked men if they had married for the purpose of begetting children. See Cicero, *Laws* 3.7; Dionysius of Halicarnassus, *Roman Antiquities* 2.25.7; Watson 1965; Treggiari 1991, 325, 439ff.

44 This is one of the few plays of Plautus that we can date with some certainty because the didascalia indicate the consuls for the year.

45 *Amphitruo* 928, *Menaechmi* 719ff., *Mercator* 784ff., *Miles Gloriosus* 1164–7; 1276–8, *Casina* 2.2.

46 Gellius 17.6; Cicero, *Republic* 3.10.7; Evans 1991, 50–71.

47 Livy 39.44.2–3; Plutarch, *Cato the Elder* 18.

48 Dionysius of Halicarnassus, *Roman Antiquities* 2.25.5; Plutarch, *Roman Questions* 20, 271 E; Treggiari 1991, 183–262; Dixon 1992, 83–9.

49 Gaius, *Institutes* 1.48–55; 108–18; 136–7a; Justinian, *Institutes* 1.9.

50 Segal (1987, 43) discusses the transgression against *pietas* in the comedies but he considers *pietas* to be an obligation of respect by the sons towards their elders only.

51 Fraenkel 1960, 153–4; Zagagi 1980.

52 The freeborn foundling is a dramatic *topos* of Greek and Roman comedy but it also reflects the disturbing reality of child exposure in antiquity. Sometimes these infants were rescued from certain death by strangers who reared them in their households to become servants. Gomme and Sandbach 1973, 34–5; Boswell 1988, 53–157; Harris 1982; Bradley 1994a, 35–9.

53 Ulpian, *Titles* 5.5 (*FIRA* 2.268); Paul, *Sententiae* 19.6 (*FIRA* 2.345). Although slaves in Rome did form partnerships (*contubernia*) and families, these unions had no legal validity and could be arranged and disrupted at will by a slave owner. Slave families were often in the slave owner's interest since slaves born on the estate would automatically come into the master's property. The unions of land overseers (*vilici*), like Olympio in the *Casina*, were especially encouraged as a means to promote stability. See Cato (*On Agriculture* 143); Columella 1.8.5. On slave-families Scaevola, *Digest* 40.4.59 [23 *Digest*]; Varro, *On the Latin Language* 9.59; Flory 1978; Treggiari 1991; Bradley 1994a, 50–1.

54 Relations with prostitutes and slaves did not fall under the definition of *stuprum*, not even under the otherwise strict Augustan legislation on sexual morality, the Julian Law. See Paul, *Sententiae* 2.26.16 (*FIRA* 2.352); Fantham 1991.

55 There was enough ambiguity to warrant debate about the status of foundlings. In a rhetorical school exercise (Seneca, *Controversiae* 10.4.13) one speaker argues that all exposed children were automatically slaves. A similar dispute is also presented in Quintilian, *Minor Declamations* 278. However, the problems surrounding the status of foundlings who claimed to have been born free were not only the stuff of rhetorical exercises. When Pliny was governor of Bithynia he wrote to the emperor Trajan to ask how he should handle cases in which a person claimed to have been born free but was enslaved (Pliny, *Letters* 65 and 66).

56 Williams 1958.

57 Saller 1994, 133–54.

58 Saller 1994, 137 with examples; Parker 1989.

59 The Romans' anxiety about possible violence from their slaves is evident in the harshness of the punishment contemplated by the law for the murder of a master by his slave: according to Tacitus (*Annals* 14.42–5), ancient laws required that all household slaves should be killed in retaliation (cf. Finley 1980, 173 n.41; Saller 1987, 65). As for drama, the grammarian Donatus (fourth century CE) observes that in drama slaves were allowed to deceive and dominate their masters only in the genre of Roman comedy known as the *fabula palliata*, "the comedy in Greek dress," where the characters and settings were "Greek," but not in the *fabula togata*, where the characters were Roman (ad Ter. Eun. 57). It is conceivable that behind the Greek mask Romans could imagine the threatening idea of rebellious slaves as a distant fantasy.

60 Treggiari 1991, 465ff.; Watson 1967, 29–31.

61 Cicero *Philippics* 2.69; Gaius [*ad edictum prov.*] *Digest* 24.2.1–2. Cf. McDonnell 1983, 54–80; Schuhmann 1976, 46–65; Treggiari 1991, 435–82.

62 Plutarch, *Romulus* 22.3; cf. Watson 1975, 31–4.

63 Cf. *Asinaria* 856ff.; *Mercator* 700–4, 784–6; *Menaechmi* (766–7).

64 See Pearce 1974; Treggiari 1991, 185–7, 220–1, 229–61. The female staff especially was the responsibility of the mistress of the household. In Tibullus' fantasy about country life (1.5.19–35) Delia is cast in the role of the mistress of the house over-

seeing the servants. Female staff were also likely to belong to the wife and to have come into the household with her (cf. Treggiari 1973; 1991, 374). The involvement of the wife with the care of her female servants is also illustrated by a case described in the *Digest* (40.4.59, Scaevola [23 *Digest*]) where a female slave owner specified in her will that some of her personal attendants (*pedisequae*) should be freed. But before she died she arranged a "marriage" of one of her servants with the bailiff. The legal question that interests the jurist here is whether the slave woman in question should still be freed, which is decided positively.

65 See Seneca, *Controversiae* 4, praef. 10.; Richlin 1993. A similar reversal of the roles of master and slave in a sexualized context occurs in the *Asinaria* (697ff.) where the two slaves demand to be addressed as *patroni* by the young man who needs their help and at the same time subject him and his girlfriend to sexual taunts.

66 Anderson 1983.

67 Despite the fragmentary state of the text in parts of this passage (especially 923–9), the phallic references are still evident in Olympio's comparisons which involve swords (909) and vegetables (911–14).

68 Pollux, *Onomastikon* 4.118; Neiiendam 1992, 81.

69 Cf. Webster 1960, 185; Neiiendam 1992, 81.

70 Adulterous matrons were forced to wear only the *toga*, like prostitutes. See Juvenal 2.68–70; Martial 2.39, 10.52; Cicero, *Philippics* 2.44; Horace, *Satires* 1.2.63; cf. Sebesta 1994.

71 The term *expalliatus* is a Plautine *ad hoc* creation. The term *palliatus* appears in the *Curculio* (288–9) in a mocking reference to Greeks in the Roman Forum.

72 The ban is documented in the *Senatusconsultum de Bacchanalibus* (The Senatorial Decree Concerning the Bacchic Rites) on *Corpus Inscriptionum Latinarum* I^2 581; Livy 39.8–18; cf. Gruen 1990, 34–78. If the line in the *Casina* is indeed alluding to these events, the play had to have been written during or after 186 BCE. If 184 BCE is correct as the date of Plautus' death, the *Casina* would be one of the last, if not the last, of Plautus' plays; cf. Buck 1940, 54–61.

73 *Mercator* 469–70.

74 Fraenkel 1960 (1922), 55–94.

8

WOMEN, SLAVES, AND THE HIERARCHIES OF DOMESTIC VIOLENCE

The family of St Augustine[1]

Patricia Clark

In Roman society the ideal of domestic *concordia* (harmony) included two pivotal concepts: first, the family was hierarchically structured in terms of power and status and second, this structure was maintained through reciprocal ties of affection and favor.[2] At the head of the family was the *paterfamilias*; other family members were ranked vertically according to the degree of dignity (*dignitas*) commanded or compliance (*obsequium*) expected. More than a simple hierarchy of authority and obedience was involved, however, for at the core of the ideal family was the conjugal pair, bound by mutual ties of marital affection (Treggiari 1991, 54–7 and chapter 8). In an affective configuration, children, dependents, freedmen and freedwomen, and assorted household slaves were envisaged as ranging outward from this centre in concentric spheres (Cicero, *On the Supreme Good and Evil* 5.65). Domestic harmony, then, included the mutually agreeable functioning of these spheres and the absence of friction between them. In sum, authority and obedience on the one hand, and familial affection and loyalty on the other, were the foundations for the orderly, stable, and harmonious ideal of the Roman household.

In reality, of course, domestic harmony was not always easily maintained. In Roman political life, it has been observed, the term *concordia* came most often to the fore when it was either threatened or absent, and this very likely held true too for the domestic realm (Bradley 1991, 6–8). Evidence of discord within Roman families is easy to find, and with it the potential for violence. Force or the threat of force always underlies hierarchies of power, the classic example being slavery, which was founded on the violent act of enslavement and maintained by the constant threat of force (Bradley 1987; MacMullen 1986, 512–19; Shaw 1987, 11–12). Within the Roman family, violence as a method of control is most clearly apparent between master and slave; it is less immediately discernible and more ambiguously presented among members of the nuclear family, but evidence for it does exist (Bradley 1984). My intention here is to focus on the manner in which this darker side of Roman family life was represented and the ways in which these representations were informed by cultural assumptions about slavery, women, and violence. More specifically, I want to ask how the social fact of slavery played into the violence against women that was a part of Roman culture.[3]

The most comprehensive and explicit description of a real domestic interior where the thread of violence weaves through the lives of its women, slave and free, is found in the *Confessions* of St Augustine.[4] Augustine's biographical sketch of his mother presents a series of domestic tableaux that provide a sustained, intimate narrative of one woman's life from childhood, through marriage and child-rearing, until death. Consciously paradigmatic and unconsciously revelatory, Monnica's biography is of great value in elucidating Roman male representations of women, slaves, and domestic violence and the ethical and literary traditions within which Augustine was writing. In addition, and in contrast to the more discrete and cryptic glimpses found elsewhere in Roman literature, Augustine's account shows us something of the dynamics of violence within the household. I shall examine Augustine's presentation of events and relationships, above all the domestic violence which formed a critical part of his mother's life, and then survey the cultural attitudes and modes of discourse perceptible here in the context of other, albeit more piecemeal, testimony from classical Roman sources.

Monnica: vulnerabilities and power

Monnica's early life as a girl and young wife was spent in a world of tense, shifting domestic power dynamics in which females slaves figured variously and importantly at every juncture. Augustine describes first young Monnica's childhood and especially her relationships with the slave women, young and old, who were charged with her care and training; next we see her as a finished product, the young wife in her husband's household, where her new domestic role required her to negotiate relationships not simply with a difficult husband but with the slave women of the house and her redoubtable mother-in-law.

Monnica was born into an African Christian family, where she and her sisters spent their early years under the austere eye of an elderly slave woman, who seems to have been a commanding presence in the household generally.

> she [Monnica] always said that her good upbringing had been due not so much to the attentiveness of her mother as to the care of an aged servant, who had carried my grandfather on her back when he was a baby, as older girls do with small children. Her master and mistress, out of gratitude for her long service and respect for her great age and unexceptionable character, treated her as an honoured member of their Christian household. This was why they placed their daughters in her care.
>
> (*Confessions*, trans. Pine-Coffin, 9.8.17)[5]

This task she carried out conscientiously, keeping the girls under strict control, correcting them when necessary "with firmness" (*vehementer*) and a "holy severity" (*sancta severitate*), and giving them instruction with "grave discretion" (*sobria prudentia*). In fact, to judge from the example given by Augustine, the severity with which she prepared the girls for their future roles was marked indeed:

> Except at the times when they ate their frugal meals at their parents' table she would not allow them to drink even water, however great their thirst, for fear that they might develop bad habits. She used to give them this very good advice: "Now you drink water because you are not allowed to have wine. But when you are married and have charge of your own larders and cellars, you will not be satisfied with water, but the habit of drinking will be too strong for you."
>
> (*Confessions*, trans. Pine-Coffin, 9.8.17)

The harshness of this instructional exercise for children in an African climate is underscored by Augustine's choice of words: *etiamsi exardescerent siti* (even if they were burning up with thirst). This aged slave woman, he says, tamed and curbed her youthful charges with formidable regulation and unassailable command (*auctoritate imperandi*). Disciplinary restraints are here assumed to be necessary to ensure that young girls would not grow up to be wasteful of their husbands' stores, and more specifically so that they would not, as wives, be overcome by a love of wine.[6] Women are presented as naturally prone to dangerous excess and unable to control themselves unless strong external limits are imposed from the outset. The language employed to describe the role of the old slave woman is more usually associated with the masculine worlds of statecraft (*auctoritas*) and the military (*imperium*). Because of her owners' trust, the length and dutifulness of her service, and her strong moral qualities, the slave woman has accrued status in the domestic sphere analogous to that of a man in the public sphere. And her responsibilities were significant, for she transmitted familial and societal values to her charges, and exerted very real power (moral and physical) over the freeborn daughters of the household. The girls very early learned subordination and obedience in this key relationship based on dominance, for the powerful slave woman with her "masculine" authority and command was, in effect, standing in for and instilling a societal pattern of male control over adult free women.

At the same time, the dominance of the slave woman involves a complicated reversal, for her primary duty was to train the girls to become mistresses (*dominae*) themselves. At some stage in their development her control over them must give way to their own control of self, and with this a concomitant capacity to control others. The concern over wine-drinking is more than a simple concern over excessive consumption or a propensity to drunken female misbehavior; it also reflects cultural anxiety about the danger to the domestic hierarchy if an adult woman and mistress of the house (*materfamilias*) should exhibit this kind of lack

of control. Then indeed would there be something to fear from the slave population whose houshold duties she supervised. This kind of potential servile threat
is implied in a subsequent scene in which Monnica is somewhat older, and the
figure of prudent, elderly slave woman has been replaced by an impudent,
quarrelsome young one, an *ancilla* (slave girl).

Despite (or more probably because of) the restrictive measures imposed by
her nurse, the young Monnica gradually developed a secret addiction to wine.[7]
The problem began when she, "a good and obedient child," was sent regularly
to the storage cellar to fill the family wine-jug. Initially she tasted a few drops
from the spout but soon increased the amount until she was gulping down whole
cups of wine. Here again, Augustine relates, it was a female slave, this time one
closer to her own age, who had a deep, lasting, and literally sobering effect
upon her mistress.

> my mother used to go to the cellar with a servant-girl. One day when
> they were alone, this girl quarrelled with her young mistress, as servants
> do, and intending it as a most bitter insult, called my mother a drunkard.
> The word struck home. My mother realized how despicable her fault
> had been and at once condemned it and renounced it.[8]
>
> (*Confessions*, trans. Pine-Coffin, 9.8.18)

The picture has changed dramatically. Gone is the powerful and aged guardian
of familial virtue; now the slave woman is a fearful, secretive, and troublesome
creature.

> For the girl had lost her temper and wanted to provoke her young
> mistress, not to correct her. She did it when they were alone, either
> because the quarrel happened to take place at a time when no one
> else was present, or because she may have been afraid of being punished
> for not having mentioned the matter earlier.
>
> (*Confessions*, trans. Pine-Coffin, 9.8.18)

Young and unruly, the slave woman has no intention of improving or instructing
her mistress; rather Augustine is emphatic that Monnica's "rescue" was inad-
vertent, the unintended result of the fierce quarrel between the two young
women. The virtuous outcome (albeit the ultimate manifestation of divine will)
is clearly in the first instance due to Monnica's own moral decision and physical
efforts of self-control. Monnica, too, has changed. She has reached a moment
of transition: having internalized the moral strictures of her old slave nurse, she
is now taking "control of herself."

Monnica's acquisition of self-control occurs in the context of a relationship
with a hostile, inadequately subservient, slave woman. Augustine assumes that
the relationship between these two young unmarried women was by its very
nature a stormy one: slave girls are accustomed to quarrel with and insult their

young mistresses, who for their part may join in the quarrel up to a point. The tension, anger, and animosity of the free girl and her slave contribute to a representation of a *domina* in training. The *ancilla* acts as a double catalyst here: as an inferior she holds up a mirror to her superior, pointing up the discrepancy between Monnica's status and her behavior; as a hostile subordinate she accelerates Monnica into the next phase of her life. Here, the slave woman's insubordination tests her young mistress as she makes her transition from immature girl to adult woman and *domina*. In this passage Monnica passes her test and emerges stronger, more in control, just as she will again in a later, similarly charged situation with the female slaves of her husband's household. But for now the tippling passage depicts Monnica as she emerges from childhood, soon to be fit mistress of her own household and fit, too, to control others – in particular the female slaves who, as the passage subtly implies, may badly require it.

By her own account (9.8.17) guided and dominated more by slave women than her mother, Monnica completed her domestic and moral education.[9] Her early training in "modesty and temperance," Augustine asserts (9.8.17), had properly prepared her for adult married life, and, at the appropriate age, she was married to Patricius. He was a man of moderate means, respectable, a town councillor in the city of Thagaste, and a suitable but not a perfect match, for among other drawbacks Patricius was not a Christian. In contrast to his detailed reminiscences about his mother, Augustine makes few allusions to his father, and these somewhat negative.[10] But he does convey some important, intimate details of his parents' married life:

> when she was old enough, they gave her in marriage to a man whom she served as her lord (*servivit veluti domino*). . . . He was unfaithful to her, but her patience was so great that his infidelity never became a cause of quarrelling between them. For she looked to you to show him mercy, hoping that chastity would come with faith. Though he was remarkably kind, he had a hot temper, but my mother knew better than to say or do anything to resist him when he was angry. If his anger was unreasonable, she used to wait until he was calm and composed and then took the opportunity of explaining what she had done.
>
> (*Confessions*, trans. Pine-Coffin, 9.9.19)

This is the first example in Augustine's account – more explicit ones are to follow – of the language of slavery used to describe the relationship between husband and wife. In effect, Patricius' mode of domestic control was based, like slavery, on the implicit threat of violence: anger was his weapon, and he achieved behavioral compliance from subordinates (specifically here his wife) simply by the threat of his explosive temper and propensity for rage. It is noteworthy, too, that the *dominus/paterfamilias* (master, head of the household), Patricius, is described as basically benevolent ("remarkably kind"), yet prone to "unreasonable" bouts of anger. This representation of the violent *paterfamilias*, one which is repeated and amplified in Augustine's general description of the husbands of Thagaste, suggests that he is fundamentally a decent man, but, alas, insufficiently in control of his passions.

In Augustine's depiction, Monnica, for her part, employs the techniques of patience, subservience, and placation that she learned as a child to achieve domestic concord, and perhaps survival. In the passages which follow she articulates the attitudes that she has internalized and promulgates them for the benefit of other abused free women. For Monnica, it seems, was not the only woman in Thagaste adjusting to married life with an ill-tempered husband. Augustine's account shows a community in which wife-battering was something of a *modus vivendi*.

> Many women, whose husbands were far more gentle than her own, bore the disfiguring marks of blows even on their faces, and so when they used to meet together and complain of the behaviour of their husbands, my mother would admonish their gossiping tongues. With a light manner but in all seriousness, she told them that ever since they had heard the marriage deed read over to them, they ought to have regarded it as a contract which bound them to serve their husbands, and from that time onward, mindful of their condition, they should not defy their masters.[11]
>
> (*Confessions*, trans. Pine-Coffin, 9.9.19, slightly adapted)

The language of domination applied to marriage here evokes not only Christianity but the institution of slavery: the marriage contract (*tabulas matrimoniales*) is equated with the purchase deed (*instrumenta*) of slavery, and wives were to understand that they had been made "slave women" (*ancillae factae essent*) to their "masters" (*dominos*). That wives were *not* exactly the same as slave women is subtly signalled by the "light manner" in which Monnica made the comparison. However, the dynamics of these two domestic relationships are sufficiently parallel to validate a discourse with some slippage between servitude and uxorial obedience.

Here again, the husbands, although obviously violent, are assumed to be essentially kind and loving, "more gentle" even than Patricius. And the appropriate female response to domestic abuse, it is suggested, is not for women to flock together for mutual support, but to display loyal and discreet obedience. Wives should not only endure, they should endure in silence; public gossip and criticism of the private behavior of their lord and master (*dominus*) is to be discouraged. Monnica's paradigm for wifely responses to violence, like her language, has notably servile resonances.

In the prescriptive discourse of Augustine, Monnica is not only marital advisor but role model:

> And when these women marvelled, knowing what a ferocious husband Monnica had, that never once had it been heard or revealed by any

indication, that Patricius had beaten his wife, or that there had been one day of domestic discord between them, and they asked her, as intimates do, the reason for this, she used to respond by teaching them her rule of conduct as outlined above: the ones who tried it out, thanked her; those who didn't continued to be cruelly humiliated.

(*Confessions*, trans. Pine-Coffin, 9.9.19, slightly adapted)

Whether or not Monnica was actually beaten by her husband is a question that cannot be answered; opinions vary and Augustine's account is ambiguously worded.[12] In fact, it was not necessary for a husband like Patricius actually to strike his wife. The shadow of his imminent violence and the vivid reminders on the bruised faces of other wives would have been sufficient to ensure that she was obedient, non-confrontational, rational, and controlled – controlled in effect by the implicit threat of violence. Many of the attitudes perceptible in this passage are not new. They belong to a traditional discourse which suggests, among other things, that women are responsible for men's behavior and for changing it: by altering their own behavior, they can stop their husbands from beating them; they must placate; they should keep quiet about domestic violence and avoid making it public; and if all else fails, they must endure.

Thus far Monnica's story has indicated some significant intersections between the worlds of free and slave women: the shifting relations between free and slave women as the young free woman matured into a *domina*, or mistress, and the parallels between the relationship of wife and husband and that of slave girl and master created by the threat of violence. Further glimpses of female intrafamilial dynamics come when Augustine recounts Monnica's entry into her new household after marriage, where she encountered first an ill-tempered husband, then a hostile mother-in-law and malicious female slaves.

Her mother-in-law was at first set against her by the whispers of malicious slaves, but she won the older woman over by her dutiful attentions and her constant patience and gentleness. In the end her mother-in-law on her own accord complained to her son about the meddlesome talk of the slave women which was spoiling the peaceful domestic harmony between herself and her daughter-in-law, and asked him to punish them. Patricius, anxious to satisfy his mother as well as concerned to preserve the good order of his home and the peace of his family, had the offenders whipped as she desired. She herself then warned them that anyone who gossiped maliciously about her daughter-in-law, in the hope of pleasing her, could expect to receive the same reward. Since none of them dared do so, the two women lived together in memorable harmony and mutual goodwill.

(*Confessions*, trans. Pine-Coffin, 9.9.20, slightly adapted)

Domestic tensions are rampant here: between mother-in-law and daughter-in-law, between the slave women and the free, and, potentially, between the *paterfamilias* and his mother. The single figure of the malicious slave woman has now been pluralized: slave women in general appear as troublesome and potent sources of domestic discord. Slave women, too, play an important role in nego-tiating tensions between free women of different ages and statuses. In effect, the potential animosity between a mother-in-law and her new daughter-in-law is denied. Rather, any ill-feeling is projected onto the slave women, who are then beaten. These beating are the cost of concord between the two free women.

Patricius' role in this passage is also new. Whereas earlier he fits the negative stereotype of the *paterfamilias* prone to ungovernable fits of rage, he now becomes the benevolent and rational *dominus* (perhaps a little in awe of his formidable mother), who assesses the threat posed by dissonant women to the *concordia* of his household and takes appropriate action. Here, he is a fit *paterfamilias* concerned to maintain an ordered household that is controlled as necessary by the rational application of physical violence. Since this control must come from the top, Monnica's mother-in-law, albeit a power in her own right, is shown behaving properly when she hands her malicious female slaves over to her son. Once he has made the judicial decision and ordered the beatings, the mother-in-law is then empowered in turn to use threats of similar punishment in the future as *her* weapon of control. Thus the hierarchy of family violence is maintained.

By her son's account, Monnica experienced a domestic world characterized by tensions and violence. Older female slaves exercised harsh disciplinary power over young free girls; slave women, young and old, quarreled with and attempted to sabotage their mistresses. Wives were beaten by husbands whom they were expected both to endure and placate. Tension and ill-feeling inform the relations between the junior and senior *matronae* (married women) of the household and plague the relations between adult free women and their female slaves. It was, taken at face value, a world in which, for women, hostility and physical violence were unexceptional.[13] At the same time Augustine suggests ways in which much of this domestic discord might be controlled. The *paterfamilias* at the top of the hierarchy was, at his best, a benevolent, rational, and effective disciplinarian; the *materfamilias* obedient, patient and placatory to the husband, firm toward her slave women. Female slaves, those at least who did not attain the cachet of loyal household retainers, could be used as scapegoats; the violence directed toward them usefully obviated domestic tensions among their free superiors.

In light of this picture, Augustine's description of the final scenes of his mother's life might give pause. Until very close to her death Monnica wanted to end her life in Africa, her native land, and to be buried beside her husband Patricius, "because the two of them had lived so lovingly (*concorditer*) together" (9.11.28). This sentiment, a stock Roman funerary convention, would have seemed unexceptional to Augustine's audience but may strike us as more surprising, coming as it did from a woman who, reportedly, spent the bulk of her life with a husband inclined to anger, abuse, alcohol, and adultery.[14] Yet Augustine finds no irony or contradiction here. To him, this laudable state of marital *concordia* had been achieved by both partners as they undertook their respective roles in the domestic hierarchy and ordered their actions and their household appropriately.

Some caveats may be raised at this point. Augustine's *Confessions* is a late source, deeply imbued with Christian values, and reflecting the life of one small locale in North Africa.[15] For my purposes, however, these are not seriously limiting factors. It is reasonable to assume *a priori* that domestic violence was not the invention of this Christian community, and, as we shall see, there is ample evidence from earlier centuries and all parts of the Roman world that the wives and slaves of Thagaste are not isolated cases.[16] Moreover, that domestic violence, while not new, is more visible in late antique sources such as Augustine is readily explicable by the fact that many of our late texts are by the church fathers, who were doing something relatively innovative: responding directly to spiritual and social problems among their dependants, questions and issues that did not simply involve, but very often were raised by, women.[17] It should then not be surprising that once women's voices began to be heard in this way, however indirectly, the mechanisms and dynamics of their lives became more visible. The glimpses these late texts provide of a domestic world in which violence is at the same time dramatic and banal are vivid but not unique.

In the next section I locate key elements in the Augustinian material in an older Roman discourse on domestic relations. The nature of the testimonials in this section is largely fictive, and the authors here, unlike Augustine, do not always claim to represent the real experiences of historical individuals. These sources do, however, articulate pervasive and enduring Roman attitudes toward women and violence, attitudes which frame and inform Augustine's account. The specific focus in the discussion that follows is on three main areas in which cultural assumptions about slavery, violence, and women intersect: marriage as a relationship of domination, the relationship between mistress and female slave, and the relationship between the older slave woman and younger mistress.

Violent intersections

Girls and wives, largely from want of evidence, have played little part in recent studies on the hierarchical power structure of the Roman family and its ultimate dependence for validation upon "corporal punishment" – either as tacit threat or real act.[18] The focus has been primarily on the *paterfamilias*: on demonstrating that the image of the stern, authoritative Roman head of house, hitherto largely derived from legal sources, is an oversimplified stereotype and that in meting out physical punishment the *paterfamilias* made significant distinctions between punishing slaves and disciplining children, especially sons who were to become the *patresfamiliae* of the future.[19]

This picture needs to be broadened through attention to daughters, who were groomed not to become heads of households, but to obey them, and through recognition that the degree to which obedience was emphasized and enforced will not have been the same among all Roman households, elite or non-elite.[20]

Ideally, among the upper classes, when a young woman married, she assumed an honored and respected role and became partner as *materfamilias* in the core conjugal unit. But she was expected also to be obedient to her husband (and father), accommodating and respectful toward senior members of the family, a firm disciplinarian to her children, and mistress to her slaves. These expectations suggest that free women were socialized to negotiate domestic subservience and dominance simultaneously, to control and be controlled. Given this bivalent role, there was always the potential for them to be both recipients and dispensors of domestic violence, and in some households this meant that physical coercion was used both against women and by women.[21]

It is precisely in households such as these that the master–slave metaphor informs the discourse of marriage; a common thread links these two relationships of domination whenever they encompass the use of force to achieve compliance. Yet while the metaphor of slavery might be used in such marital situations, it was acknowedged to be *only* a metaphor. Wives, however badly treated, were *not* slave women, and in other contexts this important distinction was preserved. Augustine's Monnica, for example, has internalized the dominance-model for marriage and promotes it, employing the language of slavery to do so. At first sight her juxtaposition of wife/slave woman and husband/master is striking and seems to contrast sharply with more traditional discourse in which these concepts are polarized, as for example in the speech Livy attributes to Valerius advocating, in 195 BCE, the repeal of the Oppian Law, a wartime emergency measure which restricted Roman women's expenditures on luxuries: "you ought to keep them [women] under control and guardianship, not in servitude, and you should prefer to be called fathers and husbands rather than masters."[22] But, viewed in context, Valerius' distinction is less clear than might first appear. In Livy's construction he argues for the stronger exertion of personal control by the *patresfamiliae* over their wives, sisters, and daughters, as opposed to mere legal constraints such as the Oppian Law. Moreover in this same passage, Livy's Valerius speaks approvingly of "women's servitude" (*servitus muliebris*) to their husbands, which is life long, and of women's detestation of the freedom (*libertatem*) which comes unbidden with the death of a father or husband (*History of Rome* 34.7.13–14). The distinction in status between wives and slave women could be maintained, it seems, in the same breath as the slavery metaphor for the dominance-model of marriage. There appears here to have been enough cross-over in the underlying concepts of subservience and obedience to allow for this kind of rhetorical interplay in the writing of history in the late first century BCE.[23]

That wives were not *the same* as slave women was signaled in various ways. Livy's Valerius might speak of *servitus muliebris* (women's servitude) metaphorically amid general observations about the status of women. But when it came to discussion of an actual law, his arguments sharply polarized Roman women and their slaves. The very real gulf between these two categories of women could also be acknowledged by language and tone: Monnica advised beaten freeborn wives to regard themselves as *ancillae* (slave women) and to respond in a placatory (and servile) manner, but she did it "*per iocem*" (tongue in cheek). In Apuleius' novel *Metamorphoses* (6.1), the efforts of the slave girl Psyche, trying to pacify her husband's anger, show that subtly distinct language was deemed appropriate for wives and for slaves, even though they were both engaged in essentially the same placatory efforts: "even if she could not soften his anger with a wife's allurements (*uxoriis blanditiis*), she could at least try to appease him with a slave's prayers (*servilibus precibus*)." One of the most significant markers distinguishing the dominated free woman from the female slave is Augustine's assertion that Monnica could wait, and later explain or justify her actions, and reason with her husband; this option, which, as we shall see, forms a part of the *topos* of the good wife, is not one that is stressed in a slave's relationship with a violent master or mistress.

In the discourse of domestic violence, Roman authors represent both husbands and wives by positive and negative stereotypes. The *topos* of the good *paterfamilias* is distinguished from that of the bad chiefly by the presence of rationality and self-control. The same holds true for wives: the good wife exhibits reason, restraint, and control; the bad wife the opposite. Each of these polarized stereotypes, however, may be shown to have the ultimate effect of reinforcing and validating the traditional domestic hierarchy.

Augustine's father Patricius, who is portrayed as violent and irascible in some contexts, and benevolent and rational in others, embodies both *topoi* of the *paterfamilias*. The first model, the angry, despotic, and violent husband, is traditionally condemned primarily because he cannot control himself or his family. In Roman moral discourse a man who could not control himself, his wife, or his household, is incapable of controlling weightier matters: "A man therefore ought to have his household well harmonized who is going to harmonize state, forum, and friends" (Plutarch, *Moralia* 144C).[24] In the early second century BCE, the statesman and censor Cato the Elder explicitly condemned spousal assault: he reckoned a good husband worthy of more praise than a good senator and announced that a man who beat his wife or child laid violent hands on what was most sacred (Plutarch, *Cato the Elder* 20.2). Not surprisingly, allegations of violence against wives, often for "trivial" offences, were used in political invective and biographical defamation to demonstrate moral inadequacy (as were stories of excessive or inappropriate punishment of slaves).[25]

The use of conjugal quarreling, intimidation, and violence to undermine a man's public standing explains the importance of concealment, which we have seen in Monnica's own behavior and her advice to her peers. Visible domestic *concordia* was, at least for the respectable classes, a social necessity. The first-century CE novelist Petronius, in his satirical portrait of Trimalchio, an obscenely wealthy ex-slave, presents scenes of marital vituperation and threats of violence as instances of extreme bad taste (*Satyricon* 74–5). In an after-dinner scene, Trimalchio throws a glass in his wife's face and makes veiled threats that he will beat her: "otherwise you'll feel my temper," and "I'll give you something to moan about in a minute" (75). His long harangue, punctutated by colorful insults, includes the forceful assertion that his wife Fortunata, a freed slave like himself, whom he takes full credit for having "elevated," must be "tamed" (*domata*) (74). This scene of marital squabbling with its violent overtones underscores the unspeakable vulgarity with which Trimalchio conducts his household. Visible and habitual domestic discord, Petronius implies, is lower-class behavior and signals unmistakably the humble origins of Trimalchio and his wife.

There was, however, one sphere in which a husband's uncontrolled feelings could be expressed with relative impunity in violence against women: romantic passion and jealousy. In Chariton's novel *Chaereas and Callirhoe*,[26] an innocent and unsuspecting wife runs to greet her young husband, who has been fed rumors that she is unfaithful:

> He could not find his voice to revile her; overcome by his anger, he kicked her as she ran to him. Now his foot found its mark in the girl's diaphragm and stopped her breath. She fell down and her maids picked her up and laid her on her bed.
>
> (Reardon 1989, 27)

In a context of overwhelming emotion the young man, enraged with his wife, attacks her and tortures her maids. His remorse when he finds that she is innocent is more sincerely stated, yet not unlike the regret expressed by the poet Ovid (*Amores* 1.7) after he has beaten up his girlfriend. She refuses to speak to him, but her scared, silent, frozen expression and her speechless tears condemn him. He talks about the attack: he could merely have shouted and threatened or ripped her dress from the neck to the waist, but instead he seized and tore her hair and scratched her cheeks. In a more flippant mood on another occasion the poet remarks: "I don't think I tore her dress, I wasn't conscious of doing so – but she said I did and the bill was paid for at my expense" (Ovid, *Art of Love* 2.171–3).[27] Assaults on women are not expressly condoned in these passages, but they are made to appear explicable and venial. Violence from lovers was to be expected (Ovid, *Art of Love* 2.565ff.), just as assaults out of rage on the part of loving husbands were deplored but essentially accepted as a part of domestic life in Monnica's world and at higher levels of society, too: the historian Tacitus does not seem to find it difficult to reconcile Nero's love for his wife Poppaea with the fact that he kicked her while pregnant, inadvertently causing her death.[28]

The second, and ideal, type of the *paterfamilias* is the benevolent, rational, controlled head of house, concerned for domestic concord, a judge and dispensor of requisite chastisement. This *topos* explicitly confirms and upholds the domestic hierarchy. Yet implicitly the negative *topos* of the uncontrolled or vicious *paterfamilias* and the recurring stories of jealous rages and excessive domestic violence also served to reinforce the structure. Such stories performed the same minatory function as the bruised faces of Monnica's women friends. The stereotypical figure of the violent and irascible husband could join the legendary accounts celebrating early Roman traditional morality with their salutary beatings and murders of family members by stern *patresfamiliae*.[29] Both *topoi* contributed to a traditional discourse that was a means of ensuring compliance by threatening violence without actually exercising it. In this way Romans managed at the same time both to condemn and accept violence against women.

There was yet another way in which free men could abuse their wives without actually laying hands on them. The use of inferiors to inflict violence was specifically recommended for beating slaves (Galen, *Diseases of the Mind = an Aff.* 4; Harkins 1963, 39), but there are also accounts in which masters and husbands used subordinates to inflict violence on free women. One such story was circulated after the death of Regilla, wife of the prominent second-century CE politician and rhetorician Herodes Atticus (Philostratus, *Lives of the Sophists* 555): it was alleged that when his wife was near full term for her pregnancy, Herodes, because of some trivial irritation, ordered one of his freedmen to beat her, and as a result of the blows to her stomach both Regilla and the child she was carrying died. Herodes' delegation of the task of wife beating to his ex-slave passes without special comment, as does a similar act of surrogate violence in Suetonius' biography of Tiberius (*Tiberius* 53): the emperor had his daughter-in-law Agrippina beaten by a centurion until one of her eyes was destroyed. In both these incidents a phenomenon more commonly encountered in the public sphere is carried over into a domestic one: the use of one's slaves or underlings to enforce compliance from others – "the ordinary inducement to obedience controlled by people who enjoyed 'clout'" (MacMullen 1986, 512).[30]

As with the positive and negative *topoi* of the *paterfamilias*, so, too, the stereotypes of good and bad *matronae* represented in the discourse of domestic violence serve in the end to maintain and enhance the established domestic hierarchy. The first of these *topoi* centers on the good wife who makes an appropriate response to male violence; the second on women who themselves dispense violence, the savage *domina*.

A rhetorical exercise of the first century CE presents the fictional case of a wife subjected to frequent beatings. At first she attempts to soften her husband's rages with a love potion, but when that fails, she divorces him. Her relatives try to convince her to return to him. When she refuses, and her husband hangs himself, the woman is accused of poisoning (Quintilian, *Oratorical Training* 7.8.2). We need not concern ourselves with the convoluted legal points at issue here: more important are the ways in which women were envisaged as responding to domestic violence. The case may be imaginary, but the assumptions are not.[31] A woman subjected to her husband's violence could attempt to gain some measure of control over her situation in several ways: as in the case above, she could try first to mollify the person in power. Love potions were not socially approved, but there were prescribed "softening" techniques which consisted in adopting a "feminine" attitude: wheedling, charming, or placating.[32] This, essentially, is the route Monnica espoused. Plutarch, the famous Greek essayist of the Roman imperial period, too, recommends that women of sense keep silent if their husbands shout in anger, and, when they are more subdued, talk to them and mollify them with words (*Moralia* 143C). Plutarch uses military imagery here, recognizing that such an approach involves a strategy in which women can attain some mastery of the situation. Similarly in Apuleius' novel of the mid-second century (*Metamorphoses* 9.25), a wife caught deceiving her husand is urged to go and stay with a woman friend quietly until "time softened her husband's seething anger." Ideally, a marital quarrel should involve both partners in its resolution, as suggested by the tradition described by the first-century moralist Valerius Maximus (*Memorable Deeds and Sayings* 2.1.6): "whenever there is a quarrel between husband and wife they go to the temple of the goddess VIRIPLACA in the Palatine; there they talk in turn, leave the quarrel behind and go home with concord recovered." It is clear that the onus in reconciliation and domestic peace-keeping lay with the wife, as indicated by the next line: *dea nomen hoc a placandis viris fertur adsecuta* (the goddess, it is said, acquired this name from husbands being placated).

Mollifying and placating were techniques inculcated early in the socialization of young girls, as may be seen, for example, in passages from the *Controversiae* of the Elder Seneca, a collection of hypothetical legal cases. In one, advice is given to a girl on how to approach her angry father: "prepare yourself for such wheedlings as you are capable of. Beg, ask his pardon. If you don't succeed, you have a means of forcing his hand – threaten to kill yourself" (10.3.2). In another, a father describes how a girl should *not* beg: "defiantly, . . . face not cast down, words not meek, as if she had not been defeated" (10.3.13). Pacification and pleading then were tactics of first resort for free women; they were also, however, central features of a slave's response. Servile, pacific, and placatory behavior in answer to violence and abuse from above appears to have been a shared expectation for many women, slave and free.

As noted above, however, markers distinguish the abused slave from the abused free woman in this discourse, and one of central importance was exhibited and extolled *par excellence* by Monnica. The capacity for self-control, endurance, and, at the appropriate time, for rational explanation of her point of view, were key elements of the *topos* of the good wife. Along with discreet public silence, such behavior clearly sustained and validated the existing hierarchy of domestic power and privilege. Against this positive stereotype we can set the negative representation of the free woman, whose behavior and character form the reverse image: here is the uncontrolled, irrational, short-tempered, and disturbingly loud woman, most clearly recognizable in the *topos* of the impulsive, savage *domina*.

Roman authors frequently portray women as physically threatening or violent in their behavior toward their slaves, especially their female slaves.[33] Galen's account of his irascible mother polarizes rational male self-control and female passionate irrationality, itself a *topos*:

My mother, however, was so very prone to anger that sometimes she bit her handmaids; she constantly shrieked at my father and fought with him – more than Xanthippe did with Socrates. When I compared my father's noble deeds with the disgraceful passions of my mother, I decided to embrace and love his deeds and to flee and hate her passions. Just as in these respects I saw the utter difference between my parents, so also did I see it in the fact that my father [seemed] never to be grieved over any loss, whereas my mother was vexed over the smallest things.

(Galen, *Diseases of the Mind* = an *Aff.* 8, Harkins 1963, 57)

Galen's mother demonstrates all the qualities of the bad *materfamilias*. Not only is she easily irritated by trivial matters, but she vents this anger in unrestrained physical abuse of her slave women. Toward her husband, who for his part exhibits all the virtues of the rational, philosophical *paterfamilias*, she is a virago. Galen's portrait of his parents nicely juxtaposes two domestic *topoi*: the wise *paterfamilias* and the savage *domina*.

The bad tempered and vicious mistress can be met over and over again in Roman literature. In the poetry of Ovid she vents her spleen over a trifle by stabbing her *ornatrix* (maid, hairdresser) during her toilette and clawing the face and jabbing the arms of her maids with needles (*Art of Love* 3.235–44, and *Amores* 1.14, 12–18). In one of the satires of Juvenal, a mistress displeased with her appearance tears her maid's hair, rips her clothing, and has her whipped (*Satires* 6.487–95). If her husband ignores her sexually, she will have her slaves professionally flogged, or she will order her husband to crucify a slave on a whim whether he approves or not (6.475–85 and 219–24). In Apuleius, a mistress is accustomed to beating her slave-girl mercilessly (*verberare saevissime consuevit*) when she fails in her tasks (*Metamorphoses* 3.16). Even the emperor Hadrian was said to have banished for five years a woman who had harmed her slave women (*Digest* 1.6.2 and *Collatio Legum Mosaicarum et Romanarum* 3.3.4, cited in Bradley 1987, 126). We can only speculate about the extent to which tensions between free men and women were displaced and vented on the slave women of the household. The poets imply that sexual and marital discord drive free women to maltreat their slaves, but as Galen's account suggests, not *all* the anger of the savage *domina* is displaced onto inferiors; the *paterfamilias*, too, must contend with his wife's hostility, and the manner with which he does so, in this case noble imperturbability, legitimates his role as head of house.

The most frequent criticism of Roman women's lack of self-control is not simply that they lose their tempers and attack their maids, but specifically that they are too violent and/or too capricious in their punishment of slaves. The Stoic philosopher and statesman Seneca speaks of a mistress who is "changeable and passionate (*varia et libidinosa*) and neglectful of her slaves, . . . capricious in both her rewards and punishments" (*To Marcia, on Consolation* 10.6). Plutarch instructs husbands to demonstrate control of anger by example and to oppose wives who punish their slaves excessively and unjustly. Wives, avid for punishment, may accuse the controlled, rational man of being lax and easy-going:

they must be resisted. An orgy of punishment followed by repentance is described as "womanish", as is anger generally: men who arouse anger with barbed remarks are "transferring anger from the women's quarter to the men's." Plutarch also explains the Roman custom of husbands giving their wives notice when returning home in terms of women's propensity to create domestic turmoil: during their husband's absence wives have more household duties and occupations "and also dissensions and outbursts against those of the household." Notice is given so that they may settle these matters and make their husbands' return undisturbed and pleasant.[34]

In addition to such explicit criticism, examples of wives who are immoderate in their punishment carry the same message indirectly: Antony's mother would have tortured all the household slaves one by one when a silver bowl went missing, had her husband, generous and kindly, not confessed that he had given it to a friend (Plutarch, *Antony* 1.3). A jealous wife in Petronius' *Satyricon* (69) tells her husband's favorite male slave she will ensure he gets branded; in contrast Trimalchio recounts that when he was a slave and got up to sexual tricks with his mistress, his master merely sent him off to the farms. Men are generally portrayed as more reasonable than women. In one of the most grisly stories of the excessive punishment of a slave, Pomponia, the wife of Quintus Cicero, had her slave Philologus tortured to death by forcing him to slice off pieces of his own flesh, roast and eat them because he had betrayed her husband and caused his death in the proscriptions of 43 BCE (Plutarch, *Cicero* 49.2–4).[35]

In sum, the message implicit in these repeated representations of irrational and uncontrolled women is that alone, women are incapable and domestic tranquility requires a competent, controlling male figure at the head of the household. Above all, the proper punishment of slaves is a task best handled by the wise *paterfamilias*, who is rational, moderate and punishes only to correct (Galen, *Diseases of the Mind* = *an Aff.* 4, Harkins 1963, 38–9; Plutarch, *Moralia* 460C; Seneca, *Letters* 2.12.2). The behavior of such women, their lack of moderation, and their propensity for creating domestic discord justifies masculine control of the household, and this stereoptye, just as much as its opposite, confirms and consolidates the traditional domestic hierarchy of power.

A modulated version of this theme informs Augustine's account of Patricius' household, where domestic concord *was* achieved at the expense of slave women, victims of the tense power negotiations between two free women of different ages. The ultimate authority to whom Monnica's mother-in-law appeals, and the one who administers the flogging to the slave women, is Patricius in his guise as the wise, discerning *paterfamilias*. Patricius' calculus of domestic *concordia* had to assess two areas in which differentials of power were creating havoc in his house: the discord between the slave women and their mistresses or owners and that between the younger woman and the older one. In this particular anecdote the tensions associated with the hierarchy of age were between the two free women, but, as we have seen with the young Monnica, other and more convoluted tensions could arise when the hierarchy of status intersected with that of age.

Monnica's mother-in-law chose initially to vent anger and hostility on her new, young, and vulnerable daughter-in-law before turning it onto her even more vulnerable slave women. A contemporary truism of domestic violence asserts that people who abuse others are the ones who *can*. Such an assumption would seem to hold true for Roman society. In Roman texts, as noted above, the free woman who opts to perpetuate a chain of dominance and domestic violence displaces her own pain, frustration, and unhappiness onto the vulnerable people under her control – above all her slaves. A psychological mechanism of this kind, about which we can only conjecture, could very well contribute, although certainly only in part, to the ubiquitous stereotype of the savage *domina*. But venting and displacement of anger should also be considered in the context of a slave society. The hierarchical structure of the slave milieu had its own dynamics, and for the slave elite, some of whom had their own slaves, there were opportunities for violent abuse of underlings (provided they avoided damaging what was ultimately their master's property) (Bradley 1994a, 72). For female slaves, who ranked low in the slave hierarchy, there were indirect avenues available for venting hostility: malicious gossip, quarrelling, and sabotage, all the tactics of the powerless which we have seen attributed to them in Monnica's story.

The vulnerable people under the "control" of female slaves were the children of the family, particularly, again as in Monnica's case, the daughters. To what extent slaves might physically punish small children is unknown, but one ancient physician warns parents to avoid using nurses with bad tempers who might in anger drop children (Soranus, *Gynecology* 2.19[88]).[36] We can only speculate whether the harsh discipline exercised over Monnica and her sisters by the elderly slave nurse could have contained elements of disguised hostility and revenge, and to what extent this might hold true of others in her situation (Bradley 1994b, 153). It is clear, however, that older slave women had a recognized role to play in the socialization of young girls and, as in Monnica's case, might well have been important in habituating and inuring them to subordination, potential physical abuse, and the perpetuation of hierarchical familial violence of all kinds.

In the domestic realm the violence, which was integral to Roman daily life, both linked and divided free women and their female slaves. The social realities of slavery and of violence toward women are represented in the discourse we have examined as intersecting at several key points: in the representation of marriage as a relationship of domination and subservience, in the servile nature of the response prescribed for women subjected to violence, in the depictions of mistreatment of slaves by the uncontrolled and vicious *domina*, and the retaliatory measures, subversive or abusive, which could be anticipated on the part of slave women. Directed toward the vulnerable, domestic violence, or the potential for it, could be used in several ways to buttress hierarchies of gender, status, and age. Consolidation of the lines of power took place when violence met with the prescribed mollifying response, and this pattern appears to have held true between wives and husbands, junior and senior *matronae*, and slaves and mistresses.

Up to this point, the representations of domestic violence examined have all been derived from male-authored texts that vary in their degree of fictionality. There remains to be heard one solitary female voice, vivid, clear, and authentic. In a fragmentary papyrus from Roman Egypt, a maltreated Christian wife complains about her husband, not only on her own behalf, but also on behalf of her foster-daughters and the family slaves, all of whom appear to have been treated with even-handed brutality:

> He shut up his own slaves and mine with my foster-daughters and his agent and son for seven whole days in his cellars, having insulted his slaves and my slave Zoe and half-killed them with blows, and he applied fire to my foster-daughters, having stripped them quite naked, which is contrary to the laws. . . . He swore in the presence of the bishops and his own brothers, "Henceforward I will not hide all my keys from her" (he trusted his slaves but would not trust me): "I will stop and not insult her." Whereupon a marriage deed was made and after this agreement and his oaths, he again hid the keys from me . . . he kept saying, "A month hence I will take a mistress." God knows this is true.[37]

The addressee of the document is missing, but it is thought to be an affidavit for use in legal proceedings against the husband.[38] As in Augustine's account of Monnica's marriage, a rare glimpse is given into the domestic life of a fourth-century Christian community in a Roman African province. Although it is written in Greek, this document must nevertheless be acknowledged here, for it demonstrates even more forcefully than Augustine's contemporaneous account, how violence within a household could be pervasive and relentless, and how, in reality, it could cut across all distinctions of age, gender, and status. The violence of this *paterfamilias* is directed toward everyone in the household, slave and free. Although the wife, for her part, tries to assert traditional and legal distinctions about property, family, and status, the husband feels empowered to ignore these. This household is an inversion of the ordered, stable, and harmonious ideal, where authority and obedience are balanced by familial affection and loyalty. Here hierarchies of status are ignored, mutual marital affection is non-existent, and authority, *dignitas*, and *obsequium* (rank, dignity, and compliance) have been denigrated to naked power, violence, and submission. Domestic violence, as we have seen, can be used to maintain a variety of familial hierarchies, yet here in its most corrosive form it eliminates all distinctions save one, the abuser and abused.

Notes

1 This paper has benefited immeasurably from the many suggestions made by Sandra Joshel and Sheila Murnaghan. I wish to thank them and my colleague Keith Bradley.

2 *Concordia*, the term regularly used for harmony between marriage partners, is applied by extension here to the domestic realm as it is, for example by Plutarch, *Moralia* 144C and Augustine, *Confessions* 9.9.20.

3 In the discussion which follows the term "domestic violence" includes any use of physical force, coercion, or restraint against any member of a household by another. In our modern society the term is avoided as having collusive overtones; a spade is more correctly called a shovel and "domestic violence" wife battering or child abuse. But since the Roman family with its hierarchical strata provides numerous convoluted possibilities for violence, it is best to retain this efficient umbrella term. Also, deliberately, I have avoided the term "corporal punishment": it is a euphemism which already asserts the viewpoint of the male head of family. Most English terms are in any case quite inadequate to encompass all acts of physical violence within the Roman family: the striking of children, the flogging and torture of slaves, and the beating of wives – whether these be deemed "discipline" or "abuse."

4 Passages cited by number only are from Augustine, *Confessions*, edition and commentary by James J. O'Donnell 1992.

5 *Saint Augustine Confessions* 9.8.17, translated by R.S. Pine-Coffin, 1961. Most major passages cited in translation are from this edition. O'Donnell, *ad loc.*, suggests that a *quasi* "brother-sister" relationship may have evolved from this early closeness; this, he infers, may account for the old woman's evident "clout" in the household – responsibility for the daughters and power over other, younger female slaves.

6 Masculine concerns about women and wine-drinking are legal and literary *topoi* with a long history. See, for example, Valerius Maximus 6.3.9; Pliny, *Natural History* 14.89. For discussion of wine-drinking as a cause for divorce see Treggiari 1991, 461–2.

7 Peter Brown (1967, 33) notes that alcoholism was a widespread problem among African congregations.

8 The term *meribibula* is rare; see O'Donnell *ad loc.*; Brown 1967, 174 gives the pleasing translation "little tippler."

9 On the duty of the *nutrix* and other child-minders to inculcate virtue see Bradley 1991, 49–55 and especially Bradley 1994b.

10 See Brown 1967, 30; Shaw 1987, 25, who calls the relationship between father and son "distant, formal, and somewhat fearful."

11 Brown (1967, 31) understands Monnica to be speaking "sarcastically"; I think this is too strong a reading of the phrase *veluti per iocum graviter admonens*.

12 Brown (1967, 31) claims that Patricius never beat her; Shaw (1987, 31) seems to think he did. Augustine's language suggests a deliberate clouding of the issue.

13 O'Donnell, at 9.9.20: "The underlying violent tenor of Roman private life is quietly taken for granted even in these incidental matters."

14 Before his death Patricius was converted and baptized. Augustine states that from this point on, late in life, Monnica "no longer had to grieve over those faults which had tried her patience before he was a Christian" (9.9.22, trans. Pine-Coffin).

15 On the "Roman-ness" of Augustine's society see Brown 1967, 21–2. On the continuity of Roman behavior and values among early Christians see now Grubbs 1995, especially chapter 2.

16 Scarce documentation for wife-beating in the classical period has led to speculation that domestic violence was lessened by the relative ease of unilateral divorce in the Republic and Principate and that the incidence of domestic violence rose in the late empire, at least among the upper classes (Treggiari 1991, 430–1). By implication, among social groups where this recourse was possibly more difficult (the lower classes at all periods and in the Christian late empire), the incidence of domestic violence may have been higher. It is impossible to substantiate this hypothesis: even today statistics on domestic violence are innaccessible and unreliable and the assumption that ease of divorce implies a diminished incidence of spousal abuse is open to

question. It should be noted too that despite the ease of divorce for Romans of the classical period, notably few of those attested were initiated by women (Treggiari 1991, 435–82, esp. 481–2).

17 See, for example, Augustine's advice to a woman whose husband has broken their mutual pact of chastity and formed an adulterous relationship, *Letters* 262; Jerome's advice to a widow on the education of her young daughter, *Letters* 123; Basil's letter concerning a woman living with a man whose wife had sent him notice of divorce, *Letters* 188.

18 Shaw (1987, 18) does discuss husbands and wives, asserting that the all-important *concordia* of the Roman household rested on a concept of patriarchal power enforced by "physical discipline" in a context of love and commitment.

19 The whip was associated more with servile punishment, while normative pressures existed, at least in elite society, for the use of words and reason in disciplining and controlling sons (Saller, 1994, 142–53). On the stereotype, see Treggiari 1991, 249–53; Saller 1994, chapters 5 and 6.

20 See Treggiari 1991, 238–41 on the changing emphasis on uxorial obedience in Roman elite society. Almost nothing is known about expectations in lower-class marriages. I would stress, however, Treggiari's note (504) that although marriage *ideals* remained relatively constant over time, even among the elite, home life would have differed in different households.

21 On the role of wife: Williams 1958, 29 and *passim*; Treggiari 1991, 414–27; childcare: Dixon 1988,104–40; slave management: Bradley 1984, 21–45. Violence between husbands and wives has been given some attention: Shaw 1987, 28–32; Treggiari 1991, 429–32; Clark 1993, 25.

22 Livy 34.7.13–14: *et vos in manu et tutela, non in servitio debetis habere eas et malle patres vos aut viros quam dominos dici*. See discussion in Treggiari 1991, 212–14.

23 See Shaw 1987, 28, and n. 104 on the language of servitude for the marriage relationship in late antiquity. In an earlier text, Musonius Rufus describes an ideal wife, a woman schooled in philosophy: "likely to be energetic, strong to endure pain, prepared to nourish her children at her own breast and to serve her husband with her own hands, and willing to do things which some would consider no better than slaves' work" (Lutz 1947, 43).

24 Unless otherwise stated all translations of primary sources are from the Loeb editions.

25 Allegations: Tacitus, *Annals* 4.22.1–2, 4.16.6; Suetonius, *Caligula* 33; *Nero* 35; Herodian, 3.13.2–3, 3.10.8, 4.6.3; *The Augustan History*, "Clodius Albinus" 11.5.7; 13.1; "Commodus Antoninus" 5.7; Libanius, *Autobiography* 190, F171. On the importance of this theme in imperial biography see especially Bradley 1985. Slaves: Galen, *Diseases of the Mind = an Aff.* 4, Harkins 1963, 38–9. Trivial offenses: Philostratus, *Lives of the Sophists* 555.

26 A Greek novel of the mid first century BCE (or possibly a later CE date), the work is part of Greco-Roman literary activity under the Empire.

27 All citations from Ovid are from Green's 1982 translation.

28 Tacitus, *Annals* 16.6; cf. Suetonius, *Nero* 35. The theme of beating a pregnant wife so that she miscarries and/or dies is an ancient *topos*. Such stories surface regularly and will have served, among others, a minatory purpose; the avoidable loss of an heir and a wife at one and the same time would have been a significant inducement to self-control. An early Greek version is Herodotus' account (3.32) of King Cambyses in a rage kicking his pregnant wife *cum* sister and causing a miscarriage and her death.

29 Traditional stories: Livy 3.47.1–48.6; cf. Valerius Maximus 6.12. Note that in historical times Augustus is said to have threatened to kill his daughter Julia for dishonor, and to have had her child exposed (Suetonius, *Augustus* 2.2).

30 Something similar can be seen, too, at a more mundane level in a story in Apuleius, in which a husband, going away on business, leaves his wife locked up and guarded

by a household slave (*Metamorphoses* 9.17; cf. also 5.4). Women, too, according to Juvenal (*Satires* 6.413–18), could exercise their own public "clout": he tells of a woman who has her humble neighbors beaten if, for example, their dog barks too loudly.

31 Quintilian's fictional woman ultimately divorced her husband. Spousal abuse could invite unilateral divorce (cf. Seneca, *On Anger* 3.5.4). Always a legal option, unilateral divorce, especially for Christian women, became more difficult in the late Empire (Treggiari 1991, 463, n. 132). Theodosius and Valentinian's list (449 CE) of just causes for divorce included wife-beating; later changes by Justinian (542 CE) simply introduced financial penalties for it (*Novellae of Justinian* 117.14 in Clark 1993, 25). Monnica's advice on endurance is echoed by Basil's comments on a Christian woman's capacity to divorce: "If she was beaten and did not bear the blows, she ought to have endured rather than separate from her husband" (Basil, *Letter* 188.9, *Patrologia Graeca* 32.677; cf. Clark 1993, 40ff.). Note that much earlier in Quintilian's fictional case (first century CE) the woman was prevailed upon by her relatives to return to her marriage. Unilateral divorce was not always the accessible, easy recourse that divorce laws make it seem.

32 The anger-softening love potion was universally condemned in antiquity, as was magic in general. Like poison (with which it was frequently identified), a magic potion was a secret source of power lurking at the heart of the household, available to women and slaves alike and potentially devastating to the hierarchy of domestic control. See also Juvenal, *Satires* 6.610–61; Suetonius, *Caligula* 50.2; Plutarch, *Moralia* 139B. Although condemned, magical recourse was none the less common: see for example, Faraone 1992; several charms to restrain anger: *Papyri Graecae Magicae* 36.35–68 in Betz 1986, 269; *Papyri Graecae Magicae* 161–77 and 211–30 in Betz 1986, 273–4. On binding spells generally see Winkler 1990; collections: Betz 1986 and Gager 1992.

33 The step-mother motif is another violent domestic stereotype; on this see Gray-Fow 1988 and Watson 1995.

34 Plutarch, *Moralia* 609C, 459C, 460C, 457B-C, 266B; cf. Seneca, *Letters* 2.14.1: women are wild and unrestrained in their passions unless they have undergone much instruction.

35 This story is surprising in two ways: it is not about one of the more monstrously colorful members of the imperial family, and it involves a woman brutally avenging a husband with whom she apparently had a most uncordial relationship: see Cicero, *Letters to Atticus* 1.2, 2.2, 6.5, and especially 17.1–5 and 94.3–4, 116.1, 117.8, 202.1–3, 207.3; *Letters to Quintus* 10.1 and cf. Bradley 1991, 186–91, 197–8.

36 Were girls subjected to physical punishment? Probably (*pace* Saller 1994, 152): in a critical letter to the Emperor, Fronto says, "it was easier for me to say this of you myself than to suffer others to speak any ill of you: just as I could more easily strike my daughter Gratia than see her struck by another" (*Letter to Caesar, 145–147 AD* 3; Vat. 131). And the daughter of Sejanus, upon being taken into custody after her father's execution, asked her captors if she couldn't be punished by a beating like other children (*posse se puerili verbere moneri*) (Tacitus *Annals* 5(6).9). On girls' being struck at school see Bonner 1977, 135–6, who cites Martial 9.68.1–2; Ausonius, *Letters* 22.33–4.

37 Oxyrhynchus Papyrus 903, in Bowman 1986, 132.

38 Grenfell and Hunt 1908, 239 (Papyrus 903).

9

MASTERING CORRUPTION

Constructions of identity in Roman oratory

Joy Connolly

In the preface to his *Institutio Oratoria*, or *Oratorical Training*, a textbook on oratory written in the last decades of the first century CE, Quintilian summarizes the aims of elite Roman pedagogy in these words: "We strive, then, for the perfect orator, who cannot be so unless he is a good man; consequently, we demand of him not merely the possession of exceptional gifts of speech, but of all the virtues of character as well" (*IO* 1 pref. 9).[1] Each of the *Institutio's* twelve books makes an attempt to put this statement into practice, to forge a seamless connection between oratorical training and ethical instruction. At the basis of its pedagogical theory lies the popular ancient notion that inner character manifests itself most clearly in self-presentation, and specifically in speech: "as a man lives, so he speaks," Quintilian says (*ut vivat, quemque etiam dicere, IO* 11.1.30). Train a youth in the techniques of speechmaking with sufficient care, the rhetorician believes, and he will evolve into a virtuous man, eager and able to "meet the demands of both public and private business, guide a state by counsel, give it a firm basis in legislation and improve it in the courts" (*IO* 1 pref. 10).

Quintilian's ideal has become the keystone of western conceptions of liberal education, retaining a good deal of influence to the present day (Lanham 1988). At the same time, however, now that written compositions have taken the place of the dramatic declamations that dominated ancient schools (Brody 1993), we as postmoderns have lost sight of the practical demands and moral complexities of public speechmaking that generated the ideal in the first place. As a result, it has grown difficult for us to grasp the hidden contradictions in Quintilian's forthright assertion that oratory furnishes an ideal pedagogy of manly virtue (**vir**-*tus* **vir**-*orum*). For while an oratorical education ostensibly inculcated the student into the conventional beliefs and behaviors of elite Roman culture, it did so by using techniques paradoxically discordant with elite Roman *mores*. On a deeper level, the pedagogical practice of oratory potentially exposed the degree to which free men owed their concept of elite selfhood to a re-articulation and re-naming of values and practices that were, according to contemporary cultural mythology, the native properties of the very groups over whom elite men exercised political and personal power: women and slaves.

Greek and Roman writers from Plato to Quintilian were well aware of the close kinship popularly believed to exist between oratory and the modes of verbal persuasion utilized by women, slaves, and groups of people who were defined, at least in part, by their "feminine" and "servile" aspects.[2] Viewed pejoratively, orators operate through lies, seduction, exaggeration, and misdirection: they exert power in a sordid fashion properly relegated, in the Greek and Roman cultural imaginary, to the intellectually inferior and socially disenfranchised. The sexual identity of eloquent men, too, in the active/passive binary paradigm that appears to govern sexual relations in Greco-Roman antiquity, is aligned markedly with the role given to women and other non-elites.[3] "They do say that of all the young men, those who are fucked the most speak the most impressively," says Praxagora, the heroine of Aristophanes' satire of late fifth-century BCE politics (*Ecclesiazousae* 112–3). According to Cicero, the Stoic Zeno distinguished rhetoric from dialectic in the following way: "closing his fingers and making a fist, he said dialectic was like that; stretching out his hand and relaxing it, he said that eloquence was like the open palm" (*Orator* 32.113). A telling gesture, the violent fist transformed into limp pliancy incarnates both philosophical and social objections to rhetoric on the grounds that it is a craft of the malleable and the weak.

Even from a comparatively favorable point of view, as a pleasurable practice designed to move and entertain as well as to instruct (*IO* 3.5.2), oratory retains certain suspect traces, an air of mannered extravagance and superfluous artificiality in which factual reality is readily sacrificed to the demands of the elegant performance. Defenders of oratory generally acknowledge from the start that oratory is above all performance art, a literal act, in which effective delivery is "first, second and third in importance," as Demosthenes was famously supposed to have said (*IO* 11.3.6). Along with this admission come a variety of justifications for oratorical performance that attempt to obscure its epistemologically and ethically problematical condition. In the *Rhetoric*, for example, Aristotle pleads for rhetoric's legitimacy with the argument that because straightforward speech is insufficient to persuade crowds (1404a1–10), the orator is by necessity compelled to assimilate artificial techniques of style (1415b1–5; 1417a32–5). Pressing Aristotle's argument even further, Quintilian contends that even when an orator speaks falsely or for the sole purpose of exciting the passions of his audience, "it is no disgrace, so long as the motive be good" (*IO* 2.17.26–7). Righteous ends, it appears, justify ornamental or even deceitful oratorical means.

But what free men may do with impunity, women and other subordinate classes cannot. Women's and slaves' acts of persuasive speech, devoid of legitimacy in the dominant political order, undergo a process of vilification in all kinds of Greek and Roman literary genres, which exaggerate and demonize their ability to persuade their manly masters. As a number of recent studies have pointed out, women in classical myth are presented as eloquent tricksters whose physical allure and native craftiness combine in irresistible acts of persuasion. Ann Bergren, for example, speaks of the tradition of "Helen and her *logos*,"

> a tradition that is part of the larger phenomenon by which a female is endowed with a degree of knowledge . . . that gives her a *metis*-like power over the utterance of both truth and imitation, a power that every male . . . must make his own.
>
> (Bergren 1983, 85)

The Hesiodic Muses, who dispense both truth and falsity; Athena, weaver of cloth and of words; Pandora; and a whole host of mythological female characters play a major role in Greek poetics, the gist of which, as Froma Zeitlin shows, is to place women "in the domain of art itself . . . the make-believe" (1981, 327). Not only do women speak eloquently, then, but also artfully, and to deceitful ends.[4]

Ancient detractors of rhetoric were swift to exploit the common perception of women as the deceitful and extravagant sex in order to enhance their own attacks on oratorical practice, regularly using female figures and feminine attributes as symbols of verbal excess and trickery.[5] Plato's seminal arguments against sophistic oratory are characteristic of this approach, and, as we know from sources as disparate as Cicero (*On the Orator* 1.47) and Aelius Aristides (*Orations* 2–4), his writings exerted a great deal of influence on rhetorical theory throughout the Roman republican and imperial period.[6] What is oratory, Plato asks in the *Gorgias*, and what purpose does it serve? He concludes that oratory is like cosmetics (465b) and gourmet cooking (466): like them, it arouses contemptible desires rooted in false perception, presenting a beautiful surface that conceals inner corruption.[7] The analogy also implies that oratory relies heavily upon bodiliness to produce its effects, both the persuasive body of the speaker, and the bodies of the audience, who fail to master their physical sensations of pity or pleasure. In several significant ways, then, oratory is like poetry: through the dramatic performance of counterfeit pleasures and pains, it saps men of the impassive self-command that is an essential sign of the manly philosopher.[8] Much of the strength of the *Gorgias'* acrimonious attack on oratory comes from gendered language like this, drawn from a large mythological vocabulary that locates all those who lack autonomous, manly status in an ontological field of deceit and hyperbole. In Quintilian and other Roman writers, Plato's specific choice of analogies evolves into one of rhetorical discourse's most powerful tropes, in which gourmet cuisine and cosmetics are closely identified with the vicious eloquence of effeminized men.[9]

Like that of women, slaves' language is suspect, and for similar reasons. The slave, Page DuBois concludes, "can apprehend reason, without possessing reason

... [thus,] incapable of reasoning, [s/he] can only produce truth under coercion, can produce only truth under coercion" (1991, 68). This discursive status quo colored most ancient opinions on the status of servile language, from philosophy to comedy, tragedy to elegy. Both ancient testimony and comparative evidence demonstrate the popular belief that slaves' talk was motivated by self-interest, a desire to flatter or to trick their owners (Patterson 1982, 90–1).[10] Aristotle's discussion of the purple passages of formal preambles exposes his associations between slaves and the duplicity, elusiveness and charm-for-charm's-sake of some modes of oratory:

> This is what Prodicus called "slipping in a bit of the fifty-drachma show-lecture for the audience whenever they begin to nod." They are popular with those whose case is weak, or looks weak: it pays them to dwell on anything but the actual facts of it. That is why slaves, instead of answering the questions put to them, make indirect replies with long preambles.
>
> (Aristotle, *Rhetoric* 1415b14–20)

The accusation that eloquence is nothing more than charm and deceit not only lies at the roots of Plato's influential critique of oratory, but continues to haunt the works written in defense of oratory by Aristotle and his intellectual descendants in Rome.

The critical idiom of Quintilian and other Roman rhetoricians stabilizes and exploits existing prejudices against women's and slaves' speech in order to promote an elite pedagogy of ethical, which is to say, manly, oratory. Their effort is rooted in the beginning of rhetoric's existence as a discipline, when Greek rhetoricians evinced a strong commitment to ethical training as a complement to oratory (Plato, *Gorgias* 460a; Isocrates, *Against the Sophists* 3–5; Isocrates, *Antidosis* 84); and Aristotle further emphasized the crucial importance of ethics in oratorical education in his *Rhetoric*, arguing that rhetoric was in fact an offshoot of ethical studies (1356a25).[11] By the first decades of Roman imperial rule, after three centuries of post-Aristotelian ethical, rhetorical and pedagogical theory, these arguments furnished the intellectual basis for a freshly conscious exploitation of oratory as an instrument of social apprenticeship. Rhetorical education became the means by which Roman youths might imbibe an ideology of manly virtue, through the processes of exemplum, repetition, and performance that were embedded in the technicalities of oratorical practice.

"Arms and legs full of numb imperatives"

To borrow the term coined by sociologist Pierre Bourdieu, it was the bodily *hexis* of the elite Roman – the intricate assemblage of particular habits of posture, gesture, dress, facial cast, and vocal range corresponding to, structuring, and structured by the ideology of his gender, class, and nation – that literally "em-bodied political mythology" and proclaimed an individual's place in the social order (Bourdieu 1977, 93). It is in this sense that Bourdieu uses Proust's description of bodies "full of numb imperatives," because, he argues, bodies literally act out the perpetuation of cultural disposition through their performative obedience to social conventions (1990, 69). According to this theory of social logic, specific beliefs about the inherent characteristics of any isolated class – for example, that the ruling elite is honest, intelligent, firm, compassionate, courageous, and so forth, in contrast to the deceitfulness, inanity, frailty, carelessness, brutality, and cowardice of the politically and socially disenfranchised – undergo a complex process of enactment in social practice through the minutiae of bodily *hexis*.

The inculcation of elite *hexis* is precisely the point of an oratorical education. Like Bourdieu, Roman rhetoricians and teachers recognized that to control the body and the tempo at which it moves is to inscribe one's whole relationship to society, or more specifically, to broadcast one's rights and privileges as a man (*vir*), free from the supervision of an owner or a husband. Hence virtuous Romans, Cicero and Quintilian agree, are supposed to pace with a steady gait, erect posture, and relaxed demeanor, looking others straight in the eye (for example, Cicero, *Orator* 18.59, *IO* 11.3.122).[12] A slave, by contrast, is imagined to be always on the run, at the owner's beck and call, his or her back weighed down by bundles, too economically and legally – and hence emotionally – impoverished to meet anyone's eye with confidence (Graf 1992, 49). And as for women: "I shall never admire a continuous flow of random talk, such as I note streams in torrents out of quarreling hussies," Quintilian says (*iurgantibus mulierculis, IO* 10.7.13). Some people believe, he writes later on, that real eloquence is the kind that resembles "the ordinary speech of life, which we use to our wives, slaves, children and friends" (12.10.40). Not at all, he argues: true eloquence demands much more. It requires a mastery over the body and its practices that only properly educated men can develop. Not surprisingly, women who speak well and responsibly – that is, like men – are rare, always appearing in rhetorical discourse as the exclusive product of close association with a male master or masters (Laelia in *Brutus* 58.211; Cornelia and Hortensia in *IO* 1.1.6).

Feminists have long recognized that nothing publicly proclaims and reiterates essentialist concepts of identity so effectively as the body. Elizabeth Grosz efficiently summarizes this claim when she writes that "bodies become intextuated, narrativized; simultaneously, social codes, laws, norms and ideals become incarnated" (1995, 35). In Roman rhetorical discourse, long-standing beliefs about the bodily practice, or the *hexis*, of slaves and women translate automatically into prejudicial concepts of the *nature* of politically disenfranchised classes. These concepts are essentialist in the most restrictive sense of the term, transforming normative, naturalized (as opposed to natural) conceptions of the natures and duties of men and women, slave and free, old and young, and so on into irrefutable notions of group and individual identity. A crucial element of social ideology, a culture's collective trust in bodily *hexis* as an index to self and society reinforces the dominant order, ultimately insulating that order from everyday consciousness and protecting it from reform. Consequently, the preoccupation of oratorical practice with bodily *hexis* made it an ideal method of initiating young elite Roman men into their place at the top, by training them in the conglomerate of behaviors suited to their dominant position in the hierarchical order of the province, the marketplace and the household. More dependable than the lessons in philosophy that Aristotle and Cicero recommended but of which the details were distressingly vague, the exercises in speechmaking of the type that Quintilian recommends combined overt object-lessons in morality with physical training in the attitudes of social mastery.[13]

Above all, the lessons of physical deportment taught by the rhetorician were aimed at obliterating any trace of bodily and vocal practices associated with women and slaves. "Instructors shall not permit the student's hand to be raised above the level of the eyes or lowered beneath the belly," runs a typical piece of Quintilianic advice, lest the youth appear to imitate the "lively movements common among maidservants and unmarried women" (*IO* 11.3.112). Erasing any traces of feminine and servile practice, disciplining his body to maintain an upright posture, unwavering gaze, restrained gestures, and other signs that enacted his social dominance, was paramount to the project of transforming a youth into a master. Having rid his body and voice of the surface flaws associated with womanly and servile carriage and speech, the good student was in an excellent position to assimilate the techniques of eloquent persuasion, however deeply rooted their association with effeminacy and servility. In fact, gaining mastery over these (renamed) techniques, exploiting and mastering the persuasive potential of language precisely without being soiled by its seductively ornamental qualities, was proof positive of his natural superiority. Just as the free man exploited women and slaves in daily life, so he appropriated their putative abilities to persuade, and thereby could effectively disown the presence of womanish or slavish qualities in his own character.

Let me expand for a moment on the theoretical implications of these prescriptions for oratory as a discipline. The strong cultural prejudices about the nature of the language used by women and slaves that I mentioned earlier play a crucial role in the conceptualization of oratory in Greek and Roman rhetorical discourse. They enable the construction of women's and slaves' speech as a metaphor for all suspect communications, including the peculiarly seductive pleasures produced by the free male profession of oratory.[14] To label certain persuasive practices as feminine and servile, and subsequently to prohibit those practices, was an effective method of sanitizing the discursive surface of oratory, because it denied its otherwise undeniable relations to unmanly eloquence. Such a disavowal, to use the term in the strict Freudian sense, occludes any latent awareness of correspondence between women's and slaves' vaunted ability to exert power through ornamented verbal blandishments and an elite Roman's dramatic oratorical performances in the senate, the assembly, or the courts.[15] Hyperformalized bodily *hexis* – certain gestures, an assertive stance, a conventional

135

costume, cultivated turns of phrase and restrained facial expressions – all served to make the elite male speechmaker in the senate, court, public assembly, or declamation hall *appear* to act differently from his social and political subordinates. In this way, manly eloquence is affirmed as essentially different from, and better than, its suspect counterparts.

For these reasons, Quintilian's rhetorical handbook engages in a persistent re-naming of the "tricks" of deceit and ornament on which women and slaves were commonly believed to rely. He provides them with technical labels, codifying them as "techniques" of professionalized manly speech. The process of labeling, which on the surface appears innocent enough to us, holds substantial ideological significance: it transforms persuasive language into a respectable science.[16] A few examples suffice to show the pervasiveness of this enterprise. Under the professionalized codes of oratorical practice, the superfluous babbling of women that Quintilian detests is transformed into periphrasis and pleonasm (*IO* 8.3.53–5); what he attacks as the crude and uneducated straightforwardness of a slave (2.11.7) reappears as the "absolute and unaffected simplicity" of *apheleia* (8.3.87). Outright deception is cloaked under a variety of labels, including the bland *simulatio* (9.2.34–6), *phantasiae* (6.2.29), and false sincerity for the sake of vividness (6.2.34–6). Theatrical miming, the literal role-playing of another, becomes *prosopopeia*, or impersonation (3.8.49–54, 6.1.25–30, 11.1.41). Giving these practices a code name, so to speak, distinguishes them from the troublesome daily practice of women and slaves, and legitimizes them through incorporation into a pseudo-scientific discourse of ethical pedagogy.

But haunting the sanitization of oratory for manly use is the incongruity I mentioned at the very beginning of this essay. Enabling the Roman youth to "play" himself, teaching him how to pass for the real thing regardless of the true nature of his character, made oratorical training at best an ethically troubling, and at worst a dangerous practice. For the student in such a curriculum was in a position to learn that identity is not ineffable, that virtue is the natural possession of no single class or gender, and that authority is not the manifestation of the natural superiority of free men. As Jacques Lacan has observed, displays of virility always seem feminine precisely because they are just that – displays (1966, 291). Paradoxically, then, the pedagogical practice of oratory generates *histrionic* acts of manliness, potentially undermining the real ideal to which it purportedly adheres.[17] Anxiety about the contamination of manly persuasion by effeminate or servile affectations does not consist of the simple concern that an eloquent man may appear to be other than that which he is supposed to be (a free man), but rather is complicated by the recognition, voiced or silent, that oratorical training itself exists in an ethically troubled state of compromise through its emphasis on the *act*, the *show*, the theatrical presentation of elite manly character to the audience. This perception introduces a certain level of panic into the rhetorical discourse of manliness, and explains, I believe, both Quintilian's obsession with the eradication of feminine and slavish bodily practice from the schools, and the preoccupation with the material dangers posed by women and slaves to virtuous Roman men that is manifested in the advanced technical exercise known as declamation.[18]

In the remainder of this essay, I want to examine two things: first, the desta-bilizing presence of women and slaves in Quintilian's vision of oratorical training, and second, the ways in which the practice of declamation demonized both groups in order to promote an ideal representation of free Roman manliness. In the first part, I have isolated three issues from Quintilian's *Institutio* that I consider particularly relevant to this study: the role of male and female slaves and free women in the upbringing of a budding orator; the doubled identification of the slave-actor as both paradigm and anti-paradigm of the free orator; and finally, the figure of the eunuch, whose existence at the interstices of man and woman, slave and free, represents Quintilian's deepest fears about the corrupting influence of oratorical eloquence. The second part addresses the practice of declamation, the central exercise of Roman oratorical training, of which, out of the hundreds that once circulated, five collections are preserved: the elder Seneca's assortment of *Controversiae* and *Suasoriae*, dated to the early first century CE, the *Major* and *Minor Declamations* falsely attributed to Quintilian, and the *Declamations* of Calpurnius Flaccus, a senator of the late first century CE. The *controversia*, the most popular exercise and the backbone of adolescent education, was a speech, either in defense or prosecution, in a fictional case produced out of a highly sensational narrative of domestic intrigue. The typical *controversia* draws on images from literature and popular culture to portray women and slaves as dangerous bodies, whose mental and bodily practices had to be avoided at all costs, and as rebellious subjects, working separately or in collab-oration to engineer the downfall of their natural masters. Through the highly theatrical dramatic declamation of these narratives, ideally performed according to the conventions of elite bodily *hexis* as prescribed by rhetoricians like Quin-tilian, the student further assimilated the naturalized configurations of authority and inferiority, masculinity and femininity, free and slave that were – as he would have already begun to suspect – essential to the smooth operation of Roman society.

Quintilian's *Institutio Oratoria*: fantasies of exploitation

The first two books of the *Institutio* address the early stages of childhood, which Quintilian insists are crucial to the development of a virtuous man (1.9.3). In this short but vitally important period, the child was nurtured almost entirely by a nurse (*nutrix*), a tutor (*paedagogus*), a grammarian (*grammaticus*), and a rhetori-cian (*rhetor*). All of these were likely to be or to have once been enslaved, and, more often than not, were Greek, an ethnicity holding deep associations with effeminacy and servility in Roman culture.[19] The boy's mother, too, was expected to play some role in her child's development (though hers was minimal in comparison to that of the *paterfamilias*). It is worth noting that Quintilian discusses her contributions in his section on slave labor, rather than in his analysis of the responsibilities of the father.

That the upbringing of a young elite boy is consigned to enslaved, female and/or foreign caretakers is a fact of Roman social practice which Quintilian does not bother to dispute. What is absolutely vital, he argues, is that these caretakers be strictly and severely monitored, so that their naturally inferior dispositions will not adversely affect their young charges. The course of supervised exploitation that Quintilian recommends is reminiscent of the program of household management outlined in the *De Re Rustica*, or *Rural Life*, of Columella, another writer of the first century CE. Written for the same class of men who would receive an oratorical education, Columella's work revolves around the virtuous man's obligation to impose order upon the naturally disordered operation of his domestic environment. Mastery is the leading motif of *Rural Life*, which returns repeatedly to the issue of dominating the land, the weather, and one's human possessions, the latter of which are the most potentially troublesome elements of domestic life. It makes for an interesting aside that Columella draws an explicit comparison between his own project and that of rhetorical pedagogy. Especially notable is Columella's placement of oratorical practice in the Platonic company of cosmetics and cookery:

> There are to this day schools for rhetoricians and, as I have said, for mathematicians and musicians, or, what is to be more wondered at, training-schools for the most contemptible vices – the seasoning of food to promote gluttony and the more extravagant serving of courses, and dressers of the head and hair.
>
> (*Rural Life* 1 pref. 5–6)

Like Quintilian, Columella displays a discursive tendency toward aggregating slaves and women in one large, inferior mass, stressing the strong similarities between the bodily practices and emotional natures of the self-indulgent, deceitful free wife and the lazy, cunning slave. "For the most part," he writes, "women so abandon themselves to luxury and idleness that they do not deign to undertake even the superintendence of woolmaking . . . and in their perverse desires they can be satisfied only by clothing purchased for large sums" (*Rural Life* 12 pref. 9). Women are careless and lazy, and they "hate the country," recalling the pleasures the city offers (12 pref. 10). Like women, slaves think constantly of "the voluptuous occupations of the city" (1.8.1), a habit that worsens their natural inclinations toward laziness (1.8.2,10) and unlimited spending (1.7.5, 1.8.6). In Columella's view, both slaves and women are necessary evils. On the one hand, their labor enables free men to pursue the virtuous fruits of leisure; on the other, their vices are a constant threat to the leisured order. The only effective way to combat their vices, Columella advises, is to transform the aberrant woman or slave, as near as his or her inferior nature allows, into some approximation of a good man (1.8.10).[20] As a good example of the profits of this treatment, Columella cites the *villica*, the steward's wife. When subjected to harsh discipline, he says, her natural addictions to wine, greediness, superstition, sleepiness, and lust (12.1.3) are obliterated in favor of a virtuous, soldier-like existence (12.2.6). Thus supervised and regulated, her femininity and slavishness mutate into the more acceptable (and exploitable) qualities of modesty and obedience, qualities visibly manifested in her chaste and submissive bodily practice.

Enforced self-transformation is the answer to Quintilian's concerns as well.

> Above all, see that the child's nurse speaks correctly. The ideal, according to Chrysippus, would be that she should be wise (*sapientes*); failing that, he desired that the best should be chosen, as far as possible. No doubt the most important point is that they should be of good character: but they should speak correctly as well.
>
> (*IO* 1.1.4)

Though the nurse's identity as an enslaved woman cannot be changed, her bodily practice may be altered to imitate that of her owners, or more precisely, of her owners' ideal, a philosopher. If the nurse is supposed to be a philosopher with perfect Latin, the grammarian becomes a Phoenix, devoted to his student Achilles (2.3.12), and the rhetorician a paragon of virtue (2.2.5).

> We must spare no effort to secure that the purity of the teacher's character should preserve those of tenderer years from corruption. . . . Nor is it sufficient that he set an example of the highest self-control; he must also be able to govern with strict discipline.
>
> (*IO* 2.2.3–4)

All this Quintilian demands of slaves and freedmen: despite the realities of their social status, they should be models of elite Roman manhood.

To women's contributions to their children's education, Quintilian devotes little time. Against his complaints about feminine garrulity, his fears that young boys will be contaminated by the langauge and bodily *hexis* of women, he offers fantasies of the dutiful mother and daughter, whose closeness to men of great eloquence transfigures their speech: Cornelia, mother of the Gracchi, and Hortensia, daughter of the great orator Hortensius (1.1.6). Such fantasizing plays a significant role in Quintilian's reconstruction of both slavish and womanly nature in the face of Roman social and economic reality. Confronted with the necessities that put women and slaves in positions of control over young elites, he chooses to re-make their natures to emphasize, like Columella, that under the proper supervision even slaves can become perfect exemplars of manly responsibility. In *Rural Life*, the steward's wife is transformed into a close approximation of an ideal man through the exercise of Columella's imagination. To insist on this is not to deny the realities of harsh treatment that surely plagued the lives of slaves, but to isolate the element of fantasy that colors Columella's coercive vision as deeply as it does Quintilian's. In reality, the *villica* could bear little real resemblance to a free man, regardless of how diligently she worked or how little she indulged her physical desires. The very inferiority of her social status, however, is precisely what enables Columella to fantasize a new identity for her, a role as a virtuous *vir*. In the *Institutio*, through a corresponding process of fantasy and mystification, education is mythologized into a noble pursuit, where the unfree status of the teacher and, consequently, the potential unreliability of his ethical character, is obscured under a veil of unreality.

Quintilian's fantasizing is made more difficult, however, by the dangerously histrionic nature of the exercises the older adolescent begins to perform, particularly the declamation. To be truly well done, this exercise calls for the advice of an actor, whose command of effective delivery, Quintilian admits, has much to offer the potential orator. The actor corrects pronunciation, refines awkward gesticulation, and recommends optimal posture and facial expression (1.9.4–8). He reveals the secrets of effective narration, using texts from the comic stage to demonstrate at what points in the speech one should amplify the voice, or let it fall to a whisper (*IO* 1.9.12). The actor's manifest usefulness in training rhetorical students creates a serious dilemma for Quintilian, who has obvious reasons for de-emphasizing the role of deception and theatrical display in oratorical practice, reasons based on the low social status of the actor in Roman society and the ethical problems raised by the mimetic play of the theater.[21] First of all, the Roman actor was virtually always a slave or a freedman. Even more important was the fact that the entertaining nature of actorly mimesis makes his status as a pedagogical model quite threatening, far more so than that of the nurse or the enslaved teacher.

Quintilian reacts to these thorny issues by setting strict boundaries on the actor's sphere of influence, and by ensuring that his readers understand the vicious consequences of breaking his rules. Again, the key to making virtuous use of the actor's learning is to exert mastery over it, placing clear constraints on its use: "the orator ought to command both [the gestures and movements of an actor] within certain limits" (*IO* 1.11.3). The prime essential, he says much later on, "is a sense of proportion" (11.3.181). When used in moderation, in circumscribed locales and exclusively for manly and noble purposes, the actor's knowledge can be transformed into virtuous practice. The student may learn to incite emotion in the judge and jury, like an actor on stage (6.1.14, 11.3.4), but only in moderation: nothing extravagant or unnecessary may be permitted (6.1.45). Movements imitating the dance (1.11.19), displays of unbridled frenzy (8.3.4), or choleric or pathetic attitudes (6.4.9–13) veer uncomfortably near to the showy staginess that is incompatible with Roman *mores*. Even the reactions of the student audience are subject to discipline, especially when the atmosphere of the theater begins to infect the schoolroom: "I strongly disapprove of the prevailing practice of allowing boys to stand up or leap from their seats in the expression of their applause. . . . This practice is unseemly, theatrical and unworthy of a decently disciplined school" (2.2.9–10). To be sure, the orator must stimulate the audience with a simulated display of feeling, but his position as a model of free *Romanitas* – far from the hysterical laughter and tears of the stage – should restrain him from operatic extravagance. "Oratory possesses a natural mien," Quintilian concludes, "which, while it is far from demanding a stolid and immovable rigidity, should as far as possible restrict itself to the expression with which it is endowed by nature" (9.3.101). By contrast, the stage is the site of prepared lines and excessive gestures, and the actor's self-presentation, artificially enhanced for the purposes of charm and entertainment, is antithetical to the bodily practice of an elite man.[22]

Quintilian's distrust and fear of extravagant, stagey behavior produces a series of harsh condemnations that soon escape the confines of the theater. As his criticism of theatrical habits builds, it grows increasingly obvious that, for Quintilian, to label something "theatrical" is, effectively, to summon up unfavorable images of servility and effeminacy in his readers' minds. In the eleventh book, which attacks these practices one by one, Quintilian repeatedly describes their similarity to the habits of slaves on stage (who may themselves, of course, be playing women or slaves). Immature students pushed too early into *ex tempore* speaking tend to develop artificial habits of self-presentation, talking to no purpose, like common entertainers (2.4.15). They and other melodramatic orators take on a slavish, effeminate appearance, through the exuberant gesticulation and crude vocal tricks of the comic actor. Vivid gestures intended to express thought, such as scratching the scalp (11.3.121), shaking the head in confusion (129), or shifting from foot to foot (128), and coarse expressions of emotion, such as jumping up with happiness (128) or slapping the thigh (123) are the actor's domain, as is effeminate posture (122, 125). Unrefined motions designed to communicate something in a visual fashion, like demanding a cup, threatening a flogging, or indicating the number 500 by crooking the thumb might cause the orator's audience to mistake him for a mime artist, another form of slave entertainment (117). From Quintilian's comments, fortified by what little we can glean from Plautus, it appears that these gestures were not only predominant on the stage, but were the slave character's special property (Graf 1992, 49). In the *Miles Gloriosus*, for example, Periplectomenus describes for the audience's benefit the cunning Palestrio in the act of cogitating some scheme. The slave beats his chest with his hand, turns to the side in an exaggerated tilt, counts on the fingers of his right hand, slaps his thigh, snaps his fingers, shifts around, shakes his head, and finally hops up, triumphant, plan in place. In short, he behaves precisely as orators should not. Only by avoiding such movements, keeping a close rein on potentially unruly verbal tropes like hyperbole, universally employed, Quintilian says, "by peasants and uneducated folk" (8.6.75), will the orator succeed in producing a manly style.

Palestrio's performance is a perfect example of the slavish rusticities of the stage that Quintilian detests. "Repeated imitation passes into habit," he warns (1.11.3). It was one thing to imitate the emphatic vocal expressions and gestures of the comic actor, which enhanced narration and held the audience's interest through a long oration. This was the main incentive to learn from the stage: its language was close to quotidian usage (2.10.13), charming (2.10.10), and full of conviction (11.3.4). It was quite different, and much more problematic, for the free man to accustom himself to playing the other, assuming the habits – and eventually, perhaps, the identity – of his inferiors.

> I do not wish the boy to talk with the shrillness of a woman or in the trembling accents of old age. Nor for that matter must he ape the vices of the drunkard, or copy the cringing manners of a slave, or learn to express the emotions of love, avarice or fear.
>
> (*IO* 1.11.1–2)

The comparative crudeness of dramatic lines, the violence of the theater's bodily practice, and the unabashed nature of its prepared speeches, Quintilian insistently differentiates from proper oratory, and strictly forbids their use. Polish and ornament must be the alternative, and so he argues (9.4.4–19).

But there are dangers here, too: and at times Quintilian seems at a loss which path is more corrupt. "I should prefer my rhythm to be harsh and violent rather than nerveless and effeminate," he says, "as it is in so many writers, especially in our own day, when it trips along in wanton measures that suggest the accompaniment of castanets" (9.4.12). By contrast, the antiquated oratorical practice of Cato and the Gracchi is admirably simple and straightforward: but it is excessively blunt, inappropriate for modern times (2.5.21–2), which, Quintilian is at pains to point out, are a general improvement on the old (10.2.4–28). The obvious quandary here, the orator's choice between effeminacy and the uncouth boorishness by now normally attributed to slaves and peasants, is quite a difficult problem. The best Quintilian can do is to recommend a middle way (*media quaedam via*, 8.5.34), "combining smoothness and polish with manly vigor" between the ends of the spectrum of social practice that slaves inhabit (2.5.9).

Quintilian's insistence that oratory must be eloquent and persuasive without being tainted by theatrical or actorly habits is best understood, as I have already implied, as arising not only out of desire to dissociate rhetoric from the overtly mimetic practices of stage entertainment, but out of centuries of distrustful associations – in popular, literary, and dramatic discourse – between acting and feminine language on the one hand and acting and slavish language on the other. As the figure that Quintilian attacks in the *Institutio*, the actor represents both himself – a slave or freedman with the power to move his audience to laughter or tears – and the cultural constructs of Woman and Slave, whose access to power is nearly always expedited by their natural ability to sway their masters with mendacious tongues. Hence the actor occupies the threshold between praise and blame. He is an educational model by virtue of his ready eloquence and dramatic virtuosity, but he is also the scapegoat of oratorical pedagogy, the anti-ideal of charming and counterfeit eloquence. His enslaved, politically disempowered condition and that of the slaves and nurses who educated the young, act in a peculiarly enabling fashion in rhetorical discourse, allowing Quintilian to mystify servile contributions to the making of a Roman man and to construct fantastic narratives of control over the realities of their influence.

Just as Quintilian chooses to forget about the enslaved status of some of the most significant shapers of Roman manliness, a mental leap that permits him to avoid answering difficult practical questions of ethical training, so he disregards the fact that forensic and deliberative practice was withering away during his own lifetime, due to the growing authority of the emperor. Partly as a result of this, the noted orators of his era performed most often in the recitation hall rather than the forum or the courts. Quintilian's insistence that any practice approximating that of the stage is antithetical to the aims and nature of rhetoric rings a false note in the face of the fact that late first-century orators performed what sounded like theatrical speeches, on what looked like stages, to audiences that behaved like the low-class crowds of the arena.

> Today a rather more violent form of delivery has come into fashion and is demanded of our orators: it is well adapted to certain parts of a speech, but requires to be kept under control. Otherwise, in our attempt to ape the elegances of the stage, we shall lose the authority which should characterize the man of dignity and virtue.
>
> (*IO* 11.3.184)

It is tempting to conclude that Quintilian's passionate attacks on the servile and effete nature of contemporary oratory stem in large part from the rise of imperial autocracy, and the ensuing loss of political autonomy by the Roman aristocracy, from the beginning of the first century CE.[23]

In the autocratic regime of the imperial period, it was all the more crucial for Quintilian and his contemporaries to *act* like free, autonomous men. If they lacked the political power of their republican contemporaries, then at least they could construct self-representations reminiscent of ancestral *dignitas*.[24] Failure to resist the elegances of the stage, to control the effete ornamentations of declamation that threatened the bodily and sexual integrity of the elite man, has especially drastic consequences in the *Institutio*. As I mentioned earlier, Plato's analogies between oratory and gourmet cuisine and cosmetics retained a strong presence in the tropics of rhetorical discourse, for instance, in Columella's discussion of oratorical training in *Rural Life*. Quintilian, too, employs vivid images of the human body's strengths and vices as metaphors for ideal oratory and its opposite. At the very start of the *Institutio*, he compares rhetorical training to gymnastics, which, pursued in a moderate manner, tones the body into manly firmness (1.11.16). Lack of exercise, he warns, leaves the body too weak and womanly to perform oratorical exertions (15). But trying to acquire the benefits of exercise without the hard work has even worse consequences.

Healthy bodies acquire grace from the same source that gives them strength, but the man who attempts to enhance these physical graces by the effeminate use of depilatories and cosmetics succeeds merely in defacing them by the very care that he bestows on them. . . . Tasteful dress lends dignity, but effeminate and luxurious apparel fails to adorn the body and merely reveals the foulness of the mind.

(8 pref.19–20)

Ornament, Quintilian emphasizes, is an essential part of oratory, but excessive ornament is repulsive, so it must be bold, manly, chaste: "free from all effeminate smoothness and the false hues derived from artificial dyes, glowing with health and vigor" (8.3.6–11). These and similar passages set the stage for a fascinating fusion of body and oratorical practice in which Quintilian isolates a single figure as the ultimate embodiment of oratorical vice: the eunuch.

Quintilian's eunuch condenses femininity and slavery into a single figure representing deceit, impotence and vice. He, or it, is the phantasmatic figuration of commodified, corrupted speech (Brody 1993, 19). The eunuch's effeminate style is complicated by his own contested identity: he is a man who is not really a man, not really a woman, but who straddles the boundary between the two.[25]

There is the same evil practice among declaimers, assuredly, as that which slave-dealers adopt, when they try to add to the beauty of young fellows by depriving them of their virility. For as slave-dealers regard strength and muscles, and more especially the beard and other distinctions which nature has appropriated to males, as at variance with grace, and they soften down, since they are harsh, whatever would be strong if it were allowed full growth, so we cover the manly form of eloquence. . . . But to me, who look to nature, any man with the appearance of virility will be more pleasing than a eunuch; nor will divine providence ever be so unfavorable to its own work as to ordain that weakness be numbered among its excellences; nor shall I think that an animal is made beautiful by the knife, which would have been a monster if it had been born in the state to which the knife has reduced it.

(5.12.17–20)

The eunuch deeply troubles Quintilian, I think, because the alleged excess of his own behavior reveals the reality beneath the art of persuasion. The monstrosity of the eunuch is intensified by his real appeal, which seduces men precisely as a harlot can (2.5.15), and as oratory does (2.15.1). Collapsing discrete categories of truth and deceit, surface and interior, the eunuch embodies a kind of bodily and linguistic indeterminacy that marks for Quintilian the extent to which rhetorical ornament may corrupt its practitioner. After all, the slave-dealer castrates his boys in order to make them more beautiful; his act is a response to public demand. Quintilian's determination to prove the unnaturalness of the eunuch's appeal only reveals the extent to which its metaphorical incarnation in oratory arouses corrupt desire in the speaker and his audience. If men can be made effeminate by oratorical performance, then where does one draw the line?

The declamations: ideology in practice

Mary Beard describes the declamation as a negotiation, and a re-negotiation, of "the fundamental rules of Roman society . . . offering an arena for learning, practising and recollecting what it is to be and think Roman" (Beard 1995, 55).[26] The average *controversia* consists of a short passage describing a legal dispute of some kind, with common reference to fictional, or at least quite archaic, jurisprudence: that is, the laws under discussion were themselves likely the stuff of myths, as the following examples will show (Bonner 1949, 84ff., Sussman 1994, 13–14). The pseudo-Quintilianic *Major Declamations* records the legal scenario, the *controversia* proper, including a complete speech for one side of the case. The other three reproduce only snippets of arguments, adding (with the exception of Calpurnius Flaccus) their own evaluations and advice. The declaimer could argue either the defense or the prosecution, though a casual glance at the collections is sufficient to prove that both types of speeches attacked erring women, slaves, tyrants, and so forth far more often than they do virtuous men.

The *controversiae* affirm conventional configurations of power and authority most plainly in their plots and stock characters, a most fertile source for elaborate myth-making. By and large, the *controversia* favors the private, not the public sphere: even the *suasoriae*, the monologues addressed to famous generals or statesmen, focus on their outstanding moral qualities rather than matters of the *res publica*. Out of the nineteen *Major Declamations* of Quintilian, all but three involve conflicts between family members: ten focus on the behavior of wives and mothers, and nine feature some form of enslavement or the treatment of free people as slaves. Seneca's *Controversiae*, too, highlight domestic feuds: out of the first two books, all the exercises but one involve disputes within the *familia*. Out of Calpurnius Flaccus' fifty-three *controversiae*, over thirty address the crimes involving women and slaves; the more fragmentary *Minor Declamations* of Quintilian follow a similar pattern. There are other kinds of debates in all four collections, most commonly over military matters, relations between the classes, the demands of tyrants and the fate of the tyrannicide, acts of sacrilege, election campaigns, and suicide. But by far the most popular *controversiae* are those that debate "family matters" involving the crimes of women who lie and betray their husbands, fathers, and lovers for the sake of the servile vices of greed, lust, disobedience and laziness. Due to the constant reiteration of women's subject status and servile nature, I think, slaves are the focus of fewer declamations. Still, a significant number of *controversiae* call for attacks on slavish characters – particularly those slaves who pass as free men, or who seduce free men and women, metaphorically enslaving them with the chains of sexual attraction and threatening the integrity of their household and estate.

Whether they are the victims of rape, murder, or incest, the participants in adultery or the agents of vindictive gossip, wives, daughters, mothers, slaves, and freedmen are the primary sources of corruption, the weak spots in the household's defenses, or, at least, the sites at which vice enters the *familia*. In literally dozens of extant *controversiae*, women cover up all kinds of illicit activity. They are aided in this, as the declaimers take the time to point out, by equally untrustworthy slaves. In one pseudo-Quintilianic declamation (*Major Declamations* 18), a father tortures his son to death in his effort to discover the truth behind the gossip that the son has committed incest with his mother. The mother later lodges a formal protest against her husband, not in retaliation for the son's death – a suit too realistic for the fantastic world of declamation – but because he refuses to reveal the dying youth's last words. In the mother's defense, the declaimer argues that the household slaves never gossiped about the pair, suggesting the regularity with which declaimers used slaves' talk as evidence of domestic intrigue. "Take a look at why adultery emerges into a hot topic of conversation: servants and go-betweens reveal it" (*MD* 7). Slaves carry messages between adulterous couples (*Controversiae* 2.7.4), conceal their mistresses' peccadilloes from the *paterfamilias* (*Controversiae* 6.6), and even sleep with them (*Controversiae* 2.1.34). They are dangerous precisely because they are fully aware of the skeletons in the family's closets (for example, *Controversiae* 3 excerpta, 8.3). Slaves and women are also allied by the tedium and limitations of their work in the household. This comment could be applied just as accurately to slaves:

> You don't go on sea voyages, you don't engage in diplomacy, you don't change your visual surroundings in constant travel, you don't serve in the army, and legal business doesn't occupy your time. On the contrary, you women always stay at home, confined to your unimportant tasks most of the time in a single location
>
> (*Major Declamations* 6.17)

Obsessed with the betrayal and transgressions of the politically and socially disenfranchised, the declamations express deep fears of potential rebellion by those groups. Not surprisingly, then, women and slaves are usually allied in their subversions of the *familia*. At times, however, women and slaves are played off each other in complex situations involving conflicting loyalties, as in the following *controversia*:

> A man with a wife and by her, a marriageable daughter, told his wife to whom he proposed to marry their daughter. She said that their daughter would die rather than marry him. The girl died before the wedding day, with doubtful symptoms that could have suggested either indigestion or poisoning. The father tortured a slave-girl, who ... revealed an affair between her mistress and the proposed husband. He accuses his wife of poisoning and adultery. [Arguments follow.]
>
> (Seneca, *Controversiae* 6.6)

The speech for the husband dwells on the sadly deceived husband's plight. This is a man whose natural reliance on his household has been utterly and abnormally betrayed: whom is he to believe? The worst aspect of the adulteress' murderous deed is the fact that she made no secret of it, but tricked her husband by saying that the girl would die before her wedding day: "One woman [the slave] says what happened, the other [the wife] what is going to happen as well." Interestingly, the few sentences that remain of the wife's defense attack the reliability of slavish speech: "The charge of adultery has been brought on the evidence of a slave-girl," the declaimer says, "the poisoning, not even on that."

Beneath the accusations of excessive passion, lust, and greed lies the implication that feminine behavior is essentially servile. Like their slavish and feminine counterparts in mythic and scientific discourse, the women of the *controversiae* lack independence and self-control. Even more frightening is their ability to drag men into a servile position, influencing their choice of lifestyle and corrupting the integrity of the free *familia*. Numerous declamations address the legal status of children illegitimately conceived through the blandishments of a female slave or a freedwoman (for example, Calpurnius Flaccus 30, 37; *Controversiae* 2.4, 6.3). Slave women themselves, or the children they bear, receive harsh treatment at the hands of declaimers, who blame feminine powers of seduction and slavish craftiness for an insidious assault on the elite household. Male slaves, too, threaten the integrity of the elite order by trying to "pass" as free men (Calpurnius Flaccus 23).

Declamations thematize the disastrous consequences of women's actions inside the household on the world of city and nation outside it. In one *controversia* (*Major Declamations* 16), two men are captured by a tyrant: the mother of one of the men loses her eyesight weeping for him (like the uncontrollably miserable women in, for instance, *Major Declamations* 6.1 or *Controversiae* 7.4). The captives make a bargain with the tyrant: if the son is released to visit his mother, he will return on a prearranged date, but if he fails to return, his friend will be executed in forfeit. Upon the son's arrival at home, the mother forbids him to return, citing a law under which it is illegal to abandon parents in distress. The declaimer accuses the mother in the strongest terms. "My mother has already filled her cup with grief, she has expended her furious emotions, she has vented her rage" (11). Which of his two loved ones did more, the young man asks, his mother, who blinded herself with useless lamentation, or his friend, now "thrust in the dark and hidden recesses of a dungeon," awaiting sure death at the hands of the man to whom he entrusted his life (9)?

This *controversia* is only one of many in which a mother's love is excessive, destroying free relationships between men with its corrupt intensity. Others attest to the predominance of incest between mothers and sons, a repulsive relationship in stark opposition to the selfless and sexless love of a father. Several declamations argue baldly that the child is simply better served by fatherly love, which builds strength and independence instead of effeminacy and servility. Fathers can and should kill sons whose relationship with their mothers becomes suspect, as did the father in this speech: "For my part, I loved my son, not with kisses, or with tears, but with manly strength, my anguish, and the capacity to face hardship. I rescued him from malice [the rumors of incest] and withdrew from infamy an only son whom I would have saved by my own death in his place" (19.4). Another declaimer argues that, even if incest is not the issue, a son who loves his mother in excess commits a sin against his father (*Controversiae* 1.4).

The primacy of male–male connections is evident in numerous small details of the *controversiae*'s plots: a son chooses to save his father instead of his mother from a fire (*Major Declamations* 2.2); a father who has lost his hands in battle invokes the strong ties of paternal love in his insistence that his son murder his adulterous mother (*Controversiae* 1.4); a man kills his son for loving him too little (*Major Declamations* 19). The heroic love between soldiers (for example, *Major Declamations* 3.14) is a very common motif, particularly interesting because it tends to ignore class lines. Differences in property, it seems, are nothing in comparison with the essential difference of gender. Women in these declamations often attempt to break such "holy bonds of surety" between male friends (*Major Declamations* 16.1, 3). As a group, they tend to obstruct the natural paths of virtuous relationships among men.

Declamation reveals the dramatic ways in which the the prosaic landscape of rhetorical pedagogy is transformed into a moralizing justification of the existing social order. Put in semiotic shorthand, Woman (the evil stepmother, the adulterous wife, the incestuous mother) and Slave (the deceitful maid, the family retainer) by their very presence, in relation to one another and to others, engender social or domestic conflicts. These figures have no dramatic persona, no character development; they are frozen into behavioral patterns of gender and class. In the pedagogical context of declamation, such figures are held up as object lessons in impropriety: killing, fornicating, and plotting as naturally as they engage in verbal trickery. By making arguments that underscore mythical aspects of feminine and slavish essence (adultery, complicity), the speaker displaces himself and his elite male audience from such acts. The transgressions of social practice he describes function like the violent episodes of Greek drama, which transport social upheaval far from the Athenian *polis* into the realm of myth. Similarly, in Roman declamation, distorted, implausible circumstances surrounding family, class, and gender, throw into harsh relief social frictions that everyday interaction does not (and cannot) resolve. In a sense, then, declamation engages in a kind of justificatory cultural mythmaking about men, women, slaves, and their proper roles, for pedagogical purposes and from an elite perspective (Beard 1993, 55).

Crucial to understanding the significance of declamatory ideology is remembering the vivid performative context in which they were performed. These speeches were not simply copied out and reread, like similar exercises in nineteenth-century American composition classes (Brody 1993, 11ff.), but vocally and dramatically delivered with all the passion and conviction the student could possibly muster. Declamation provided the Roman student with an opportunity to hone his knowledge of the rich semantic field of myth and literature that defined women and slaves as natural inferiors, and to pair that ideological expertise with a trained bodily *hexis* that literally put free men's sense of natural superiority into social practice. The modes of behavior in which declaimers engaged, according to the elder Seneca, Tacitus, and others – the younger Pliny describes them as "a different species" (*Letters* 1.5.11–13) – was enabled by the specific combination of self-righteousness and raw hatred that colors the declamations. This combination continues to operate today, in the outrageous posturing, emphatic gestures, contorted facial expressions, and vocal pyrotechnics performed by hate-mongers of certain brands of American fundamentalism.

In his *History of Sexuality*, Michel Foucault argues that power is everywhere, that it is not used by one person against another in any strict sense, but rather exists as an inalienable part of society, available to everyone for subversive or conventional ends. He proceeds to argue that the rhetorical and philosophical "techniques of the self" utilized by elite Roman men are excellent examples of the way in which power is used as an act of self-creation: Roman men learned to shape themselves, their bodies and minds, in accordance with an ideal that, Foucault says, valorized self-mastery and restraint. Foucault's own attitude is far from uncritical: his aim in the *History*, after all, is to map out the origins of social control in the private sphere, demonstrating meanwhile the perniciousness of that control when it moves into, and dominates, the realm of the individual. Still, Foucault's influential study glosses over the extent to which the shaping of the self that he finds so compelling is neither simple nor exemplary, that it in fact relied on the exclusion and demonization of the two groups who made rhetoric, as a leisured practice, possible in the first place.

The younger Seneca, whom Foucault treats as a fair representative of elite philosophy in the imperial period, advises his friend Lucilius that the best time to relax, clear one's head, and meditate is at night, when one's wife is asleep and the household is silent (*On Anger*, 3.36). At that time, a man can contemplate the ethical progress of his day, particularly those moments when he grew unreasonable, angry, passionate, or violent. In a sense, Seneca is checking himself for signs of femininity and slavishness in a house made restful by the exhausted labors of the people whose putative characteristics he most deeply hates and fears. Due in part to the stories told by rhetorical theory and declamation about women and slaves, the two groups were trapped in a web of stereotypes that constrained them as completely as the legal and social laws that denied them legitimate authority. And men, meanwhile, considered themselves free to employ the practices of women and slaves that they considered useful, secure in the fact that the speech they called "rhetoric" was a manly pursuit.

Notes

1 All three numbered citations to Quintilian's work refer to his *Institutio Oratoria*, here generally abbreviated to *IO*. I would like to take this opportunity to express my

gratitude to the editors of the collection for their conscientious readings of this piece. Thanks also go to Michael Strevens for his comments and support. All quotations, unless noted otherwise, are adapted from the widely available Loeb Classical Library.

2 The situation here partakes somewhat of the chicken and egg: are the socially disenfranchised – especially foreigners – defined as womanly and servile because of their social status? Or are womanliness and servility themselves given further dimension by the characteristics of other inferior groups (foreigners, for example)? Pierre Bourdieu writes suggestively of a "confusion of spheres" in cultural belief-systems, concluding, "the universe of discourse in relation to which a given class (and therefore the complementary class) is constituted can remain implicit, because it is implicitly defined in each case in and by the practical relationship of the situation" (1990, 86–7).

3 The standard works on the subject are now K. J. Dover, *Greek Homosexuality* (Oxford 1989), Michel Foucault, *History of Sexuality* (New York, 1986) and David M. Halperin, *One Hundred Years of Homosexuality* (New York and London 1990).

4 If the popular mythology promotes this, we should remember how fantastic, how distant from reality its picture is, keeping in mind the strong element of anxiety-transference operating here.

5 This tendency persists into the Renaissance: see Erasmus' *Praise of Folly*, in which a female Folly defends rhetoric's worst qualities.

6 Plato's critique of rhetoric and its practice, oratory, reflects widespread ancient anxiety over the power of persuasive speech, concerns as relevant in the societies of the Roman republic and early empire as they were in the Greek democracies of the fifth and fourth centuries BCE: this being the case, the Platonic critique set the terms of the debate for centuries into the Roman era. All criticism of rhetoric as a discipline might be called "a footnote to Plato," borrowing Whitehead's famous label for philosophy. For further discussion, see Vickers 1988, chs. 1 and 2.

7 Ornamentation, in Plato's telling words, is "fraudulent, deceitful, petty and servile" (*Gorgias* 465c). For further discussion of women and the cookery motif, see DuBois 1991, ch. 6.

8 The triangulation here of oratory, poetry, and archetypal feminine attributes of concealment, ornament, corporeal pleasure, deception, and bodiliness needs little explication here, especially in the light of recent work by Froma Zeitlin, Ann Bergren, and Page DuBois, among others.

9 It is worth noting that not all constructions of oratory as feminine were derogatory: in the second book of his earliest rhetorical work, Cicero draws a lengthy analogy between the beautiful bodies of women and the "figures" of oratory that he thinks most effective (*On Invention* 2.1–3).

10 I am grateful to Rebecca Frost for drawing my attention to the following passages in Plautus, where the comedian underlines the slave's seemingly natural aptness for deception and flattery (*Cistellaria* 729–30; *Mercator* 157–66; *Amphitryuo* 198; *Casina* 635ff.).

11 Thomas Cole argues that ethics makes its first important entrance into rhetorical discourse with Aristotle (1995, 151, 156ff.).

12 See the fascinating comparison between the ideal *hexis* of the Roman orator and John Wayne, made by Gary Wills (1996, 38–49): "[Wayne's] physical autonomy and self-command – the ease and authority of his carriage – made each motion a statement of individualism, a balletic Declaration of Independence" (44). "His body spoke a highly specific language of 'manliness,' of self-reliant authority. ... The Roman Empire dreamed constantly of John Wayne" (45, 47). For further discussion, see Gleason 1995, ch. 3.

13 As Bourdieu comments, "every society provides for 'structural exercises' tending to transmit this or that form of practical mastery" (1977, 88).

14 Of course, such prejudices also serve to justify women's and slaves' legally and socially disenfranchised status by essentializing their inability to engage virtuously in the participatory practices of ancient politics.

15 Sigmund Freud, "Fetishism," in Vol. 21 of *Standard Edition of Complete Psychological Works* (London 1961, Hogarth Press), 152–7.

16 As one scholar of post-Enlightenment oratory has written, "a profound cultural legacy, misogynist and self-celebrating, undergirds the patriarchal transmission of rhetorical lore and safeguards virtuous language as manly." She proceeds to observe that this legacy consists of a set of beliefs about the essentially masculine nature of scientific discourse (Brody 1993, 29).

17 See Bersani 1995, ch. 1–3 for a fascinating discussion of the effect of hypermasculine displays of selfhood that mark gay male culture in contemporary America. He suggests that what passes for reality "self-destructs from within its theatricalized replication" (18), questioning whether the gay man's act of playing a virile soldier, a hardbodied biker, or some other paradigm of extravagant and showy manliness destabilizes those images in mainstream culture.

18 I refer to Eve Kosofsky Sedgwick's theory of panic in *Between Men: English Literature and Male Homosocial Desire* (New York 1985), ch. 5, "Toward the Gothic: Terrorism and Homosexual Panic."

19 This association is ancient, and impossible to unpack in this limited context. For further discussion, see Balsdon (1979, 30–58) and chapters 1 and 4 of Kaplan 1990. R. Kaster provides a useful commentary on the identity of enslaved and freed teachers (1995, 82–3, 116–17, 183).

20 Columella's suggestion is reminiscent of that offered by Ischomachus for the rehabilitation of his wife in Xenophon's *Oeconomicus*, in which, Sheila Murnaghan argues, Ischomachus honors his wife for "her capacity not to represent but to transcend those qualities conventionally identified as female" (1988, 18). Neither Xenophon nor Columella phrases his solution in these terms, but their meaning is clear.

21 See Shadi Bartsch's discussion of the great scandal provoked by Nero's participation in the theatre in ch. 2 of *Actors in the Audience* (Cambridge 1994).

22 The emphasis here is on the obvious artificiality of the actor's performance: Quintilian, like Cicero, insists simultaneously (and paradoxically) first, that art is not the basis of oratory, and second, that the orator's art must be concealed. Like so many aspects of oratory, ornament is interesting because it requires the orator to deny its very existence even as he makes use of it.

23 Winterbottom (1964) highlights the political undertones of the *Institutio*: "I suggest then that Quintilian was, like Plato, led to a moralistic view of the function of rhetoric by what he saw going on around him. He found himself disgusted by the way rhetoric was being misapplied" (96). In my view, Quintilian writes in response to a much longer tradition of philosophical and social criticisms of rhetoric, of which Plato's was the most important; but Winterbottom's point about the particular political pressures existing during Quintilian's lifetime is well taken.

24 Pliny provides an excellent example of imperial encomium masquerading as republican oratory in his *Panegyricus*, an early second-century CE speech in honor of the emperor Trajan.

25 Note that those who were castrated were likely to be slaves: see Martial 9.6 for explicit discussion.

26 Declamations came in two varieties, the *controversia* and the *suasoria*: but because only a few examples of the latter survive, I will concentrate on the former.

10

LOYAL SLAVES AND LOYAL WIVES

The crisis of the outsider-within and Roman *exemplum* literature

Holt Parker

Tales of Loyalty

I want to look at a striking series of stories about loyalty and betrayal on the parts of slaves and wives that Roman men told each other. These stories form their own subgenre in Roman literature and show a consistent set of narrative patterns, characteristics, and tropes for both slaves and wives. These "Tales of Loyalty" provide us with powerful testimony to the ambiguous position shared by slaves and wives in Roman society, the Roman family, and the Roman male mind, a liminal position that these stories, as they were told and retold, help construct and maintain.

Although images of faithful slaves and faithful wives appear in a wide range of genres – comedy, history, elegy, letters – these comfortable words form their own subgroup within the extraordinarily popular genre of *exemplum* literature.[1] The *exemplum* is a self-contained short story, illustrating a particular cultural value. *Exempla* are found scattered throughout Latin literature, providing a resource for oratorical illustration and historical narrative. They are the never-failing spring for the "heroes, villains and fools" of Roman culture.[2] As Richard Saller notes (1994, 109), "the Romans traditionally perpetuated their moral values through retelling such *exempla* (rather than through systematic moral philosophy or sacred texts)." The *exempla* are a type of popular narrative that forms part of the cultural encyclopedia. As a repository of standard narratives, categories, symbols, scripts, and types on which the poet, orator, or historian might draw, they offer unique insights into the fundamental ways in which the Romans organized their universe. *Exempla* serve as guides to the cognitive map of Rome, to the shared norms, values, and symbols that made up Roman culture.

Each story purports to be about real events but each is told for specific rhetorical purposes and responds to specific psychological needs. Far from being value-free, their great interest to us lies precisely in the values they embody, the conception of slave and wife, and hence of master and husband, that they reveal. The nature of the "event" changes depending on the teller's purpose and need. Thus in one of the earliest stories, with one of the earliest historical settings, Coelius Antipater (writing after 121 BCE) tells us that the life of Scipio at the battle of Ticinus (218 BCE) was saved by his faithful slave (Livy, *History of Rome* 21.41.10). So does Macrobius (*Saturnalia* 1.11.26). Polybius says that Laelius told him that the son, the future Africanus, alone was responsible (10.3.2). Valerius Maximus (*Memorable Deeds and Sayings* 5.4.2) and many others repeat this version (Walbank 1967, II: 198–9). Livy says he would *prefer* the story about the son to be true (21.41.10). We will never know the truth, for the purpose of the story varies: a slave's devotion or a son's bravery.[3]

Exempla represent a form of cultural capital that masters and husbands can use to create social order and reproduce cultural values. By providing a repository of narrative patterns and *topoi*, *exempla* give both writer and reader intellectual control over complex and terrifying events. They are ready-made devices for showing the effects of the breakdown of society, while simultaneously offering an affirmation of its fundamental values. To those in power, to husbands and masters, the *exempla* offer a way to deal psychologically with conscious and unconscious fears. The Tales of Loyalty are a palliative against the anxiety roused both by the actual events of a crisis and the master's realization of the inherently unstable nature of his society revealed by that crisis: slaves and wives are good to think with. In addition, these stories provide a means of shoring up that threatened stability, by offering to the female and servile reader a paradigm of rewarded behavior and a series of heroes/heroines with whom identification is encouraged. They thus give the masters not only mental but also physical control over what they perceive as the danger spots of their society.[4]

Since *exempla* are repositories for normative cultural values, they tend to be deployed in times of crisis when those fundamental values are most in danger. The stories appear most often to describe and illustrate precisely those moments of societal stress when elite men are faced with loss of their manhood, their liberty, status, and lives. Thus these Tales of Loyalty tend to be set in two volatile periods of Roman history: the collapse of the Roman Republic, especially the proscriptions of the triumvirate, and the days of the bad emperors, especially Tiberius and Nero.[5] Other favored periods are the Social Wars (91–87 BCE) and the Marian and Sullan proscriptions (88–87 BCE).[6] Later authors can draw on the cultural capital of the *exempla* by representing new crises in terms of older ones, using the same narrative units, and affirming the same value systems. In these crises, immediate fears about the breakdown of social order intersect with old anxieties about status, which are repeatedly figured as the reduction of the free male to slave or woman.[7] The masters-husbands-authors demonstrate an awareness of the discordant elements and potential fissures which have always existed in their society's fundamental institutions.

Family structure and liminality

Of these institutions the most fundamental in Roman thought was the *familia*. And within the culturally normative Roman family – a man, his children, his wife, and his slaves – slaves and wives stand out as the discordant and therefore dangerous elements.[8] This split in the composition of the *familia* is encoded in the standard legal definition: "The various persons who are subject either by law or nature to the legal power (*potestas*) of a single person, namely the father of the family (*paterfamilias*)."[9] The law thus recognizes two distinct groups: children, subject to the father's power by the natural bond of blood kinship, and his wife and slaves, subject to his power only by law and lacking any "natural" kinship (so too Gaius, *Institutes* 1.52, 108–9). Slaves and wives differ greatly in power and status, but they are united by one important factor. Both slaves and wives are brought into the family from *outside*.

Rome was founded on slavery and slavery was founded on a paradox, for the slave was the outsider brought in, simultaneously the Same and the Other. Rome was also founded on the exchange of women and the exchange of women is founded on a paradox, for women are simultaneously the Same and the Other. Both slaves and wives are intimate parts of the family, yet both are still thought of as foreign, as outsiders (Wiedemann 1987, 25–6). Thus both slaves and wives share the feature of *liminality*: they are both interior and exterior, family and not family.

The liminality of slaves, their position on the edge of society and the family, has been a powerful tool of analysis in recent scholarship. Orlando Patterson's concept of "social death" as "the essence of slavery" is perhaps the most famous formulation: "The slave, in his social death, lives on the margin between community and chaos, life and death, the sacred and the secular" (1982, 5 and 51; also 7, 45–51; Joshel 1992a, 55–6). Slaves were outsiders, the complete Other. Yet they were also insiders, tied to their master by bonds of "fictive-kinship" (Patterson 1982, 63). In Roman society slaves shared every aspect of life with their masters (Joshel 1992a, 43–5; Bradley 1994a, 58–75); they shared his family's cults (Bömer 1981, I: 32–56), his family's tomb (Hopkins 1983, 216–17, 229; Dixon 1992, 26; Saller 1994, 95–101), and, if freed, his family's name (Wiedemann 1987, 23).

Slaves are thus pre-eminently liminal (Bradley 1994a, 76–7) but how can we say the same of wives? Judith Hallet has written of "Women as *Same* and *Other* in the Classical Roman Elite" (1989). Wives are manifestly the Same; they are fully human, as slaves are not. They are often beloved partners, the mothers of their husbands' children, central to the existence of the family and society. Yet wives are also the Other. Like slaves, they too are outsiders brought in.

The obvious differences between slaves and wives only serve to underscore the similarity of the cultural categories into which both were placed, a similarity explicitly acknowledged by Roman males on occasion (Livy 34.7.12–13; cf. Dionysius of Halicarnassus, *Roman Antiquities* 2.25.4; Juvenal, *Satires* 6.140). To put a complex matter briefly, the role of Woman as Sign has led to the role of Woman as Stranger.[10] The exchange of women is part of the founding legend of Rome. Livy's tale of the rape of the Sabine women illustrates the positive side of this mediation. Torn from their natal families by rape, they become, by their love and loyalty to their new husbands, the medium of exchange and reconciliation between men and families.[11] However, the very interchangeability and exchangeability of women on which Rome was based necessitated that a woman be still attached to, a member of, her father's family for her to have any value as an exchange, as a conduit of the society's life. She is connected vertically, up to her natal family and down to her husband's children. However, *horizontally* the wife remains an outsider to her husband's family; she is in her husband's household, but not kin to her husband's *familia*.[12] As a result, she is still a stranger in her new family by marriage, and can be resented, suspected, and feared as a stranger. Thus slaves and wives share the liminal position of outsider-within. Both are intimate strangers.

Liminality, vice, and danger

Like all liminal creatures, slaves and wives are potentially dangerous (Douglas 1966, esp. 41–57; Murray 1983). Wiedemann (1987, 25) suggests that the marginality of wives "raises the question of whether there were analogies between their treatment and that of slaves." However much their daily lives and physical treatment may have differed,[13] slaves and wives received analogous symbolic treatment: the cultural categories in which they were placed were markedly similar. Wiedemann (1987, 25) observes that "ancient literature ascribes to slaves an assortment of vices and shortcomings which are not unlike those ascribed to women." The reverse is equally true: ancient literature ascribes to wives the vices of slaves (Just 1985).

A society justifies its exclusion of certain groups from full participation in society by depicting the members of these groups as needing constant paternalistic supervision and domination in precisely those areas from which they have been excluded.[14] Roman society denied slaves any natural right to a share in food, drink, and sex. The slave was therefore depicted as unnaturally gluttonous, bibulous, and libidinous (Bradley 1987, 26–30; Wiedemann 1987, 12). The slave's vices were seen as endangering the master's goods and household (for example Seneca, *Tranquillity of the Soul* 8.8). Most importantly, slaves were socially dead, without any ties to ancestors or descendants. They had no parents; they were legally incapable of marriage; their children belonged to their master and might be removed from them at his whim (Finley 1980, 75–6; Treggiari 1991, 43, 52–4). Consequently, slaves were depicted as morally incapable of social relations. They were seen as ignorant of *pietas* (devotion, duty), lacking in *fides* (faithfulness), and imbued with treachery, imperiling their master's very life. Appian intended his description of social breakdown, when slaves were free to give in to the specifically servile vices of greed and disloyalty, as a general lesson:

155

People were more afraid of their domestic slaves than of assassins. ... They immediately changed from domestics into enemies, either because of festering hatred [i.e. disloyalty] or the rewards which had been announced to them or the gold and silver in the house [i.e. greed]. So for these reasons each one immediately became faithless to the head of the house.

(Civil War 4.14)

Roman wives also were denied autonomy in just these areas. Their access to food and sex was controlled by their husbands; they had no legitimate access to wine at all (Durry 1955; Cantarella 1987, 118–19; Treggiari 1991, 423). In these areas, the husband's legal power extended to life and death (Pomeroy 1975, 153–4). Wives were consequently and consistently portrayed as gluttonous, bibulous, and sex-crazed, and thus in need of constant supervision. Their greed imperiled the husband's goods, their lust imperiled his honor.[15]

So too in her role as Stranger, the wife can exhibit the servile vice of treachery. This fear, though best known as centering on the figure of the step-mother, was not confined to her. Rather, since for Rome the children were the husband's, both legally and biologically, all mothers were step-mothers, fostering another's children (Noy 1991; Watson 1995). Anthropological data from a variety of cultures demonstrate the way in which witchcraft accusations are frequent against brides brought into virilocal or patrilineal villages.[16] For Rome, a single example may serve to illustrate this nexus of witchcraft, betrayal, and adultery. According to Plutarch (*Romulus* 22.3), the laws of Romulus specified that a husband might divorce his wife only for poisoning his children, counterfeiting his keys, or adultery.

Tales of loyal slaves

Rome, of course, feared more than merely the vices of slaves. A series of slave wars, rebellions, and domestic murders seared themselves into the Roman imagination (Crook 1967, 57; Bradley 1989; 1994a, 76–7, 107–31). The slave who held the razor daily to his master's throat was always a potential traitor and murderer (Cicero, *On Duties* 2.25). Stories of loyal slaves provided the audience with the psychological reassurance that *their* slaves, in any case, would be loyal to them. Such tales resolved a cognitive dissonance at the heart of Roman society: slaves are still inherently disloyal and must be kept slaves for their own good, yet the audience's slaves will be not betray or murder them. So Valerius Maximus (6.8 pref.) finds in his collection of *exempla* "a loyalty all the more praiseworthy since it is the less expected," allowing the Roman master to have his cake and eat it too (cf. Seneca, *Benefits* 3.19.3; Donatus on Terence, *Brothers* 301). The master's slaves will overcome the specifically servile vices of greed and disloyalty, their hearts won by his firm but fair treatment. So the Stoic philosopher Seneca, in recommending a more relaxed attitude towards slaves, makes the generalization that those slaves who talked not only in their masters' presence but even with their masters, whose mouths have not been sewn together, have been prepared to offer their necks for their master, to turn a danger threatening him onto their own head. They talked during dinner, but kept silent during torture.

(Letters 47.4)

In one of the two most frequently recorded stories, the slave of Antius Restio, even though he had been branded for misconduct, secretly followed his master, hid him, brought him food, and, when soldiers approached, killed an old man in his place, claiming to the soldiers that he had taken revenge on his master for branding him (Valerius Maximus 6.8.7; Appian, *Civil War* 4.43; Cassius Dio, *Roman History* 47.10.4–5; Macrobius 1.11.19–20). Contrasting this tale with two others of self-sacrificing slaves, the historian Cassius Dio (cf. Macrobius 1.11.18) makes the moral clear:

In these incidents, perhaps the slaves, because of some previous act of kindness, were repaying those who had treated them kindly. But a certain slave who had been branded not only did not betray the man who had branded him, but enthusiastically saved him.

(Cassius Dio 47.10.4)

The slave was loyal because his punishment was just. Restio's slave was more than merely loyal; like the clever slave of comedy, he was actively and creatively devoted, even at risk of his life (cf. the comments of Seneca, *Benefits* 3.23; Macrobius 1.11.23).

The theme of the just master dominates the tale of loyalty. Thus Seneca (*Letters* 47.18; cf. 47.11–15) offers what he considers practical advice: "He who is respected, is also loved: love can't be mixed with fear." This notion of disinterested paternalism winning the hearts and minds of the people is, of course, a staple of imperialist dogma and literature. One thinks of Kipling's, and even more of Hollywood's, Gunga Din (including the notion of a slave's ability to achieve *virtus* [courage, manliness]: "You're a better man than I am" and his proof of loyalty by dying), or the family retainers, faithful even after the war, in *Gone with the Wind*. The tales of loyalty are, not least, projections of the master-husband's own idealized self: just, fair, beloved by those he rules.

In demonstrating the slave's loyalty to his idealized master, these stories repeatedly deploy three common *topoi*: (1) betrayal by others, (2) help with suicide, and (3) pretended disloyalty in the service of true loyalty. Many of the stories emphasize the good slave's loyalty by contrasting it with the disloyalty of others. When the others are fellow slaves, the contrast helps demonstrate the innately treacherous nature of slaves, which can nevertheless be overcome in exceptional instances by the influence of a firm but fair master. The master resolves the cognitive dissonance, projects an idealized image of himself, and demonstrates the ideology and rewards of *fides*. When the master's friends and relatives are the betrayers, the slave serves to draw a contrast between those who have power and reason to observe *fides* and *pietas* (especially sons, see below) and those who have no power and no good reason. So in the second of the two most popular stories, Urbinius Panapio, betrayed by his slaves, was saved by one faithful slave, who put on his master's clothes and ring and was patiently killed in his place (Valerius Maximus 6.8.6; Appian, *Civil War* 4.44; Seneca, *Benefits* 3.25.1; Macrobius 1.11.16; Cassius Dio 47.10.2–4). Panapio survived to set up a monument with an inscription to his slave's *pietas* (Valerius Maximus 6.8.6). These authors tell the same story about the slave of Menenius. Other stories show similar motifs. The unnamed slave of an unnamed wealthy master tried the same ruse, but was betrayed by a fellow slave. The townspeople successfully appealed to the triumvirs to have the loyal slave freed, and the traitor crucified (Appian, *Civil War* 4.29). Haterius was betrayed by a slave, whose uppity pride on being freed as a reward was punished by being made a slave again to the sons of Haterius (4.29). After conspiring against Augustus, Fannius Caepio was smuggled out of Rome by one of his slaves, who survived shipwreck to hide him in Naples, and was unmoved by rewards or threats to betray his master to the centurion (Macrobius 1.11.21; 22 BCE). He was freed by Caepio's father; a second slave, who had abandoned his master, was paraded through the Forum with a placard announcing why he was to be crucified (Cassius Dio 54.25.7). According to Cassius Dio (62.13.4), when Nero falsely accused his wife, Octavia, of adultery, all of slaves deserted her except Pythias, who remained loyal even under torture, insulting Nero's henchman, Tigellinus, to her last.[17]

Helping the master to commit suicide is a common *topos*, a benefit performed by Philocrates (also called Euporus), slave of Gaius Gracchus (133 BCE; Valerius Maximus 6.8.3; Macrobius 1.11.25); by the slave of Gaius Vettius during the Social War (Seneca, *Benefits* 3.23.5; Macrobius 1.11.24); and by Pindarus, slave of Gaius Cassius after Philippi (Valerius Maximus 6.8.2).[18] I will return to these cases below. In a story of successful escape from Marius, Cornutus was saved by his slaves who threw another body on the funeral pyre, claiming that their master had committed suicide (Appian, *Civil War* 1.73). In a similar tale set during the triumviral proscriptions, Cestius was concealed by faithful slaves, tricked them into building a pyre by claiming that he would try the same ruse, and then jumped on (Appian, *Civil War* 4.26). Although Valerius Maximus (6.8.3) makes it clear that he regarded the use of slaves' help in committing suicide as a shameful necessity, it is a marked feature many stories: Brutus (Appian, *Civil War* 4.131), Flavius Fimbria (Appian, *Mithridatic War* 59), Antony (Plutarch, *Antony* 76.7), and Nero (Suetonius, *Nero* 49.3) (see Vogt's remarks 1975, 137).

In the *topos* of feigned betrayal, a reversal of circumstances leads to the reversal of what actions constitute true loyalty. Both Seneca (*Benefits* 3.23.2–4) and Macrobius (1.11.23) relate the story of a woman of Grumentum, whose two slaves saved her by pretending to lead her out of town to be killed in vengeance for cruel treatment. The slave of Restio pretended to murder his master. The slave of Ventidius pretended to shackle his master in order to smuggle him out safely (Appian, *Civil War* 4.46). In order to die for their masters, the slave of Panapio put on his master's ring; the slave of Menenius traveled in his master's litter; the slave of Appius exchanged clothes with his master (Appian *Civil War* 4.44); and the slave of Piso claimed to be his master (Tacitus, *Histories* 4.50.8). Acts that would normally be examples of unbearable effrontery are transformed into proofs of heroic loyalty. Indeed the entire *topos* of help with suicide is an example of the notion of pretended disobedience. The slave kills the master, but only at his master's command and in order to save his master from the pain and humiliation of becoming a slave.[19]

Seneca's theoretical discussion in *Benefits* 3.18.1 provides a framework for analyzing the meaning of the Roman Tales of Loyalty. He distinguishes *beneficia* (benefits) performed by outsiders (who are under no obligation to do anything), from *officia* (duties) performed by wives and sons (who have a duty to those in their family), and from *ministeria* (services) performed by slaves (who can have no claim on the one for whom they do the good deed). The distinction lies in the right or ability to refuse (19.1), so that a slave may, in ordinary circumstances, confer a benefit only in things that are neither specifically required or forbidden by law (21.1–2), or in extraordinary circumstances in which he has acquired the ability to refuse.

The *exempla* show slaves performing three *beneficia* in particular. The first demonstration of loyalty, arising from the setting of many of these stories during the chaos of the end of the Republic, is accompanying their masters into exile. Due to the exigencies of the time, slaves could seldom be compelled to perform this normal duty. The slaves in these stories therefore evidence a voluntary desire to continue living with their masters, which constitutes a genuine *beneficium* and is singled out as proof of loyalty. Even in exile the proper hierarchy is maintained. The slave shows that his love for the good master outweighs his immediate desire for material advantage: the slave has overcome the servile vice of greed. Direct appeals are made to this vice:

> Virginius, a good speaker, taught his house slaves that if they killed him for a small amount of money and uncertain rewards, they would be filled with great fear afterwards; but if they saved him, they would enjoy glory and piety and good expectations and later on a much greater and more certain amount of money.
>
> (Appian, *Civil War* 4.48)

The truly loyal slave, however, needs no such encouragement, since he is motivated by love of a good master. Antius Restio's slave followed his master of his own accord. The slave of Marius killed his master in order to save him from Sulla's cruelty, despite the great reward offered for him alive (Valerius Maximus 6.8.2), calling forth the ironic comment that this act of *pietas* was no less great than that of those slaves who had saved their master, since death had become a *beneficium*. The slaves of Marcus guarded him in his own house, while those of Hirtius formed the nucleus of a small protective army (Appian, *Civil War* 4.43). Lucretius, husband of Turia, was accompanied by two faithful slaves, one of whom offered himself to robbers to let his master escape (4.44). Pomponius disguised himself as a praetor and his slaves as his attendants (4.45), while Apuleius, Aruntius, and Ventidius dressed themselves as centurions and their slaves as soldiers in pursuit of the proscribed (4.46). Fannius Caepio's slave stayed loyal in exile. Similarly, Asinius Pollio's slaves refused offers of money and freedom to betray their master (Macrobius 1.11.22), as did the slaves of Calenus and Marcus Terentius Varro (Appian, *Civil War* 4.47).

The second, and more powerful, proof of loyalty was provided by the willingness of a slave to suffer torture or to die on behalf of his master. Here, obedience to the master triumphs even over self-preservation and the slave overcomes the servile vice of cowardice. When the great orator Marcus Antonius was accused of incest, his slave demanded, over his master's protests, to be tortured so that he could give evidence of Antonius' innocence (Valerius Maximus 6.8.1). The slaves of the proscribed Gaius Plotius Plancus endured torture until he gave himself up to stop it (6.8.5) – the only master to do so. The freedmen of Quintus Labienus refused under torture to give up their master's hiding place (Macrobius 1.11.18). Aesopus, freedman of a certain Demosthenes, denied under torture the charge brought against his master of adultery with Augustus' daughter Julia (Macrobius 1.11.17). Similar stories of loyalty under torture feature the slaves of Lentulus, charged with treason against Tiberius (Tacitus, *Annals* 4.29), and Pythias together perhaps with other servants of Octavia. Willingness to die in the master's stead is immortalized in the stories of the slaves of Urbinius Panapio and Menenius. The pedagogue of a proscribed orphan wrapped his arms around the boy and died protecting his charge (Appian, *Civil War* 4.30). I have already mentioned the slave who tried to die in his master's place, but was betrayed by a fellow slave, resulting in the loyal slave's freedom and the traitor's crucifixion.

The third and most impressive proof of all was suicide after the master's death. The slave's suicide, an act normally motivated by wickedness (said the masters), becomes instead the ultimate proof of loyalty, an act unconstrained even by the master's presence.[20] Appian singles it out in his introduction to his set of tales of loyalty (*Civil War* 4.15): "Equally remarkable were the zeal and virtue of others, wives, children, brothers and slaves, who rescued them, came up with many plans, and died with them, when they did not succeed in their hopes. Some even killed themselves over the bodies of those who had been killed." Philocrates (or Euporus), the slave of Gaius Gracchus, and Pindarus, slave of Gaius Cassius, already mentioned, helped their masters with suicide and then committed it themselves. They, together with Octavia's Pythias, are uniquely remembered by name, an honor not given even to the slaves of Restio or Panapio. The slave of Naso, who could have escaped, instead killed the centurion who had murdered his master and then himself, addressing his final words to his master's body: "You have consolation" (Appian, *Civil War* 4.26). The slave of Vettius helped his master with suicide and then killed himself "lest he survive his master" (Macrobius 1.11.24).

For the slave owners, suicide is psychologically the most satisfying demonstration of loyalty, for it represents the conversion of the master's dependence into the slave's dependence. Hegel in his analysis of the master–slave relation pointed out the paradox that total personal power becomes a form of total dependence on the object of that power (Hegel 1910, 228–40; Patterson 1982, 50; Joshel 1992a, 53–5). The Romans were acutely aware of their daily dependency on slaves, a paradox which forms the basis of many a Stoic homily (for example Seneca, *Letters* 47; cf. Horace, *Satires* 2.7; Joshel 1992a, 152). The tale of loyalty transforms this anxiety into a comforting wish-fulfillment. The master, *in extremis*, is brought up against the fact that he is utterly dependent on his slaves, that he literally cannot live without them. Yet the slaves, by their suicide, demonstrate that they are utterly dependent on him to give their lives meaning, that they literally cannot live without him.

Besides this comforting psychological dimension, we can observe two additional reasons for the popularity and the usefulness of these tales of loyalty, each relating to a different aspect of the power relation of slavery: one directed inwardly to the masters themselves, the other outwardly to the slaves. Weber (1946, 245–52, 295–301), and many others subsequently, have divided the notion of power into three components: a social aspect, force (the ability to employ coercion to gain one's will); a psychological aspect, influence (the ability to persuade another); and a cultural aspect, authority ("the means of transforming force into right and obedience into duty"). The tales of loyal slaves have a special role in conferring authority on the masters, in the particular form of a culturally recognized position of *honor*. Hegel's paradox, that power confers honor only to the extent that those dominated themselves have honor, reaches an "existential impasse" in the extreme of slavery (Kojève 1969, 19). Ownership of slaves may confer *status*, as a demonstration of the power and wealth of an individual, but it cannot in itself confer *honor*, a fact which Petronius' depiction of the vulgarian Trimalchio vividly demon-strates.[21] Honor, therefore, can be conferred by a slave only when the slave's obedience ceases to be a *ministerium* and becomes a *beneficium*, that is, when the slave's obedience ceases to be obedience to force and becomes obedience to authority. Then the slave's obedience becomes a testimony to the moral char-acter of the master, who inspires willing slavery, proved ideally by death. According to Seneca:

> The usual hatred of his status as slave was conquered by a master's kindness. ... So, far from ceasing to be a benefit because it was performed by a slave, it is all the more so, because not even his slavery was able to keep him from it.
>
> (*Benefits* 3.19.4; cf. Cassius Dio's comments above, 47.10.4)

161

This role of slaves in conferring honor is implicitly demonstrated by the fact that, although these profess to be tales of the virtues of slaves, they are equally (if not more so) memorials to the fame of the masters. Except for three instances already cited (Philocrates/Euporus, slave of Gaius Gracchus; Pindarus, slave of Gaius Cassius; Pythias, slave of Octavia), the master's name alone is recorded. The monument to the *pietas* of Panapio's slave is as much a public testament to the master's virtue as to the slave's. This function of the Tales of Loyalty is sometimes explicitly acknowledged, as in Seneca's story of the woman of Grumentum:

> She manumitted both on the spot and did not think it unworthy that she had received her life from those over whom she had the power of life and death. Rather, she could congratulate herself that if she had been saved in any other way she would have had a gift of the usual and ordinary mercy, but saved in this way, she was the story and the example of two towns.
>
> (*Benefits* 3.23.3)

The tales of loyalty thus resolve a disturbing paradox, for the noble slave is like the noble master. In times of crisis, he begins to act like his master. In many of the stories he literally imitates his master or takes his place. The good slave is brave (even to the point of death); he is resourceful (rich in stratagems); he is noble (preferring death to dishonor). In short, he shows all the characteristics of the ideal Roman citizen-soldier. Not only does this threaten to undo the distinction between slave and free, it rouses the terrifying specter of the brave, clever, armed, autonomous slave.

Pliny, recounting the vivid story of the murder of Larcius Macedo by his slaves, bears anxious witness to the pervasive fear of reversal, the recasting of victimizer as victim which formed part of the conscious background to the Romans' relations with their slaves (3.14): "You see how many dangers, how many insults, how many mockeries, we are exposed to. Nor can anyone be safe, just because he's considerate and gentle. Masters are murdered not by reason (*iudicio*) but by crime (*scelere*)."[22] This reversal is embodied and at the same time assuaged by the figure of the slave of Appius, who died in his master's bed, dressed in his master's clothes, while Appius stood by dressed as the slave (Appian, *Civil War* 4.44; cf. the general statement at 4.13). The tales of loyalty (especially through the *topoi* of feigned disloyalty and suicide) allow an airing of these fears and then can allay them by telling a story in which seeming "crime" is merely disguise for reassuring loyalty.[23] The Tales grant the slaves volition and autonomy while confirming their status as mere instruments of the master's will. Like the clever slave of comedy, the loyal slave puts his threatening "reason" at the master's disposal (Parker 1989). The slave enacts the role of master only to enable the master to escape the role of slave. The narrative is similar to the pattern of Saturnalia: reversal is the means for a return to normal hierarchy.[24]

162

The Tales of Loyalty also make another contribution to authority, directed outwardly to the slave. Patterson (1982, 1–2) perceptively locates authority in the ability to manipulate the dominant public and private symbols of a society, and the loyal slave is a potent symbol (Cartledge 1985). He can be not only a source of reassurance but also a source of moral authority through which the master can secure the obedience of other slaves. Patterson, though he disagrees with some of Hegel's analysis, follows it in concluding:

> This leads us to one of the most remarkable features of slavery. What does the master make of the slave's yearning for dignity? . . . The master exploits this very yearning for his own benefit . . . by manipulating it as the principal means of motivating the slave, who desires nothing more passionately than dignity, belonging, and release.
>
> (1982, 101)

The slave can thus achieve "freedom through collusion" (Cox 1969, 145; Barton 1993, 134).

The model of the loyal slave is held up constantly to slaves, as well as masters, in the literary forms of comedy (which slaves attended: Plautus, *Poenulus* 23) and *exemplum*; in the private rituals of the *familia*; and especially in the public rituals of burial with the *familia*, often including an epitaph, meant to be read by all passers-by, praising the slave for *fides* (Lattimore 1942, 282–5). Patterson claims that "the slave as an active instrument was recognized only when he behaved in a criminal manner" (1982, 200). However, the tales of loyalty also show the slave as an autonomous subject, but they represent that autonomy as exercised only in the service of the master. The masters hold up these exceptional deeds of loyalty as the only possible way for a slave to achieve a vicarious share in honor, which is the exclusive characteristic of the free man. Cassius Dio explicitly states that the slave of Restio both saved his master and gained honor for himself (47.10.5). Further, not only may the slaves in the stories be treated with the honor of a free man but they may be given freedom itself, as are, on equally infrequent occasions, the clever slaves of Roman comedy (Segal 1987, 164–9). The slaves of the woman of Grumentum were manumitted on the spot, while the loyal slave who tried to die for his master only to be betrayed by a fellow slave was freed by the intercession of the townspeople and the traitor crucified. Thus the slave not only might achieve public recognition, but might by acting like a citizen become one.[25] The loyal slave served both as a source of psychological comfort and honor for his master and as powerful model to invoke obedience in other slaves.

Tales of loyal wives

Roman marriage, like Roman slavery, was not based solely on fear, but on affective ties as well. Of the genuine love that could, despite all societal pressures, exist between husband and wife we have some (if scanty) testimony (Treggiari 1991, 229–61; Dixon 1991; 1992, 83–90; Saller 1994, 5–7). But as in the case of slaves, it is clear that the marginal status assigned to women by Roman society forced its members into a severe cognitive dissonance. The wife of one's bosom is also a potential adulteress, a murderer of her husband and children (Monaco 1984; Purcell 1986, 95; Santoro L'Hoir 1992, 41–2; Edwards 1993, 51–2; Parker 1994). To resolve that dissonance, a psychological necessity for the Roman male is a repertoire of Tales of Loyal Wives, balancing the figure of the adulteress.

Valerius Maximus (6.6–8) implicitly acknowledges the parallelism of the two sets of stories within the genre of *exemplum* literature by giving first examples of tales of loyalty to the state, then tales of faithful wives, and finally tales of faithful slaves. The historians also explicitly acknowledge the parallelism; for example, Tacitus in the preface to the *Histories*:

> Nevertheless, the age was not so barren of virtue that it did not produce good examples: mothers who accompanied proscribed sons, wives who followed their husbands into exile, brave relatives, constant sons-in-law, loyalty of slaves unyielding even in the face of torture.
>
> (1.3.1)

Velleius (2.67.2) ranks wives and slaves above sons, who as blood relatives with a full share in society should have good reason to observe *fides* and *pietas*.[26] "It must be noted however, that towards the proscribed the loyalty of the wives was the highest; that of freedmen, moderate; that of slaves, somewhat; that of sons, nonexistent." Appian's comments (*Civil War* 4.15) about the fidelity and courage of "wives, sons, brothers and slaves," who rescued the proscribed, helped them, died with them, or committed suicide after their death, have already been quoted; he uses the outsiders, wives and slaves, to frame the insiders, sons and brothers. Appian also begins his list of *exempla* (4.36) by framing the sons with the wives and slaves: "Remarkable instances were seen of wives' love for their husbands, and goodwill of sons toward fathers and of slaves, beyond nature, toward masters." The language is revealing: the loyalty of slaves is simply *hyper physin*, "unnatural."[27]

In the tales of loyal wives, we can note the same three *topoi* found in the tales of loyal slaves: betrayal by others, help with suicide, and pretended disloyalty in the service of true loyalty. The wife of Ligarius hid him, but was betrayed by a slave (Appian, *Civil War* 4.23), as was the wife of Acilius (4.39). Many wives help their husbands with suicide, most famously Arria, the wife of Paetus (Pliny, *Letters* 3.16; Martial 1.13; Cassius Dio 60.16.5–6). Arria indeed achieved a type of semi-divine status, welcoming dead brides together with Laodamia, the Greek heroine who committed suicide after her husband's ghost told her of his death at Troy (*Inscriptiones Latinae Selectae* 6261). Arria also testifies to a type of the *topos* of betrayal by others, when she upbraids the wife of Scribonianus for not dying with him (Pliny 3.16). Paxaea, wife of Pomponius Labeo, and Sextia, wife of Mamercus Scaurus, encouraged their husbands and joined them in suicide (Tacitus, *Annals* 6.29). Here, however, we notice an important difference between the stories told of wives and slaves. No wife aids the suicide of her husband without committing suicide herself, or at least attempting it. The slave, being a mere *instrumentum*, might be used by a master as a tool to commit suicide, but a wife, if she is to avoid the suspicion of murder and adultery, must join her husband in death. Tacitus (*Annals* 15.63–4) records the calumny and distrust that fell on Pompeia Paulina for daring to survive Seneca, and takes considerable pains to explain that she was sent from the room at her husband's own command and that her wounds were bound up against her will.

The *topos* of pretended disloyalty features in the stories of the wife of Apuleius, who threatened to inform on him if he left without her (Appian, *Civil War* 4.40), and Sulpicia, wife of Lentulus Cruscellio, who though forbidden by her husband and guarded by her mother kept watch on him to try and join him when he left for Sicily and finally succeeded dressed as a slave (Valerius Maximus 6.7.3; Appian, *Civil War* 4.39). The praise given them is in sharp contrast to the blame attached to the wife of Coponius who purchased his safety with her chastity (Appian, *Civil War* 4.40). The moral is clear: pretended disloyalty in order to fulfill the husband's true wishes is utterly different than betrayal, which includes sexual betrayal, even from good motives.

The tales of loyal wives also share the three proofs of loyalty found in the tales of loyal slaves. Accompanying a husband into exile is singled out as exceptional behavior many times (cf. the general statement of Tacitus, *Histories* 1.3.1 quoted above). This act not only provides evidence of love but moves the wife from the possibility of independent action into her proper subordination. The story of Sulpicia is strikingly parallel to that of the slave of Restio: not only did she accompany her husband, but she had to do so by stealth in order to circumvent his orders and the watch placed on her by her mother. The wives of Apuleius and Rheginus escaped with their husbands (Appian, *Civil War* 4.40). Virginius' wife brought a ship to take him to Sicily and money to bribe the soldiers (4.48). Under Nero, Antistia Pollitta accompanied her husband, Rubellius Plautus, into exile (Tacitus, *Annals* 14.22), as did Artoria Flaxilla, wife of Novius Priscus, and Egnatia Maximilla, wife of Glitius Gallus, who also gave up a considerable fortune to do so, "both of which actions enhanced her glory" (15.71.3). Most famous are the cases of Arria and her granddaughter Fannia. Arria, denied the right to act as slave to her husband, followed his ship in a tiny boat; Fannia, wife of Helvidius Priscus, followed her husband into exile twice and was herself banished a third time (Pliny, *Letters* 3.16, 7.19). The stories of Arria, the wife of Lentulus, and Sulpicia point to another *topos*: the parallelism of the tales of loyal slaves and loyal wives is intensified by the detail of wives dressing up as slaves, or being willing to act as slaves, in order to follow their husbands.

Arria's willingness to die for her husband was shown not only by the famous and much praised "Paete, non dolet," ("It doesn't hurt, Paetus," said after she stabbed her herself, drew out the sword, and handed it to her husband) but by the grotesque detail of her trying to dash her brains out against a wall, when denied surer means of suicide (Pliny, *Letters* 3.16). Pliny (6.24) also records a local story of the mutual suicide of a husband and wife when his genital cancer proved incurable and compares the deed to Arria's. Pompeia Paulina attempted a mutual suicide with Seneca. Although some accounts do not specify exactly who committed suicide first (Tacitus, *Annals* 6.29: Paxaea with Pomponius Labeo and Sextia with Mamercus Scaurus), the Romans preferred a wife who committed suicide after her husband's death. Thus Calpurnia stabbed herself to death with the sword that had been used to execute her husband Antistius during the Marian massacres (Plutarch, *Pompey* 9; Velleius, *Compendium of Roman History* 2.26.3). The wife of Aruntius starved herself to death after the death of her husband and son (Appian, *Civil War* 4.21). Porcia committed suicide, following her father's example, by swallowing live coals on hearing the news of Brutus' death (Valerius Maximus 4.6.5; Cassius Dio 47.49.3).[28] The same bizarre means (or the same *topos*) is used in the story of Servilia, who committed suicide after the death of her husband, Marcus Lepidus, who had conspired against Octavian (Velleius 2.88.3, who compares Calpurnia and Servilia). After the suicide of her husband Gaius Fufius Geminus under Tiberius, Mutilia Prisca stabbed herself with a dagger inside the senate chamber itself (Cassius Dio 58.4.5–6). The case of the wife of Ligarius deserves to be quoted in full:

> While his wife was hiding Ligarius, she let a single maidservant into the secret, and when she was betrayed by the slave, she followed her husband's head as it was being carried out, crying, "I sheltered him, the punishment is the same for those who gave shelter." When no one killed her or denounced her, she came before the triumvirs and denounced herself, and when even they overlooked her because of her love for her husband, she killed herself by starvation.
>
> (Appian, *Civil War* 4.23)

Here again the *topos* of suicide motivated by loyalty provides emotional satisfaction to the men in the audience. It resolves deep anxiety about the exercise of power by converting the husband's dependence into the wife's dependence. The husband, *in extremis*, is forced into the feminine role. He is protected and sheltered by his wife. He discovers that he literally cannot live without her. Yet the wife, by suicide, demonstrates that she is utterly dependent on him to give her life meaning. The methods of suicide are various, but death by starvation is markedly popular. Though not an exclusively feminine method,[29] its significance in these stories is plain: it is a symbolic enactment of the belief that the husband is life and the means of life. The role of starvation is made manifest in an anecdote told by Pliny the Elder (*Natural History* 39.18.6). A wife who had taken the keys to the wine storage was forced by the family council to starve herself to death.[30] Here, lack of self-control, the typical vice of slaves and wives, threatens the husband's household goods. Since she has violated her role in the new family, her husband and her agnates remove her from the literal nourishment of that family. Indeed, the story of Julia (Valerius Maximus 4.6.4), who miscarried and so died at the sight of her dead husband, Pompey, shows that this motif is designed to present the woman's social dependence as rooted in nature. A wife's inability to live without her husband is made to have a physical basis.

However, the archetype of the wife who commits suicide as the ultimate proof of loyalty is at variance with the realities of a wife's duty to care for her husband's children and with another equally powerful Roman stereotype, the *univira*, a word which significantly combines the wife of one husband and the widow who refuses to remarry. Three solutions to this dilemma are found. First and most commonly, no mention is made of children, and so the wife is left free to kill herself. Second, she can be persuaded by her husband, but only by her husband, to go on living. In this way her survival is made almost as great a testimony to her loyalty as her suicide would be. The younger Arria had to be begged by her husband, Thrasea Paetus, not to commit suicide but to go on living for the sake of her daughter Fannia (Tacitus, *Annals* 16.34), and Seneca was forced to banish Pompeia Paulina from the room so that she might live (15.63–4). A third, and most significant, solution is found in a ritual form of living death, where the wife proves her loyalty by keeping herself on the edge of death and starvation. So Pompeia Paulina after her suicide attempt is described as living out the rest of her life (15.64) "in the praiseworthy memory of her husband, and with a face and limbs white with a degree of pallor that showed how much vital spirit [*vitalis spiritus*] she had lost." Tacitus also relates how Antistia Pollitta, who had accompanied her husband into exile, and after his murder "had embraced his bleeding neck and kept his blood-spattered clothes. She remained a widow, neglecting her appearance, with continual lamentation and only enough food to ward off death." She only remained alive in order to save her father and when her masculine attempts (*aliquando sexum egressa voce*) to persuade Nero failed, she committed suicide, together with him and her grandmother Sextia (*Annals* 16.10–11). The stories of suicide (especially by starvation) and these tales of living death present a biological theater in which the wife publicly enacts the Aristotelian metaphor of the man as soul [*vitalis spiritus*] animating the mere matter of the woman's body.[31]

The psychological purpose of these tales is clear: they serve to reassure the husband that despite the inherently vicious and treacherous nature of women, *his* wife at least will be loyal. Thus the familiar dissonance is resolved: wives are still inherently disloyal and must be kept under guard for their own good, yet the audience's wives will be not betray or murder them. As with the loyalty of slaves, Valerius Maximus can both use and deprecate the loyalty of women: Turia, who hid her husband, the proscribed Quintus Lucretius Vespillo, acted with "unique faithfulness" (6.7.2). Like the story of the loyal slave, the story of the loyal wife shows an idealized husband engendering in his wife a love which is able to overcome the innate feminine vices of lust, vanity, and greed. Women's avarice, especially for jewels, and its connection with other vices, especially adultery, was a deeply founded stereotype (Livy 34.1–8; cf. Seneca, *Helvia* 16.3–4). Thus, the wife of Acilius (Appian, *Civil War* 4.39), the wife of Virginius (4.48), and Egnatia Maximilla (Tacitus, *Annals* 15.71.3) all sacrifice their own jewels and money, that is, specifically their inalienable dowries, to follow their husbands. The wife in the so-called "Laudatio Thuriae" (*Funeral Eulogy of Turia*) sends her jewels and money to her husband in exile.[32] Sulpicia values her husband not only more than money, but more than her own mother, whom she defies to accompany Lentulus. This story offers a profound example of psychological consolation, which goes to the heart of the fear of the wife as stranger: a woman proving that her love for her husband is more powerful than her ties to her agnatic family. So in the "Laudatio Thuriae," the wife is praised not only for her devotion to her agnatic family but for her love for her mother-in-law as well.

As with the Tales of Loyal Slaves, the Tales of Loyal Wives also contribute to the husband's authority, first by granting him fame and honor for the loyalty of his wife (so explicitly Velleius 2.26.3 on Calpurnia), and second, by offering a model to other wives. Returning to Seneca's distinctions (*Benefits* 3.18.1), an *officium* is the part of "the son, the wife, of those persons whom *necessitudo* [both 'necessity' and 'relationship'] encourages and orders to give help." Just as honor can be conferred by a slave only when the slave's obedience ceases to be a *ministerium* and becomes a *beneficium*, so honor can come from a wife only when her *officium* become a *beneficium*, that is, when she acts not because of necessity but because of her husband's moral authority. A few husbands may achieve fame by dying for their wives (Valerius Maximus 4.6.1–3), but far more husbands gain far greater fame by having their wives die for them. The wife's virtue is proof of her husband's virtue (even as her adultery is proof of his weakness) and the tale is told equally about him.

Like the Loyal Slave, the Loyal Wife resolves a contradiction. The good wife is like the good husband and in times of crisis becomes increasingly masculine. She shows a man's courage (especially in following him into exile), a man's resourcefulness (especially in feigned disobedience), a man's nobility (especially in suicide). She thus threatens to become that object of masculine dread, the phallic woman, while the man in crisis, powerless, dependent, weak, is in danger of being effeminized.[33] The tales of loyal wives offer a way of dealing with these fears. The stories grant wives freedom, but freedom placed at the service of their husbands. The "masculine daring" despised in Sempronia is praised in Porcia (Sallust, *Conspiracy of Catiline* 25; Plutarch, *Cato the Younger* 73.4; Hallett 1989, 65–7). The effrontery of public speaking, condemned when Amasia Sentia and Gaia Afrania asserted themselves in the law courts,[34] is praised when Mutilia Prisca, Antistia Pollitta, and the unnamed wife of Ligarius professed their wifely *fides* in the forum or senate. As in the case of the loyal slave, the exceptional woman who transcends her nature allows the Roman male to resolve the contradiction of his desire for willing (and hence autonomous) servants, and his fear of them.

The loyal wife is also a potent symbol, displayed for emulation in literature from Roman comedy to private letters. So, explicitly, Pliny (*Letters* 7.19) writing about Fannia's imminent death: "Will there be anyone now whom we can hold up as a model to our wives?" The symbol is enacted ritually in the public cults of chastity (Cantarella 1987, 150–5) and in the act of burial. The public statement of the loyalty of the wife is enshrined in numerous epitaphs.[35] The most famous of all these epitaphs, the "Laudatio Thuriae" stands as a monument to the virtue of her husband,[36] to the virtue of the wife, and as an ideal to be emulated. Nor should we ignore the psychological satisfaction these stories might offer the women in the audience. The Tales of Loyal Wives show brave, powerful, autonomous women. They are heroines who have adventures, yet do not lose their "femininity." They violate accepted gender roles, yet are rewarded with praise. Even noble suicide provides the deep emotional pleasures of courage and pathos.

Roman men defined Roman women only in relation to a man. This was a fact of law as well as a fact of life (Gardner 1986, 5–80). Like the slave, the woman was dependent on others for her status and her very existence (hence the symbolic force of suicide by starvation and life in semi-starvation). Yet this dependence opened a way for her to achieve honor, recognition, and humanity. She could become honored as a daughter, from a famous father; as a mother, from famous children; and as a wife, from a famous husband.[37] Cornelia served as a paradigm of womanly honor derived from these three sources, but there is a difference among them.[38] She achieved honor and fame because she *was* the daughter of Scipio Africanus, because she *was* the "mother of the Gracchi." But as the wife of Tiberius Gracchus, she must *do* something. She must remain an *univira*, demonstrating her loyalty to her husband's memory, actively maintaining her socially constructed role of wife. The tale of the loyal wife holds out the fame of Cornelia as an achievable goal to all women. By loyalty to her husband, by overcoming the vices inherent to her nature, a woman can gain a vicarious share in a man's honor. The loyal wife, like the loyal slave, provides the ruling class with psychological comfort, a source of honor, and a symbolic means of coercion.

Conclusion

Nothing, it would seem, could be less like a Roman slave than a Roman matron: the one a possession, socially dead, natally alienated, without rights; the other a human being, a link between households, a medium of transmission of life and property, a citizen with well-defined (if limited) rights. There is a clear hierarchy: wives rule slaves. However, in the Tales of Loyalty, whose purpose is to maintain the master in *his* place in the hierarchy, the differences between slaves and wives are submerged in their similarities. Both are seen solely in relation to the master, emphasizing their dependence and obedience to him.[39] The parallelism is implicitly and explicitly marked not only in a series of shared motifs but in the specific *topos* of the wife acting as or offering to become one of her husband's slaves.

Slaves and wives are conceptually united. Because Roman men defined themselves negatively – not a woman, not a slave, not a child, not a beast – there is a tendency for these negatives to merge. Slaves are bestialized, infantilized, effeminized; women are likened to beasts, children, and slaves. Most importantly, slaves and wives share the feature of liminality. They are both intimate strangers. Slaves and wives are members of the family, intimate, sometimes loved, always necessary. They are in daily and physical contact with their masters. Yet they are the Other; they come from outside. Lacking any tie by blood and nature to their new household, they remain potentially dangerous. They are given to the vices of laziness, lust, drunkenness, and disloyalty. They are capable of the most heinous crimes: betrayal, adultery, murder. To balance the tales of horror, the Romans devised the Tales of Loyalty. In these, slaves and wives enact the same *topoi*, show the same desire to prove their loyalty by overcoming their vices, even to the point of death. These tales calm the masters' fears, bring them honor, and serve as an ideological weapon. The legends of loyal slaves and loyal wives are a fund of stories that Roman men told each other so that they could sleep at night, surrounded by those they most trusted and most feared.

Notes

1 Throughout Roman comedy, clever slaves, with their potentially disruptive behavior, act only under the orders and from love of their young masters (Segal 1987, 164–9; Parker 1989). For the popularity of *exemplum* literature, see Appian, *Civil War* 4.16. See also Bramble 1982, 610; Klotz 1909 and 1942; Helms 1939; Maslakov 1984; Bloomer 1992. There is a tendency to think of "*exempla*" as confined to "rhetoric." In fact, they penetrate the whole of Latin literature and life.

2 See Burke 1978, 149–77: "A culture's heroes, villains and fools form a system . . . they reveal the standards of that culture by surpassing them, threatening them and falling short of them respectively." Burke employs the analysis of Klapp 1962.

3 A further example is Cassius Dio's remarkable tale of Tanusia, wife of Titus Vinius, who hides her husband and with the help of Octavia and a faithful freedman, Philopoemen, produces him out of a chest in the theater before Octavian (47.7.4–5): a stunning bit of mime. Dio tells the story to illustrate Octavian's clemency. Appian tells the tale to illustrate the loyalty of the freedman, here called Philemon, without the wife or Augustus or the theater (4.44).

4 *Exempla* thus constitute a "field" in Victor Turner's analysis: "abstract cultural domains where paradigms are formulated, established, and come into conflict" (1974, 17).

5 The tales are not confined to these periods. The figures of the Loyal Slave and the Loyal Wife persist from the beginnings of Roman literature (for example, the plays of Plautus) and are still showing up in 359 CE (Ammianus Marcellinus 19.9).

6 In the analysis, the groups of stories and sources are arranged chronologically.

7 A running theme of Syme 1939, esp. 154–6, and Barton 1993. The masters and husbands in the various tales that follow are confined to the elite, usually senatorial,

170

class. The narratives of the proscriptions emphasize the dishonor not only of those who survived by shameful methods but of those who died as well.

8 For *familia* as the fundamental unit of society, see Cicero, *On Duties* 1.54. For the differences between "family" and *familia*, and the danger (as well as the legitimacy) of speaking of *the* Roman family, see Rawson 1986, esp. 7; Bradley 1991, 162–5; Dixon 1992, 7–9 and 22–3; Saller 1994, 74–101, esp. 74–6 and 82.

9 Ulpian, *Digest* 30.16.195.2. So too in everyday usage; see Saller 1994, 76–9 (contra Dixon 1992, 2).

10 See Cowie 1978 and the succinct statement by Arthur 1973, 24. The anthropological idea of the exchange of women (first articulated by Lévi-Strauss 1949/1969) has had a profound effect on feminist anthropology (Rubin 1975; Lerner 1986, 46–9; Strathern 1988; Joplin 1991, 40–2). It has had little impact on Roman studies, where exchange is viewed narrowly in terms of "politics." Dixon (1992, 42–3) rightly draws attention to the suspicion which arises from the exchange of women but explains their marginality primarily in economic terms.

11 Livy 1.9; see also Ovid, *Art of Love* 1.101–34; Hemker 1985; Stehle 1989; Brown 1995.

12 The most obvious and important external sign of this is the fact that she keeps her father's gentilic name (Pomeroy 1975, 152, 165; 1976, 225–6; Hallett 1984, 67; Saller 1994, 79–80). On the importance of the difference between *familia* and *domus*, see Saller 1994, 74–101, esp. 76–7.

13 On the role of "discipline and punishment," see Saller 1994, 133–53.

14 Patterson 1982, 77–91, 93–4. Paternalism in American slavery is a running theme of Genovese 1976, esp. 3–7, 88–93, 118–23, 142–7.

15 These fears of vice and disloyalty are an ancient *topos* (Homer, *Odyssey* 15.20–3; Hesiod, *Works and Days* 695–705, *Theogony* 590–612) and a frequent topic in what has come to be called "Mediterranean anthropology." See the brilliant analysis of Giovannini 1981 and her critical survey of 1987. The classic statements are Peristiany 1965; Schneider 1971; Davis 1977; Pitt-Rivers 1977, esp. 126–71.

16 The title of Winter's article (Middleton and Winter 1963), "The Enemy Within," neatly sums up the problem. See Gluckman 1956, 98; Middleton and Winter 1963, 14–17, 86–7, 278, 287–8; Epstein 1967, 135–54, esp. 150; Harper 1969; Marwick 1970, 252–63 (esp. 261), 280–1; Rosaldo 1974, 32–4. See also Giovannini 1981.

17 In Tacitus, *Annals* 14.60.4, the majority of Octavia's slave women are loyal, although a few are forced to make false confession under torture; he includes the story of the retort but gives no name. Suetonius, *Nero* 35.2 says that all maintained she was innocent under torture. The differing versions show their differing rhetorical purposes.

18 The law is also interested in the case of slaves helping with their masters' suicides: *Digest* 29.5.1.22 provides that the slaves who do not prevent it are to be punished with death, which lends a possibly different motive – from the slaves' point of view – for their own subsequent suicides (see below).

19 Cf. Valerius Maximus 6.8.2. Seneca's story of the slave doctor who kept his master from suicide for Caesar's ultimate clemency (*Benefits* 3.24.1) is the rule-proving exception: under the guise of disobedience, he saved the master and so performed the master's true wish.

20 Seneca, *Letters* 4.4; *Digest* 14.2.2.5; Bradley 1994a, 111–12.

21 So a large retinue of slaves is frequently blamed as ostentatious and luxurious, for example, Apuleius, *Apology* 17; Pliny, *Natural History* 33.6; Seneca, *Letters* 47.2–3.

22 Pliny, indeed, seems terribly concerned about the danger posed by slaves. Cf. his speculation that his friend Metilius Crispus was murdered on the road by his slaves (6.25) or the account of the case of Afranius Dexter who may have been murdered by his freedmen and slaves (8.14).

23 The technique is similar to that used by Plautus in the great figure of Tyndareus in *The Captives*. Tyndareus is a slave who acts loyally and heroically. In a time of war, when Roman citizens are actually being enslaved by the enemy, he reassures the audience of the loyalty of their slaves, even when they are free from compulsion, even unto death. Yet this action breaks down the distinction between slave and free, between the *ingenium servile* and the *ingenium liberale*. The comic solution, that Tyndareus acts like a son because he is a son, resolves the contradiction while still upholding the opposition.

24 In Turner's analysis, such tales are a device for engendering *communitas*. Masters and slaves are stripped of their status, suffer together, reverse social roles, but the end result of this liminal state is reintegration and restoration of the hierarchy (see Turner 1974, 38–45).

25 Yet this story of reward is followed immediately by the warning about the freedman of Haterius who betrayed him, got too uppity, and was made a slave again (Appian, *Civil War* 4.29). The *controversia* reported by the Elder Seneca is an interesting case (7.6): slaves are encouraged by a tyrant to kill their masters and rape their mistresses. Only one slave refuses and keeps his master's daughter safe. The master rewards him not merely with manumission but with his daughter. Occasional recognition that the slave's action was good and perhaps deserving of freedom (11, 12, 15, 19) is swallowed up in a storm of indignation at the marriage. Here we can note the theme of the single loyal slave, but also the arguments that he was motivated only by fear or hope of reward (14–15). His action is acknowledged as good – for a slave (10), but even so Latro refuses to call it a *beneficium* (13): "It is not a benefit to abstain from a crime."

26 Cf. Hallett 1984, 226. So Appian provides a series of stories of disloyal sons (*Civil War* 4.18) and wives (4.23–4); the treachery of slaves and freedmen is too common to be singled out. Interestingly, all the stories about brothers are of loyalty.

27 The implication is not merely that the slaves' acts were remarkable but that "goodwill" is not in the makeup of the slave by nature.

28 Again, the rhetorical ends sought determine the stories told. Valerius lists his under the heading "Conjugal Love." Plutarch, *Brutus* 53.4–7 (citing Valerius and the philosopher Nicolaus) tells how she was guarded by friends to prevent her suicide but nevertheless managed to kill herself. He seems reluctant to accept as genuine a letter from Brutus himself, which told that Porcia had already committed suicide rather than endure an illness, because it runs counter to the *exemplum*. See Hallett 1984, 224–5 and 1989, 63.

29 For example Appian, *Civil War* 4.15; Pliny 1.12; Suetonius, *Augustus* 53.

30 Note too how the story, specifying misuse of keys (symbolizing control over the house), is made to reflect the fears embodied in the laws of Romulus (quoted above).

31 The connection with theories of conception and social hierarchy from Aristotle onward and the role of woman as *materia* for man is obvious (Parker 1992, 110 n. 32 for a bibliography and citations); cf. Myerowitz 1985, 104–28.

32 Edited by Durry (1950), Wistrand (1976), and Flach (1991); see also Horsfall 1983. A useful translation in Lefkowitz and Fant 1992, 135–9.

33 See Parker 1997 for the first theme; Syme 1939, 154–6; Brunt 1988, 281–350; and Barton 1993 for the second.

34 Valerius Maximus 8.3. Hortensia is exempted for her connection to her father, but even here it seems she is more a stick to beat the men of the family than a model for emulation; Hallett 1989.

35 Treggiari 1991, 237–8, 243–9. A convenient selection in Lefkowitz and Fant 1992, 16–20.

36 A fact which he takes great pains to deny and point out.

37 So Cicero, *Roscius Amerinus* 147 for a splendid example. This is the running subject of Hallett 1984; see also Hallett 1989.

38 For Cornelia: Plutarch, *Tiberius Gracchus* 1.2–4 and *Gaius Gracchus* 4, 19; Appian, *Civil War* 1.20; Cicero, *Brutus* 211; Quintilian, 1.1.6; Valerius Maximus 4.4.1.

39 The stories ignore the other relations of wives. Even children are mentioned only in the case of the wife of Aruntius; in the generational sagas of Arria, Arria the Younger, and Fannia; and in the case of Antistia Pollitta, her father, and grand-mother (even here the defining relationship is to the dead husband, Rubellius Plautus). Julia's death by miscarriage is likewise a demonstration.

Acknowledgments

I wish to acknowledge the support of the Semple Fund of the Department of Classics of the University of Cincinnati. My thanks are also due to the editors, Sandra Joshel and Sheila Murnaghan, for extraordinary help and engagement with this paper. Only space has prevented me from following up many of their ideas and suggestions.

11

SERVITIUM AMORIS:
AMOR SERVITII

Kathleen McCarthy

Roman love elegy collectively constitutes a story of loss, but not a story of resignation. The surviving elegies of Propertius, Tibullus, and Ovid take as their central organizing viewpoint the experience of a young man deeply, disastrously in love with a woman who is either uninterested in or incapable of the kind of faithfulness he seeks from her. The elegiac poet's world is permeated with a melancholy longing for that perfect oneness with the beloved that is always just beyond his reach. This perfect oneness may have existed in the past or may in the future, but the present is an existence of strife, longing, and complaint. And yet, although the elegists may explicitly admit that their mistresses are unworthy of love bestowed on them, they never give up the attempt to win them over, to prove themselves victorious in the erotic contest of wills. In this tangled web of desire and disappointment, one of the most prominent images is the servitude of love (*servitium amoris*). The poets of this genre describe their situation of endless wanting and endless striving by writing themselves into the poems as the slaves of their beloveds. The poet-lover does not imagine himself as a slave in order to renounce his claims on the beloved, but both to express his dissatisfaction and to attempt to overcome the beloved's resistance.[1]

Within the narrow range of recounting the vicissitudes he meets in pursuit of a coldly indifferent woman, the elegiac poet depicts the ever-shifting relations of domination that define his world, the world of an elite Roman man in the late first century BCE and early years of the first century CE. Although all elite men enjoyed a privileged position in two of the most obvious hierarchies (male/female and free/slave), many other bases of status, such as wealth, inherited political prominence, and the cultural prestige attributed to old Roman families (versus those in other Italian towns or in the provinces), served to differentiate within the group of elite men. Elegy plays with these hierarchies that shape the relationships between men and women, between masters and slaves, and among elite men. When the elegiac poet depicts himself in the thrall of his mistress, and therefore alienated from respectable men, he sets himself on the powerless side of all three of these hierarchies. And yet, this powerlessness is not unalloyed: the overwhelming effect of this poetry is the exalted, almost heroic, position of the poet, through whose eyes the reader sees these tableaux.

Neither the suffering lover nor the triumphant poet alone reflects the position of the real author; it is the author's stake in both of these identities that promotes elegy's "male project of selfhood."[2] This poetry reflects the elegist's attempt to stake out a place for himself in the complex hierarchies that shape Roman life, in keeping with the traditional competition for status within the oligarchy. Because slaves and women represent socially excluded persons, in contrast to whom the elite male establishes his own identity and authority, they can be objectified (that is, emptied of their own subjectivity) and used as instruments to express the selfhood of the author. This use of the socially subordinate as Other has already been established for the female characters of elegy, especially in the work of Maria Wyke. In this essay, I would like to concentrate on the ways that the slave and the woman in elegy illuminate both the powers and the vulnerabilities that the elegists felt in their social relations with peers, inferiors, and superiors.

An expression of *servitium amoris* from Ovid will illustrate the symbiosis of authority and submission in this genre.[3] This poem (*Amores* I.3) begins with the lover expressing subordination to the goddess of love and having to accept what she chooses to impose on him: an asymmetric love affair in which he is utterly compelled to love his mistress, while she merely allows herself to be loved (lines 1–4). The next section describes the "servile" selflessness and renunciation that is packaged up in the image of the lover as slave, but also yokes this humility with grandiose claims about the power of the poet.

> accipe, per longos tibi qui deserviat annos;
> > accipe, qui pura norit amare fide.
> si me non veterum commendant magna parentum
> > nomina, si nostri sanguinis auctor eques,
> nec meus innumeris renovatur campus aratris,
> > temperat et sumptus parcus uterque parens,
> at Phoebus comitesque novem vitisque repertor
> > hac faciunt et me qui tibi donat Amor
> et nulli cessura fides, sine crimine mores,
> > nudaque simplicitas pupureusque pudor.
>
> > > (5–14)

Have for your own one who will devote himself to you throughout the years, one who knows how to love with sacred constancy. If I have no illustrious names of ancient ancestors to recommend me to you, if it was just second-class gentry who fathered our stock, and my land is tilled by a less-than-infinite number of plows, and both my frugal parents count their pennies, still Phoebus and his nine companions and the inventor of the vine are on my side, and also Love who gives me to you as a gift, and a constancy that will yield to none, blameless character, open candor and blushing modesty.

Here Ovid claims that the favor shown him by Apollo, the Muses, Dionysus, and Amor more than compensate for his lack of worldly status: through poetry and servile humility he proposes to construct this inverted heroism of love. But it is at the end of this poem that this heroism truly aggrandizes itself.

> te mihi materiem felicem in carmina praebe:
>   provenient causa carmina digna sua.
> carmine nomen habent exterrita cornibus Io
>   et quam fluminea lusit adulter ave
> quaeque super pontum simulato vecta iuvenco
>   virginea tenuit cornua vara manu.
> nos quoque per totum pariter cantabimur orbem
>   iunctaque semper erunt nomina nostra tuis.
>
> (19–26)

Offer yourself to me as rich inspiration for my poetry: the poems that result will be worthy of their source. Io, frightened by the horns she saw on her head, is famous in poetry, as is the girl whom the adulterer deceived in the guise of a swan, and the one who, as she was carried over the sea by a make-believe bull, held the curving horns in her virginal hand. We too will be recited all over the world, and my name will always be joined with yours.

Ovid makes it abundantly clear that the goal of this poetry is neither a *cri de coeur* nor the real conquest of a real beloved, but his own fame as a triumphant craftsman of fiction. The implicit comparison of himself to Jupiter (Curran 1966, 48–9) offers a clever allegorical statement for Ovid's view of himself as poet: just as Jupiter was able to rape women through disguising himself as an animal (and so put the women off-guard; who ever would worry about being raped by a swan?), Ovid's disguise as an unassuming slave, whose only desire is to devote himself to his *domina* (mistress), accomplishes pretty much the same thing (cf. Olstein 1975, 245–6). Like the victims of Jupiter's lust, Corinna will win her place in literary history, a place made possible by a power greater than herself.

In its movement from the humility of the slave to the poet's proud confidence in his own immortality, this poem forces our attention on the irony implicit in elegy: while the fictive lover renounces his claim to any effective expression of his own desire, the poetry itself is understood to be the validated self-expression of the poet. Although Ovid (characteristically) constructs his poem to lay bare this irony, this same irony is implicit in the other poets as well and can be further illustrated, for example, through the famous lines from Propertius' opening poem:

fortiter et ferrum saevos patiemur et ignis,
   sit modo libertas quae velit ira loqui.
(I.1.27–8)

Bravely will I bear steel and raging fire, just so I may have the freedom
to speak what anger bids.[4]

Propertius claims (paradoxically) that he is willing to suffer servile punishments
in order to be freed from his present servitude to his mistress and, in particular,
to have restored to him an important mark of his freeborn status, the freedom
to speak from the heart, not to rein in his speech to please a mistress.[5] The
almost magical effect that Propertius has managed in these lines, and in his
corpus as a whole, is to speak what anger bids (to speak his own subjective view
of the woman he has created) while making it seem that he is under constraint.
The poetry itself is the author's assertion of his *libertas* (freedom), even though
its content seems to be a chronicle of his *servitium* (servitude). But the irony
extends further: while the lover claims to be silenced and yet "speaks" to us
through the text itself, we are told that the mistress enjoys untrammeled
autonomy, yet she never speaks for herself.

If we focus on the story of the love affair and let ourselves forget the text
through which we get access to this story, we will see the lover as silenced and
humiliated, while the mistress revels in her power. If, on the other hand, we
take a step back and consider the medium through which this story is transmitted to us, then we will realize that we have only the poet's point of view,
and the mistress comes to look like a beautiful mannequin. Although it is
tempting to stabilize these contradictions by designating one level (the fictional
or the metafictional) as more important or more authentic, I think a more thorough reading of elegy will result if we resist that temptation. The "lover" (who
suffers *servitium*) and the "poet" (who declares his *libertas*) share the first-person
voice, the "Ego" of this poetry.[6]

In emphasizing the author's stake in both of these figures, and in choosing
not to privilege one or the other as a more authentic expression of the real
author's voice, I am trying to reconcile the contributions of two influential views
of elegy. One view sees the lover and the pain he expresses as the primary focus
of the poetry; although almost no one today would argue that these poems give
a reliable account of some real love affair (*pace* Veyne 1988), some scholars
believe that the lover's sense of discontent, his rebellion from mainstream values,
and his idealized devotion to love offer an index to the author's feelings about
his marginalized place in the world (for example Griffin 1985; Hallett 1973;
Lyne 1978; Stahl 1985). The other view focuses on the poet and his masterful
control of the fictive world, seeing his love-pangs as invented either to amuse
himself (Veyne) or to exalt himself and the power of his poetic art (Wyke 1987,
1988, 1994a; Kennedy 1993; Sharrock 1991). On the political level, this second
view sees the elegist as like other elite men (in his desire and ability to control

women), rather than as an outsider rebelling against them. Rather than assuming either that the author is marginalized or that he has complete control, I propose to read this poetry as an *attempt to gain control*.[7]

When we take seriously both the lover and the poet, we can ask the more challenging question of why and how the author is invested in both powerlessness and control, both submission and domination, in both being objectified and being a validated subject. The very conjunction of these two personae exemplifies the genuine situation of the elegiac poets as "men in the middle": men who were privileged with respect to the vast majority of the Roman populace, but who nevertheless felt keenly their relative humility with respect to the wealthy and politically powerful men of the elite's inner circle.[8] Thus it should come as no surprise that the poetic output of such men makes use of their control over their subordinates (slaves and women) to frame a case for respect from their superiors.

However, the exact mechanism of this use of subordinates against superiors is far more complex than we might have predicted. I will argue here that the real practice of objectifying slaves and women creates in the minds of elite men images of these "outsiders" that are powerful for their very opaqueness. We may doubt whether real slaves and women would agree with this perception of their "advantages", but to the elite man, so conscious of the need to establish both his mastery and his masculinity by constant display of the correct behaviors, being objectified seems to offer both a vacation from this vigilance and a chance to achieve control in more round-about ways.[9] In his campaign for respect from other elite men, the elegist constructs a dynamic fictional situation through which, by constantly shifting his closeness to and distance from the fictional characters depicted, he can use as weapons both his own authority and the subversive potential he perceives in his subordinates.[10] Recognizing that masters fear becoming dependent on their slaves, the author imagines a slave's elaborate show of deference having the power to reduce the mistress's independence. Recognizing that it is the combination of autonomy and inscrutability that makes a rebellious woman seem threatening, the author creates a mistress who never explains or excuses herself to her lover, and uses this mistress as a vehicle for his own rebellion. By identifying with the slave in his role as lover, and by using the mistress to characterize his poetic voice, the author gains the "advantages" he sees in these objectified figures, but also maintains his mastery and masculinity by asserting his control over them.

"Your humble servant"

A passage from Ovid's didactic *Art of Love* will illustrate the advantages and disadvantages the author seeks to maximize and minimize, respectively, when he depicts the Ego as a powerless slave. At *Art of Love* II.339–72 the didactic narrator begins by recommending absence as a way to make the heart grow fonder, using mythological exempla such as Penelope and Ulysses. He then goes on to recount how Helen made use of Menelaus' absence, a story which clearly preaches the advisability of presence over absence (see especially 357–8). The trick that the lover should learn, then, is to have enough presence to remain in the forefront of the woman's mind, but without becoming so familiar as to be taken for granted. In these lines (which precede the mythological exempla), it becomes clear that it is by repeatedly adopting and abandoning the selfless devotion of the slave that the Ego tries to bring off this trick:

> fac tibi consuescat: nihil assuetudine maius,
>   quam tu dum capias, taedia nulla fuge.
> te semper videat, tibi semper praebeat aures,
>   exhibeat vultus noxque diesque tuos.
> cum tibi maior erit fiducia, posse requiri,
>   cum procul absenti cura futurus eris,
> da requiem: requietus ager bene credita reddit,
>   terraque caelestes arida sorbet aquas.
>
>   (II. 345–52)

See to it that she grows accustomed to you; nothing is greater than constant attendance; to which end, avoid no trivial tasks. Let her always see you, let her always hear you, let night and day show her your face. When you are quite sure that you will be asked for, when you are in her thoughts even while she's away, then give her a rest: the fallow field gives better return on what has been entrusted to it; the earth when dry soaks up the heaven-sent rain.

In being like a slave (giving up his right to absent himself), the lover gains closeness, trust, familiarity. Thus the slave embodies an ability to disarm others' resistance, to conquer almost from within; this is not the power of coercion or even of seduction, but the power that comes from allowing oneself to become objectified, to be thought of as a nobody. But any control achieved in this underhanded way involves being taken for granted: he can only maintain her trust if he refrains from expressing his own desires. This kind of control will never be satisfying because only her open acceptance of his authority will confer on him the external mark of an authoritative man. Therefore, the *Art of Love* elaborates on the advantages of making oneself look like a slave, only to argue that this pretence must always be followed by an assertion of one's "true" independence, the marker of both mastery and masculinity. As often in this parodic handbook, the didactic narrator's advice describes the textual practice of the poets of elegy.

The poets of elegy take on and then abandon the personae of slaves in relation to their fickle mistresses because, counter-intuitive as this may seem, their experience as masters leads them to believe that slaves have certain powers which are denied to themselves. In texts authored by Roman slaveholders, we can see that the ideological assumptions of masters result in certain internal contradictions. Chief among the contradictions I will consider here is the fact that, since masters demand that slaves appear cheerfully obedient and do not give any evidence of their own wishes and desires, it becomes very difficult for masters to read slaves' motives.[11] The result is that masters never know whether slaves are obedient because they accept the masters' absolute authority over them or just because they have realized that they can manipulate the system of rewards and punishments by apparent compliance. Thus, slaves stand in masters' minds as figures who can achieve their own desires precisely by seeming not to have any.

The inscrutability of obedient slaves takes on even greater importance when we realize that slaves often act as surrogates for their masters. The logic of surrogacy requires instruments that are as efficacious as possible; yet, especially when the power of these instruments consists in going where the principal cannot go and doing what s/he cannot do, the more powerful these instruments become, the more obviously they threaten either to escape control or to supplant the principal. The author's use of slaves in elegy is an attempt to exploit the surrogate's potential powers, while neither wholly assuming the surrogate's selflessness, nor wholly admitting that such powers are possible. This accounts for the fact that while the servility of the lover is proposed as the solution to the hard-hearted mistress, the conquest is never achieved but continually deferred.

In general, our evidence for the ideology of Roman masters shows that they were caught in a recurrent paradox. Although it may seem that slavery operates only by de-humanizing slaves, a slave is useful precisely because he or she has the human attributes of knowledge, judgment, reasoning. By acknowledging (in practice, if not in theory) slaves' subjectivity, masters can use slaves for tasks that require these mental and social capabilities, such as skilled clerical work, financial administration, or business negotiations (on the variety of work performed by slaves see Bradley 1994a, 57–80; Finley 1980, 81). Furthermore, if masters act on the premise that slaves maintain their subjectivity, they can motivate slaves to serve the master's interests by means of offers to their own interest, most obviously manumission, but also other privileges or compensation (Bradley 1994a, 158–65). Therefore masters can make slaves both more useful and more tractable by exploiting slave subjectivity, even if the openly-used ideology of mastery goes as far as possible towards reducing this subjectivity to a minimum.

Thus, although acknowledging slave subjectivity may seem superficially to confound masters' interests rather than support them, the practice of mastery can be aimed less at erasing the slave's subjectivity than at harnessing it for the master's advantage. The anthropologist Igor Kopytoff emphasizes that the slave's place cannot be reduced to that of either a unique, validated subject or that of a fungible, commodified object: the slave is defined by his/her position as the crossing point of subjectivity and objectification.[12] This formulation would not hold for all slave societies, but it does describe well what Finley has called "the ambiguity inherent in slavery" in the ancient world, the tension between the human and non-human aspects of the slave (Finley 1980, 97).[13]

That the slave was simultaneously a subject and an object was, in fact, central to the way Romans conceived of slavery, as can be seen in the definition of a slave as "a speaking tool" (*instrumentum vocale*: Varro, *Rural Life* I.17). If Roman masters (implicitly) treated slaves as subjects while continuing to describe them as objects, this does not necessarily imply that they felt any pangs of conscience at their enslavement of fellow-human beings (Finley 1980, 99), but it does make the task of mastery a very delicate project, one that could never be explicitly codified but existed only in practice. Therefore, although we cannot find this difficulty expressed explicitly in master-class sources, we might expect to find traces of it in the way the practice of mastery is praised or criticized.

The discourse of mastery at Rome constantly harps on those sad figures who, thinking they are in full control of their armies of slaves, degenerate, in fact, to mere appendages of their powerful slaves who do everything and make all the decisions. This form of "bad mastery" not only includes masters who are tricked or cheated by their slaves, as is the hypothetical master in Cicero (*Verrine Orations* 2.3.50) who allows a smooth-talking slave overseer (*vilicus*) to permanently ruin the value of the estate, for the sake of large temporary profits (most of which the slave himself pockets). There are others who, like the mistress Ovid imagines in the *Art of Love*, are almost imperceptibly robbed of their authority, falling prey to obedient slaves: for example, Trimalchio's former masters who let him become "master of the house" (Petronius, *Satyricon* 76), or those masters who, the elder Pliny tells us (*Natural History* 29.19), lost any ability to secure their own health because of their reliance on slave doctors.

One instance of this topos is particularly striking: in his *Letters to Lucilius* (27.5–8) the first-century CE Stoic philosopher Seneca describes Calvisius Sabinus, a man whose reliance on slaves is so complete that he cannot even think for himself. He has bought slaves and has had them trained to memorize poetry so that he can be cultured while having nothing in his head.[14] This is an extreme caricature of the more general Roman anxiety about slaves: by taking it to the extreme of slaves usurping even the mental function of their master, Seneca makes the point about the need for masterly vigilance against becoming dependent on slaves,[15] but also provides his reader with the comforting impression that good masters, those who do not go to such extremes, are insulated from the horrifying spectacle that the life of Calvisius Sabinus represents. In fact, Seneca has managed to distance this example even further from the ideal elite reader by implying that Sabinus is actually servile himself, since his fabulous wealth was inherited from a freedman (27.5: *et patrimonium habebat libertini et inge-nium*). The boldness of this characterization draws our attention to the consistent, though illogical, strategy of this story: Seneca denies the very possibility of "real" masters being reduced to parasites of their own slaves by labeling this parasitical behavior servile, even though the content of the story shows very clearly that mastery itself, with its emphasis on the leisure of masters and the instrumentality of slaves, is the very root of the problem.[16]

The lover-as-slave in elegy thus employs to his advantage a vision of slaves already present in the anxieties of Roman masters: a vision of the slave as someone who undermines, rather than assaults, who achieves control by a show of obedience and selflessness rather than by claiming authority outright. Thus the lover of elegy can deflect attention from his motives, under the cover of servile objectification, while the poet of elegy maintains an ironic distance from the degraded slave, and signals his control of the fictive situation by never allowing the slave's underhanded attempt to succeed. The overall effect is the author's skill at exploiting both the imagined strategy of the objectified and the strategy of the authoritative.

This view of the lover-as-slave metaphor is corroborated by a pair of poems in which we see the elegiac poet, in his own persona as elite man, interacting with a slave character.[17] In Ovid's *Amores* I.11 the lover wheedles and charms Nape, the slave woman who dresses Corinna's hair and who carries messages between the lovers.[18]

> Colligere incertos et in ordine ponere crines
>   docta neque ancillas inter habenda Nape
> inque ministeriis furtivae cognita noctis
>   utilis et dandis ingeniosa notis,
> saepe venire ad me dubitantem hortata Corinnam,
>   saepe laboranti fida reperta mihi,
> accipe et ad dominam peraratas mane tabellas
>   perfer et obstantes sedula pelle moras.
>
> (I.11.1–8)

> Expert at gathering together and ordering unkempt hair and not to be counted among slave-women, Nape, proven[19] in the services of night-time rendezvous, useful, too, and clever at carrying messages, you who have often ordered Corinna to come to me when she hesitated and who have often been found faithful to me in my troubles, take these tablets I inscribed this morning and bring them to your mistress and assiduously dismiss those delays that stand in my way.

The lover's deference to Nape foregrounds the ironies of an elite man being dependent on a slave. The conceit of this poem is that Nape can bring about what the speaker himself would not be able to, even were he admitted to Corinna's bedroom. Because she is a slave, whose own self-interest will be discounted, she can speak the very words the lover might speak, but much more effectively. The letter itself cannot compel Corinna's reply: without Nape's insistence that Corinna write back, the message would merely fall without effect

– all it can do is present the lover's words, it cannot compel Corinna to answer them (or even to read them). This poem, in the tensions it displays between wanting the instruments to be almost magically effective and wanting them to be controllable, eloquently expresses the dilemma of surrogacy. When the Ego imagines himself as a slave, then, he grants to himself all the positive opportunities offered by this dilemma, rather than the pitfalls the dilemma presents to masters.

But it is significant that the next poem in Ovid's collection (*Amores* I.12) forcefully retracts this potential for persuasive slave messengers: there we learn that Corinna has remained unconvinced by the message and the messenger.[20]

> Flete meos casus: tristes rediere tabellae;
> infelix hodie littera posse negat.
>
> (1–2)

> Bewail my misfortune: the tablets have come back dreary indeed; the cursed letter says "not today."

In this second poem, the Ego declares his independence by claiming it was madness to trust slaves and writing tablets to carry out important business (lines 21–2). The first poem of this pair saw in Nape and the tablets the powers of speech, especially the powers of performative speech (ordering). The second poem sees her as a body, clumsy with drink (5–6), and the tablets as merely wax and wood (9–20). Neither of these one-sided representations is truer than the other: slaves are both bodies and potentially persuasive speakers; tablets are both physical entities and the means of communication. The conjunction of these two poems shows the dual nature of the instruments through which the speaker tries to exert his will in the world: each poem is an exaggerated emphasis on one side of this nature or the other; together they show the continual flux of belief in which masters find themselves with respect to slaves.

These two poems also reveal the specifically literary stakes of the use of slaves as surrogates. In the first poem (*Amores*. I.11), the female slave messenger is assimilated to the message itself. Not only do the epithets used for her echo qualities of Ovid's writing (*docta* [2], *utilis et dandis ingeniosa notis* [4]; see Henderson 1991, 77), but her very function echoes the function of writing: persuasively to convey his thoughts to Corinna and to bring about the desired effect. Furthermore, the poem ends with the speaker's confident assertion that he will dedicate to Venus the tablets that will have brought him such success, using for the tablets language that unmistakably identifies them with the slave-woman: "faithful handmaids" (*fidas ministras* [27]). Thus one could reasonably associate his hopes for the success of his writing with his hopes for the slave woman's success in the fictive situation he has designed.

What, then, should we think about the powers attributed to his writing when the slave woman dismally fails at her task? The second poem (*Amores*. I.12) is mostly taken up with a curse against the tablets, in terms that almost personify them.[21] The important point of this second poem is that it separates out the poet's transcendant art from both of the material instruments which might seem to affect its success: writing and slaves. At the fictional level, the lover's inability to achieve what he wants through a slave "proves" that the surrogate is not more powerful than the principal. At the metafictional level, the fact that the poet appeals directly to us the readers ("I never should have entrusted my *Amores* to those tablets" [21–2]) implies that his voice (and subjectivity) transcend the material carriers of his words, that he can speak directly to us without the intervention of wood and wax. Thus, these poems sum up the inconsistent attitude towards instruments that I have argued is fundamental to the elegist's strategy: both writing and slaves are acknowledged to have power as surrogates, but in the end the poet asserts his independence of them.

As a female slave, Nape also prefigures the role of the elegiac mistress that I will explore in the next section: she is an instrument that is useful to the poet precisely because she escapes the control of the fictive lover. Even Corinna, Ovid's wayward mistress who has only the most shadowy presence in these two poems, can give us a clue as to the textual role of women in this genre. She is logically necessary to the scheme that these poems set out, since she is the object of desire and the frustrator of that desire, but almost no energy is expended in describing her or her behavior; instead, as I have shown above, the instruments with which the lover attempts to win her over occupy center stage. All we know is that Ovid wants her to read what he wrote and to write back a single word "Come!" (I.11.24). Instead she writes back a rather wordy letter "stuffed with naysaying" (*negaturis cera referta notis*; I.12.9). Both her refusal and the long-winded way she expresses it indicate that she is not controlled by the speaker, nor by his instruments.[22] We could even say that in her autonomy and her control of both the slave messenger and the message, Corinna achieves what the Ego wants: full and untroubled use of the instruments of slaves and writing. After all, it is her slave woman who was set up as the instrument of the lover's conquest: Corinna apparently is impervious to the undermining strategy of slaves. Further, unlike the Ego's written tablet that was unable to bring about what he wanted, her message does exactly what she intends, puts him off and shows that she is not at his beck and call.

Corinna's power to resist the Ego's attempts has (at least) two functions. Because the master-poet wants to believe that, in the end, instruments are never as powerful as those who wield them, this poetry continually re-asserts the primacy of masters by denying the efficacy of slaves. At this level, we could say that she represents masters in general. But, because the mistress "is constituted in the elegiac text as a means to define the uniqueness of her male narrator as both lover and poet" (Wyke 1994a, 111), her ability to shake off the slave's attempts to control her redounds not to her own benefit but to the benefit of her creator, the poet. Specifically, this powerful woman represents the unapologetic authority with which he hopes to endow his own poetry.

The mistress and the elegiac self

quicquid ero, dicam "Cynthia causa fuit."
(Propertius, I. 11.26)

Whatever I am, I will say, "Cynthia was the reason."

If the Ego of Roman love elegy is a speaking subject telling us about his own objectification, the mistress is in the converse situation, having subjectivity attributed to her, even while she is objectified: we see her through the poet's eyes as willful and autonomous, but never hear her own voice.[23] Her silence acts in two complementary ways. On the one hand, she never explains herself to the lover, and this proud indifference puts him into a position of submission, and it also makes her inscrutable, an embodiment of the indefinable femininity which is both powerfully attractive and threatening.[24] On the other hand, because she never speaks for herself we are constantly reminded of the poet's control over her, she becomes a vehicle for the poet's own voice.[25] By constructing her as an uncontrollable force and also showing his control over her, the elegist writes the mistress in a way that declares his own rebellious selfhood.

While I agree with the accepted view that the elegiac poets compare themselves favorably to those men who devote their lives to war, money, and politics, I would not agree with either of the two usual ways of seeing this contrast: either that the elegiac poet revels in his bohemian existence just for the shock value (Lyne 1979; Griffin 1985), or that he is subversive, questioning either the unfair hierarchies of Roman society (Hallett 1973; Gold 1993), or the oppressive regime of Augustus (Stahl 1985; Wallace-Hadrill 1985). Rather, I believe he is playing a subtle strategy in the traditional competition for standing within the elite: the elegiac poet's depiction of his mistress shows an attempt to gain two traditional markers of elite status: autonomy and "the instrumental use of a woman."[26] What is innovative about the elegists' foray into elite competition (though Catullus is a clear precursor in this respect) is the use of poetry, itself a suspect activity (Fitzgerald 1995, 48, 51 *et passim*), as a weapon. Poetry itself is the real hero of elegy; it is the means by which the author both obtains instrumental use of a woman and helps himself to the spirited rebellion she enacts.

Even though, on the face of it, the author's site of identification in the fictive situation is the Ego, and this Ego is defined in contrast to the mistress (as the victim of her faithlessness), he is also identified with her in a certain way. This identification does not arise through metaphor, as in the case of the lover-as-slave, but through metonymy. The Ego never takes on the characteristics of the hard-to-handle mistress, but his very association with her helps to characterize him. This relation of metonymy crystallizes in the idea that the mistress and the poetry are two sides of a single entity: she is an eroticized personification of the poetry, and the poetry is a literary textualization of her (Wyke 1987, 1989; Sharrock

1991; Keith 1994). This relationship is famously illustrated in the doubleness of "Cynthia", the name of the mistress and of the book of poetry.[27] Thus, although the Ego is never actually represented *as* either the mistress or the poetry, he is consistently represented *by* the mistress and the poetry.

The more shocking, rebellious, and uncontrollable Cynthia is, the more all these attributes apply to *Cynthia* , the poet's creation; this uncontainable woman, indifferent to the judgments of others, betokens an uncontainable poetic voice. Her most salient characteristic is her autonomy: she may sometimes be very loving and tender and at other times heartless and greedy, but the poetry tells us over and over again that what pains the Ego is the fact that she refuses to abide by the pact he thinks he has made with her. She takes the gifts (jewels, money, poetry, devotion) of all her lovers, but will not grant in return the expected loyalty. In other words, she disturbs the honorable understanding of reciprocity on which Roman society depends, both among equals (*amicitia*) and between those of unequal status (*clientela*).[28] She opts out of the "gentlemen's agreements" that ordered relationships in Roman society, and thereby shows that one needs only audacity to take what is given but decline the implications. And yet, because the Ego is so obviously her victim (and therefore aligned against her as well as with her), the author can distance himself from the taste-less social heresies the mistress commits.[29]

These qualities of the mistress characterize the stance of elegy towards other, more "respectable" poetic genres and towards the whole world of male civic life against which it defines itself. Like the mistress, the genre of elegy is conscious of its bad reputation, the fact that it has utterly alienated itself from its betters by refusing to accept the more usual values.[30] The lover endlessly complains that she should have a care for her reputation, but she is massively indifferent. Like the mistress who continues on her course despite the lover's hand-wringing over her reputation, elegy itself does not try to argue against the scale of values on which it is being judged, but it also does not change to suit them (for example Ovid, *Amores* II. 4. 1–4).[31]

Elegy's depiction of the struggles of the main character against the wider community of his peers, a community that is imagined as scoffing at his unpro-ductive devotion to a life of love and poetry, draws our attention to the fact that elite men must struggle to secure their own status in the oligarchy.[32] This poetry is the author's attempt to transcend his potential to be subordinated to other elite men; this risk is most obvious in the case of his patron, but includes the wealthy and politically powerful in general. His lack of independence in the real world becomes a catalyst for his poetry, the means by which he will ultimately achieve not only independence, but an immortality that will put him beyond the reach of all rivals – poetic, erotic, social, political.[33] Therefore, both the elegist's control of women, showing that he is capable of obtaining instru-mental use of a woman, and the metonymic identification with the assertive qualities that woman possesses, allow the male poet to fight back against those who would reduce his autonomy without ever admitting that this danger exists.

A brief look at one poem, Tibullus I.5, will demonstrate these two functions of the objectified mistress: an instrument "proving" the author's status as elite man, and an embodiment of his own desired autonomy. Although this poem begins with Tibullus' characteristically masochistic enslavement to Delia, after asking to be tortured in order to tame his wild words, he then reminds her of all she should be bound to him by: not just the pact of their secret love (*furtivi foedera lecti* [7]) but (at great length) the many medical, magical and religious acts through which he secured her good health (9–16). He sums up with the result of this devotion:

> omnia persolui: fruitur nunc alter amore
> > et precibus felix utitur ille meis.
> > > (17–18)

> I fulfilled all these vows: now another man enjoys your love and happily reaps the profit from my prayers.

Here, then, is the tyranny of the mistress that I have suggested is central to the overall project of elegy: she takes all that the Ego can give to her and lavishes her attentions on another man.

I call attention to this theme here because it highlights by contrast the most famous section of this poem, the mad dream (*fingebam demens* [20, cf. 35]) of a happy pastoral life with Delia (19–36). In this dream, Delia performs matronly duties, such as making the proper sacrifices, and she is a loving mistress (*amantis . . . dominae* [25–6]) to a prattling slave child; here, Delia's *dominatio* (mastery) is not an offence against propriety as it usually is in Tibullus' poetry, but the control exercised by a proper *materfamilias* (mistress of the household), who rules the household but bows to her husband (cf. Johnson 1990, 103). Her role in the household is made explicit in lines 29–34, where she is pictured as being in complete control, but she also serves the visiting Messalla.

> illa regat cunctos, illi sint omnia curae,
> > at iuvet in tota me nihil esse domo.
> huc veniet Messalla meus, cui dulcia poma
> > Delia selectis detrahat arboribus;
> et tantum venerata virum hunc sedula curet,
> > huic paret atque epulas ipsa ministra gerat.

> Let her control everyone, let everything be in her management; let it please me to be nothing in the whole house. My own Messalla will come here, for him let Delia pick sweet fruit from the best trees; and, in awe of so great a man, let her pamper him, let her prepare for him banquets and herself as servant serve them.

She rules the house, but only as a proper wife does, to relieve its master of cares. Messalla's presence here foregrounds another function of the dream-Delia: to solidify Tibullus' relations to other elite men. In her, Tibullus has not just a generous hostess but also a beautiful and properly deferential servant, an unambiguous marker of his right to a place among elite men. This passage allows Tibullus to show his respect for Messalla, but also to claim his own right to respect, since his household is run by a woman so perfectly desirable in every way: her beauty, her matronly authority, and her deference to men.[34]

What the dream-Delia does for the fictive lover, the hard-hearted Delia does for the poet. Even though elsewhere she is not deferential, she is still an *objet d'art* over which men can define their masculinity and their fellowship, as they exchange knowing glances over the heads of the fictive characters. And, further, the elegiac poet gets the credit for creating this incomparable object of desire, and so establishes himself as a valued member of the masculine community that forms around her. The dream offers an instance where Delia is obedient to the lover, and so establishes his value among men; elsewhere, even though on the fictional level she scorns the lover's attempt to control her, on the metafictional level she is under the control of the poet, and so performs the same function of "proving" his masculinity and creating a bond with other men.

It is true that this dream is framed by indications that Delia would never "really" be so compliant. But, if we accept that the author defines his identity as much through his role as poet as through the figure of the lover, then the very fact that the mistress usually escapes the control of all the fictional characters highlights the autonomy he and his poetry gain through their association with her. This autonomy is emphasized in this poem by the fact that even the wealthy lover will not ultimately control her, but will be pushed out in his turn after she has taken his gifts (69–76). In a poem where the author has earlier mentioned his respectful attitude towards his patron, the implication that even wealth cannot reduce the stubborn autonomy of this high-handed *domina* can serve obliquely to declare the author's ultimate independence: though he accepts the worldly assistance of others, he does not necessarily accept the strings that may be attached to those gifts.

Elegy grows out of the atmosphere of competitive honor that prevailed among the male elite of Augustan Rome. But more than merely reacting to this atmosphere, elegy acts as a gambit in this competition. This poetry that arises from the mistress's imagined indifference and refusals becomes a monument to the poet's own subjective point of view and, even more importantly, constitutes a powerful play for the readers' assent to this subjective point of view. The seductive experience that elegy grants us is to feel what it would be like to be objectified while maintaining the voice and authority of one whose subjectivity is affirmed by others. Thus, it allows us (and the author) the illusion of being utterly sovereign, but without the work involved in maintaining this sovereignty against those above and below.

The success of the elegiac strategy involves the poet displaying his worries about his own status but only allowing these as a catalyst, a springboard to his own triumphant self-definition. If we readers look too closely at his depiction of submission, there is the danger that we will see in it, not just a necessary fiction that frames the poet's transcendant subjectivity, but the admission on the part of the poet that he really is, or could be, subordinated. Well may Ovid ask us, then, to bewail his misfortunes (*Flete meos casus* ...): only by making us feel that our own subjectivity is at stake and is redeemed by the aesthetic triumph of this poetry can the poet be assured of our uncritical acceptance of his self-presentation.[35]

The objectification of slaves and women that I have argued is central to the genre's project obviously maintains the practices and values that were accepted as normal in this culture. Furthermore, the elite man's ultimate inability or unwillingness to relinquish his right to speak for himself and to be heard with attention also testifies to the importance of his authoritative voice. In these ways, the elegiac poets act much as we might expect them to act, knowing that they are male elite Romans, who have benefited from the hierarchies that order Roman society. But to accept this as the only answer to what these authors are doing would be to close our eyes to the complexity of both elegiac poetry itself and the social position of the authors. The attraction that being objectified holds for these authors and the desire to, at least partially, live through the objectified figures of the slave and the woman reveal both an understanding of the potential resistance of subordinates and a stake in resistance on the poet's own behalf.

Notes

1 This metaphor appears in two different forms: first, in passages where it is developed systematically (for example Tibullus II.4.1–6; Propertius I.9.19–30; Ovid, *Amores* I.3.5–18), with images of torture, fear to speak openly, devoted service, etc. Second, words such as *domina* and *servitium* migrate out of specific metaphorical passages to become normal elegiac language for "girlfriend" and "affair." Murgatroyd (1981) has the fullest listing of examples of both types. Recent scholarship on elegy has recognized this paradox of submission as a means to domination, but has not explained why the metaphor of slavery should work this way: Kennedy 1993, 73; Labate 1984, 214. By contrast, earlier analyses of this metaphor (Copley 1947; Lyne 1979; Murgatroyd 1981) accepted the idea that humiliation was the fundamental meaning of the metaphor.

2 The term "male project of selfhood" is taken from Froma Zeitlin's (1996, 347) description of Greek tragedy's function. The usefulness of this notion for elegy has already been noted by Wyke (1994a).

3 I will use the following texts in my citations: for Tibullus, Postgate (1915); for Propertius, Barber (1960); for Ovid, Kenney (1994). All translations are my own.

4 On the importance of silencing oneself as evidence of one's servile deference, cf. Propertius II.18A.1–2 (*Assiduae multis odium peperere querelae: / frangitur in tacito femina saepe viro.*), Tibullus I.5.1–6. Cf. Propertius' declarations of poetic heroism and immortality, for example I.7. 21–6, but especially in the programmatic poems (II.1.71–8,

II.34B, III.1–5), what Barchiesi (1991, 3) characterizes as "Propertius' great innovation, his elevation of the poet to the status of a star in his own production."

5 Lyne (1979, 129) relishes the paradox and usefully compares Tibullus I.9.21–2; he also rightly allows that the imagery of medical treatment is also present; elsewhere in this article (125) he stresses that freedom of speech was an important mark of civic status for the Romans. Shackleton Bailey (1956, 6) asserts that the imagery of medical treatment is the primary impetus behind this line, but even here describes the sufferer as "a slave who cannot even voice his anger."

6 In using the term "Ego" to denote the speaker of the poetry, and keeping this speaker separate from the real author, I am following Veyne's terminology (1988). But while I agree with Veyne that we should not see the events reported as historically accurate, I think that he goes too far in imagining the poetry as a "game" in which we (the savvy readers) are invited by "Ego's editor" (=the poet) to share his ironic amusement at the foibles of the silly Ego. This may well be the image the authors of this genre are attempting to create; but if we allow ourselves to be seduced into this game (by the desire to show what clever readers we are), we give up our ability to question the author from a point of view other than his own.

7 Clover's (1992, 209–10) application of the Lacanian distinction between the "look" and the "gaze" offers a good analogy for the distinction between the real historical author and the character "the poet" in elegy: "The gaze . . . is the transcendental ideal – omniscient, omnipotent – which the look can never achieve but to which it ceaselessly aspires."

8 All three of the surviving elegists (all four if we count Gallus) belonged to the equestrian census class (second only to the senatorial class), and all except Tibullus came from outside Latium. Cf. Skinner 1989, 18–19 on Catullus' similar position and its role in defining the power relations in his poetry.

9 Skinner (1993, 111) emphasizes the vigilance needed to maintain one's masculine identity. She also considers the possibility that identification with the feminine may have been for ancient men "a channel for imaginative escape" (1993, 120)

10 Although the details of the process here are quite different, I have found Clover's (1992) argument about identification across gender lines very helpful in formulating this idea of "fluid identification."

11 Scott (1990, 32): "We are in danger of missing much of their significance if we see linguistic deference and gestures of subordination merely as performances extracted by power. The fact is they serve also as a barrier and a veil that the dominant find difficult or impossible to penetrate." See also (1990, 132–3).

12 Kopytoff (1986, 65): "In brief, the process has moved the slave away from the simple status of exchangeable commodity and toward that of a singular individual occupying a particular social and personal niche. But the slave usually remains a potential commodity: he or she continues to have a potential exchange value that may be realized by resale."

13 The similarity between the African slave societies studied by Kopytoff and those of the ancient Mediterranean may have to do with the personalized form of power dominant in both. Bourdieu remarks (1980, 126): "Because the pre-capitalist economy cannot count on the implacable, hidden violence of objective mechanisms which enable the dominant to limit themselves to reproduction strategies (often purely negative ones), it resorts simultaneously to forms of domination which may strike the modern observer as more brutal, more primitive, more barbarous, and at the same time as gentler, more humane, more respectful of persons." See also Scott 1990, 21.

14 27.7: *ille tamen in ea opinione erat, ut putaret se scire, quod quisquam in domo sua sciret.*

15 Elsewhere (*On the Tranquillity of the Mind* 8.8) Seneca emphasizes the dependence of slaves on the master for food, clothing, etc.

16 Patterson (1982, 334–42) on slavery as human parasitism; Joshel (1992a, 152, 158–9). Eve Kosofsky Sedgwick has argued in her study of English literature: "Only women have the power to make men less than men within this world. At the same time, to be fully a man requires having obtained instrumental use of a woman, having *risked* transformation by her" (Sedgwick, 1985, 40; emphasis in the original). Below, in my consideration of the elegiac mistress, I will pursue the implications of this formulation for the elegiac poets' definition of themselves as men, but here we can see that the same logic applies to their definition of themselves as masters.

17 Other poems with slave characters: Propertius III.6, III.15; Ovid, *Amores* I.6, II.2/3, II.7/8 (these last examples are, like I.11/12, paired poems)

18 Cf. Propertius II.23.3–4. Of course we are free to imagine that the speaker is really in control of the situation, that he has carefully gauged Nape's vulnerability to flattery and so is pulling out all the rhetorical stops as he manipulates her into doing what he wants her to do (DuQuesnay 1973, 30–1). This reading would imply that it is Nape's shallow vanity that is being exposed, rather than the lover's grovelling. This reading is absolutely defensible as far as it goes. But even if we accept it, we are left with the fact that the speaker *needs* Nape, he must have her on his side in order to get his way. So even if we think that she is shallow enough to fall for this ploy, the necessity for the ploy itself mitigates any argument that the speaker is completely in control of the situation. Further, DuQuesnay (1973, 36–7) implicitly admits that the elite man is beholden to the slave by saying that in the next poem, the reason he curses the tablets instead of her is because that allows him to maintain her goodwill for future projects (see also Davis 1977, 81).

19 Or "known" (carnally)? Cf. *Heroides* 6.43. If we accept this as a double entendre, Nape's situation comes to look like that of Cypassis in II.7 and 8, on whose plight see Henderson 1991–2.

20 Davis' (1989) third chapter, "Dropping the Mask", analyzes the Ovidian pattern of revealing the insincerity of what has preceded, focusing especially on the paired poems, such as I.11 and 12. Note that this idea of "dropping the mask" implies that the worldly voice of the second poem is the "real" Ovid, and that the naive voice of the earlier poem was just a set-up; this recreates in microcosm the overall effect of Ovid's poetry that the "poet" is in complete control.

21 The tablets are bloody, rather than blushing (11–12); and, in the final lines of the poem, the speaker ends by wishing that the tablets will be gnawed at by the decay of old age, and that the wax will grow white with disuse (29–30), making them look like one of the villains of elegy, the hag-like bawd (Davis 1977, 83, n.28)

22 This effect is strengthened when we note that in the first poem (I.11.19–22) he wavered before asking for this brief reply; he considered first the pleasures that a long full letter from Corinna would bring, but then opted in favor of reducing her writing to its most boiled-down communicative function. However, on the dangers of this imperative as an extreme example of a message that cannot secure its own reading, see Henderson 1991, 80–1.

23 When a woman speaks in elegy (for example Propertius I.3; Ovid, *Heroides*), she is never characterized as the powerful mistress, but as the helpless abandoned lover (cf. Catullus' Ariadne). Notice in the Ovid poem above that we were told that Corinna wrote a long letter, but we never get access to her words.

24 Gold (1993, 88): "[Cynthia] is – or becomes – what Propertius wants or fears for himself, and her identity in the poetry changes depending on whether she is the fulfillment of his erotic desires or the embodiment of all the traits that men fear in women (instability, fickleness, violence, inscrutability, wiliness, deception)." I agree with the second part of Gold's description ("embodiment of all the traits men fear in women"), though I question the first part since fulfillment of erotic desires plays a surprising small role in this genre. Also, I will argue that the function of this

fearsome Cynthia is to turn against other men "what Propertius . . . fears for himself."
An interesting corroboration of my interpretation of the mistress's silence comes
from Kaja Silverman's argument that one of the ways mainstream film exerts control
over female characters is consistently to align a woman's speaking voice with an
image of a woman's body: "To permit the female subject to be seen without being
heard would be to activate the hermeneutic and cultural codes which define woman
as a 'dark continent', inaccessible to definitive male interpretation" (1984, 135).

25 Wyke (1994a, 114) calls the poet's control of the mistress "discursive mastery"; see
also Sharrock 1991.

26 Sedgwick (1985, 40); the full context of this term is quoted above in note 16.

27 Slightly different uses of this doubleness are made by Veyne (1988, 3); Wyke (1989,
33–4); Gold (1993, 88–9).

28 Gibson (1995) describes the ways that the elegists position themselves towards their
mistresses as "humbler friends" do towards potential patrons, and also notes the role
of assumptions about reciprocity that shaped such patronage relations; see also White
1993, 91.

29 Oliensis (1995) describes Horace's relation to his personified book in *Letters* I.20 in
ways that strikingly parallel the elegists' relations to their textualized mistresses. An
important parallel to the argument here is that Horace both distances himself from
the book's whorish desire for public admiration, and yet "[a]s the book disobeys its
master, so Horace in the opening poem of the collection – a dedication that is also
a *recusatio* . . . – resists the desire of his patron" (222).

30 For example Propertius I.7, II.1, II.10, II.13A, II.34B, III.2, III.3, III.9; Ovid, *Amores*
I.1, I.15, II.1, II.4, II.17, II.18, III.1.

31 Furthermore, it is significant that readers seem never to have been able to fix the
social status of these women – are they freedwomen or loose-living aristocrats? are
they prostitutes or married women? Since the mistress represents the poetry, the
(intentional, I think) blurriness of her status helps to configure the poetry itself as
slipping through the usual borders of high and low genres.

32 For example Propertius I.12.1–2, II.3.1–4, II.24A, II.30B, III.11, III.19; Ovid, *Amores*
I.15.1–8, II.1.1–4, II.17.1–4; Tibullus I.1.53–8.

33 Fitzgerald (1995, Chapter 7, "The Ruse of the Victim") has recently made a similar
claim for the humiliated speaker of Catullus 10 and 11. "The poet's staging of his
persona's victimization is the means of locating the exorbitant position from which
the lyric poet speaks" (169).

34 Johnson characterizes Messalla as the "Roman male *par excellence*" (1990, 97), and
argues that Tibullus' relation to his patron is as to a "father-figure all young men
worship and resent, strive to imitate and strive to reject, love and hate" (96). My
argument is that this mix of respect and resentment is not just Tibullus' attitude
towards Messalla, but the general attitude of the elegists towards men of the inner
circle of the elite.

35 Fitzgerald on Catullus: "But doubtless it is the implication of this weakness with a
form of power that wins over readers of these poems, for the poetic power that the
poems finally exhibit is one with which the reader, as a reader of poetry, is already
implicated" (1995, 184).

Acknowledgments

I am very grateful to the editors for their thoughtful suggestions on both the sub-
stance and the form of my argument. I would also like to thank Mark Griffith,
Leslie Kurke, Deborah Shaw and Yasmin Syed, who read and commented on
various drafts.

12

REMAINING INVISIBLE

The archaeology of the excluded in Classical Athens

Ian Morris

Archaeology and the histories of gender and slavery

Where can we find the lost history of women of earlier cultures? Central
to our search is the discovery of new sources and the reevaluation of
traditional ones.

(Bridenthal and Koonz 1977, 2)

In calling their collection of essays *Becoming Visible*, Bridenthal and Koonz were
making a point about the politics of historiography. The only reason that the
history of women had seemed invisible was that historians had not thought it
worth looking for. Raboteau suggested much the same about the cultural history
of American slaves: "We should speak of the 'invisibility' of slave religion with
irony: it is the neglect of slave sources by historians which has been the main
cause of this invisibility" (Raboteau 1978, x; cf. Levine 1977, ix–xi). To Bridenthal and Koonz, the obvious response was for historians to assemble the neglected
evidence which would make visible the excluded – "baptismal certificates, hospital
and asylum records, indices of nutrition and health such as harvest and
butchering records, deeds, wills, tax registers, marriage contracts, and burial
records" (1977, 6).

Woe to the ancient historian wanting to follow the lead of the modernists,
burning to recover the lost voices of Athenian women and slaves. The hellenist's
myopia has been as acute as anyone's when it comes to seeing women in the
past (see Pomeroy 1975, xii), and as the contributions to this volume show,
scholars in the last twenty years have done much to reread the already well
known literary sources against the androcentric grain. But, with the possible
exception of epigraphy (see Saller, this volume), going into the archives and
bringing to light the obscured testimony of the oppressed is simply not an
option.

In this essay, I suggest that one response is to turn to archaeology. Feminist art historians have made extensive use of vase painting as a source for Athenian representations of gender and sexuality (for example Kampen 1996). With a few recent exceptions, such as Miller's analysis of Persians on Athenian vases (1997, 192–215), the study of images of slaves has not progressed much beyond the cataloging stage. But in this paper I consider a different kind of archaeology. Artifacts with writing or representational art make up only a tiny proportion of what we excavate, and in the 1990s, archaeologists outside the classical tradition began to make important progress in using these "mute" data as evidence for the history of gender and slavery (Conkey and Gero [1991] and Ferguson [1992, xxxiii–xlv] discuss why these developments are so recent; and Brown [1993] why they have still had little impact in classical archaeology). I suggest here that it is in the humble sherds of plain cooking ware and the scanty remains of mudbrick walls that the greatest potential lies.

But as will quickly become clear, this paper is highly speculative, more an exercise in possibilities than a set of rigorously tested hypotheses. Classical archaeologists have, on the whole, not collected and published the kinds of evidence we would need to produce a proper archaeology of slavery or gender in Athens. But interpretation and fieldwork are inseparable. Decisions about what kinds of sites to excavate and which data to collect are driven by the debates that are in the air, and that fact alone makes this exercise worthwhile.

The argument

Despite the rapid growth of feminist scholarship in archaeology in the 1990s, there is still a feeling in some quarters that gender is not a legitimate topic of inquiry because (with the exception of burials) archaeologists cannot "detect" women. This betrays a certain confusion. Scott rightly points out

> this is not so much a methodological problem as theoretical nonsense. If we cannot locate women in the past, then how can we be sure we have located men? And children? Logically, *everyone* in the past is therefore invisible – an intolerable proposition.
>
> (Scott 1997, 5)

We know that there were men and women, free and slave, in Classical Attica, and that we can therefore observe the material residues of their actions: the real methodological problem is how we can attribute gender or legal status to the agents who produced specific parts of the archaeological record. Finley summed the problem up in discussing a papyrus describing the complex arrangements involving leasing, labor, and capital for a pottery kiln:

> I merely wish to make the simple point that archaeological evidence or archaeological analysis *by itself* cannot possibly uncover the legal or

economic structure revealed by the Oxyrhynchus papyri or the alternative structures in Arezzo, Puteoli, Lezoux or North Africa. The burst of polemical rhetoric with which Carandini closes his survey of the North African ware in the final centuries of antiquity serves only to divert attention from the absence of data about the "social mode of production" of that ware, and, in my view, the impossibility of ever overcoming that gap in our knowledge from archaeological evidence alone.

(Finley 1985, 25. Emphasis in original)

Finley was quite right, but the words he emphasized – "archaeological analysis *by itself* " – are crucial. We can rarely know whether a particular room was used mainly by men or women, or by free or slaves. Conkey and Gero (1991, 11–14) have argued that archaeologists do not necessarily need to be able to attribute gender, but for many important questions, this does remain an issue (for example Costin 1996). I suggest in this paper that the Athenian literary evidence provides important indications which allow us to bypass some of the most severe problems of attribution. Our sources all agree that the mining and processing of silver in the Lavreotiki, the hilly area of southeast Attica around the town of Thorikos (Figure 12.1), was overwhelmingly carried out by imported chattel slaves (by the 340s BCE, tens of thousands of them). When we excavate silver washeries and the residences associated with them, most of the rooms we dig up, and the objects in them, were used chiefly by these slaves. Archaeologists working in slave quarters on plantations in some parts of the United States have discovered handmade pottery and simple houses which combine European, African, and native American traditions in solid material evidence of creolization or the continuity of slave lifestyles. Most of the slaves in the Lavreotiki probably came from Asia Minor and the Balkans, areas which have ceramic and housing traditions very distinct from those of Attica. The evidence is painfully inadequate, but there is currently absolutely no indication whatsoever that slaves retained any significant element of their native material cultures once they reached Attica. Even when we know we are in their presence, Athenian slaves remain archaeologically invisible.

I devote more than half of this paper to the archaeology of slavery, because so little work has been done in this area. The archaeology of gender in domestic space has already been the subject of some important essays (Walker 1983; Jameson 1990a; 1990b; Nevett 1994; 1995), so I treat it more briefly. But the issues of visibility involved are very similar to those raised by slavery. Lysias (1.9–10) and Xenophon (*Oeconomicus* 9.5) tell us that Athenian houses were divided into women's quarters (the *gynaikonitis*) and men's quarters (the *andronitis*), and a number of fourth-century orators reinforce this picture of strongly gendered domestic space. Modern historians have traced in detail how the ideology of a distinctive feminine sphere in nineteenth-century Europe and North America was buttressed by the development of equally distinctive male and female material cultures within

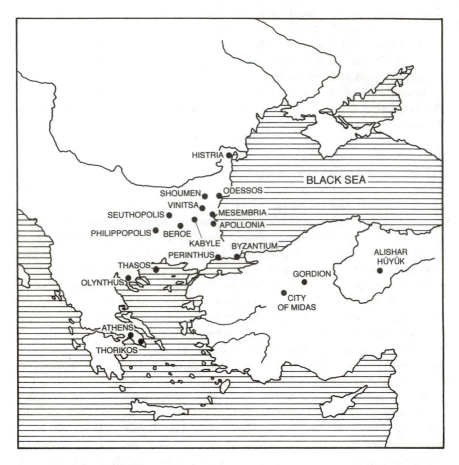

Figure 12.1 Main sites discussed in the text

bourgeois houses; and prehistorians have made plausible arguments that such developments can be observed archaeologically. Yet when we excavate Athenian houses, in spite of all the importance Athenian male writers attached to the gendering of space, we find no clear material correlates at all (although once again, the evidence leaves much to be desired).

At one level, the continuing invisibility of Athenian slaves and women, even in the places where we most expect to find them, is simply another cautionary tale, illustrating the difficulty of gender and status attribution in archaeology. But the evidence may also tell us something about the nature of male citizen dominance in Classical Athens. There is no sign of the excluded constructing alternative material cultures, and even the limited forms of resistance that may imply. As a tentative hypothesis, I suggest that the "mainstream" material culture of Athens was so pervasive because Athenian male citizen culture as a whole was unusually hegemonic, filling every corner of the conceptual landscape, allowing no space for alternatives.

The formation of identities is always a dialectical process. The antebellum white male planter's sense of who he was took shape in his daily interactions with his slaves, wife, and daughters, as well as with other white male planters. The Athenian citizen's notion of himself must have been formed in the same kinds of encounters; but the relative strength of the groups involved in these interchanges varies from case to case. In Classical Athens, I suggest, the excluded remain invisible not just because of methodological problems, but because the dominant male citizens wanted them so.

Slavery

I. A comparative case: the archaeology of American slavery

In the 1970s, historians of American slavery shifted their research toward trying to understand how slave culture functioned as a form of resistance to exploitation (see Elkins 1976, 267–93), and in the 1980s archaeologists followed suit. Their experiences suggest ways in which classical archaeologists might come to grips with the cultural dimensions of slavery.

A generation ago Ivor Noël Hume (1962) drew attention to a class of hand-built, unglazed, and low-fired pottery from late seventeenth- and eighteenth-century levels at Williamsburg. He noted that some of its shapes imitated glazed European vessels, but that the clay and technology seemed to develop out of native traditions. He concluded that these pots, which he called Colono-Indian ware, were made by native American craftsmen for sale to Europeans. But since European imports were cheap at this time, Noël Hume concluded that colonists would only have bought this native pottery to give to their African slaves.

This interesting hypothesis rapidly broke down. As often happens, once an anonymous coarse ware had been defined, excavators noticed it everywhere. By the 1970s Colono ware was known from Virginia to Florida, and particularly from South Carolina. Leland Ferguson (1980) argued that some of the Carolina Colono ware had parallels in Ghana and Nigeria, and that African slaves in the New World not only used Colono ware but also made it.

This hypothesis, too, ran into difficulties of a kind common in archaeology. For example, to take a well known classical case, if we wanted to demonstrate that in the twelfth century BCE there had been a Dorian invasion from the Balkans into Greece, we would need to identify clearly intrusive elements in the Greek material record that had equally clear predecessors in the Balkans. In practice, things are rarely so clear cut. The "Barbarian ware" of twelfth-century Greece seems not to have a single geographical point of origin, yet it is so consistent from site to site across Greece that we have to assume that it took shape in a population movement which blended a whole group of ceramic traditions, none of which encompassed the new "Barbarian ware" but all of which contributed to it (see Rutter 1990).

The situation in colonial America is similar, but on a larger scale. Slaves were imported from a vast region, stretching from Senegal to Angola, which included very varied ceramic traditions. Only some of these seem to be relevant to American Colono ware, and even then, only in limited ways. It seems, for example, that the shapes favored by potters along the Gambia river may have survived in South Carolina Colono ware, but the Gambian vases are highly decorated, while Colono ware is normally plain (Hill 1987). Nor is Colono ware uniform within America. In Virginia, it makes up no more than 5–10 percent of the ceramic assemblage at any site, and most sherds come from pots imitating European shapes. But in Florida something like 65 percent of ceramic finds are Colono ware. Some of it imitates Spanish majolica pots and olive jars, but most of it has strong links to native American traditions. In South Carolina, where Colono ware has been studied most carefully, it ranges from less than 20 percent of the assemblage at plantation houses like Utopia to nearly 90 percent in what are probably slave quarters at Yaughan and Curriboo (Ferguson 1992, 37–41, 44–55, 82–92).

Given that we are comparing enormous and internally varied regions on each side of the Atlantic, it is not surprising that few one-to-one correlations can be made (Ferguson 1992, 9–18). The varied forms of eighteenth-century Colono ware were generated by complex, regionally distinct processes of creolization (Orser 1996, 117–23). In Florida, Africans (often runaways from South Carolina) tended to live among the numerically dominant Apalachee Indians, and this mixed population probably produced most of the Colono ware for sale to Spanish soldiers (Vernon 1988; Vernon and Cordell 1993). In Virginia, the native population was greatly reduced by 1700, and most Africans lived in small groups under direct European supervision; while in South Carolina, by 1740 blacks outnumbered whites roughly two-to-one, and often lived in large groups with only minimal contact with whites (see Wood 1974). Slave houses in South Carolina also had much more in common with west African styles than did comparable houses in Virginia (Garrow and Wheaton 1985; Ferguson 1992, 55–9, 63–82).

In different areas along the Atlantic coast, Colono ware was created out of different blends of African, European, and native American traditions. Archaeologists have put such emphasis on this pottery because it was associated with cooking (Ferguson 1992, 93–107; Yentsch 1994, 196–255; Singleton 1996), which nineteenth-century reporters saw as central to slaves' sense of themselves as distinct from whites (Rawick 1972, 71–2; Genovese 1976, 540–9). Ferguson suggests that "In their foodways, the slaves of South Carolina were not surrounded by an everyday symbolic environment that reinforced and explained their position in a hierarchy . . . the building of an African-American culture, different in kind from that of Southern whites, maintained an unconscious resistance to slavery and the plantation system" (Ferguson 1991, 37), what he calls "struggling with pots."

The archaeology of American slavery is a new field, and much remains unclear about Colono ware. But all the same, the work of the last ten years suggests new ways to think about the archaeology of Greek slavery. When we can examine the artifacts against a textual record that tells us that certain areas were demographically dominated by slaves, as in South Carolina, we can side-step some of the problems of attribution. We cannot say that a specific hut belonged to a slave or that a particular pot was made by a European, but we can say that certain kinds of assemblage appear in regions or sites where we know that slaves predominated. We might even be able to say, as Ferguson does, that the character of these assemblages tells us something about the extent to which slaves constructed cultural worlds which stood apart from those of the master class. Other interpretations are certainly possible, as the debate over Colono ware has shown. But the first step is to draw attention to the potential significance of such evidence.

II. Slaves in the Lavreotiki

I turn now to Attica and the one region where we can confidently assert that there was an extraordinary concentration of imported chattel slaves: the silver-mining area of Lavreotiki.

Cupellation of silver is attested at Thorikos as early as the ninth century BCE (Bingen 1967, 38–42), but large-scale extraction only began late in the sixth century (see particularly Spitaels 1978, 39–89; Mussche 1990, 17–24, 36–8). The town of Thorikos expanded rapidly, and southeastern Attica is honeycombed with a network of fifth- and fourth-century mining facilities (Ardaillon 1893 and Conophagos 1980 are the main accounts). By this time, rights to mineral resources were owned collectively by the polis, and at least by 424 (Aristophanes, Knights 362) mines were leased by individuals, to be worked for their own profit. We know little about the mines in the early fifth century apart from the story of the great silver strike of 483 (Herodotus, Histories 7.144), but according to Xenophon (Ways and Means 4.14–15), Nicias and other rich men rented out gangs of hundreds of slaves to work in the silver mines, presumably in the 430s and 420s. Mining probably declined after 404, but revived after 370, reaching its peak around 340. A series of mid- and late-fourth century inscriptions recording state leases of mining rights survives (Crosby 1950; Hopper 1953).

Athenian writers take it for granted that the laborers in the mines would be slaves, because such work was banausic. Mining country was the wild west of Attica, and needed special laws forbidding lease holders from cutting into each others' mines, smoking out rivals' shafts, or making armed attacks on another man's mine (Demosthenes 37.35–6). Any involvement in mining could be turned against a man, as a sign that he lacked the true values of the citizen (Demosthenes 21.167; the implication at 23.146 is less clear). Only one speaker ever admits to personally working a silver vein, telling a jury that "Formerly I made a lot of money from working the silver mines, laboring myself, from the pains of my own body; I confess it" ([Demosthenes] 42.20). He presents his labors as somewhat shameful, but presumably raises the issue as part of his strategy of creating an image of himself as a humble, hard-working man to throw into sharp relief his portrait of his enemy Phainippus as a man who grows fat by selling the surplus from his suspiciously large estates at inflated prices. Given these attitudes, it may be that more of the smaller mine lessors dug out silver with their own hands (either alone or alongside slaves) than the literary sources would lead us to believe. But this does not alter the most important point, that the vast majority of mine workers were slaves. In 355, Xenophon simply took it for granted (*Ways and Means* 4.14–15, 23–5) that an expansion of the mines would call for lots of slaves – maybe up to 10,000 to be provided by the state – and the inscriptions from the Lavreotiki regularly refer to slaves (Gauthier 1976, 273–5; Lauffer 1979, 122–40).

The individual groups of slaves at work in the mines were probably quite small. The largest mentioned in the literary sources is thirty slaves (*andrapoda*) in a single *ergasterion* in Maroneia (Demosthenes 37.4). Demosthenes (37.22) goes on to say that this lease cost 1.5 talents (that is, 9,000 drachmas, in a period when a skilled wage-laborer might expect to earn one drachma per day). Of the seventy-six lease prices to survive in the fourth-century mining inscriptions, thirty are for 150 drachmas and twenty-two for just 20 drachmas. Crosby (1950, 202) suggested that 20 drachmas was the standard price for a new (and therefore risky) mine cutting, and 150 drachmas the norm for leasing an old mine, with the higher prices in Demosthenes (as well as the 1.5 talents at 37.22, we hear of three talents – 18,000 drachmas – for three mines [42.3]; and a loan of 2,000 drachmas for "some" mines [40.52]) representing particularly productive veins. She concluded that these properties consisted of just a single mine shaft, often in association with a washery (1950, 194, 202).

If Crosby's argument is correct, the mine with thirty slaves was probably unusually large. However, archaeological evidence shows that mines and washeries could occur in large clusters. Several fourth-century washeries were found together at Souriza (Conophagos 1980) and Agrileza (Jones 1984/85), and probably several dozen early fifth-century examples nearby in the Bertseko valley (Kakavoyiannis 1989). Thorikos was a town of hundreds of people by 350, with washeries and other mining facilities mixed among the houses (Mussche 1975, 48–54). We do not know how many of its inhabitants were slaves, but their numbers must have been substantial. The evidence is sketchy, but Lauffer's judicious review (1979, 140–71) points to something like 25,000 slaves in the mines around 420, and maybe 35,000 around 340. Whatever margin of error we allow – even if we were to cut Lauffer's figures by 50 percent – we cannot avoid the conclusion that the majority of the people in the Lavreotiki were slaves. Osborne (1987, 79) concludes that "The presence of the mines and the miners entirely reshaped the local community whose lands were being exploited." This region was as different from the rest of Attica as was South Carolina from Virginia.

200

III. Origins of the Attic mine slaves

Identifying the slaves' geographical origins is crucial, but once again the evidence is problematic. Slave owners often gave their chattels new names, and many of the recorded slave names seem to be ethnic designations. Reconstructing the slave trade from such allusive information is of course risky. A passage in Varro (*On the Latin Language* 8.21) says that Romans might name a slave according to where they bought the slave, not where the slave originally came from. In the Attic Stelai, set up some time between 415 and 413 BCE (Pritchett 1956, 276–86; 1961), thirteen of the thirty-two slave names with ethnic implications are Thracian, seven Carian, and most of the rest scattered over Asia Minor and the Balkans (Figure 12.2). Lauffer (1979, 123–32) lists 104 names from inscriptions in the Lavreotiki, most of them dating to the fourth century. Thirty-three of

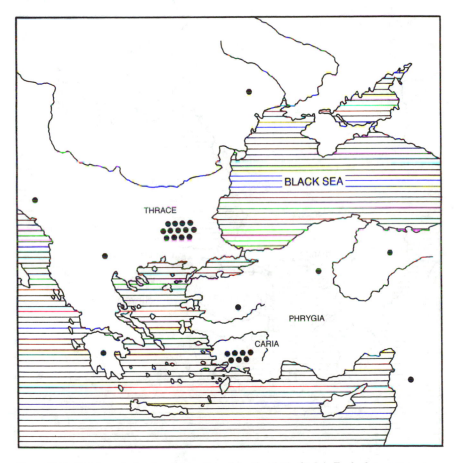

Figure 12.2 Origins of the slaves mentioned in the Attic Stelai. Each dot represents the point of origin of one slave

these names have ethnic associations: nine are Phrygian, six Paphlagonian, and two each Thracian, Semitic, Thasian, and perhaps Iranian. Most of the rest, as in the Attic Stelai, come from Asia Minor and the Black Sea coasts (Figure 12.3). The overwhelming impression created by the ancient literary sources is also that the main supply areas were the regions around the Black Sea (Velkov 1964; Finley 1981, 168–73). Herodotus (5.6) particularly noted the Thracians' willingness to sell even their own children into slavery, and Xenophon (*Anabasis* 7) refers several times in his account his adventures in Thrace in 399 to the activities of slave traders from Byzantium. Around 150 BCE, Polybius (*Histories* 4.38) commented that the areas around the Black Sea still "provide both cattle and slaves in the greatest quantities and of the highest quality," and that Byzantium had grown rich by serving as a market for the Greeks.

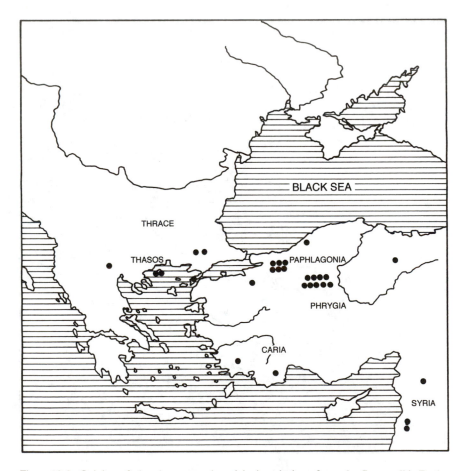

Figure 12.3 Origins of the slaves mentioned in inscriptions from the Lavreotiki. Each dot represents the point of origin of one slave

IV. Slave material culture

The mine slaves, then, came from a large geographical area. This included a great variety of material cultures, which complicates analysis enormously, as Americanists have discovered. But in Greece there is a still more serious problem, which is that cooking wares and other plain pottery from mining sites have rarely been published in detail. It is quite possible that Anatolian or Balkan influences have simply been overlooked, and that more detailed study of this material may change the picture radically.

The account I offer here can only be provisional. But even in the face of such fragmentary evidence, I believe that we are in a position to formulate initial hypotheses for further analysis, chiefly because the pottery and housing traditions of the regions from which most slaves probably came are highly distinctive. The time pressures of salvage excavation may prevent careful study of handmade or plain wheelmade pottery, but some washeries have benefited from more controlled excavation (for example Conophagos 1980; Jones 1984/85), particularly in Thorikos (Mussche 1965, 93–6; 1967, 61–71; 1969, 121–30; Mussche and Conophagos 1973; Spitaels 1978, 65–107). Overall, these finds seem typical of those from contemporary settlements in other parts of Attica (for example, Jones *et al.* 1962; 1973; Stavropoullos 1938; Young 1951). And if we turn from pottery to housing, the absence of connections with the Balkans or Anatolia is much harder to put down to the excavators' lack of attention. It is possible that if slaves lived in flimsy huts of the kinds typical in the Balkans excavators expecting only to find substantial stone foundations and cement floors might have missed them; but overall that does not seem like a very convincing explanation of the silence.

In the interests of space, I restrict myself to the two categories of pottery and housing. I also limit my description to Phrygia and Thrace, the two regions best represented in the ethnic origins of slave names illustrated in Figures 12.2 and 12.3.

Pottery

PHRYGIA

The Late Phrygian style is known particularly well from settlement finds in the City of Midas at Yazilikaya (Haspels 1951, 43–85) and Alishar Hüyük (Schmidt 1933, 40–53; von der Osten 1937, 19–88). A little imported East Greek and Attic pottery turned up on these sites, but the vast majority of finds were local, wheelmade gray monochrome wares. Haspels (1951, 85) suggests that "despite everything, [the ceramic tradition] guarded its Anatolian character; Anatolian from the beginning, during its independence the heir of the Hittite empire, it turned back there in the final period, under Persian domination" (von der Osten [1937, 88] draws similar conclusions).

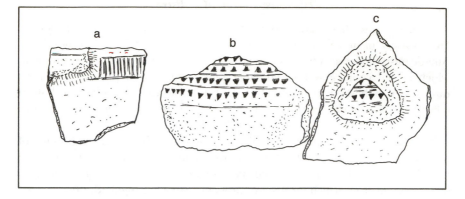

Figure 12.4 Fragments of Late Phrygian handmade pottery from the city of Midas (after Haspels 1951)

The construction of Late Phrygian pots is distinctive. They are simply made, with the handles attached poorly. Figure 12.4 shows several examples; and 12.4c illustrates another typical Late Phrygian practice: attaching the handles after applying impressed decoration to the surface of the vase. There are imprints from fingers and wooden tools on many vessels. Most pots are plain, but the surface treatment is very different from what we find in Greece. There were four main techniques: wet-smoothing with the hand; burnishing with a pebble; applying a slip after firing; and adding a mica surface.

Flat-bottomed wide bowls were particularly common at all these sites. A few vases could also be directly linked with beer-drinking, having a spout and a strainer to catch impurities. Xenophon (*Anabasis* 4.5.26–7) noted this practice in 399, and at Gordion a late eighth-century beer-drinking set has been identified, with strong similarities to Old Assyrian beer sets from eastern Anatolia a millennium earlier (Sams 1977; 1994, 74–6).

THRACE

Wheelmade pottery only became common in Thrace in the sixth century, but in the fifth it was the typical indigenous fineware. This tradition may have been influenced by Aeolian gray bucchero in the Archaic period, but developed in new ways in Classical times. By 450, potters had introduced a faster wheel and began to imitate Greek shapes more closely. In the late fifth- and early fourth-century cemetery at Ravna, wheelmade gray pots outnumbered handmade (57 percent to 43 percent), and Greek shapes were common (Ljubenova 1984). The hellenization of Thracian pottery accelerated in the fourth century, particularly after the Macedonian conquest in the 340s. Imported Greek finewares were already quite common in the medium-sized settlement at Shoumen in the fifth century; in the fourth, imported Attic Black Glaze and Thasian wine amphoras were in use even in the small village of Vinitsa (Hoddinott 1981, 106–10; Archibald 1983).

Thracian wheelmade finewares are most readily distinguishable from Attic by their fabrics, and if Thracian slaves in the Lavreotiki were making such vessels out of local Attic clay, these pots might look very like plain Attic pottery. But on Thracian settlements throughout the fifth and fourth centuries, gray handmade pottery formed a much larger part of the overall assemblage than wheelmade wares (Cicikova 1963). Most importantly, handmade wares dominated cooking and storage. Their shapes were more conservative than those in the wheelmade repertoire, and changed little between the sixth and late fourth century BCE, although in Hellenistic times there were rapid developments, and handmade wares virtually disappeared from southern Thrace by 200 (Dimitrova and Gizdova 1974). Greek styles had little influence on handmade wares. The settlement finds consist mainly of crude conical cups, biconical jugs, and mugs (Figure 12.5). The fabric is very coarse, with large grit and mica inclusions. The commonest decoration is attached relief bands marked with finger impressions, or incised swastikas and spirals. By 400, the vessel shapes were very standardized (Cicikova 1977).

Housing

PHRYGIA

Fifth- and fourth-century Phrygian settlements are characterized by dense clusters of small rectilinear rooms, with mudbrick walls on low foundations of fieldstones. In the City of Midas (Figure 12.6) many rooms contained semi-circular hearths or ovens, and in two cases a gray pot containing the bones of a sheep or goat had been built into a wall (Haspels 1951, 16–18; Gabriel 1952). At Alishar Hüyük the excavators disagreed on dating, but the clearest area (Mound C, level 1) was rather similar, with clusters of small mudbrick rooms separated by narrow corridors (Figure 12.7). No information was recorded on roof materials, which suggests that they were made of thatch, wood, or clay.

THRACE

Xenophon (*Anabasis* 7.4) describes fighting in Thracian villages near Perinthus in 399. His comments on the settlements are vague, but are certainly consistent with the remains of small villages found at Vinitsa, Brestak, and Devnja. Vinitsa was a fourth-century hamlet of twenty or twenty-five one-roomed rectangular wattle-and-daub huts. The roofs would have been pitched and made of thatch. The huts ranged from 3 × 3 m to 4.5 × 4.5 m, and most were "Halberdhütten," in which the floor level inside the hut had been dug out some 30–90 cm deeper than the ground level outside, to give more headroom. Most huts had a small internal hearth in or near one corner, and an oven built against an outside wall,

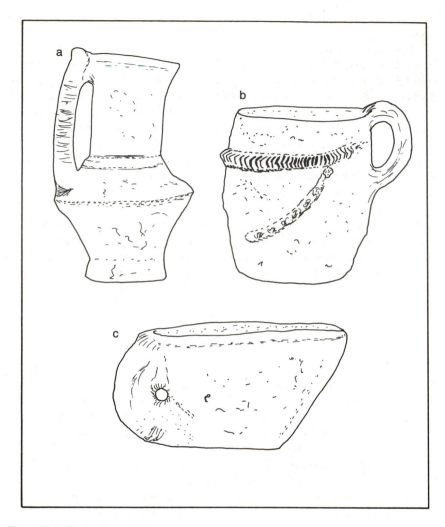

Figure 12.5 Sixth- through fourth-century BCE handmade vessels from Thrace (after Cicikova 1977)

often under a simple lean-to. There were numerous round pits, some for garbage, but most for grain storage. These villages would have had 100–200 inhabitants (sites described in Milcev 1980, 349–52; Hoddinott 1981, 110–11). There were also some bigger and longer-lived sites, such as Shoumen, which was partly protected by double stone walls; and recent work at Adjiyskaya Vodenitsa has revealed houses built from monumental stone blocks (Archibald 1994, 456–7). This site was bigger than Shoumen, and may have been a princely seat within the Odrysian kingdom.

Figure 12.6 Late Phrygian house plans from the City of Midas (after Haspels 1951)

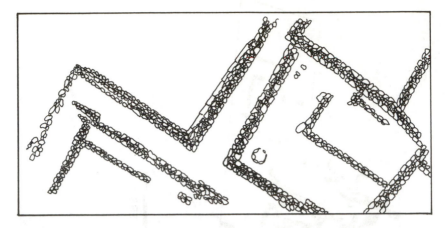

Figure 12.7 House remains from Alishar Hüyük, Mound C, level 1 (after Schmidt 1933)

There had been Greek cities on the Black Sea coast at Apollonia, Mesembria, Odessos, and Histria since Archaic times, but most Thracians went on living in tiny villages. As with the handmade pottery, it was only in Hellenistic times that traditional ways changed significantly. Philip II founded cities at Beroe, Kabyle, and Philippopolis in 342/1, and Aegean-style urban life began to penetrate Thrace. Late in the fourth century, the Thracian rebel Seuthes established Seuthopolis. This small town was filled with very Greek-looking large courtyard houses, but they were organized around a distinctively Thracian palace complex. The houses had mudbrick walls on low stone foundations, faced with plaster on lath, and tile roofs (Dimitrov and Cicikova 1978). In the third and second centuries, the kind of villages Xenophon had seen became less common.

V. Material culture in the Lavreotiki

The houses in which Thracians and Phrygians would have lived before being sold to Greeks were very different from those which have been excavated in the Lavreotiki. The houses of fourth-century Thorikos were multi-roomed, rectilinear structures, with mudbrick walls on stone socles and tile roofs, grouped in rectangular insulae (Figure 12.8). They have much in common with the grand structures of Hellenistic Seuthopolis, but not with the humble dwellings of Vinitsa. The basic technology (mudbrick upper walls on stone foundations) also resembles Alishar Hüyük, but their regular planning around courtyards and the use of tile roofs do not. The Thorikos houses belong to a wider tradition of Classical Greek housing (for which see Hoepfner and Schwandner 1986), and seem to owe nothing to Phrygia or Thrace.

Several of the excavated silver washeries had substantial courtyard houses attached to them, which presumably (since no other facilities have been found)

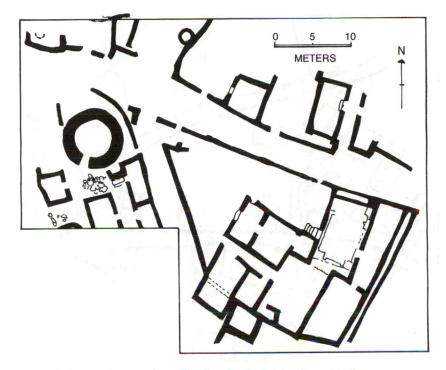

Figure 12.8 Classical houses from Thorikos Insula 3 (after Jones 1975)

housed the slaves. In a recently excavated example near Thorikos, a kitchen and bathroom could be identified, as well as an *andron*, presumably so that the mine lessors should not be denied the kind of lifestyle they would have enjoyed back in Athens while they were present at their mines (Second Ephoreia 1991). Areas of these houses were given over to the processing of silver, but in most ways their spatial organization is typical of fourth-century houses elsewhere in Attica (Figure 12.9).

There is, however, one unusual feature in the architecture of the Lavreotiki, which is shared by washeries, the town of Thorikos, and rural farmsteads alike. This is the presence of towers (J. H. Young 1956; Lohmann 1993, 138–61). Xenophon (*Anabasis* 7.2) says that he visited Scuthes in a tower in Thrace in 399, but towers are not prominent in the Thracian archaeological record. There may also have been a fortification tower on Alishar Hüyük Mound A in Late Phrygian times (Schmidt 1933, 12; von der Osten 1937, 1–2), though this might in fact have been built much earlier. And while we do not know exactly what Greek towers were for, Demosthenes (47.56) has a story that in one house a group of female slaves lived in a room in a tower. Towers were thus known in Thrace and Phrygia, and while they are found in many parts of Greece (Nowicka 1975), they are particularly concentrated in the Lavreotiki, Thasos, and Siphnos,

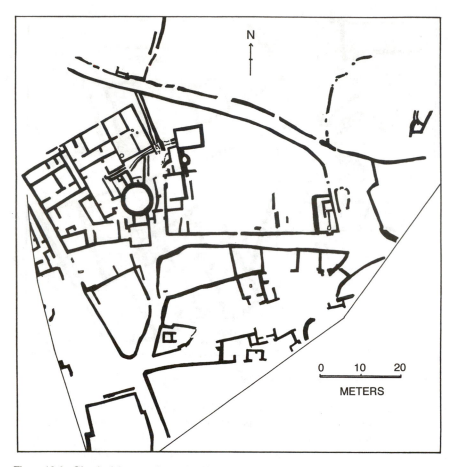

Figure 12.9 Classical houses from the Kalamboka property, Alai Aixonides (after Andreou 1994)

all areas associated with mining and therefore slavery. If anything in the architecture of the Lavreotiki can be connected with the slaves' homelands, it is these towers, but the link is not compelling. Towers are not a major feature of the archaeological record of either Phrygia or Thrace, and the most plausible hypothesis is that the towers of the Greek mining districts are purely local functional adaptations by the free citizens to the problems of living surrounded by a potentially hostile population.

VI. Discussion

The slaves of the Lavreotiki lived very differently from those in most other parts of Greece. Most obviously, they were involved in mining rather than in agriculture, domestic service, or petty commodity production. It is also likely that they were overwhelmingly male; their life expectancy in captivity may have been short, and manumission unusual. Given these peculiarities, it is unwise to extrapolate from the Lavreotiki to the lives of slaves in other parts of Greece. A serious gender imbalance among mining slaves might explain some of the peculiarities of the archaeological record. If women had been primarily responsible for cooking, pottery manufacture, or house building, it would hardly be surprising that these traditions would abruptly disappear among large groups of men sold into slavery. Alternatively, regardless of the gendered division of labor, the conditions of the mine workers may simply have been so brutal that there was no possibility of them maintaining their native customs, as Elkins (1976, 81–139) argued of American slavery, in his notorious theory of the formation of the "Sambo" personality type.

Whatever the causes, though, on current evidence it seems that in the one case in which we know we are excavating the homes of slaves, the material cultures of their homelands seem to have disappeared completely. This, I believe, is important. Certainly other things may have mattered more to Thracians and Phrygian than the kinds of pots they used or the houses they lived in. In the antebellum South, folk songs (Levine 1977) and religion (Genovese 1976; Raboteau 1978) clearly mattered a lot more to slaves than did Colono ware, for all its associations with cooking. But when we are dealing with ancient Greece, the archaeological record, for all its imperfections, is the only evidence we have for slave culture and identity. And what it seems to indicate is that the material culture of the Athenian master class was unusually pervasive.

The material world of fourth-century Athenian mining slaves was very different from that of eighteenth-century American plantation slaves, particularly those in South Carolina, and the one American archaeological case that does resemble the Athenian situation only heightens the contrast. Excavations on coastal plantations in Georgia have produced almost nothing that can be linked with Africa. However, these sites date after 1800, by which time the proportion of American slaves actually born in Africa had fallen to 25 percent or less (Figure 12.10). Slavery was changing rapidly in these years, and Colono ware died out everywhere, being replaced by cheap mass-produced pots made primarily for white tastes (Fairbanks 1984). In Attica the outcome was the same – the absence of pottery made in the slaves' native traditions – but the background was very different. While we have no figures on rates of slave imports into Attica, given the demographic structure of the Lavreotiki slaves and the hard conditions in the mines, it is very likely that there would have been steady imports from overseas throughout the Classical period. Athenian slaves seem to have abandoned their native ways more abruptly than those in early modern North America.

Gender

Aristotle (*Politics* 1252b5–9) drew a sharp distinction between Greeks and the benighted barbarians, who believed that women and slaves held the same rank.

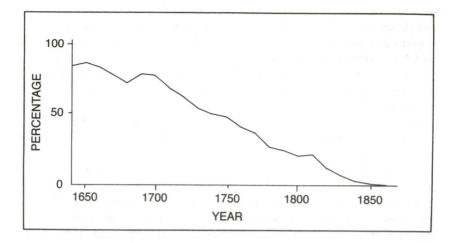

Figure 12.10 African-born blacks as a proportion of all blacks within the United
States, 1640–1860 (after Fogel 1989)

Yet the archaeological evidence for the gendering of domestic space in Athens
has much in common with that for distinctions between free and slave.

Male Athenian writers drew extremely strong gender distinctions, and repeatedly
asserted that domestic space was strongly gendered. Once again, comparative
studies reveal some of the analytical possibilities of such a situation. In her study of
furniture in modern France, Leora Auslander (1996, 277–305) was able to document the material dimensions of the emergence of distinct male and female spheres
in nineteenth-century bourgeois society. The home as a whole was increasingly
defined as a feminine space, which women were to organize in their new role as the
consumers of fashion; but within the house certain areas were more feminine and
private than others. Furniture and wall decoration emphasized this. "Masculine"
sitting and dining rooms should send messages about wealth and social position,
ideally through a combination of Louis XIV furniture and sober, heavy, and
modern decoration. "Feminine" apartments and bedrooms should say more about
a woman's age and coloring than her public standing, with a preference for delicate
Louis XVI furniture and eighteenth-century draperies. In another suggestive study,
Vickery (1993) has traced rather different developments in eighteenth-century England through a case study of a single Lancashire consumer, Mrs Shackleton.

Historical archaeologists have had some success in applying similar categories
of analysis (see Samson 1990; Parker Pearson and Richard 1994a, 1994b; Johnson
1993; 1996). Charles Redman (1986) has shown how the Portuguese take-over of
Qsar es-Seghir in Morocco in 1458 was swiftly followed by the transformation
of the values associated with rooms. While Arabs had occupied the town, houses
tended to have a strict public/private boundary associated with strong gender
distinctions. In the late fifteenth century, although the Portuguese did not normally

alter the house plans, these boundaries became much more permeable. Redman relied on rich textual documentation and material features which could be easily and reliably gendered; Gilchrist (1994) went still further in sidestepping the problems of gender attribution by focusing on medieval English nunneries. Knowing that the particular religious sites she studied were rigidly gendered either male or female, Gilchrist was able to show that male and female spaces were fundamentally different.

I. Lysias and Xenophon on male and female space

Lysias (1.9) and Xenophon (*Oeconomicus* 9.5) distinguish clearly between the *gynaikonitis* and the *andronitis* in the houses they describe. They use the words slightly differently. Xenophon's *gynaikonitis* and *andronitis* are both on the ground floor, separated by a bolted door, with female slaves restricted to the former and male to the latter; and his wife needs to be introduced by him to the *gynaikonitis*. The *andronitis* in Lysias is downstairs and his *gynaikonitis* upstairs, and until she gave birth Euphiletus' wife apparently normally slept in the *gynaikonitis* with a female slave. But both authors take the distinction for granted.

In an important and highly original paper, Susan Walker (1983) divided the plans of several excavated classical Greek houses along the lines suggested by Lysias and Xenophon, between public, male areas and zones of female seclusion (Figure 12.11). But any rigid division between male and female space faces obvious problems. Lysias (1.9–10) himself comments that this strict division broke down when Euphiletus' wife became a mother, since she had to keep coming downstairs to wash the baby. Soon Euphiletus abandoned the plan altogether and swapped bedrooms with his wife.

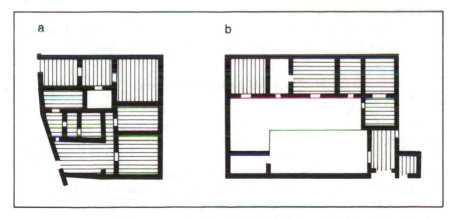

Figure 12.11 Susan Walker's division of space along gender lines (a) in a house from the North slope of the Areopagus in Athens and (b) in the Dema farmhouse. Vertical shading represents male space and horizontal shading female space (after Walker 1983)

Walker takes Lysias and Xenophon too literally. Lysias was engaged in constructing a viable persona for Euphiletus, who was at pains to present himself as a perfectly reasonable Athenian citizen. He said that he kept his wife under close watch at first, but after the child was born he had relaxed his control, since she was such an excellent housewife. It was at this point that the outsider Eratosthenes struck into his household, poisoning his wife's mind (1.6–8). The arrangement of *gynaikonitis* and *andronitis* expressed the citizen's world at its ordered best; the corruption introduced by Eratosthenes literally turned that world upside down. Under such circumstances Euphiletus could hardly be blamed, either for marrying such a wife (since she had originally seemed so fine) or for killing Eratosthenes, who had wrought such damage, committing a crime which all constitutions in Greece punished with the death penalty (1.2).

Xenophon was involved in a rather different but equally complex effort. He explicitly presented Ischomachus as a model of the best way for a man to live, having Socrates tell Critoboulus that Ischomachus "seemed to me to be among those men who quite justly (*diakaios*) are given the name 'gentleman' (*kaloskagathos*)" (*Oeconomicus* 6.12). After setting up Ischomachus as an ideal man, Socrates had him explain the best way to run a farm, choose an overseer, and train a wife. Foucault (1985, 152–65) and Johnstone (1994) show in detail how the *Oeconomicus* functions as a prescriptive text, setting out an ethical code for upper-class gentlemen.

Lysias' and Xenophon's *pre*scriptive models may also be good *de*scriptive models of what most Athenians actually did, but given the aims of the authors, it would be rash simply to assume this. There is indeed abundant testimony that Athenian women not only associated with men on a regular basis within houses, but also traveled between houses, sharing knowledge about comings and goings in their neighborhoods (Cohen 1991b, 84–90, 148–70). Walker's rigid spatial analysis is an important first step, but overlooks the generic constraints of the literary sources. Her gender attributions rest heavily on uncritical analogies with Nigerian houses, without much regard for the Greek data.

II. The archaeological remains

But that is hardly surprising. If most Athenians lived in houses like the one Euphiletus describes, we would never be able to observe a *gynaikonitis*, because the second floor never survives. And even if Ischomachus' model were normal, we would have severe problems, since very few excavated rooms have good evidence for functions. The one exception is the *andron* or dining room (literally "men's room"), which has distinctive architectural features – walls lined with an odd number of couches, an off-center door, and a tendency toward relatively elaborate floor decoration. We can see *andrones* in many (though by no means all) Classical Athenian houses (Figure 12.12).

The literary sources consistently associate women with cooking and weaving, so the positions of facilities for these activities might be useful (though neither

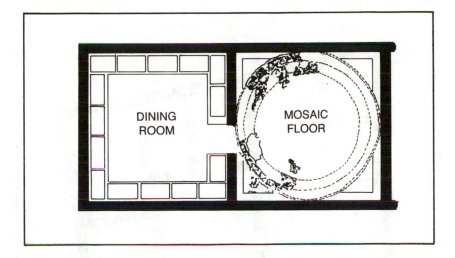

Figure 12.12 The *andron* from a partially excavated fourth-century house at 9 Menandrou Street, Athens (after *Archailogikon Deltion* 22:2 [1967] 98–100; 30:2 [1975] 24–7)

Lysias nor Xenophon associate the kitchen with the *gynaikonitis*). But even in the best-preserved Athenian houses, the evidence is ambiguous. I take just two examples. In the fifth-century phase of Agora House C (Figure 12.13), Young (1951, 206) suggested on the basis of the drainage system that room 6 was a bathroom, and the small room 7 next to it a kitchen. He identified room 3, the largest roofed space in the house, as an *andron*, although it has an unusual shape for such a room. The house was entered via corridor 1, which let out into the courtyard (2). Room 7, if Young interpreted it correctly, was at the back of the house, and male visitors coming to parties in the *andron* would have no particular reason to go near it. Rooms 4 and 5, tucked away in the corner, might have made an excellent *gynaikonitis*, which could be locked up (as Xenophon recommended) simply by barring the narrow entrance to 5. However, Young suggested that 9 was in fact "the room in which the women did their weaving and other work" (1951, 206), because he found twenty loomweights and a spindle whorl overlying its floor. Again we face a basic problem of interpretation: spinning equipment may have been kept in a storeroom (like the orderly one evoked in *Oeconomicus* 8.17–23) rather than in the room where the work was done.

In the Dema farmhouse (Figure 12.14), room I – the farthest room from VII, the entrance to the courtyard – seems likely to be an *andron*. Jones *et al.* (1962, 77–9, 110–11) suggested that room III was a kitchen, largely on the basis of an area of floor discolored by fire. They found bathtub fragments above the floor of room IX, but were unsure whether they got there by accident or whether

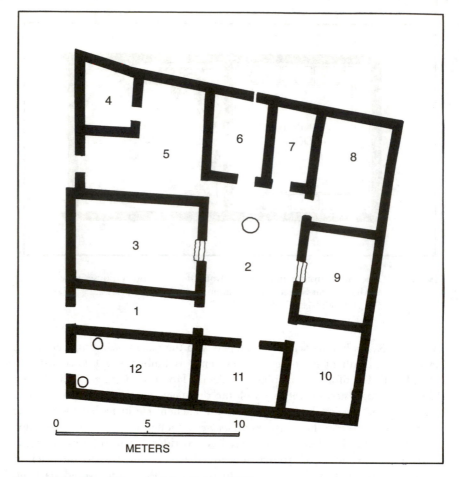

Figure 12.13 Agora House C (after Young 1951)

this really was a bathroom. Rooms V and VI may originally have been a single long room. "[O]ne or two spindlewhorls and loomweights" were found here, and the excavators suggest it was "a utility room or work-room."

The inadequacy of the evidence is clear. House C and the Dema House both had walls strong enough to have supported a second storey, though no evidence was detected. And the abandonment of Athenian houses seems normally to have involved a very thorough clean-out, reducing interpretation even of the ground-level remains almost to guesswork. If the guesses are right, there generally seems to be no clear pattern in the placement of kitchens, *andrones*, and work areas, relative to each other or to the house entrance. The fourth-century houses at Olynthus in Chalcidice were much less carefully emptied out than those in Attica, making it much easier to identify kitchens, storage areas, and *andrones*.

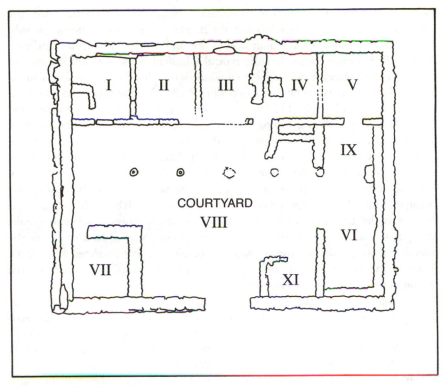

Figure 12.14 The Dema house (after Jones *et al.* 1962)

Here the main pattern seems to have been that the kitchen was near the *andron*, though the details varied enormously (Robinson and Graham 1938). Overall, there are no archaeological grounds to identify a *gynaikonitis* in Athenian houses.

III. Asymmetrically gendered space

Michael Jameson infers from this that "With the exception of the *andron*, which is at once distinctively male and oriented to the outsider, the architecture of the Greek house does not reflect the powerful social and symbolic distinctions between the two genders" (1990a, 104). But it may be an error to interpret the lack of evidence for space gendered female as meaning that the house was not a major locus for the construction of gender roles. Nevett (1994) suggests instead that what we see in Athenian houses is a pattern of gender asymmetry. Space was not rigidly divided into male and female, but into male and non-male; and space was conceived as having varying degrees of maleness, lying along a gender spectrum rather than falling into one of two distinct categories.

Athenian men regularly spoke of the house as a unit, set in opposition to the public world (*ta demosia, ta koina*) of politics (for example Isocrates 15.282;

Demosthenes 3.25–6; 23.206–8). Euripides (*Trojan Women* 645ff.) used the threshold of the door as the symbol of the dividing line between the two worlds. The physical remains of Athenian houses are fully consistent with this attitude. Nevett (1995) rightly insists that the typical Classical house was inward-turned, with the rooms opening off an internal courtyard with access limited to a single narrow door, often at the end of a corridor or alley. Yet the threshold was regularly crossed by visitors; and in other contexts, Athenian men present a different view of the house, distinguishing between the male, relatively public space of the *andronitis*, and the female, particularly private area of the *gynaikonitis*. To cross another citizen's threshold without his invitation was an act of hubris (for example Lysias 12.30; Demosthenes 18.132; 24.197), but to penetrate further, into the very heart of the house, was the ultimate attack on his honor (for example, Lysias 3.23; Demosthenes 37.45–6). Cohen (1991b, 74–5) suggests that the best model for understanding Athenian oppositions between male and female, and public and private, is the layers of an onion. Any given layer could be interpreted as public or private, male or female, relative to some other layer. At the "center of the onion" is a vague notion of the *gynaikonitis*, a female area of the house where no outsider should go.

The apparent paradox between Athenian writers' insistence on the privacy of a *gynaikonitis* and the impossibility of identifying such areas in the archaeological remains of Athenian houses is resolved once we approach the evidence in the Athenians' own terms. There was no core female area; only a series of areas defined by men as increasingly inappropriate for other men to enter.

Female space is as archaeologically invisible as servile space, and for much the same reasons. There is no reason to challenge Jameson's and Nevett's negative conclusion that we cannot find the *gynaikonitis*. But that is an important fact for any history of gender ideology at Athens. The material culture of gender relations was much like the material culture of relations between citizens and slaves. In each case, we see Athenian citizen men constructing a space from which another group is excluded, but in neither case do we see the excluded constructing alternative material cultures, definable from within on their own terms. We see instead a pair of genuine asymmetries: outside the civic, male core, we see nothing.

Conclusion

Throughout this essay I have stressed the weakness of the evidence. Without careful study of the forms and find spots of plain pottery from the Lavreotiki, or the discovery of less thoroughly cleaned out Athenian houses followed by more careful examination of floor deposits, we can only talk in terms of vague hypotheses. But all the same, both of the analyses I offer in this chapter seem to point in the same direction, which is that difficulties of attribution are not just unfortunate results which make it impossible to talk about slavery and gender. They are indications that in Classical Athens we face an unusually pervasive male citizen culture, which systematically undermined the formation of alternative value systems. This is what Ober (1989) has suggested for Athenian democratic rhetoric, and what Hedrick (1994) sees in Aristotle's account of the relationships between citizens and non-citizens. Here I suggest that the same principles applied in material culture.

In Athens we see no struggling with pots, no room of one's own. That does not, of course, mean that Athenian women and slaves never perceived male citizen domination as an oppressive fact, or that they did not resist it with the time-honored weapons of the weak, such as deliberate incompetence, lethargy, and carelessness. Ober suggests that

> It seems probable that critics of the status quo existed at every level of Athenian society; it is not hard to imagine that in each village and neighborhood of the polis there were men and women who could be counted on to interrogate, humorously or angrily, various aspects of the current order of things. The voices of these "local critics" are now lost, and we cannot say to what extent they were able to (or desired to) get outside that order.
>
> (Ober 1996, 143)

As he goes on to suggest, the one area of resistance to democratic norms we can observe in our written sources is among wealthy men, who, starting in the late fifth century, produced a series of literary works criticizing the ignorance of ordinary citizens (Ober, forthcoming). Obvious traces of the rich almost (but not quite) disappear from the fifth-century archaeological record. There are very few burials which stand out from the simple, restrained norms; houses are extremely uniform; and the elaborate silver and gold plate which, as we know from examples found in the burials and hoards of Thracian chiefs, Athenian craftsmen were producing in these years never show up in excavated houses or graves. But in the last quarter of the fifth century, just as the literary evidence for elite intellectual critiques of the democracy begins, this changes. Elaborate peribolos tombs come into use, getting ever more expensive until the 340s; and in the fourth century more imposing houses, some with fine mosaics in the *andron* and even with double peristyle courtyards, appear in Athens and the countryside. All over the Greek world, the rich begin to become archaeologically visible around 400 BCE in a way they had not been since Archaic times (Morris 1992, 108–55).

The archaeological invisibility of sections of the population is a long-term feature of the Greek record, but the changing nature of the groups so obscured is fundamentally important. I have argued that through much of the Dark Age, rituals in central Greece systematically drew adult/child and rich/poor distinctions within the community, in such a way that only relatively well-off adults entered the archaeological record (Morris 1987; forthcoming, ch. 6). In the eighth century these forms of ritual began to collapse, and by 500 many parts of Greece were characterized by a symbolic system privileging a vision of the community as an internally homogeneous, egalitarian, restrained group of men. In their deployment of material culture, Athenian citizens systematically denied the very real social distinctions within their polis: between men and women, free and slave, adult and child, rich and poor. Women and slaves remain invisible not because of the inevitable methodological problems with attributing gender and legal status to excavated remains, but because Athenian male citizens wanted it that way.

Acknowledgments

I would like to thank Sandra Joshel and Sheila Murnaghan for their patience, and John Ellis Jones for inviting me to take part in his excavations at the silver washery of Agrileza in 1983.

13

CRACKING THE CODE OF SILENCE

Athenian legal oratory and the histories of slaves and women

Steven Johnstone

Both men insisted that the other's desire for the woman ignited the conflict. The accuser claimed that the defendant, a longstanding enemy who had been captivated by the charms of the accuser's mistress, had barged into his house, seized the woman, and tried to kill him with a piece of pottery. The defendant admitted there had been a melee, but contended that he had been invited to a drinking party at the accuser's house – slaves, flute girls, and wine had been promised – to celebrate their reconciliation. The accuser, the defendant continued, was the first to attack him in a drunken, jealous fit over the woman, who was not a free mistress but a slave whom they jointly owned (Lysias 4).

Our knowledge of this dispute comes from a speech delivered in a fourth-century BCE law court that seems to open a window onto the social world of slaves and women in classical Athens. The evidence it offers, however, presents serious difficulties for historians. As with most Athenian legal orations, only one litigant's speech has survived. With only the defendant's plea (in fact, only part of it) and no independent information, it is impossible to evaluate the factual claims of either side; indeed, even the accuser's arguments must be inferred from what the defendant said. Faced with such factual quandaries, historians have noted that though speakers may have lied to Athenian juries, they are unlikely to have invented implausible lies. Although we cannot know what actually happened in this case, we may assume (so this reasoning goes) that the defendant's speech represents the type of things that were likely to occur. Thus, we may understand this conflict in the context of amorous and honorific rivalries between aristocrats: each of these men, whose honor was bound up with his sexual achievements, was quick to react to a competitor.

Compelling as such an interpretation is, however, it fails to ask an obvious question: What about the woman? What were her interests in this conflict? At one point the defendant admitted (in an offhand remark) that the woman cared much

221

more for the accuser than for him and had actually done him wrong in league with his opponent (Lysias 4.17). What was her complaint against this man? Was it related to his claim that she was not free, as the accuser said, but a slave? Had she, in fact, incited the conflict? Is it possible that this case originated less in aristocratic male rivalry than in a woman's assertion of her own interests? Despite this tantalizing hint, the possibilities of providing answers look dim. The defendant's narrative, focused as it is on his conflict with the other man, provides little evidence for uncovering the woman's interests in the dispute. Against the reality of litigation between men, it seems as if the woman's subjectivity must remain entirely speculative. Indeed, the substantial body of legal speeches extant from classical Athens consistently represents conflict between citizen men; slaves and women figure largely incidentally. If there is any hope of getting beyond this silence of the sources, some methodological ingenuity is necessary.

Subjects and silence

Despite their great treasure of details about slaves and women, in one fundamental way Athenian legal speeches remain silent about them. They are silent because marginalized people did not appear as agents in their own right, but only in relationship to the free men who were the subjects of the law's stories. The narrative conventions of a legal story consistently suppressed full accounts of the agency, experience, interests, and subjectivity of women and slaves. The danger of these sources, then, is that all they do say about these groups will obscure their fundamental omissions, and that we will unwittingly adopt their narrative constraints as our own in writing history. The silences themselves must be interrogated.

The silences of the sources present obstacles to writing the history of marginalized people, of course, but such silences are much more than just inconvenient accidents that cloak these people's experiences. Rather, they were essential features of ancient modes of representation which actively constituted and produced those experiences. As Joan Scott notes, "It is not individuals who have experiences but subjects who are constituted through experience" (Scott 1991, 779). There is no "authentic" subject outside history. An essential part of recovering slaves and women as historical subjects is problematizing the subject: that is, recognizing the degree to which subject positions are constituted through unique historical forces (cf. Hunter 1992). This is true not only for slaves and women, moreover, but for masters and men as well – an insight which provides a basis for a critical evaluation of the sources for writing history, sources which do not merely reflect social structures (although they certainly do that), but which also were part of the complex process of reproducing them (cf. Johnstone 1994). Silences, then, are not (or not only) the result of hierarchy and oppression, but also one of the means through which these were reproduced. Although to us these silences occlude marginalized subjects, they were also one of the ways these subjects were created.

People make their own history, as Marx almost said, but not under conditions of their own choosing. The project of problematizing subjects does not mean annihilating them, but analyzing them. Although an extreme poststructuralism would see subjects as pure effects, as only illusions, some of the best work has sought to temper this tendency: writing in the wake of Michel Foucault, for example, Judith Butler (1990) uses French psychoanalytic feminism to reanimate a sense of agency in Foucault's theories, and John Law (1994) argues that since attempts at imposing order (Foucault's "discourses") cannot be as totalizing as Foucault sometimes suggests, there is always room for individual action. The inhabitants of Athens who were not male citizens did exercise agency, even if in limited ways (Maurizio, forthcoming). Thus, the analysis of subjects should see them as both effects and agents – in historically specific ways. A full account of marginalized subjects (or, indeed, of hegemonic ones) should reveal not only what they experienced, but also how they were constituted as experiencing subjects. It should show how subject categories – female and male, slave and master – were created and reproduced. A history of slaves or women, then, should explicitly consider the gaps in the evidence because these gaps did not merely reflect social hierarchies – as systemic, structuring elisions they actively constituted them.

Situating these silences within a theory of the creation and reproduction of subjectivities, then, may provide a way to advance our understanding of marginalized groups. Scholarship on slaves and women has usually employed one of two strategies. The first has attempted to recover the "voices" of marginalized groups, whether that means their experiences, their subjectivities, their agency, or texts they themselves wrote; the second has sought to study the ideology, representations, or discourses concerning marginalized groups (cf. Scott 1988). Both approaches have yielded substantial insights, but both can be extended by more fully confronting and interrogating the gaps in the evidence. The first method, in constructing a traditional historical narrative with a new subject, has not always acknowledged its precarious evidentiary foundations. Pomeroy's groundbreaking book on women in antiquity, for example, briefly acknowledges in the introduction the problems the evidence presents (1975, x–xi), but its body is a seamless narrative unbroken by epistemological considerations. The second method focuses on a subject for which there is much more secure evidence. In the case of Athenian women, then, the study of gender – of the socially perceived differences between the sexes – sidesteps questions which traditional literary texts cannot answer well. Tragedy, for example, does not reveal much about how most Athenian women actually lived, much less what they thought, but it does provide rich representations of gender. The considerable insights of this approach, however, do not necessarily shed light on the historical reality of the lives of actual women (cf. Smith-Rosenberg 1986, 31–2). Confronting the gaps in the evidence not as epistemological problems but as facts to be understood and incorporated into historical accounts provides one way to build on these two approaches and to link ideology with lived experience.

Law and narratives

As one of the best sources of Athenian social history, legal speeches provide an opportunity to examine these silences and their operation. Instead of ignoring or even inadvertently reproducing their omissions, I want to examine these speeches in light of the anthropological theory of disputes which recognizes that legal representations are not reality, but one of many competing ways of constructing experience. A dispute is, broadly, a conflict between people (Comaroff and Roberts 1981; Mather and Yngvesson 1980–1; Yngvesson and Mather 1983). One of the great advantages of thinking of disputes rather than legal cases is the recognition that conflict can take many forms, only one of which is legal. The particular shape of a conflict is an outcome of the parties' struggles to impose competing meanings on the dispute. Thus the meaning or shape of the dispute is part of what is at stake in a conflict. The transformation from one shape to another (say, from a domestic quarrel to a legal case) is strategic. It is not inherent in the conflict, but the outcome of a party's interested claim. Such transformations, however, are also structural and systemic. The ability of parties to impose a definition is in part an outcome of structural factors (class, gender, status, etc.). The degree to which a particular definition has been accepted as authoritative in turn determines the resources available at any given moment to different parties.

From the perspective of dispute theory, no shape, even the most authoritative, is the "correct" one – indeed every shape represents the interested perspective of particular parties. One person hitting another could be seen as a criminal assault, an excusable peccadillo, an instance of domestic discipline, a manifestation of a psychological problem; all definitions are contestable, and dispute theory, rather than assuming that one is authoritative, seeks to understand how each of these definitions might be imposed. Dispute theory also conforms to what John Law calls a "modest sociology" by beginning with as few assumptions as possible (Law 1994, 13–14). For example, rather than unreflectively assuming a difference between litigants and third parties (witnesses, interested relatives, etc.), it sees this very distinction as the effect of a particularly legal way of narrating the dispute. The law, as a narrative mode, creates and differentiates disputants. Disputes, then, are not legal cases. The important point is not that only a small fraction of all disputes ever go to law,[1] but that the law imposes a particular shape on a dispute. It systematically transforms it.

The shape that Athenian legal stories took derived from the context in which litigants told them. The Athenian judicial system differed radically from our own.[2] Litigants who faced Athenian juries did so with minimal professional help. There were no legal experts, no lawyers, in Athens. Litigants found and cited whatever laws they thought relevant and the jury alone interpreted them. Litigants usually addressed the jury themselves, sometimes supported by friends or relatives who appeared as witnesses, added a brief plea, or showed solidarity by sitting with them. Now and then, if a party to a suit claimed to be unusually disadvantaged in speaking for himself (old age and youthful inexperience were the most common reasons), a close friend or relative might speak for him. Though there were no lawyers, some litigants paid an expert in legal rhetoric to compose their speech; such professionals wrote most of the hundred or so speeches that survive. There were no police and no public prosecutors; cases were investigated, initiated, and conducted by private citizens.[3] Each litigant had only a limited amount of time in which to speak, and trials never lasted more than a day. There was no judge; although a magistrate presided at the trial, his role was negligible. Without legal experts, the jurors were the heart of the system. All citizens over thirty could serve as jurors. Each jury consisted of hundreds of randomly selected jurors (usually 201 or 501, sometimes more, very rarely up to 6,000), the majority of whom determined the verdict. They voted immediately after the litigants' presentations without deliberation.

The legal capacity of slaves and women was extremely circumscribed. Neither ever spoke before a jury. Slaves could neither sue nor be sued except insofar as they were the instrument of their owner who would have conducted the case himself (Todd 1993, 186–7, 192–4). Women were occasionally defendants and inheritance cases were often initiated on their behalf, but in every case their male guardians spoke for them. Even suits where a male represented a woman or slave seem to have been rare: of the extant speeches, except for inheritance cases, only two involve female defendants and none concern slaves. Neither slaves nor women could appear as witnesses.

The law abridged the voices of women and slaves not just by preventing them from speaking, but, through the conventions governing stories told in courts, by refiguring disputes as legal cases (Johnstone, forthcoming). The law worked through simplification. Its conventions required that the dispute be between only two parties, a prosecutor and a defendant; however many parties might have a stake in a dispute, a legal story attempted to impose a dyadic structure on the conflict. Because in almost all cases only adult male citizens could act as litigants, these stories also defined the dispute as fundamentally between male citizens; the interests of other parties – of women and of slaves – were eclipsed. A legal narrative (for prosecutors, at least) also had to focus on a specific act which allegedly violated the law; although many disputes involved ongoing relationships of hostility or a general dissatisfaction, a legal story had to tell of a single, illegal act. Thus legal narratives required a story which might differ from that told by a party who was not a litigant and even by what the litigant himself might say in a nonlegal context. There is often a tension between specifically legal and lay modes of narration (Conley and O'Barr 1990, 12–19, 172; Merry 1990, chapter 5), and Athenian litigants often told a story fuller than the law required. This is important because details which were irrelevant from the perspective of the law often provide the clues for understanding the degree to which litigation imposed a particular meaning on a complex set of events. The boundaries of the law's stories thus imposed silences on slaves and women not by suppressing all information about them, but rather by making it impossible in court to narrate from their perspectives.

Although litigants commonly represented cases as arising from conflict between citizen men, there are strong reasons for believing this was often not the case. Scholars have recognized that it would be naive to read the orations as presenting truthfully historical accounts. Instead, because litigants had to appeal to the audience of jurors, they have suggested that events (even if untrue) must have been plausible to be persuasive (E. Cohen 1992, 36–40; Millett 1991, 2). Thus, they infer, even if we cannot be certain of what happened in this particular case, we can know the kinds of things that commonly happened. But care is required: a story may seem plausible not because it corresponds to the way things normally happen, but because it follows the way stories are usually told (Dershowitz 1996; cf. Ober 1989). It would be wrong to assume, therefore, that most conflict in Athens was between citizen men, or that only this type of conflict spawned litigation, even though most speeches represent it this way. Nevertheless, much of the best recent work (for example Hunter 1994; Cohen 1995) implicitly retains the perspective of the evidence: though it situates litigation within a broader social context ("social control" for Hunter, "elite competition" or "feuding" for Cohen) it still sees this context as the litigants represented it. It therefore suggests that conflict in Athens was fundamentally between men, and that it was only this conflict between male citizens that generated litigation. Dispute theory suggests, on the contrary, that for a dispute to be litigated it had only to be plausibly transformed, and represented as a conflict between men.

Omissions and theories

Euphiletus' defense (Lysias 1) on a charge of murdering Eratosthenes illustrates how a legal narrative represented conflict in a particular, selective way and how it both suppressed and gave shape to women's subjectivity. Euphiletus told the jury that he and his young wife were living a happy married life, made even more intimate and trusting by the birth of a child. But then one day an old woman lurking near his house accosted Euphiletus. Sent by a woman, a lover whom a certain Eratosthenes had discarded, she warned him to watch out for this man: "He's seduced not only your wife, but many others as well. He's a real professional" (Lysias 1.16). Euphiletus told the jurors he was stunned by this news, so he interrogated his housemaid, a slave whom, the old woman had identified as his wife's accomplice. When she disclaimed knowledge, he threatened torture. When she persisted in her denial, he mentioned the name Eratosthenes and claimed he knew everything. The servant broke down, begged Euphiletus not to harm her, and revealed a continuing liaison between Eratosthenes and Euphiletus' wife. Euphiletus demanded she help him catch Eratosthenes in the act. Days passed. Then, one night, the servant awoke Euphiletus to tell him that Eratosthenes was in the house, in his wife's room. Euphiletus went out, rounded up some friends who lived nearby, returned home, and burst into the room. Naked, Eratosthenes jumped up. Euphiletus knocked him to the ground, pinned his arms behind his back. Eratosthenes implored Euphiletus, he begged him to let him pay compensation, but Euphiletus told him he had broken the law. "Thus," Euphiletus euphemistically told the jury, "that man got what the laws prescribe for people who do such things" (Lysias 1.27). (Euphiletus here referred to the law which excused a husband who impulsively killed a man caught in the act of adultery with his wife. The law certainly did not require such a response.)

The traditional analysis of this case conforms closely to Euphiletus' narrative: a conflict between two men over adultery ultimately spawned a lawsuit. More generally, David Cohen has argued that adultery figured in contests of honor between men, that the male adulterer gained honor at the cuckolded husband's expense (D. Cohen 1990). Although there is much to recommend Cohen's understanding, by adopting the law's perspective, it has made adultery a transaction between men through a woman. Cohen, it is true, admits that wives must have had reasons for taking lovers (D. Cohen 1990, 164), but it is necessary to go further: Within the Athenian courts at least, it was impossible to tell the story of adultery as a conflict between a husband and a wife. The very decision to litigate crystallized the dispute, focusing it on two men. The reasons Cohen suggests for wives taking lovers – loneliness, dissatisfaction – were not merely structural features of women's lives in Athenian society; they are also ways of describing wives' disputes with their husbands. Thus adultery may have been not only the *cause* of a dispute between two men, from another perspective – unspeakable in legal terms – it may have been the *result* of a dispute between a wife and a husband.

The legal narrative failed to relate the stories that other parties to this dispute might have told, but in this case enough traces of them remain to begin to see how they might have represented the dispute differently. From these suppressed perspectives, the conflict was less about a contest of male honor as trouble between women and men. Euphiletus first learned of Eratosthenes' activities through a messenger sent by one of his previous lovers who was evidently jealous that he was neglecting her. From one perspective, then, the whole affair was the outcome of the discord between Eratosthenes and his earlier lover, which, however, could be told in a legal venue only as a footnote to the subsequent conflict between citizen men. Moreover, Euphiletus himself admitted to trouble with his wife: he revealed that she was angry because she believed he had been forcing their maid to have sex with him (Lysias 1.12). If the absence of a denial indicates Euphiletus' culpability on this point (Carey 1989, 70), it is reasonable to understand his wife's involvement with a paramour as a stage in an ongoing dispute between wife and husband. But such a conflict could not itself take legal form. Because the conditions of legal discourse mandated that citizen men privilege each other as the primary, even exclusive, disputants, other possible narratives, other possible understandings of the events, were elided. The problem with the evidence, then, is not merely that women could not speak for themselves, but that even male speakers could not fully represent a woman's interests.

Figuring adultery as primarily about men and their honor repeats this systematic silence of the sources.

This speech shows, too, that legal narratives allowed a certain room for women's subjectivity, but that it was always reinterpreted in terms of men's interests, especially as these were bundled in the idea of the household or *oikos*. During his defense, Euphiletus quoted the law which allowed a husband to kill an adulterer caught in the act and the law that set monetary damages for rape. Considering these two laws together he concluded:

> In this way, gentlemen, [the lawgiver] thought that those who use force merit a lesser penalty than those who use persuasion: He sentenced the latter to death, but made the damages for the former double [than if they had raped a slave]. He did this because he thought that those who accomplish their ends by force are hated by those who are overpowered, but that those who use persuasion corrupt the souls of their victims. The consequence is that the wives of others are more attached to their seducers than to their husbands, that the whole *oikos* is in their control, and that it is unclear whether the husbands or the adulterers are the fathers of the children.
>
> (Lysias 1. 32–3)

Thus the law recognized that a woman's interests mattered, but not in the same way that they may have mattered to her: her interests were admitted only in terms of the *oikos* – in her relationships to the husband, the property, and the children. Even her amorous interests were interpreted in light of these, so that her consent to extra-marital sex was significant (it determined the difference between adultery and rape), but it was significant only because of its implications for the *oikos*, not because of its effect on her (whether she suffered violence or not). The law recognized the woman's desire not as an aspect of her experience, but only for its implications for the relationship between her husband and her lover.

As mothers, wives, and daughters of citizen men, women were recognized as having an interest in the preservation or disposition of the property of the household. Although women could not own property in the same way men could (though they may have informally controlled it (Hunter 1994)), they were recognized as depending on it. Generally, therefore, citizen women appear prominently in legal speeches in two contexts. First, in inheritance and guardianship cases women played a prominent role (for example Demosthenes 27–9; Lysias 32). Second, in instances where the defendant faced a possible dire penalty – especially death or confiscation of property – he sometimes invoked the citizen women who depended on him as objects of pity should the punishment be inflicted (Demosthenes 19.283; 25.84; 27.65; 53.29). It is easy to imagine, of course, that most women did take an interest in their households, husbands, and children, but in the law's stories, these were the only interests women had.

Thus the *oikos* was an ideological construct which, far from representing the "sphere" of women, was employed in legal narratives to attribute to women subject positions which reinforced male dominance – precisely by constructing a realm where women's agency could support or oppose only male interests.

The law bolstered this representation of women's interests as defined by the *oikos* by providing the resources to express men's anxiety about it. The most notoriously vague Athenian law nullified wills made by a man who was "deranged on account of insanity, old age, drugs, or illness, or because of the influence of a woman, or forced by necessity or by being held captive" (Demosthenes 46.14; Rhodes 1981, 443–4). Speakers could thus attack the validity of a will alleging the nefarious influence of a woman (for example, Isaeus 6.21, 48; cf. Isaeus 2.19–20, Hyperides 3.17–18). While such claims depended upon highly negative depictions of women (which equated their influence with insanity), like the positive portrayals of good women, they limited female subjectivity to the way it effected a man's interests. Male litigants might represent the expression of women's interests as good or bad, but in either case they were largely circumscribed by the *oikos*.

Slaves and women

Slaves appear in Athenian legal orations in three notable contexts. First, disputants often dared their opponents to torture a slave as a way of formalizing the settlement of a dispute.[4] Certainly slaves must have considered that this impinged on their interests, but this symbolic, sadistic displacement of hostility onto their bodies was possible because they were legally depicted as largely devoid of humanity and therefore of interests. Indeed, the common claim that "truth" spontaneously issued from slaves under torture posits the slave not as a subject but as a body with a reflex (for example Isaeus 8.12). Second, slaves appear frequently in litigation on mercantile matters. But since male slaves often worked as free men's representatives in trade, especially in running banks, they were represented as having no interests of their own. Third, speakers mentioned slaves in the context of the household. In many of these cases, there is enough information to suspect that slaves may have been disputants with interests of their own. In Ariston's suit against Conon for assault, for example, he traced the hostility that led to their brawl back two years to when he was serving in the army on the frontiers and Conon's drunken sons used to attack his slaves and urinate on them (Demosthenes 54.4).

Generally, however, despite hints that slaves may have taken an active part in disputes (for example, Demosthenes 55.31–4 or Lysias 4.17, referred to at the beginning of this paper), the speeches fail to represent them with even the limited subjectivity allowed to women. In Euphiletus' narrative, for example, the slave who brokered the trysts between Euphiletus' wife and Eratosthenes (conveying secret messages, distracting Euphiletus in a jam) and who subsequently collaborated in Euphiletus' plan to ensnare the lovers, was represented as entirely without loyalty, affection, or interests – except for her fear of being tortured by Euphiletus (Lysias 1.19). Similarly, the young slave Euphiletus' wife accused her husband of molesting was depicted merely as an object. Indeed, Euphiletus made it clear that his wife raised the subject not out of a concern for the girl, but for its effects on her own relationship with her husband. This incident in a slave's life entered the legal narrative, then, only because it had been appropriated by the wife for her own interests, which the legal narrative took account of because of their impact on the *oikos*.

With slaves, too, silence was constitutive: the law reproduced the distinctions between slaves and free people. By this I do not mean the true but unremarkable claim that the law formally distinguished the two categories, but rather that although the law was capable of recognizing a citizen woman's interests in certain cases and in limited ways, it was altogether impossible for it to acknowledge those of a slave. The law's representation of slaves was interested and selective. It is sometimes said that, because they were property, slaves were considered part of the household, but not part of the family (MacDowell 1989; Pomeroy 1994, 65). This reflects more the limits of legal narration than reality. Indeed, it is hard to imagine that slaves had no interests simply because they were sometimes considered property. Nor, in fact, did free individuals always consider slaves property: there are indications that free individuals could form deep affectionate bonds with slaves, bonds of trust, even of love (for example, Lysias 3; Demosthenes 36.8; 47.59ff.). But, although the confiscation of a man's property would certainly affect his slaves (in some ways more than his immediate family), no litigant ever asked the jurors to pity the fate of his servants. It was not that slaves had no interests because they were property, but that they were constituted as property in part because legal stories could not be told which attributed interests to them.

The law does, however, provide glimpses into slaves' involvement in disputes in one kind of situation: when a slave or ex-slave (usually a woman) became the lover of a citizen. The frequency of such references probably has less to do with how often it actually occurred than with certain structural features which allowed for a legal narration, features illustrated by Callistratus' prosecution of his wife's brother Olympiodorus (Demosthenes 48). When a mutual relative died, these two conspired to keep his fortune to themselves. Other relatives demanded adjudication. When the court awarded Olympiodorus the entire estate, he kept it for himself, so Callistratus sued him demanding half in accord with their previous agreement. The legal case thus gave a specific shape to the dispute: Callistratus had been wronged by his brother-in-law when he refused to honor their agreement to split the loot. Yet the legal narrative contains hints that the dispute was much broader than this: during his speech, Callistratus defamed Olympiodorus for living with an ex-slave whose freedom he had bought. "Olympiodorus here, men of the jury, never married an Athenian woman in conformity with your laws, nor has he ever had children. Instead, he bought the freedom of a mistress and keeps her at home. She's the one who insults us all and makes Olympiodorus more and more insane" (Demosthenes 48.53). Callistratus' sudden reference to Olympiodorus' mistress – whom he then blames for the whole trouble – suggests a dispute wider and more complex than a merely legal narrative would reveal. In keeping with the law's conventions for negatively representing the effects of a women's assertion of her interests, Callistratus characterized the mistress's influence as insanity. But there was more. Callistratus then began speaking of his own wife (Olympiodorus' sister) and daughter – who were apparently involved in the dispute more than the legal case alone revealed:

> Aren't they being wronged, aren't they suffering terribly when they see this rich man's mistress in gold jewelry and fancy clothes going around in luxury and acting with hubris with our money – meanwhile my wife and daughter are worse off in every way – aren't they being wronged even more than I am? Isn't he obviously crazy and out of his mind in devising such things for himself? So that he cannot allege, men of the jury, that I am saying these things out of slander because of this suit, I will read to you a deposition from his relatives and mine.
>
> (Demosthenes 48.55)

There was clearly more at issue here than the simplified story the law would tell. Even in Callistratus' account, from the perspective of his wife and daughter, the dispute hinged on Olympiodorus' lover, a former slave whose elevated status inspired considerable jealousy. But the law allowed expression of the women's interests in this case only in so far as they could be represented as concerning the *oikos*, Callistratus' property.

Agency and anxiety

The prominent appearance in this account of Olympiodorus' unnamed lover reflects an important structural conjunction between the categories of slaves and women: she seems to have changed her status from being a slave to being a woman. Elizabeth Spelman (1988) has suggested that for Aristotle gender was a privilege of the free: the difference between females and males did not matter among slaves, whom he treated without discriminating by sex. Similarly, in Athenian legal oratory, though slaves took part in many events, both sexes alike were regularly represented without even the circumscribed subjectivity of women.[5] In this case, Olympiodorus' lover had acquired the ability to have her interests expressed indirectly, even if negatively – an ability free women had, but slaves did not. This woman's status changed not merely because Olympiodorus had legally freed her; her legal freedom, in fact, was in part an *effect* of becoming his lover. Scholars have argued that acts of sex for the Greeks were invariably hierarchical, that they established relationships of power (Halperin 1990, following Foucault 1985). In doing so, they have usually focused on the ways in which sex elevated

231

the male at the expense of the woman, slave, or boy. But since power can both constrain and enable – since subjects are both effects and agents – what we see in the case of Olympiodorus' lover is the ability of one oppressed person to strategically deploy its enabling capacity. Far from being only limited or stigmatized by being treated "like a woman" in this sexual relationship, this female slave actually *became* a woman.

Though the law imposed a particular, interested, and contestable shape on conflict, the authority of this assertion carried consequences even for those with different perspectives. The subject positions of slaves and women did not exist beyond the law, but were profoundly affected by it, as is shown by a story Apollodorus told when he prosecuted Neaera on a charge of passing herself off as the wife of a citizen (Demosthenes 59.30–40, 45–8). When Neaera, who began her life as a slave in a brothel, felt abused by her lover Phrynion, who had earlier helped her buy her freedom, she fled Athens taking some of their household goods. Wanting to return to Athens but fearful of Phrynion, she enrolled her subsequent lover Stephanus as her patron and went back to live with him. There, when Phrynion tried to seize her, Stephanus asserted her freedom ("in accordance with the law," as the narrative states) and bond was posted with a magistrate pending adjudication. Phrynion brought charges against Stephanus both for wrongly claiming Neaera was free and for holding property stolen from him. Here friends intervened and persuaded each man to submit their quarrel to a group of three arbitrators, one chosen by each man and a neutral third. These reconciled the men, affirmed Neaera's freedom, returned the goods to Phrynion, allowed Neaera to keep her own, and stipulated that Neaera should be shared between them.

The invocation of the law fundamentally transformed the shape of this dispute. It allowed for only two disputants, it insisted each be a legally competent male, and it focused on specific acts defined by the law (a formal assertion of freedom and the theft of property). Even in the settlement, the aim of the arbitrators (chosen because of their relationships to the men) was to reconcile Stephanus and Phrynion – they were, after all, the legal adversaries. Neaera's future became just another condition stipulated by their reconciliation. The language of the law formulated the dispute (and its resolution) as a dyadic conflict between citizen men about a wrong one did to the other.

The inability of a legal narrative to represent Neaera as a subject stands as an obstacle to recovering her experiences as a slave and as a woman; more than this, though, it partially constituted those experiences. Neaera does not seem to have been an impotent pawn of the men around her. Indeed, she enrolled Stephanus as her protector precisely to more effectively stand up to Phrynion. In seeking the leverage of the law against Phrynion, however, Neaera had to displace her interests because a legal narrative could express them only insofar as they were subsumed by a citizen male's. To invoke the law she had to effect this displacement herself. Neaera did not merely require a patron to champion her interests; more importantly, she had to sublimate those interests into someone else's, she had to mediate her relationship with her own interests through a citizen male. Stephanus was not her representative or advocate in a direct sense: he did not bring a suit against Phrynion on her behalf for legal wrongs she had suffered. Rather, Stephanus' formal legal intervention – actively sought by Neaera – decisively transformed the dispute: he now spoke for himself in his dispute with Phrynion which was partially (but only partially) *about* Neaera. His interests subsumed hers. The silence of Athenian legal speeches was part of what caused women like Neaera to live alienated from their own interests.

The ability of either slaves or women, even within the relationships that constrained them, to exercise agency could provoke considerable anxiety. Near the close of his prosecution of Neaera on the charge of passing herself off as married to a citizen (Stephanus), Apollodorus asked the jurors to imagine what they would say to their wives, daughters, or mothers after the trial if they acquitted Neaera. If that happened, Apollodorus warned,

> the laws will be annulled; the habits of whores will reign supreme. So you should look out for the women of citizen status as well so that the daughters of poor citizens don't end up unmarried. As it is now, if nature has allowed a girl anything like an average appearance, even if she is poor, the law contributes a sufficient dowry. But if you drag the law through the mud and make it invalid by acquitting this woman, the daughters of citizens who cannot be married because of poverty will certainly be drawn into the business of prostitution and prostitutes will assume the status of free women if they get the right . . . to share in the religious rites, the sacred ceremonies, and the honors in the city.
>
> (Demosthenes 59.112–13)

Apollodorus suggested that the anxiety about slaves becoming citizens was keenly felt by citizen women, especially those near the bottom whose difference from slaves was least apparent. Yet Apollodorus' imaginary feminine consciousness looks suspiciously like male subjectivity in drag: it concerns itself with public standing, honor, and competition with others. Even his concern for marriage and the *oikos* was not for the bonds of affection this might foster, nor for the economic subsistence it could provide (indeed, Apollodorus envisions an alternative means of support for these unmarried, poor women), but rather for the status it bestowed (cf. Vilatte 1986). In fact, Apollodorus himself imagined a very different reaction by some women: while the most decent would react to Neaera's acquittal with anger, he claimed, those women who lacked discretion would take it as permission to do as they pleased without regard to the laws or their male guardians (Demosthenes 59.111). Neither of Apollodorus' imaginary feminine consciousnesses provides strong evidence that women did – or did not – think like this. In fact, free women's reactions must have varied. In some cases, women and slaves became allies in their conflicts with men (Lysias 1 or Antiphon 1); in others, hostility flared between slaves and women when their interests conflicted, perhaps especially when female slaves gained the status of women through their relationship with free men (Demosthenes 48). But though it may be unclear to what extent Athenian women took part in a culture of public, competitive honor like men or, on the contrary, how far they found their virtues within the *oikos* (Foxhall 1996 and Versnel 1987, both relying on comparative anthropological studies, come to diametrical conclusions), it is clear that neither slaves nor women could pursue their interests in the same ways as men. The silence of the sources in fact constituted part of the structural conditions within which such people acted.

Conclusion

Histories of disputes must allow for a plurality of perspectives, including those of slaves and women, without privileging any as authoritative. Neaera's perspective on her conflict with Phrynion, for example, was no more authentic than the legal formulation; the legal case between Phrynion and Stephanus was not merely a shadow of the "real" dispute between Neaera and her former lover. In fact, the dispute was about different things to different people – a complexity the legal narrative entirely failed to capture. The law gave a particular shape to conflict, a shape which consistently excluded the direct representation of slaves or women as subjects.[6] The law also asserted the authority of its own representations, an authority augmented by the failure of any evidence but the legal orations to survive. Historical accounts of women and slaves must work against both of these features of legal narratives, yet these accounts must also recognize that these characteristics of the law carried important consequences for the lives of slaves and women. The silence of the sources was not merely an unfortunate effect of free men's power; it was also one of its foundations. Yet is was within the structure of the power relations constituted by these silences that women and slaves recognized and pursued their interests, that they became subjects.

Notes

1 The study of these other ways of pursuing disputes is the subject of a literature on "social control": Ellickson 1991; Black 1984. Hunter 1994 considers this form of social control in classical Athens.
2 In trying to give a brief summary of the Athenian legal system, I have had to flatten considerably its procedural complexity. MacDowell 1978, chapters 2, 4, and 16, provides a much fuller introduction.
3 There was a significant distinction among cases based on who had the right to prosecute: in one kind of case, a *dike*, only an aggrieved party himself could sue; in another, a *graphe*, any citizen had the right to initiate proceedings. Scholars often name these suits "private" and "public" respectively. The distinction does not correspond to the division between civil and criminal cases in American law.
4 The practice of challenging someone to torture a slave has usually been understood as a way of introducing the testimony of the slave to the court (for example, Todd

1990, Gagarin 1996). Against this view I argue elsewhere (Johnstone, forthcoming) that although litigants found a rhetorical advantage in having dared their opponent to torture a slave, such dares were used primarily outside the law as a way of conducting a dispute. The torture of a slave in response to an opponent's challenge was a way of formalizing the settlement of a conflict. It was, moreover, quite different from simply torturing one of your own slaves to extract information (as, for example, Euphiletus threatened to do).

5 In the many discussions of the torture of slaves, for example, no distinction was made between the bodies of males and of females (for example, Lycurgus 1.29–32).

6 It may be that men who brought cases arising from disputes involving women and slaves represented them as "really" about conflicts with other men in part because it was not honorable to litigate with someone of lower status. It seems to have been perfectly acceptable to say that a suit against a female ex-slave was really about her male guardian (Demosthenes 59.1), but in no extant speech did a litigant claim his suit was ultimately aimed at a slave or a woman.

Acknowledgments

The criticisms and suggestions of the volume editors were invaluable in improving this essay. I would also like to thank my friends who read it and responded with helpful comments: Mark Edwards, Mike Jameson, Lisa Maurizio, Ian Morris, and especially Adam Geary.

14

NOTES ON A *MEMBRUM DISIECTUM*

Shane Butler

A slave of Quintus Servilius Caepio castrated himself in honor
of the Idaean Mother and was shipped away across the sea, that
he might never return to Rome.

(Obsequens 44a)

Passing stranger! you do not know how longingly I look upon you,
You must be he I was seeking, or she I was seeking, (it comes to
me as of a dream,) ...

(Walt Whitman, "To a Stranger")

This is the story of a chance encounter.

It begins with the loss of a book, in Venice in 1508, on what is now the
rio terrà Secondo, number 2311, in the little gothic *palazzo* where Aldus Manutius
once had his printshop. There the famous Renaissance publisher prepared
his edition of an obscure classical text, the *Prodigiorum Liber* (*Book of Prodigies*)
of Julius Obsequens, setting words from a medieval manuscript into his
signature italic type. The exemplar, Aldus tells us in a prefatory letter, was
a gift from Giovanni del Giocondo, a curiosity to tuck into the forthcoming
Aldine edition of the letters of the younger Pliny. The printed volume may still
be found in libraries, though it is especially rare,[1] but the codex from which
Aldus copied, which seems to have been the only manuscript of the *Prodigiorum
Liber* to survive to the Renaissance, subsequently vanished without a trace. With
the manuscript disappeared any clues it may have held about the text's earlier
history.

The *Prodigiorum Liber* as it survives catalogues events that were formally recognized (*suscepta*) and expiated (*procurata*) as prodigies by Rome, from 190 to 11
BCE, when Augustus seems to have ended the practice.[2] The list is striking both
for its staccato style of reportage and for the relatively quotidian nature of the
"prodigious" events it describes, as in this entry for 179 BCE:

236

Several statues on the Capitoline overturned by relentless rain-storms. Many spots in and around Rome struck by lightning. On the banquet couch of Jupiter, the heads of the gods moved as the result of an earth-quake; the blanket with the coverlets which had been provided for Jupiter fell off. Mice nibbled olives from the table.

(7)[3]

Animal behavior was given prodigious interpretation often enough to prompt a parody by Terence: "Someone else's black dog came into my house," etc. (*Phormio* 705–10). The heavens, however, were by far the most fertile source of prodigious events. Among the celestial disturbances recorded in the *Prodigiorum Liber* are, on occasion, sightings of multiple suns and showers of blood or milk, but most of the prodigies report ordinary meteors and simple bad weather like lightning, hail storms, floods, and wind. So careful are these reports that R. Frei-Stolba has used the meteorological prodigies recorded by Livy and Obsequens as evidence for reconstructing the climate of Republican Rome.

In their search for supernatural disorder, the nervous Romans were exceedingly careful observers of nature, a fact which makes the prodigies historical documents of uncommon value. Their realism and immediacy is sometimes remarkably poignant, as in this description of the complications of a twin birth in 108 BCE:

At Nursia, twins born to a free-born woman: a girl, with all her members intact; a boy, born with his belly open in the front so that his exposed intestine could be seen, but with his rear orifice closed up, who uttered a cry and breathed his last.

(40)

History, despite itself, has forgotten speeches of magistrates and songs of poets, but it preserves this child's gasp. Centuries later, a more famous brother-sister pair, Saints Benedict and Scholastica, were born in the same village, but not even the former, who had a pope as hagiographer, left a relic of equal realism in his lengthy *Vita*.

Birth defects, both human and animal, comprise a large category of Roman prodigies. Some are fantastic, such as the matron who gave birth to a serpent (57), but most involve only a reduction or multiplication of the ordinary number of limbs, organs, or heads, and some of these refer to what must in fact have been Siamese twins (humans: 12, 14, 25, 27a, 50, 51, 52, 53, excluding hermaphrodites, who receive a fuller discussion later in this paper; animals: 5, 14, 15, 24, 28, 32, 50, 53, 104). A slightly different defect is shared by the boy at Nursia and two others born with missing orifices (26, 53). These stories tell us much about Roman anxieties about the natural boundaries of the human body, but some also connect us to powerful and particular moments of human suffering. Terribly eloquent are three mentions of hermaphrodites "discovered" (*inventi*) and put to death when they reached puberty, after childhoods in which their condition presumably had been concealed by their families (3, 34, 36).

Some of the prodigies listed by Obsequens do not fall into large categories. Among these are, for example, the man who devoured a fellow slave or convict in the quarries (40) and the girl who giggled before she was sacrificed to the Furies (55). There are the dreams of Caecilia Metella (55) and of Calpurnia (67), the latter on a March night in 44 BCE on which, by the way, the sky was clear.[4] The assassination of Julius Caesar is itself recorded as a prodigy, with a conspicuous emphasis on his perforated body: "Caesar himself riddled with twenty-three wounds by conspirators in the senate-house of Pompey" (*ipse Caesar viginti tribus vulneribus in curia Pompeiana a coniuratis confossus*, 67).

Who was the compiler to whom we owe the preservation of this peculiar record? A weak scholarly consensus assigns Julius Obsequens to late antiquity, making him a pious pagan who sought to glorify Rome's religious past in the face of state-sponsored Christianity.[5] But given the prodigies themselves, which scarcely could have competed with the rather more impressive miracles of the Christians, crucial parts of that hypothesis seem highly unlikely. The mystery of when and why Obsequens wrote is further deepened by uncertainty about the sources he used. It has long been observed that, where the text of Livy survives for a year chronicled by Obsequens, the prodigies in the latter can by and large be found in the former, in similar or identical language. The theory that Obsequens based his list on the text of Livy seems obvious and reasonable.[6] But since Livy himself probably derived his prodigies from annalistic compilations of the second and first centuries BCE,[7] such a theory assumes that a catalogue, perhaps only of prodigies, was incorporated into Livy's massive history only to be extracted subsequently by Obsequens. This A–B–A' genealogy is not impossible, but it has required rejecting the more elegant possibility that the text is based not on Livy at all, but rather on one of his possible sources.[8]

The earlier history of the prodigy records is equally obscure, but it nevertheless converges on a single source where most prodigies were first inscribed: the *tabula dealbata* (sometimes called the *tabula pontificum*), the "whitened board" which hung in the *Regia* (official residence of the chief priest) at the eastern end of the Roman Forum to record events requiring action by the pontifical college, among which were prodigies (*prodigia*) and their expiations (*procurationes*). But how much of the actual wording of those original inscriptions does the text of Obsequens finally preserve? The language of Roman prodigies undoubtedly derived from the delicate linguistic balance struck between vagueness (to avoid omission) and precision (to insure effectiveness) in archaic Roman religion. But it quickly developed a poetics of its own, including a tight and highly nominalized syntax bound up with the formulaic *procurationes* by which each *prodigium* was finally contained. C. Santini has shown that Obsequens is supremely sensitive to the syntax, vocabulary, and rhythms of what Santini dubs *sermo prodigialis*, or "prodigy-style" (1988). Of course, that sensitivity might suggest that elements

of the text are only products of deliberate archaism on the part either of Obsequens himself or of one of his sources.[9] But ancient writers who concerned
themselves with prodigies – whether out of piety or simple antiquarianism –
must have recognized the importance of citing their sources with care equal to
that with which priests long before them had recorded the prodigies themselves.
In the case of Obsequens, if the actual wording of the *tabula dealbata* had not
been important to him (for whatever reason), it is hard to imagine why he would
have written the book that he did. In the end, the text given under the name
of Obsequens in the Aldine edition probably preserves more or less the actual
words of the *tabula dealbata*. However obscure the path that connects them, the
distance from the *Regia* on the *via Sacra* to the printshop on the *rio terrà Secondo*
may not be very great after all.

Thus encouraged, we turn at last to my epigraph, found on page 510 *verso*
of the Aldine text:

> *seruúsq; Seruilij Cæpionis matris Ideæ se præcîdit, et trans mare exportatus ne unquá*
> *Romæ reuerteretur.*

Apart from the expansion of abbreviations and the standardization of orthog-
raphy more or less according to ancient practice, modern editions emend
the text in two places, reading an abbreviated *praenomen, Quintus,* in place of the
abbreviated enclitic *-que,* and correcting the nonsensical genitive *matris Idaeae* to
the more logical dative *matri Idaeae.* Both changes would undo very common
scribal errors, and the text thus corrected reads as follows:

> Servus Q. Servilii Caepionis Matri Idaeae se praecidit et trans mare
> exportatus ne umquam Romae reverteretur.
>
> (44a)

> A slave of Quintus Servilius Caepio cut himself off in front in honor
> of the Idaean Mother and was shipped away across the sea, that he
> might never return to Rome.[10]

The slave castrated himself in 101 BCE,[11] and there is a curious way in which,
at the end of the textual history sketched above, his act seems to be itself a
kind of writing, a message for the goddess that somehow was instead conveyed
to the authorities, referred to the priests, inscribed as a prodigy, and set on an
untraceable journey to Venice, whence it came at last to us, its unintended
recipients. But is this a precious postcard from a slave, or is it only an official
communiqué from the pontifical college? In other words, if the Aldine edition
of Obsequens connects us to the *tabula dealbata,* does the latter really connect
us to the slave whose body it transcribes and circumscribes in the language of
prodigies? The following five notes, glosses on the separate words and phrases
of which the slave's record is composed, may suggest some answers. Since each

gloss tends to represent a different discourse of knowledge about the past, I have added, in parentheses after each word or phrase to be glossed, a name for the epistemology or method that seemed most in evidence in my note.

1 Servus (history)

Roman slaves seldom won much attention from Roman historians except when they revolted. Several such slave rebellions were recorded not only as history but also as prodigies (Obsequens 27, 27b, 43, 45), and one of these was in progress when the slave of Caepio castrated himself. The most detailed account of its causes and events is given by Diodorus.[12]

In 104 BCE the king of Bithynia refused to supply the Roman consul and general Gaius Marius with an allied army against two Germanic tribes, the Cimbri and Teutoni, explaining with wry humor that all of his male subjects of military age had been enslaved by Roman tax collectors. The embarrassed senate subsequently decreed the freedom of all slaves on Roman territory who were citizens of nations then allied with Rome. In Sicily the provincial governor initially complied with the senate's order, but later, under pressure from local slave-owners, he abruptly ended the large-scale liberation in his province, precipitating a rebellion by the remaining slaves. The revolt, which eventually would grow to massive proportions, closely followed three smaller uprisings on the Italian mainland and came only thirty years after a previous Sicilian slave war.

The principal events of the war were as follows. First, slaves in the region of Halicyae revolted and seized a fortified position; betrayed by treachery, all were killed or committed suicide. Almost immediately thereafter, a larger group of slaves gathered on Mount Caprianus. After they successfully defeated the first Roman force that came against them, their numbers swelled considerably and, with horses requisitioned from territory now under their control, began to include cavalry. Meanwhile, a second rebellion began in the territory of Segesta and Lilybaeum. Eventually, the participants in this revolt joined forces with the slaves from Caprianus. By this time, the uprising had grown to include not only slaves but also poor freedmen. Conspicuous in the account in Diodorus, though reported with some contempt, is the high degree of religiosity among the rebels, including that of the man they named their first king, who "was thought to be skilled at divination and who played ecstatic music on the flute at festivals for women" (*gunaikeíais théais*, perhaps "effeminate spectacles," Photius 388b).

The war saw several Roman defeats, and those of 102 BCE were particularly humiliating. Finally in 101 BCE the consul Manius Aquilius was sent against the rebels; within a year he had crushed their revolt. Diodorus adds a picturesque touch: a remaining group of 1000 slaves was taken to Rome to fight wild animals in public games, but rather than enter the arena, they killed one another, the last one alive committing suicide. Obsequens, who records the final defeat of the slaves as a prodigy for the year 100 BCE, reports only that they were "slaughtered through battles" (*proeliis trucidati*, 45), which, however, could refer as easily to the arena as to war. In any case, the slave of Caepio, driven across the sea the year before, was not in Italy for the war's final outcome.

Did slaves in Rome follow these events, and if so, where were their allegiences? Does the rebels' religiosity, derided as effeminate by Diodorus, suggest that transgender identification by slaves was itself a type of rebellion? Might the self-castration of the slave of Caepio have been an act of solidarity with the distant rebels? Such questions are unanswerable, and all we can do here is to place the slave against a hastily painted backdrop of events that just as possibly may have meant nothing to him at all.

2 *Q. Servilii Caepionis* (prosopography)

The slave's anonymity does not disentangle him from the prosopographical thicket of the late second and early first centuries BCE.[13] The difficulties begin with the obvious identification of Servilius Caepio (with or without the emendation of the *-que* to *Q.*) as Quintus Servilius Caepio, the consul of 106 BCE. In that year Caepio commanded the Roman army that captured the city of Tolosa and rescued the gold that according to legend had been stolen from Delphi by the Gauls. Later, when the Roman guard that escorted the sacred treasure from Tolosa (modern Toulouse) was hijacked and its precious cargo was spirited away under mysterious circumstances, many turned suspicious eyes on the consul himself. Then in 105 BCE Caepio's insubordination to his successor Gnaeus Mallius Maximus helped to bring about the disastrous Roman defeat by the Cimbri at Arausio (Orange). Caepio may or may not have been punished by a special commission that investigated the loss of the Tolosian gold, but he certainly was prosecuted for his role in the disaster at Arausio, becoming the first defendant charged, under a new law, with the crime of *maiestas minuta*, an offense incorporating a broad range of treasonous actions. In the end his property was confiscated, and he himself escaped imprisonment only by fleeing to Smyrna with the tribune Lucius Reginus. The trial and conviction of Caepio for *maiestas* occurred during the tribunate of Gaius Norbanus, which has been dated to 103 BCE. In other words, by 101 BCE, the year in which the slave castrated himself, the man named in the record as his owner may have owned little more than his own life and the precarious liberty of an exile.

Why then is the slave said to be "of Quintus Servilius Caepio"? The easiest solution to the apparent conundrum would be to doubt the date of 103 BCE for the tribunate of Norbanus; all that we know with certainty is that it occurred before 94 BCE, when Norbanus himself was prosecuted for his own prosecution of Caepio, ironically under the same charge of *maiestas*. But the reasons for the early date, first given by F. Münzer (1920) and then refined by T. R. S. Broughton (1951–60), are attractive. Another simple explanation, not previously considered, is that the slave belonged not to Quintus Servilius Caepio senior but rather to his son of the same name, who survived his father's exile to enjoy a political career of his own. But the record surely would have distinguished the younger

Caepio from his more famous (and infamous) father. Still less probable is the identification of the slave's owner as Gnaeus Servilius Caepio, quaestor in 105 BCE.

Vindication of the traditional attribution is really very simple, for the reports of the prodigies are in general so bitingly laconic that it is highly unlikely that the owner of the slave would have been named at all unless his very name lent ominous meaning to the portent, and this points to the elder Caepio and his demise. Of course, the connection would have been particularly meaningful if made deliberately to strengthen the case against Caepio during his trial, which we might be tempted to date to the same year. But I wish to advance a rather more complicated explanation, consistent with the earlier date for the trial.

Some Latinists will have found taking the dative *Matri Idaeae* to mean "in honor of the Idaean Mother" after *se praecidit* somewhat generous, even in the terse dialect of the *Prodigienliteratur*. There is, in fact, an even deeper problem here. It is the nature of prodigies simply to "happen" by ambiguous agency ultimately divine. The heavens flash, statues crumble, strange animals are spotted behaving ominously, and in the prodigy immediately preceding that of the slave, normally inert objects mysteriously move – "sacred shields moved of their own accord, with a rattling noise" (*ancilia cum crepitu sua sponte mota*). The slave, because he *castrates himself*, has an uncommon authorial presence in his own prodigy. But this is an inconsistency only if we understand that the slave *decided to castrate himself*; clearly we are meant to read instead that he castrated himself *sua sponte* (like the rattling shields), i.e., that he "spontaneously castrated." As a prodigy, the slave's self-castration is a (super)natural phenomenon, not the deliberate act of a thinking being. This necessary condition, however, is undermined entirely by attributing to him a motive: "in honor of the Idaean Mother." Such thoughtful participation in a prodigy is unparalleled in the *Prodigiorum Liber*.

Aldus Manutius, however, read not *Matri Idaeae* but *Matris Idaeae*; as is explained above, the dative is a later editor's emendation of a genitive with nothing to modify in the sentence. A better solution is to keep the genitive and to mark a lacuna after *Caepionis*.[14] The missing word or words might tell us, for example, that the slave castrated himself "[under the influence] of the Idaean Mother," but this is unlikely, since specific divinities almost never are named as agents of prodigies, which instead reflect only a vague and general disruption of the *pax deorum* (orderly relations between gods and humans). What Obsequens almost always does tell us, however, is the place where the prodigy occurred; within Rome, he usually gives the specific location, which often is a temple. There is good reason to suspect that an earlier text reported simply that the slave castrated himself "[in the sanctuary] of the Idaean Mother."[15] But what was the slave of Caepio doing in the sanctuary of the Idaean Mother? Unfortunately, we are not told what happened to the property confiscated from Caepio, but it is likely that his private slaves became public slaves and that some were assigned to the service of the official state cults. One such cult was that of the Idaean Mother, also known as the Magna Mater or Cybele. It would not be at all surprising to

242

find one of Caepio's former slaves in the precinct of Cybele two years after the trial and conviction of his master.

All of this is rather conjectural, but the text contains a second peculiarity, the *procuratio* of the prodigy: "shipped away across the sea that he might never return to Rome." The first part (*trans mare exportatus*), as will be shown in my fifth gloss, is nearly formulaic, though it may imply additionally that the slave was sent to the cult center of the goddess in Asia Minor, but the injunction that follows (*ne umquam Romae reverteretur*) is unparalleled in similar *procurationes*. Something must be behind this melodramatic addition. Two years earlier, Caepio himself had fled east across the sea (to Smyrna, in Asia Minor), to the chagrin of his prosecutor Norbanus. But despite his exile, the ex-consul remained influential in Rome, and as we have seen, Norbanus himself later was prosecuted for his own prosecution of Caepio. In the years following Caepio's conviction and escape, those who had orchestrated his downfall must have feared his possible return. When one of his former slaves committed a prodigious act, Caepio's enemies in the pontifical college must have conspired to send him a message in exile. It is Caepio – and surely not a mere slave – who is warned "never to return to Rome again." Even if the message never reached Caepio himself, it would not have been lost on his friends still in Rome.[16] Much, therefore, of the text of the prodigy merely enables the slave to re-enact his master's humiliation, and this is why he is said to be "of Quintus Servilius Caepio" well after he had ceased in fact to be so.

This conclusion raises grave doubts about the possibility of learning anything about the slave from the words that survive to describe him, since they rewrite his act for the political ends of the *pontifices*. It is disheartening to consider that even after the exile of his master, even after he castrated himself, even after the two thousand years since, the slave still "belongs" to Caepio, to whose biography he is little more than a footnote – note 8, to be exact, in Broughton's entry for Caepio in *The Magistrates of the Roman Republic*.

3 *Matri[s] Idaeae* (religion)

A century before the events thus far considered, the Sibylline books had warned the nervous Roman populace that the war with Hannibal would not be won until the "Idaean Mother" of the gods was brought to Rome.[17] In 204 BCE a high-level diplomatic mission arrived at Cybele's central sanctuary in Pessinus, in Asia Minor, and with the help of King Attalus I of Pergamon, the envoys were allowed to carry off the cult statue of the goddess. Attalus had good reason to cooperate: though Rome's military involvement in the Eastern Mediterranean had begun only a few years earlier, by 190 BCE it would be the region's dominant political power. Indeed, by 200 BCE Rome would renew hostilities with Macedon at the request of none other than Attalus himself.

Two thousand years later, Franz Cumont would write, "When the Senate became better acquainted with the divinity imposed on it by the Sibyls, it must have been quite embarrassed by the present of King Attalos" (1956, 51). Cumont's sympathy represents neither the first nor the last attempt by a modern historian to purify the conscript fathers of any culpability in the introduction of "Eastern" rites into Rome. Such efforts usually have obscured the clear evidence that the adoption of Cybele was deeply implicated in struggles among Roman aristocratic families. The Delphic oracle instructed that the goddess should be received onto Italian soil by the "best man" (*vir optimus*) of Rome, and a Scipio was chosen for the honor. Lest such glory be bestowed solely on a rival family, a Claudia was said to have freed the barge carrying the goddess when it became trapped by an offshore sandbar at the mouth of the Tiber. A line of matrons conveyed the statue from Ostia to Rome, where it remained in the temple of Victory until that of the Magna Mater (Cybele's usual name in Latin) was dedicated on the Palatine in 191 BCE.

Most aspects of the annual festival founded in honor of the Magna Mater, the *Megalesia*, were deeply Roman and aristocratic in nature. Only free Romans could attend: foreigners and slaves were banished from the central festival of one of the only foreign divinities admitted into the Roman *pomerium* during the Republic, the only festival with a foreign name (Cicero, *On the Response of the Haruspices* 11–12). Aristocratic families invited each other to dinner parties and snacked on *moretum*, a dish of rustic simplicity designed to mark the antiquity of their bloodlines (Ovid, *Fasti* 4.367–72; *Corpus Inscriptionum Latinarum* I.316). At the sanctuary itself, revelers enjoyed comic plays (the *Pseudolus* of Plautus premiered here at the opening of the new temple in 191 BCE) and laughed at the staged antics of slaves and the lower classes.[18]

Of course, it was not to this respectable celebration that Cumont was referring. M. J. Vermaseren, the great Cybele scholar of our era, expresses the same sentiment in more detail:

> The Romans had brought their ancestral Goddess to the new country and provided her with proper accommodation, only then to discover how widely and profoundly their own attitude differed from the Asian mentality. They were shocked by the *Eastern rites*, with their loud ululations and wild dances, with their entrancing rhythms, which by pipe and tambourine whipped up the people into ecstasies of bloody self-flagellation and self-injury.
>
> (Vermaseren 1997b 96, italics my own)

What Vermaseren says is officially true; that is to say, during the Republic, Romans were forbidden by law from participating in these *other* rites. But the image of stunned Roman authorities who got more than they bargained for is absurd, if picturesque. In the first place, Rome did not scruple to jettison unsavory rites of other imported religions; if temple practices traveled from Pessinos to Rome, they must have done so with a Roman passport.[19] But what renders the scenario depicted by Vermaseren and others even more suspect is the elaborate care with which the Romans constructed and maintained the authenticity of the "Easternness" of these so-called Eastern rites. Priests were imported directly from Pessinus; except for an annual procession, their practices seem to have been confined to the sanctuary proper and shrouded in a secrecy that surely served to heighten public anxiety about their foreignness. The extraterritoriality of these rites was such a fixture of the cult that when the bull-sacrifice included among them in the Empire was moved to the Vatican hill, the area designated for its practice was renamed the "Phrygianum," after the region surrounding Pessinus.

If the Palatine sanctuary offered a little plot of "genuine" Eastern danger in the heart of Rome, its visible encapsulation by the rest of the city, and particularly by the aristocratic houses that surrounded it, demonstrated that this danger was well under control. At the festival each year, the aristocracy invaded this space and fashioned *romanitas* itself out of the shapeless East. This colonial fantasy is embodied in the goddess herself, with a dual name to suggest her bifurcated identity: Phrygian Cybele emerges as Roman Magna Mater. The desired appearance is that Rome fills the feminine lack of the East; we prefer to read instead that it is precisely this "East" which completes the idea of Rome.

The "East" was let out only once a year, on April 4, for the annual procession of the goddess during the *Megalesia* (Ovid, *Fasti* 4.179–372). Here, at last, are the "pipe and tambourine" Vermaseren had in mind:

> They thump tense tom-toms with open palms, and concave cymbals, all around. Horns bellow a growling menace, and the hollow flute trips minds with Phrygian cadence. The front line bears arms, symbols of violent fury poised to terrify the thankless souls and impious hearts of the crowd with the dread will of the Goddess. And so from the moment when, carried in through great cities, she, silent, grants humankind her mute benediction, the crowd tosses silver and bronze up and down the streets in her way, enriching her with extravagant alms, while they shower rose-petals, like snowflakes, to shade Mother and her band.
>
> (Lucretius, *On the Nature of Things* 2.618–28)

K. Summers has now shown that Lucretius derives his account not from Greek sources, as was previously thought and as Lucretius himself seems to suggest, but rather from the processions in Rome which the poet himself would have witnessed. In fact, the parade (*pompa*) of the goddess has no parallel in Greece or Phrygia, and though it undoubtedly seemed as exotic to Roman spectators as it has to modern Roman historians, it was a wholly Roman addition to the cult (Summers 1996, 342–51). On parade were not only Cybele but the entire cult ensemble, including the eunuch priests, the *galli*, who attended the goddess in Rome as at Pessinus. If my suggestion in gloss 2 is correct, then in 103 BCE the Roman *galli* were the new masters of the slave of Caepio. If the confiscation of the ex-consul's property occurred before April, the new temple-slave could have taken part in the *pompa* of that year.

Rome's carefully choreographed spectacle of Cybele's "Eastern side" was decidedly upstaged in the following year by the sensational surprise visit to Rome of the Battaces, priest-king of her sanctuary in Pessinus. The story survives in the *Bibliotheca* of Photius, the scholarly ninth-century Patriarch of Constantinople, in an extract from a now lost book of Diodorus. Francis Walton's 1957 translation manages to capture Diodorus' evident delight in relating the scandalous series of events:

> A certain man named Battaces, a priest of the Great Mother of the Gods, arrived, says Diodorus, from Pessinos in Phrygia. Claiming that he had come by command of the goddess, he obtained an audience with the consuls and with the senate, in which he stated that the temple of the goddess had been defiled and that rites of purification to her must be performed at Rome in the name of the state. The robe he wore, like the rest of his costume, was outlandish and by Roman standards not to be countenanced, for he had an immense golden crown and a gaudy cape shot with gold, the marks of royal rank. After addressing the populace from the rostra, and creating in the crowd a mood of religious awe, he was granted lodging and hospitality at the expense of the state, but was forbidden by one of the tribunes, Aulus Pompeius, to wear his crown. Brought back to the rostra by another of the tribunes, and questioned as to what ritual purity for the temple required, he couched his answers in words evocative of holy dread. When he was thereupon attacked in a partisan spirit by Pompeius, and was contemptuously sent back to his lodgings, he refused to appear again in public, saying that not only he, but the goddess as well, had been impiously treated with disrespect. Pompeius was straightway smitten with a raging fever, then lost his voice and was stricken with quinsy, and on the third day died. To the man in the street it seemed that his death was an act of Divine Providence in requital for his offenses against the goddess and her priest, for the Romans are very prone to fear in matters of religion. Accordingly Battaces was granted a special dispensation in regard to his costume and the sacred robe, was honoured with notable gifts, and when he started homeward from Rome was escorted on his way by a large crowd, both men and women.
>
> (Photius *Bibliotheca* 390b-391a)[20]

Plutarch, who gives a shorter version of the story in his biography of Marius (17.5–6), says nothing about the Battaces' fashion *faux pas*, but he does preserve the insulting name which the tribune called the priest as he dragged him from the Rostra: *agúrtês*, "beggar," a reference to the *galli* and their practice of soliciting alms from worshippers.[21] Behind the insults, it is highly likely that both the tribune and the Battaces had deeply political aims, at the center of which was the growing power of the consul Marius. In Plutarch's version, the Battaces prophesies imminent military victory for the Romans. In 99 BCE Marius himself, having fulfilled that prophecy by defeating the Cimbri and Teutoni, would undertake a pilgrimage to Pessinus to repay earlier vows he had made to the goddess (31).[22]

The Battaces probably presided at the *Megalesia* while he was in Rome in 102 BCE, and perhaps the former slave of Caepio was in attendance. If the Battaces' motives were in fact political, then the slave of a former consul might have proved a useful informant. But the Battaces may also have had a religious effect, not only on the slave but also on others. Archeological evidence suggests that at the end of the second or beginning of the first century BCE, that is, around the time of the visit of the Battaces, a form of the cult of Cybele alternative to that celebrated at the *Megalesia* achieved popularity in Rome. That its iconography seems to have been confined to terracotta votive statues, at a time when the state cult was represented in the costly commissions of the wealthy, suggests that its adherents were poor or middle-class; other evidence hints that among them were slaves and freedmen, and that these may have included women.[23] Central to this "subcult" was Attis, a companion of Cybele as worshipped in Asia Minor. A number of figurines representing Attis have been found by excavators in the area of the Palatine sanctuary of the goddess.[24]

Modern studies of Cybele and Attis in art unanimously fail to note the obvious: Attis as represented in this find and elsewhere is a penis; his "Phrygian cap" its foreskin; his round cheeks, those of its *glans*; his billowing cloak traces the outlines of its testicles. Along with the statues of Attis were found votives of the heads of penises, both covered by foreskin and not, and of terracotta cypress cones, with conspicuous resemblances to the *glans*.[25] In the absence of truly careful historiography of the Attis myth, it is difficult to know whether the makers of these votives knew Attis as the consort of Cybele who, driven mad by the jealous goddess, castrated himself and died, or whether that story is a later, perhaps Roman, re-writing of an Attis who began merely as a personified penis unattached to any (other) body.[26]

Beneath the very noses of the Romans in attendance at the *Megalesia* were strata of religious meaning much deeper than the rather shallow myth they had crafted for themselves. The figurines, squatters who have outlived the temple in front of which they were buried, reveal that the Roman cult of Cybele opened up a field of significance subject to appropriations and occupations by those excluded from the annual festival. But what exactly did Attis mean to these other worshippers? Was he connected solely to practices of worship brought to Rome from elsewhere, or did he in some way respond to the Roman state cult, interrogating its appropriation of the foreign goddess or, perhaps, claiming a piece of its aristocratic prestige? His figurines, phallic homunculi which are carved with singular expressiveness, smile coyly, as if they know the answer – perhaps they even know why the slave of Caepio castrated himself – but are not telling.

247

4 *se praecidit* (the body)

The slave castrated himself in imitation of the *galli*, cutting off his own testicles, probably with a jagged potsherd. Of course, the euphemism "he cut himself off in front" (*se praecidit*) presents a certain anatomical vagueness. For the Romans castration had the same ambiguity that it has in English usage: surgically it usually referred to the testicles, but on occasion, and quite often in the popular imagination, it referred to the penis. Thus when Juvenal jeeringly suggests that *cinaedi* (men who assume a passive role in sexual intercourse with other men) follow the lead of the *galli* by cutting off their "superfluous flesh" (*caro supervacua*), he almost certainly is referring to the penetrative penis rather than to the reproductive testicles, though he could, of course, intend either or both (2.116).

A slave's penis was not entirely superfluous, for it was at least valuable as a source of *vernae*, slaves born within the household. But it was not a phallus – that is, it did not signify the sexual and political domination exercised by adult male Roman citizens. The *symbolic* superfluousness of a slave's penis was translated into its sexual insignificance, from the master's point of view, from which the only penis that really mattered was the phallus, that is, the one he shared with the other free men of Rome. Slaves of both genders were supposed to be only the passive objects of their masters' will and desire, though in practice (and even in theory), things seldom were really that simple (Richlin 1992, xiv ff.).

When Michel Foucault writes about "the penis," he is in fact referring to the phallus, the significant penis attached to the body of a free Roman man:

> The penis . . . appears at the intersection of all these games of mastery: self-mastery, since its demands are likely to enslave us if we allow ourselves to be coerced by it; superiority over sexual partners, since it is by means of the penis that the penetration is carried out; status and privileges, since it signifies the whole field of kinship and social activity.
>
> (Foucault, 1986, 34)

None of these "games of mastery" was available to a slave, who stood quite literally at the other end of what Foucault somewhat alarmingly calls "our" penis. In such an account of Roman sexuality, penises that are not phalluses are meaningless loose ends, and the slave of Caepio is to be thanked for neatly trimming one away. Foucault leaves us to conclude that the slave possessed no more than a grotesque simulacrum of the Roman phallus described above; his act marked a momentary contradiction between masculinity and slavery, resolved (with or without his castration) by his emasculation by status.

The account of the Roman penetrative hierarchy offered by Foucault and his followers does allow a political reading of the slave's self-castration, but only one in which he merely *traces* an already implied text of his own subordination. The problem is this: if we view the body of this particular slave as a document he did not author, we perform on it a hermeneutic operation not unlike that performed by the Roman priests who recorded it as a prodigy. That is to say, we take his body from him and give it over to a significance larger than that body, a significance that the slave himself therefore need not comprehend. For them, the slave's body was a sign written in the familiar language of prodigies; similarly for us it becomes a recognizable symptom of the "discourse of masters and slaves."

But if instead we take the slave seriously as author of his own castration, then we must allow his body to mean in unexpected, even poetic ways. Perhaps the act alludes to Attis, and by castrating himself the slave unleashes the god latent in his own body. Divinity, however, may have been less at stake than personhood. The slave was himself a kind of *membrum disiectum*, torn from his former context by the political and economic castration of Caepio. And this may not have been his first dislocation, especially if he was not born a slave – a distinct possibility, since the triumphant general Caepio certainly would have reckoned foreign slaves among his spoils. Suppose that the slave borrowed the metaphor that made him an extension of his master, but that he used it for the purposes of his own analogy, in order to see himself in his own genitals at the moment that he made himself master of his own body. *Se praecidit*, "he cut himself off in front": here the language seems confused about just where the "self" of the slave was located, as if transcribing a schizophrenia that the slave had mapped onto his body, making two bodies, and two selves, where Rome had seen less than one. Alas, the slave does not tell us which (part of his) body he hoped to free from which.

5 *et trans mare exportatus ne umquam Romae reverteretur* (gender)

This *procuratio* is discussed above in the note on Caepio, but a connection to *procurationes* of prodigies involving hermaphrodites merits an additional note. Several prodigies reported by Obsequens over a fifty-year period concern the discovery of a hermaphrodite: "At Luna, hermaphrodite (*androgynus*) born, carried away on the sea by order of the soothsayers" (22), 142 BCE. "In Ferentine countryside hermaphrodite found and thrown into the river" (27a), 133 BCE. "In Forum Vessanum hermaphrodite born, he was carried away on the sea" (32), 122 BCE. "Eight-year-old hermaphrodite found in the Roman countryside and sent away on the sea" (34), 119 BCE. "At Saturnia, ten-year-old hermaphrodite found and plunged into the sea" (36), 117 BCE. "A hermaphrodite carried away on the sea" (47), 98 BCE. "Prayers offered in the City because a hermaphrodite had been found and carried away on the sea" (48), 97 BCE. "A hermaphrodite born at Urbinum carried away on the sea" (50), 95 BCE. "At Aretrium two hermaphrodites found" (53), 92 BCE. The formulaic *procuratio* of death by drowning (the children apparently were set adrift in rafts in order to avoid the religious pollution associated with drowning them directly) offered simple sympathetic magic for these creatures of "fluid" sex.[27] Not surprisingly, water figures prominently in the fanciful origin of the god Hermaphroditus as later described by Ovid (*Metamorphoses* 4.285–388).

The self-castrated slave was awkwardly fitted into the pre-existing category of the hermaphrodite by the priests who sought precedent for his case. The slave, however, was not set adrift to drown (*in mare deportatus*, as in most of the examples above) but rather was placed in a ship bound for a distant destination (*trans mare exportatus*), with the warning never to return. If the hypothesis advanced in my second gloss is correct, then the variation in the formula served primarily to establish the connection to Caepio, but it nevertheless is likely that the slave really was sent across the sea rather than drowned. A reasonable guess is that the destination was Pessinus, where he could have entered the service of Cybele at her ancient cult center, perhaps honored as a *gallus*.[28] Ironically, the slave probably departed Italy from the Roman port of Ostia, where Cybele had landed a century before.

> *Servus Q. Servilii Caepionis* <. . .> *Matris Idaeae se praecidit et trans mare exportatus ne umquam Romae reverteretur.*

My notes once ended here, with the slave receding from view, leaving behind nearly the same sixteen Latin words with which I had begun. For a long time I wandered this nearer shore in search of a "conclusion," a frame for the imperfect sketch I had attempted in my notes. But how could I complete what could be no more than a dim outline? I knew that it was useless to comb the beach from which the slave had departed for other fragments to flesh out the picture; despite promising results by others in reassembling "the Roman slave" from pieces found here and there, I had lost interest in such a creature, at once all slaves and no slave, and could not bear the thought of thus re-membering. Nor was I likely to find, floating in a Venetian canal, a manuscript in a bottle more complete than that conveyed to Aldus Manutius, one that contained an intact portrait of the particular slave in whom I was interested. Such a book had not been lost, for it had never been written. But in that city I did find a picture of a slave, painted not long after the text of Obsequens was first pressed into the pages of a printed book.

Tintoretto's *Miracle of St Mark* depicts a slave lying on a pavement surrounded by an angry mob (Figure 14.1). The slave, the story goes, was condemned to have his legs broken and his eyes gouged out because he had slipped away to visit the relics of St Mark without his master's permission. In the painting, though unseen by the slave's eager tormentors, the saint himself has descended from heaven to protect his follower from harm. The painting captures the moment at which the crowd's weapons suddenly and miraculously crumble into splinters. The body of the slave is preserved intact, saved as much by the painter's art as by the saint's miracle.

The painted scene is powerful – and it is unforgettably so – not because of its *deus ex machina*, but rather because it preserves a *moment*, a story collapsed

Figure 14.1 Tintoretto, *Il Miracolo di S. Marco.* (Alinari Art Resource, NY)

into an image frozen in time. In a similar way, time stands still for the slave of Caepio – his time? our time? the difference matters little. His past and our present are for a moment simultaneous, in what Walter Benjamin calls "an image which flashes up at the instant when it can be recognized and is never seen again ... a memory as it flashes up at a moment of danger" (1968, 255). We have many such momentary memories in the *Prodigiorum Liber*: the cry of the boy at Nursia, the last laugh of the girl destined for sacrifice, a hermaphrodite's exposure. ... Deprived of past and future, these moments have only *presence*, and we do not so much read them as live them. "History" may be more complete, but it can never offer such immediacy.

In vain does history or any of the other sciences represented by these notes try to prevent the slave of Caepio from vanishing "across the sea" in the words that immediately follow his castration. They might just as well try to stay his hand the moment before. But even as the slave escapes epistemological certainty, we catch a glimpse of him as of a stranger seen momentarily in a crowd: a fleeting vision, a moment of contact, enough.

Notes

1 Firmin-Didot 1875, 304. A particularly precious copy, preserved in the Berg Collection of the New York Public Library, contains a dedication in the hand of Erasmus.
2 The full surviving title, *Iulii Obsequentis ab anno urbis conditae DV prodigiorum liber*, indicates that the catalogue once began with the year 249 but that the beginning of the work was missing from Aldo's manuscript.
3 Citations are to the only widely available modern edition of the *Prodigiorum Liber*, that of A. C. Schlesinger in the fourteenth volume ("Summaries, Fragments, and Obsequens") of the Loeb edition of Livy, first published in 1959. The important critical editions remain those of Otto Jahn (Leipzig 1853) and Otto Rossbach (Leipzig 1910).
4 Shakespeare could have derived his "tempest dropping fire," etc., from Obsequens, but not from the entry for 44 BCE, in which we are told that Calpurnia was awakened by the bright moonlight. Plutarch, Shakespeare's only proven source, alludes to celestial disturbances on the night of March 14 (*Caesar* 63.1), though he does so somewhat vaguely, perhaps to gloss over their absence in his own sources.
5 The first to attribute the *Prodigiorum Liber* to late antique pagan–Christian tension was Mommsen, in the letter to Jahn which the latter includes in his critical edition. Mommsen, however, believed that Obsequens was a Christian who, on the analogy of Orosius, sought to glorify Christianity with examples of the gloom and barbarity of the Roman past. Subsequent historians have tended to make Obsequens a pagan and a participant in the so-called "pagan Renaissance" of late antiquity; and thus *The Oxford Classical Dictionary* (2nd edn, 1970) says only that he is "probably 4th c. A.D." (revised to "late 4th or early 5th" in the new, 3rd edn) and that his book "represents late heathen justification of the forms of the old faith."
6 P. L. Schmidt (1968), who accepts the reconstruction of Obsequens as a late antique pagan, presents a complex view of his working method, arguing that he added historical material (chiefly reports of military victories) from other sources to the prodigy material he took from Livy. Schmidt rejects the views of some that Obsequens used an epitome of Livy rather than the full text.
7 These may have included the *Annales Maximi*, copied directly from the *tabula dealbata*, though, for a skeptical view, see Rawson 1971, refuted by MacBain 1982, 8ff.

8 That argument apparently was last seriously made by K. W. Nitzch in 1873 (237ff).

9 Santini himself hedges almost charmingly on this last question, concluding that Obsequens "ci conserva l'eco di testi prodigiali che per noi sarebbero irrimediabilmente perduti" and that his style is "lo specchio di una realtà autentica e consistente della civiltà di Roma repubblicana" (1988, 224, 226). In his emphasis on formulaic regularity in the language used by Obsequens, Santini overlooks important irregularities. For instance, in his discussion of prodigies concerning hermaphrodites (216–18), Santini does not include the slave of Caepio (see my discussion of the slave's *procuratio*, below), nor does he note a lexical change concurrent with a change in *procuratio* (cf. my note 27). The former reflects an intrusion into the language by historical events, as I will show; the second must trace subtle religious and linguistic evolution. These irregularities cannot plausibly be attributed to Obsequens himself, who must sometimes be an even more faithful "echo" and "mirror" than Santini suggests.

10 The phrase *se praecidit*, "he cut off (in front) himself," is difficult to translate. For *praecidere* referring to castration, compare Martial 2.45, *praecisa est mentula*, humorously connected to the castration of the priests of Cybele. I have favored the most literal translation possible, since "he castrated himself" undoes the euphemism, while a more elaborate translation like "he severed his forward appendage" muddles the simplicity of the original. I discuss more fully the ambiguities of *se praecidit* later in this paper.

11 In the Aldine edition, the sentences which Schlesinger numbers 44a (*ancilia cum crepitu sua sponte mota. servus Q. Servilii Caepionis . . . urbs lustrata. capra cornibus ardentibus per urbem ducta, porta Naevia emissa relictaque. in Aventino luto pluit. Lusitanis devictis Hispania ulterior pacata. Cimbri deleti.*) end the preceding section, which records events from the consulship of Gaius Marius and Quintus Lutatius (102 BCE). Obsequens tends to end his lists for each year with important military actions, and so modern editors indicate a lacuna after the defeat of the Teutoni, which happened in 102, and place the immediately following text *ancilia . . . deleti* in the next year, when the defeat of the Cimbri is known to have occurred. Schlesinger adopts the missing textual division supplied, he says, by Oudendorp (though not in his 1720 edition) – the names of the consuls for 101, Gaius Marius and Manius Aquilius, which may be the only omission. The emendation must be correct, and the castration of the slave thus should be dated to 101.

12 The fragments of book 36, in which the account of the slave war appears, have been collected by F. R. Walton in the Loeb edition of Diodorus. On the initial causes of the rebellion, compare the version of Cassius Dio, 27.93.

13 The thicket is one of analysis, not of evidence, which for the period in question is notoriously spare. The patient reader should consult, from the bibliography at the end of this book, Münzer 1920, 283–302, and Broughton 1951–60, 562–6 (where additional bibliography is summarized). See also Münzer's articles in Pauly-Wissowa, *Realencyclopädie der Classischen Altertumswissenschaft* ("Servilius" 49 and 50) as well as those by E. Badian in *The Oxford Classical Dictionary* (2nd edn, 1970), "Caepio" 1 and 2, with references in the latter to two more recent analyses. In the new, third edition of the *OCD* (1996), Badian revises his entry on Quintus Servilius Caepio 2 (now listed under "Servilius," as in Pauly-Wissowa) to make him only a "relative" (i.e., not necessarily the son) of number 1.

14 Probability is lent to this alternate explanation by the almost certain loss of text only a few words earlier, explained above, note 11.

15 I.e., *[in templo* or *aede] Matris Idaeae*, if the sanctuary was the temple precinct on the Palatine hill, or *[in campo] Matris Idaeae*, if the reference is to a yet unknown *campus* of Cybele at Rome, such as that known to have existed at Ostia and elsewhere.

The second possibility might even explain the scribal eye-skip (*Caepionis in campo*) that produced the error.

16 For the use of Roman prodigies to send political "messages," though in a very different context, see MacBain 1982, especially chapter 3, "Expiations as Vehicles for Communication."

17 Bibliography on Cybele and its salient controversies over more than a century were summarized by G. Thomas in 1984. M. J. Vermaseren's five-volume *Corpus Cultus Cybelae Attidisque* has since been completed. Recently published is a collection of essays dedicated to Vermaseren after his death, edited by Eugene N. Lane: *Cybele, Attis and Related Cults: Essays in Memory of J. J. Vermaseren*, (1996). As the present article was going to press, Philippe Borgeaud kindly shared with me an early copy of his new book, *La Mère des Dieux: De Cybèle à la Vierge Marie*, Éditions du Seuil, 1996, which casts long overdue light on the cult's political roles in Rome and elsewhere.

18 The date of the premier of the *Pseudolus* is preserved at the beginning of the oldest manuscript of the text: *M. IUNIO M. FIL[O] PR[AETORIBUS] URB[ANIS] AC[TA] ME[GALESIIS]*, "Acted at the Megalesia when M. Junius and M. Filus were urban praetors (=191 BCE)."

19 Compare the roughly contemporary adoption of the worship of Venus Erycina from Sicily. Among other changes, the temple prostitution central to her worship in Sicily was abandoned (Schilling 1982, 249).

20 The translation appears as section 36.13 in Walton's (Loeb) edition of the fragmentary remains of the last twenty books of Diodorus (1957–8).

21 The word is used elsewhere as an apparently neutral epithet for the alms-seeking *galli*, but here it clearly is an insult, probably directed at the priest's extravagent (and regal?) appearance. If the tribune assailed the priest in Latin that Plutarch has translated into Greek, then the word presumably was *mendicus*, though it seems more likely that the tribune would have wanted the Battaces, who surely spoke only Greek, to understand the jibe.

22 The Battaces' visit came at the end of a decade of highly politicized references to the goddess in Rome, reconstructed in detail by M. G. Morgan (1973), beginning with the struggle to control the rebuilding of her Palatine temple, destroyed by fire in 111. Morgan believes that the priest's visit wrested Cybele's public favor from the Metelli, who were financing the reconstruction of the Roman temple, and bestowed it on the more powerful Marius (243). D. G. Glew (1987) differs somewhat with Morgan's reconstruction; he also argues that the desecration to which the Battaces alludes in Diodorus (the allegations are not mentioned by Plutarch) had taken place in Pessinos (i.e., not in Rome) and that the priest had traveled to the capital to seek redress.

23 Evidence of connections between *galli* and the freed class is found in a legal dispute in 77 BCE regarding the right of the *gallus* Genucius to inherit property (Valerius Maximus 7.7.6). Evidence of involvement by slaves and women is largely to be assumed by reasoning backwards from later evidence (of which there is a great deal), unless the story of the visit of the Battaces quoted above offers earlier evidence for widespread participation by the latter.

24 The entire find of terracotta fragments is Vermaseren 1977a 12–199; for Attis, see especially 12, 141, 142, 151, 157, 161, 162. For a later but better-preserved bronze figurine found in Rome, see 305.

25 Vermaseren 1977a 13, 68–77.

26 By the first century CE, the alternative iconography was sufficiently widespread to prompt an intervention by the emperor Claudius, who co-opted the worship of Attis into the state cult in the guise of democratizing the worship of Cybele. The earlier Attis disappeared, at least temporarily, in the onslaught of a new state festival in which he appeared as a youth with classicizing features – and this time, a hat was only a hat.

27 The only earlier reference to a hermaphrodite among the prodigies seems to pre-date *procuratio* by drowning: "In Umbria hermaphrodite (*semimas*) almost twelve years old found, killed by order of the soothsayers" (3), 186 BCE. Here only does Obsequens use the word *semimas* for "hermaphrodite," as does Livy in his mention of the same prodigy (39.22.5). Obsequens later uses only the Greek word *androgynus*, which, however, refers to the same condition. The earliest reference to the birth of a hermaphrodite as *prodigium* is the one in Livy 27.11.4–5 (209 BCE), which may gloss the *semimas* that Livy had for the first time found in his sources: *et Sinuessae natum ambiguo inter marem ac feminam sexu infantem, quos androgynos uolgus, ut pleraque, faciliore ad duplicanda uerba Graeco sermone appellat.* For the later supplanting of the term *androgynus* by *hermaphroditus*, see Pliny *Natural History* 7.34, repeated by Aulus Gellius 9.4.16.

28 One wonders whether Catullus was inspired to write his "Attis" poem by the story of the slave of Caepio, though he reverses the order of events:

> Born in a swift craft over deep seas, Attis,
> when eagerly he set nimble foot inside Phrygian wood
> and entered the vaulted shade of the Goddess's precinct,
> there goaded by a seething madness, and out of his mind,
> with a sharp flint let tumble the burdens of his groin . . .

> (63.1–5)

BIBLIOGRAPHY

Anderson, William S., 1983, "Chalinus *Armiger* in Plautus' *Casina*," *Illinois Classical Studies* 8: 11–21.

—— 1984, "Love-Plots in Menander and His Roman Adapters," *Ramus* 13: 124–34.

—— 1993, *Barbarian Play: Plautus' Roman Comedy*, Toronto.

—— 1995, "The Roman Transformation of Greek Domestic Comedy," *Classical World* 8: 171–80.

Archibald, Sofia, 1983, "Greek Imports: some aspects of the Hellenic Impact on Thrace," in *Ancient Bulgaria I*, G. Poulter, ed., Nottingham, UK.

—— 1994, "Thracians and Scythians," in *The Cambridge Ancient History VI: The Fourth Century B.C.*, 2nd edn, David M. Lewis, John Boardman, Simon Hornblower, and Martin Ostwald, eds, Cambridge.

Ardaillon, Edouard, 1893, *Les mines de Laurium dans l'antiquité*, Paris.

Arrowsmith, William, trans., 1959, *Hecuba*, in *The Complete Greek Tragedies*, David Grene and Richmond Lattimore, eds, Chicago.

Arthur [Katz], Marylin B., 1973, "Early Greece: The Origins of the Western Attitude toward Women," *Arethusa* 6: 1–24. Reprinted (1984) in *Women in the Ancient World: The Arethusa Papers*, John Peradotto and J. P. Sullivan, eds, Albany, NY.

Auslander, Leora, 1996, *Taste and Power: Furnishing Modern France*, Berkeley, Calif.

Austin, M. M. and Pierre Vidal-Naquet, 1977, *Economic and Social History of Ancient Greece: An Introduction*, M. M. Austin, trans., 1973, *Économies et sociétés en Grèce ancienne*, 2nd edn, Berkeley, Calif.

Babcock, Barbara, ed., 1978, *Reversible World: Symbolic Inversion in Art and Society*, Ithaca, NY.

Bacon, Helen H., 1961, *Barbarians in Greek Tragedy*, New Haven, Conn.

Bakhtin, Mikhail M., 1984, *Rabelais and His World*, H. Iswolsky, trans., Bloomington, Ind.

Balsdon, J.P.V.D., 1979, *Romans and Aliens*, Chapel Hill, NC.

Baltrusch, Elisabeth, 1988, *Regimen morum. Die Reglementierung des Privatlebens der Senatoren und Ritter in der römischen Republik und frühen Kaiserzeit*, (Vestigia 41), Munich.

Barchiesi, Alessandro, 1991, "Discordant Muses," *Proceedings of the Cambridge Philological Society* 37: 1–21.

Barker, Ernest, ed. and trans., 1962, *The Politics of Aristotle*, Oxford.

Barthes, Roland, 1980, "The Old Rhetoric: An Aide-Mémoire," in *The Semiotic Challenge*, Richard Howard, trans., New York.

Barton, Carlin A., 1993, *The Sorrows of the Ancient Romans: The Gladiator and the Monster*, Princeton, NJ.

Beard, Mary, 1993, "Looking (harder) for Roman myth: Dumézil, Declamation, and the Problems of Definition," in *Colloquium Rauricum 3* (*Mythos in mythenloser Gesellschaft: Das Paradigms Roms*), Fritz Graf, ed., Stuttgart.

Beare, William, 1964, *The Roman Stage*, 3rd edn, London.

Beckles, Hilary, 1996, "Black Female Slaves and White Households in Barbados," in *More Than Chattel: Black Women and Slavery in the Americas*, David Barry Gaspar and Darlene Clark Hine, eds, Bloomington, Ind.

Benjamin, Walter, 1968, "Theses on the Philosophy of History," in *Illuminations*, Harry Zohn, trans., Hannah Arendt, ed., New York.

Bergren, Ann L.T., 1983, "Language and the Female in Early Greek Thought," *Arethusa* 16: 69–98.

Beringer, Walter, 1961, "Zu den Begriffen für 'Sklaven' und 'Unfreie' bei Homer," *Historia* 10: 259–91.

—— 1982, "'Servile Status' in the Sources for Early Greek History," *Historia* 31: 13–32.

Bersani, Leo, 1995, *Homos*, Cambridge, Mass.

Bettini, Maurizio, 1982, "Verso un'antropologia dell'intreccio. Le strutture semplici della trama nelle commedie di Plauto," *Materiali e discussioni per l'analisi dei testi classici* 7: 39–101.

Betz, H.D., 1986, *The Greek Magical Papyri in Translation*, Chicago.

Biezunska-Malowist, Iza and Marian Malowist, 1989, "L'Esclavage antique et moderne. Les possibilités de recherches comparées," in *Mélanges Pierre Lévêque* 82, Marie Madeleine and Evelyne Geny, eds, Paris.

Bingen, Jean, 1967, "L'Établissement géométrique et la nécropole ouest," *Thorikos III, 1965*: 31–56, Brussels.

Black, Donald, 1984, "Social Control as a Dependent Variable," in *Toward a General Theory of Social Control*, vol. 1, Donald Black, ed., Orlando, Fla.

Bloomer, W. Martin, 1992, *Valerius Maximus and the Rhetoric of the New Nobility*, Chapel Hill, NC.

—— 1997, *Latinity and Literary Society at Rome*, Philadelphia, PA.

Blundell, Sue, 1995, *Women in Ancient Greece*, Cambridge, Mass.

Bömer, Franz, 1981, *Untersuchungen über die Religion der Sklaven in Griechenland und Rom*, 2nd edn, Wiesbaden.

Bonner, Stanley F., 1949, *Roman Declamation in the Late Republic and Early Empire*, Berkeley, Calif.

—— 1977, *Education in Ancient Rome*, Berkeley, Calif.

Boswell, John, 1988, *The Kindness of Strangers. The Abandonment of Children in Western Europe from Late Antiquity to the Renaissance*, New York.

Bourdieu, Pierre, 1977, *Outline of a Theory of Practice*, Cambridge.

—— 1990, *The Logic of Practice*, Stanford, Calif.

Borgeaud, Pierre, 1996, *La Mère des Dieux: De Cybèle à la Vierge Marie*, Paris.

Bowman, Alan K., 1986, *Egypt after the Pharaohs. 332 BC–AD 642 from Alexander to the Arab Conquest*, London.

Bradley, Keith R., 1978, *Suetonius' Life of Nero: An Historical Commentary*, Brussels.

—— 1979, "Holidays for Slaves," *Symbolae Osloenses* 54: 111–18.

—— 1985, "Ideals of Marriage in Suetonius' *Caesares*," *Rivista Storica Dell'Antichità* 15: 77–95.

—— 1987, *Slaves and Masters in the Roman Empire: A Study in Social Control*, New York and Oxford.

—— 1989, *Slavery and Rebellion in the Roman World, 140 BC–70 AD*, Bloomington, Ind.

—— 1991, *Discovering the Roman Family*, New York and Oxford.

—— 1992, "'The Regular, Daily Traffic in Slaves:' Roman History and Contemporary History," *Classical Journal* 87: 125–38.

—— 1994a, *Slavery and Society at Rome*, Cambridge.

—— 1994b, "The Nurse and the Child at Rome: Duty, Affect and Socialisation," *Thamyris* 1.2: 137–56.

Bramble, C.J., 1982, "Martial and Juvenal," in *Cambridge History of Classical Literature II: Latin Literature*, E.J. Kenney and W. V. Clausen, eds, Cambridge.

BIBLIOGRAPHY

Bridenthal, Renate, and Claudia Koonz, 1977, "Introduction," in *Becoming Visible: Women in European History*, Renate Bridenthal and Claudia Koonz, eds, Boston, Mass.
Brody, Miriam, 1993, *Manly Writing: Gender, Rhetoric, and the Rise of Composition*, Carbondale, Ill.
Broughton, T. Robert S., 1951–60, *The Magistrates of the Roman Republic*, New York.
Brown, Peter, 1967, *Augustine of Hippo: A Biography*, Berkeley, Calif.
Brown, Robert, 1995, "Livy's Sabine Women and the Ideal of *Concordia*," *Transactions of the American Philological Association* 125: 291–319.
Brown, Shelby, 1993, "Feminist Research in Archaeology: What Does It Mean? Why Is It Taking So Long?" in *Feminist Theory and the Classics*, Nancy Sorkin Rabinowitz and Amy Richlin, eds, New York and London.
Brunt, P.A., 1988, "*Libertas* in the Republic," in *The Fall of the Roman Republic and Related Essays*, Oxford.
Buck, Charles Henry, Jr., 1940, *Chronology of the Plays of Plautus*, Baltimore, Md.
Burke, Peter, 1978, *Popular Culture in Early Modern Europe*, New York.
Bush, Michael L., ed., 1996, *Serfdom and Slavery: Studies in Legal Bondage*, London.
Butler, Judith, 1990, *Gender Trouble: Feminism and the Subversion of Identity*, New York.
Cantarella, Eva, 1987, *Pandora's Daughters*, Baltimore, Md.
—— 1996, *Passato Prossimo: Donne romane da Tacita a Sulpicia*, Milan.
Carby, Hazel V., 1987, *Reconstructing Womanhood*, New York.
Carey, C., ed., 1989, *Lysias: Selected Speeches*, Cambridge.
Carson, Anne, 1990, "Putting Her in Her Place: Women, Dirt, and Desire," in *Before Sexuality: The Construction of Erotic Experience in the Ancient Greek World*, D.M. Halperin, J. J. Winkler, F. I. Zeitlin, eds, Princeton, NJ.
Cartledge, P.A., 1985, "Rebels and *Sambos* in Classical Greece: A Comparative View," in *CRUX: Essays presented to G.E.M. de Ste. Croix*, P.A. Cartledge and F.D. Harvey, eds, Exeter, UK.
Cicikova, Maria, 1963, "Développement de la céramique thrace à l'époque classique et hellénistique," *Acta Antiqua Philippopolitana*: 35–54, Sofia.
—— 1977, "Céramique thrace fabriquée à la main du VIe au Ie s. avant notre ère," *Thracia* 4: 123–40.
Clark, Gillian, 1993, *Women in Late Antiquity. Pagan and Christian Lifestyles*, Oxford.
—— ed., 1995, *Augustine Confessions. Books I-IV*, Cambridge.
Clifford, James, 1986, "Introduction: Partial Truths," in *Writing Culture*, James Clifford and George E. Marcus, eds, Berkeley, Calif.
Clinton, Catherine, 1982, *The Plantation Mistress: Woman's World in the Old South*, New York.
—— 1985, "Caught in the Web of the Big House: Women and Slavery," in *The Web of Southern Social Relations: Women, Family, and Education*, Walter Fraser, Jr, R. Frank Saunders, Jr, and Jon L. Wakelyn, eds, Athens, Ga.
—— 1991, "Southern Dishonor: Flesh, Blood, Race, and Bondage," in *In Joy and in Sorrow: Women, Family, and Marriage in the Victorian South, 1830–1900*, Carol Bleser, ed., New York.
Clover, Carol, 1992, *Men, Women and Chain Saws: Gender in the Modern Horror Film*, Princeton, NJ.
Cohen, David, 1990, "The Social Context of Adultery at Athens," in *NOMOS: Essays in Athenian Law, Politics, and Society*, Paul Cartledge, Paul Millett, and Stephen Todd, eds, Cambridge.
—— 1991a, "The Augustan Law on Adultery: The Social and Cultural Context," in *The Family in Italy from Antiquity to the Present*, David I. Kertzer and Richard P. Saller, eds, New Haven, Conn.
—— 1991b, *Law, Sexuality, and Society: The Enforcement of Morals in Classical Athens*, Cambridge.
—— 1995, *Law, Violence, and Community in Classical Athens*, Cambridge.

258

Cohen, Edward, 1992, *Athenian Economy and Society: A Banking Perspective*, Princeton, NJ.

Cohn-Haft, L., 1956, "The Public Physicians of Ancient Greece," *Smith College Studies in History* 42.

Cole, Eve Browning, 1994, "Women, Slaves, and 'Love of Toil' in Aristotle's Moral Philosophy," in *Engendering Origins: Critical Feminist Readings in Plato and Aristotle*, Bat-Ami Bar On, ed., Albany, NY.

Cole, Thomas, 1991, *The Origins of Rhetoric in Ancient Greece*, Baltimore, Md.

Collins, Patricia Hill, 1991, *Black Feminist Thought: Knowledge, Consciousness, and the Politics of Empowerment*, New York and London.

Comaroff, John L. and Simon Roberts, 1981, *Rules and Processes*, Chicago.

Conacher, D. J., 1987, *Aeschylus' Oresteia: A Literary Commentary*, Toronto, Buffalo, and London.

Conkey, Margaret W. and Joan M. Gero, 1991, "Tensions, Pluralities, and Engendering Archaeology," in *Engendering Archaeology: Women in Prehistory*, Joan M. Gero and Margaret W. Conkey, eds, Oxford.

Conley, John M. and William M. O'Barr, 1990, *Rules versus Relationships: The Ethnography of Legal Discourse*, Chicago.

Conophagos, Constantin, 1980, *Le Laurium antique*, Athens.

Copley, Frank O., 1947, "*Servitium Amoris* in the Roman Elegists," *Transactions of the American Philological Association* 78: 285–300.

Corbett, Percy E., 1930, *The Roman Law of Marriage*, Oxford.

Corbier, Mireille, 1991, "Divorce and Adoption as Roman Familial Strategies," in *Marriage, Divorce and Children in Ancient Rome*, Beryl Rawson, ed., Oxford.

—— 1992, "Family Behavior of the Roman Aristocracy, Second Century BC–Third Century AD," in *Women's History and Ancient History*, Sarah B. Pomeroy, ed., Chapel Hill, NC.

Costin, Cathy Lynne, 1996, "Exploring the Relationship Between Gender and Craft in Complex Societies: Methodological and Theoretical Issues of Gender Attribution," in *Gender and Archaeology*, Rita P. Wright, ed., Philadelphia, Pa.

Cowie, Elizabeth, 1978, "Woman as Sign," *m/f* 1: 49–63.

Cox, Harvey, 1969, *The Feast of Fools*, Cambridge, Mass.

Crook, J.A., 1967, *Law and Life of Rome*, Ithaca, NY.

Crosby, Margaret, 1950, "The Leases of the Laureion Mines," *Hesperia* 19: 189–312.

Culham, Phyllis, 1982, "The Lex Oppia," *Latomus* 41: 786–93.

Cumont, Franz, 1956, *The Oriental Religions in Roman Paganism*, New York. Trans. of *Les Religions orientales dans le paganisme romain*, 1905, Paris.

Curran, Leo, 1966, "*Desultores Amoris*: Ovid *Amores* I.3," *Classical Philology* 61: 47–9.

Daitz, Stephen G., 1971, "Concepts of Freedom and Slavery in Euripides' *Hecuba*," *Hermes* 99: 217–26.

Daviault, André, ed., 1981, *Comoedia Togata. Fragments*, Paris.

Davis, Angela, 1971, "Reflections on the Black Woman's Role in the Community of Slaves," *The Black Scholar* 3: 2–15.

Davis, John H., 1977, *People of the Mediterranean: An Essay in Comparative Social Anthropology*, London.

Davis, John T., 1977, "Dramatic Pairings in the Elegies of Propertius and Ovid," *Noctes Romanae*, Bern.

—— 1989, *Fictus Adulter: The Poet as Actor in the Amores*, Amsterdam.

Dean-Jones, Lesley, 1987, "Morbidity and Vitality," unpublished dissertation, Stanford University, Stanford, Calif.

—— 1994, *Women's Bodies in Classical Greek Science*, Oxford.

Deichgräber, Karl, 1982, *Die Patienten des Hippokrates. Historisch-prosopographische Beiträge zu den Epidemien des Corpus Hippocraticum*, Wiesbaden.

Della Corte, Francesco, 1967, *Da Sarsina a Roma: Ricerche plautine*, 2nd edn, Florence.

—— 1975a, "Maschere e personaggi in Plauto," *Dioniso* 46: 163–93.

—— 1975b, "La tipologia del personaggio della *palliata*," *Association Guillaume Budé. Actes du IXe congrès. Rome 13–18 avril 1973*, Paris.

Demand, Nancy, 1994, *Birth, Death and Motherhood in Classical Greece*, Baltimore, Md.

Denniston, John Dewar and Denys Page, eds, 1972, *Agamemnon*, Oxford.

Dershowitz, Alan M., 1996 "Life Is Not a Dramatic Narrative" in *Law's Stories: Narrative and Rhetoric in the Law*, Peter Brooks and Paul Gewirtz, eds, New Haven, Conn.

Dimitrov, D. P. and Maria Cicikova, 1978, *The Thracian City of Seuthopolis*, British Archaeological Reports, International Series 38, Oxford.

Dimitrova, A. and N. Gizdova, 1974, "Der Charakter der thrakischen Kultur während der jüngeren vorrömischen Eisenzeit in dem Gebiet des Sredna-gora Gebirges," *Thracia* 3.

Dixon, Suzanne, 1985a, "The Marriage Alliance in the Roman Elite," *Journal of Family History* 10: 353–78.

—— 1985b, "Polybius on Roman Women and Property," *American Journal of Philology* 106: 147–70.

—— 1988, *The Roman Mother*, Norman, Okla.

—— 1991, "The Sentimental Ideal of the Roman Family," in *Marriage, Divorce and Children in Ancient Rome*, Beryl Rawson, ed., Oxford.

—— 1992, *The Roman Family*, Baltimore, Md.

Doherty, Lillian Eileen, 1995, *Siren Songs: Gender, Audiences, and Narrators in the Odyssey*, Ann Arbor, Mich.

Dougherty, Carol, 1991, "Linguistic Colonialism in Aeschylus' *Aetnaeae*," *Greek, Roman, and Byzantine Studies* 32: 119–32.

Douglas, Mary, 1966, *Purity and Danger*, London.

Dover, K. J., 1989, *Greek Homosexuality*, Cambridge, Mass.

DuBois, Page, 1991, *Sowing the Body*, Chicago.

—— 1995, *Sappho Is Burning*, Chicago.

Duckworth, George E., 1952, *The Nature of Roman Comedy: A Study in Popular Entertainment*, Princeton, NJ.

DuQuesnay, I. M. Le M., 1973, "The *Amores*," in *Ovid*, J.W. Binns, ed., London.

Durry, M., 1950, *Eloge funèbre d"une matrone romaine*, Paris.

—— 1955, "Les femmes et le vin," *Revue des Études Latines* 33: 108–13.

Edelstein, L., 1942, "The Hippocratic Oath: Text, Translation and Interpretation," Supplement to the *Bulletin of the History of Medicine*, vol. 1, Baltimore, Md.

Edwards, Catharine, 1993, *The Politics of Immorality in Ancient Rome*, Cambridge.

Eichenauer, Monika, 1988, *Untersuchungen zur Arbeitswelt der Frau in der römischen Antike*, Frankfurt a.M.

Elata-Alster, Gerda, 1985, "The King's Double Bind: Paradoxical Communication in the Parodos of Aeschylus' *Agamemnon*," *Arethusa* 18: 23–46.

Elkins, Stanley, 1976, *Slavery: A Problem in American Institutional and Intellectual Life*, 3rd edn, Chicago.

Ellickson, Robert C., 1991, *Order Without Law: How Neighbors Settle Disputes*, Cambridge, Mass.

Epstein, S., 1967, "A Sociological Analysis of Witch Beliefs in a Mysore Village," in *Magic, Witchcraft and Curing*, J. Middleton, ed., New York.

Evans, John K., 1991, *War, Women and Children in Ancient Rome*, London and New York.

Evans-Grubbs, Judith, 1993, "'Marriage More Shameful than Adultery': Slave-Mistress Relationships, 'Mixed Marriages,' and Late Roman Law," *Phoenix* 47: 125–54.

Ewans, Michael, 1982, "The Dramatic Structure of Agamemnon," *Ramus* 11: 1–15.

Fairbanks, C. H., 1984, "The Plantation Archaeology of the Southeastern Coast," *Historical Archaeology* 18: 1–14.

Fairweather, Janet, 1981, *Seneca the Elder*, Cambridge.

Fantham, Elaine, 1975, "Sex, Status and Survival in Hellenistic Athens: A Study of Women in New Comedy," *Phoenix* 29: 44–79.

—— 1991, "*Stuprum*: Public Attitudes and Penalties for Sexual Offences in Republican Rome," *Echos du Monde Classique* 10: 167–91.

Fantham, Elaine, Helene Peet Foley, Natalie Boymel Kampen, Sarah B. Pomeroy and H. Alan Shapiro, eds, 1994, *Women in the Classical World*, New York and Oxford.

Faraone, Christopher A., 1992, "Sex and Power: Male-Targetting Aphrodisiacs in the Greek Magical Tradition," *Helios* 19: 92–103.

Faulkner, William, 1986, *Absalom, Absalom! The Corrected Text*, New York.

Feichtinger, Barbara, 1991, "Zur Kassandra-Szene in Aischylos' *Orestie* und ihren poetischen Funktionen," *Würzburger Jahrbücher für die Altertumwissenschaft* 17: 49–67.

Ferguson, Leland, 1980, "Looking for the 'Afro' in Colono-Indian Pottery," in *Archaeological Perspectives on Ethnicity in America*, Robert L. Schuyler, ed., New York.

—— 1991, "Struggling with Pots in South Carolina," in *The Archaeology of Inequality*, Randall H. McGuire and Robert Paynter, eds., Oxford.

—— 1992, *Uncommon Ground: Archaeology and Early African America, 1650–1800*, Washington, DC.

Finley, M.I., 1968 [1960], "Was Greek Civilization Based on Slave labour?" *Historia* 8 (1959): 145–64, reprinted in *Slavery in Classical Antiquity: Views and Controversies*, M.I. Finley, ed., New York.

—— 1973, *The Ancient Economy*, Berkeley, Calif.

—— 1978, *The World of Odysseus*, rev. edn, New York.

—— 1980, *Ancient Slavery and Modern Ideology*, New York.

—— 1981, *Economy and Society in Ancient Greece*, Brent D. Shaw and Richard P. Saller, eds, London.

—— 1985, *Ancient History: Evidence and Models*, London.

Firmin-Didot, Ambroise, 1875, *Alde Manuce et L'Hellénisme à Venise*, Paris.

Fitzgerald, William, 1995, *Catullan Provocations: Lyric Poetry and the Drama of Position*, Berkeley, Calif.

Flach, Dieter, 1991, *Die sogenannte Laudatio Turiae*, Darmstadt.

Flory, Marleen B., 1978, "Family in 'Familia': Kinship and Community in Slavery," *American Journal of Ancient History* 3: 68–95.

Fogel, Robert W., 1989, *Without Consent or Contract: The Rise and Fall of American Slavery*, New York.

Foley, Helene P., 1995, "Penelope as Moral Agent," in *The Distaff Side. Representing the Female in Homer's Odyssey*, Beth Cohen, ed., New York and Oxford.

Fortenbaugh, William W., 1977, *Articles on Aristotle*, vol. 2, *Ethics and Politics*, Jonathan Barnes, Malcolm Schofield, and Richard Sorabji, eds, London.

Foucault, Michel, 1985, *The Use of Pleasure*, New York.

—— 1986, *The Care of the Self*, New York, trans. of *Le Souci de soi*, 1984, Paris.

—— 1986–88, *History of Sexuality*, 3 vols, New York.

Fox-Genovese, Elizabeth, 1988, *Within the Plantation Household: Black and White Women of the Old South*, Chapel Hill, NC.

Foxhall, Lin, 1996, "The Law and the Lady: Women and Legal Proceedings in Classical Athens," in *Greek Law in Its Political Setting: Justifications not Justice*, L. Foxhall and A.D.E. Lewis, eds., Oxford.

Fraenkel, Eduard 1922 [1960], *Plautinisches im Plautus*, Berlin, trans. F. Munari as *Elementi plautini in Plauto*, Florence.

—— 1937, *Die Kassandraszene der Orestie*, Stuttgart.

Frank, Tenney, 1933, *An Economic Survey of Ancient Rome I*, Baltimore, Md.

Frei-Stolba, Regula, 1987, "Klimadaten aus der römischen Republik," *Museum Helveticum* 44: 101–17.

Gabriel, Albert, 1952, *Phrygie II. La cité de Midas: Topographie; le site et les fouilles*, Paris.

Gagarin, Michael, 1975, "The Vote of Athena," *American Journal of Philology* 96: 121–7.
—— 1996, "The Torture of Slaves in Athenian Law," *Classical Philology* 91: 1–18.
Gager, John, 1992, *Curse Tablets and Binding Spells from the Ancient World*, Oxford.
Gardner, Jane F., 1986, *Women in Roman Law and Society*, Bloomington, Ind.
Gardner, Jane F. and Thomas Wiedemann, eds, 1991, *The Roman Household. A Sourcebook in Translation*, London.
Garlan, Yvon, 1988, *Slavery in Ancient Greece*, revised and expanded edn, Janet Lloyd, trans., Ithaca, NY and London.
Garrow, P. and T. Wheaton, 1985, "Acculturation and the Archaeological Record in the Carolinas," in *The Archaeology of Slavery and Plantation Life*, Tessa Singleton, ed., Orlando, Fla.
Gaspar, David Barry, 1996, "From 'The Sense of Their Slavery': Slave Women and Resistance in Antigua, 1632–1763," in *More Than Chattel: Black Women and Slavery in the Americas*, David Barry Gaspar and Darlene Clark Hine, eds, Bloomington, Ind.
Gauthier, Philippe, 1976, *Un commentaire historique sur les Poroi de Xénophon*, Geneva.
Genovese, Eugene D., 1976, *Roll, Jordan, Roll: The World the Slaves Made*, New York.
—— 1991, "'Our Family, White and Black': Family and Household in the Southern Slaveholders' World View," in *In Joy and in Sorrow: Women, Family, and Marriage in the Victorian South, 1830–1900*, Carol Bleser, ed., New York.
Gero, Joan M. and Margaret W. Conkey, eds, 1991, *Engendering Archaeology: Women and Prehistory*, Oxford.
Gibson, R.K., 1995, "How to Win Girlfriends and Influence Them: *Amicitia* in Roman Love Elegy," *Proceedings of the Cambridge Philological Society* 41: 62–82.
Gilchrist, Roberta, 1994, *Gender and Material Culture: The Archaeology of Religious Women*, London.
Giovannini, Maureen J., 1981, "Woman: A Dominant Symbol within the Cultural System of a Sicilian Town," *Man* 16: 408–26.
—— 1987, "Female Chastity Codes in the Circum-Mediterranean: Comparative Perspectives," in *Honor and Shame and the Unity of the Mediterranean*, David D. Gilmore, ed., Washington, DC.
Gleason, Maud W., 1990, "The Semiotics of Gender: Physiognomy and Self-Fashioning in the Second Century CE," in *Before Sexuality: The Construction of Erotic Experience in the Ancient Greek World*, D.M. Halperin, J.J. Winkler, F.I. Zeitlin, eds, Princeton, NJ.
—— 1995, *Making Men: Sophists and Self-Presentation in Ancient Rome*, Princeton, NJ.
Glew, Dennis G., 1987, "Publicans or Sinners? Why the Battaces Came to Rome in 102 BC," *Klio* 69: 122–37.
Gluckman, Max, 1956, *Custom and Conflict in Africa*, Oxford.
Gold, Barbara K., 1993, "'But Ariadne was never there in the first place': Finding the Female in Roman Poetry," in *Feminist Theory and the Classics*, Nancy Sorkin Rabinowitz and Amy Richlin, eds, New York and London.
Golden, Mark, 1984, "Slavery and Homosexuality at Athens," *Phoenix* 38: 162–78.
—— 1985, "*Pais*, 'Child,' and 'Slave,'" *L'Antiquité Classique* 54: 91–104.
—— 1990, *Children and Childhood in Classical Athens*, Baltimore, Md.
Goldhill, Simon, 1984, *Language, Sexuality, Narrative: the Oresteia*, Cambridge and New York.
—— 1986, *Reading Greek Tragedy*, Cambridge and New York.
Gomme, A.W. and F.H. Sandbach, 1973, *Menander: A Commentary*, Oxford.
Graf, Fritz, 1992, "Gestures and Conventions: The Gestures of Roman Actors and Orators," in *A Cultural History of Gesture*, Jan Bremmer and Herman Roodenburg, eds, Ithaca, NY.
Gratwick, A. S., 1982, "The Origins of Roman Drama," in *The Cambridge History of Classical Literature*, vol. 2., E.J. Kenney and W. Clausen, eds, Cambridge.
—— 1984, "Free or Not So Free? Wives and Daughters in the Late Roman Republic," in *Marriage and Property*, E.M. Craik, ed., Aberdeen.

Gray-Fow, M.J.G., 1988, "The Wicked Stepmother in Roman Literature and History: An Evaluation," *Latomus* 47: 741–57.

Green, Peter, trans., 1982, *Ovid. The Erotic Poems*, London.

Grenfell, Bernard P. and Arthur S. Hunt, eds and trans, 1908, *The Oxyrhynchus Papyri, Part VI*, Oxford.

Griffin, Jasper, 1985, *Latin Poets and Roman Life*, Chapel Hill, NC.

Grosz, Elizabeth, 1995, *Space, Time and Perversion: Essays in the Politics of Bodies*, New York.

Grubbs, Judith Evans, 1995, *Law and Family in Late Antiquity: The Emperor Constantine's Marriage Legislation*, Oxford.

Gruen, Erich, 1984, *The Hellenistic World and the Coming of Rome*, Berkeley, Calif.

—— 1990, *Studies in Greek Culture and Roman Policy*, Leiden.

—— 1992, *Culture and National Identity in Republican Rome*, Ithaca, NY.

Gschnitzer, Fritz, 1976, "Studien zur griechischen Terminologie der Sklaverei. Zweiter Teil: Untersuchungen zur Älteren, insbesondere homerischen sklaventerminologie," *Forschungen zur antiken Sklaverei* 7, Wiesbaden.

Guardì, T., ed., 1974, *Cecilio Stazio. I frammenti*, Palermo.

Gundersen, Joan Rezner, 1989, "The Double Bonds of Race and Sex: Black and White Women in a Colonial Virginia Parish," in *Women and the Family in a Slave Society*, Paul Finkelman, ed., *Articles on American Slavery* vol. 9, New York and London. First published in *Journal of Southern History* 52 (1986): 351–72.

Guyot, Peter, 1980, *Eunuchen als Sklaven und Freigelassene in der griechisch-römischen Antike*, Stuttgart.

Gwin, Minrose C., 1985a, *Black and White Women of the Old South: The Peculiar Sisterhood in American Literature*, Knoxville, Tenn.

—— 1985b, "Green-eyed Monsters of the Slavocracy: Jealous Mistresses in Two Slave Narratives," in *Conjuring: Black Women, Fiction, and Literary Tradition*, Marjorie Pryse and Hortense J. Spillers, eds, Bloomington, Ind.

Haley, Shelley P., 1993, "Black Feminist Thought and Classics: Re-membering, Re-claiming, Re-empowering," in *Feminist Theory and the Classics*, Nancy Sorkin Rabinowitz and Amy Richlin, eds, New York and London.

Hall, Edith, 1989, *Inventing the Barbarian: Greek Self-Definition through Tragedy*, Oxford.

Hallett, Judith P., 1973, "The Role of Women in Roman Elegy: Counter-Cultural Feminism," *Arethusa* 6: 103–24.

—— 1984, *Fathers and Daughters in Roman Society*, Princeton, NJ.

—— 1989, "Women as *Same* and *Other* in the Classical Roman Elite," *Helios* 16: 59–78.

Halperin, David, 1990, *One Hundred Years of Homosexuality*, New York and London.

Halporn, James W., 1993, "Roman Comedy and Greek Models," in *Theater and Society in the Classical World*, Ruth Scodel, ed., Ann Arbor, Mich.

Hammond, N.G.L., 1972, "Personal Freedom and its Limitations in the *Oresteia*," in *Aeschylus: A Collection of Critical Essays*, Marsh H. McCall, Jr, ed., Englewood Cliffs, NJ. First published in *Journal of Hellenic Studies* 85 (1965): 42–55.

Handley, E.W., 1968, *Menander and Plautus: A Study in Comparison*, London.

Hanson, Ann Ellis, 1975, "Hippocrates: Diseases of Women 1," *Signs* 1: 567–84.

—— 1987, "The Eight Months' Child and the Etiquette of Birth: *Obsit Omen!*" *Bulletin of the History of Medicine* 61: 589–602.

—— 1989, "Diseases of women in the epidemics," in *Die Hippokratischen Epidemien: Theorie–Praxis–Tradition. Verhandlungen des V Colloque International Hippocratique*, G. Badder and R. Winau, eds, Sudhoffs Archiv, Beihefte 27, Stuttgart.

—— 1990, "The medical writers' woman," in *Before Sexuality: The construction of Erotic Experience in the Ancient Greek World*, D.M. Halperin, J.J. Winkler, and F.I. Zeitlin, eds, Princeton, NJ.

—— 1991, "Continuity and Change: Three Case Studies in Hippocratic Gynecological Therapy and Theory," in *Women's History and Ancient History*, Sarah B. Pomeroy, ed., Chapel Hill, NC.

—— 1992, "Female Nature in the *Corpus Hippocraticum*," *Helios* 19: 31–71.

Harkins, Paul W., trans., 1963, *Galen on the Passions and Errors of the Soul*, Columbus, Ohio.

Harmon, D.P., 1978, "The Family Festivals of Rome," *Aufstieg und Niedergang der römischen Welt* II, 16.2, Berlin.

Harper, E.B., 1969, "Fear and the Status of Women," *Southwestern Journal of Anthropology* 25: 81–95.

Harriott, R.M., 1982, "The Argive Elders, the Discerning Shepherd and the Fawning Dog: Misleading Communication in the *Agamemnon*," *Classical Quarterly* 32: 9–17.

Harris, William V., 1982, "The Theoretical Possibility of Extensive Infanticide in the Graeco-Roman World," *Classical Quarterly* 32: 114–16.

Harrison, A.R.W., 1968. *The Law of Athens*, 2 vols, Oxford.

Hartsock, Nancy, 1983, "The Feminist Standpoint: Developing the Ground for a Specifically Feminist Historical Materialism," in *Discovering Reality: Feminist Perspectives on Epistemology, Metaphysics, Methodology, and Philosophy of Science*, Sandra Harding and Merrill B. Hintikka, eds, Dordrecht.

Haspels, C.H. Emilie, 1951, *Phrygie III: La cité de Midas. Céramique et trouvailles diverses*, Paris.

Hedrick, Charles, 1994, "The Zero Degree of Society: Aristotle and the Athenian Citizen," in *Athenian Political Thought and the Reconstruction of American Democracy*, J. Peter Euben, John R. Wallach and Josiah Ober, eds, Ithaca, NY.

Hegel, G.W.F., 1910, *Phenomenology of Mind*, J. B. Baillie, trans., London.

Helms, R., 1939, "Valerius Maximus, Seneca und die 'Exemplasammlung,'" *Hermes* 74: 130–54.

Hemelrijk, E.A., 1987, "Women's Demonstrations in Republican Rome," in *Sexual Asymmetry*, Josine Blok and Peter Mason, eds, Amsterdam.

Hemker, Julie, 1985, "Rape and the Founding of Rome," *Helios* 12: 41–7.

Henderson, John, 1991–2, "Wrapping Up the Case: Reading Ovid, *Amores*, 2.7 (+8)," *Materiali e Discussioni* 27: 38–88 and 28: 27–83.

Hester, D.A., 1981, "The Casting Vote," *American Journal of Philology* 102: 265–74.

Heubner, Friederike, 1981, "Kassandra in Aischylos' und Senecas' 'Agamemnon,'" *Aischylos und Pindar: Studien zu Werk und Nachwirkung*, Ernst Gunther Schmidt, ed., Berlin.

Hill, Matthew, 1987, "Ethnicity Lost? Ethnicity Regained? Information Functions of 'African Ceramics' in West Africa and North America," in *Ethnicity and Culture*, R. Auger, M.F. Glass, S. MacEachern and P.H. McCartney, eds, Calgary, Alberta.

Hoddinott, Ralph F., 1981, *The Thracians*, London.

Hoepfner, Wolfram and Ernst-Ludwig Schwandner, 1986, *Haus und Stadt im klassischen Griechenland*, Munich.

Holladay, A.J. and J.C.F. Poole, 1979, "Thucydides and the Plague of Athens," *Classical Quarterly* 29: 282–300.

Hopkins, Keith, 1978, *Conquerors and Slaves*, Cambridge.

—— 1983, *Death and Renewal*, Cambridge.

—— 1993, "Everyday life for the Roman Schoolboy," *History Today* 43: 25–30.

Hopper, R.J., 1953, "The Attic Silver Mines in the Fourth Century B.C.," *Annual of the British School at Athens* 48: 200–54.

Hornblower, Simon, 1987, *Thucydides*, London.

Horsfall, N., 1983, "Some Problems in the *Laudatio Turiae*," *Bulletin of the Institute of Classical Studies* 30: 85–98.

Hull, Gloria T., Patricia Bell Scott and Barbara Smith, eds, 1982, *All the Women are White, All the Blacks Are Men But Some of Us Are Brave: Black Women's Studies*, Old Westbury, NY.

Hunter, Virginia J., 1989, "Women's Authority in Classical Athens," *Echos du Monde Classique* 8: 39–48.

—— 1992, "Constructing the Body of the Citizen: Corporal Punishment in Classical Athens," *Echos du Monde Classique* 11: 271–91.

—— 1994, *Policing Athens*, Princeton, NJ.

Jacobs, Harriet, 1987, *Incidents in the Life of a Slave Girl*, in *The Classic Slave Narratives*, Henry Louis Gates, Jr, ed., New York.

Jameson, Fredric, 1971, *Marxism and Form*, Princeton, NJ.

Jameson, Michael H., 1990a, "Domestic Space in the Greek City-State," in *Domestic Architecture and the Use of Space*, Susan Kent, ed., Cambridge.

—— 1990b, "Private Space and the Greek City," in *The Greek City from Homer to Alexander*, Oswyn Murray and Simon Price, eds, Oxford.

Johnson, Matthew, 1993, *Housing Culture: Traditional Architecure in an English Landscape*, Washington, DC.

—— 1996, *An Archaeology of Capitalism*, Oxford.

Johnson, W.R., 1990, "Messalla's Birthday: The Politics of Pastoral," *Arethusa* 23: 95–113.

Johnston, Patricia. A., 1980, "*Poenulus* 1.2 and Roman Women," *Transactions of the American Philological Association* 110: 143–59.

Johnstone, Steven, 1994, "Virtuous Toil, Vicious Work: Xenophon on Aristocratic Style," *Classical Philology* 89: 219–40.

—— (forthcoming), *Disputes and Democracy: The Consequences of Litigation in Ancient Athens*, Austin, Tex.

Jones, J. Ellis, 1975, "Town and Country Houses of Attica in Classical Times," in *Thorikos and the Laurion in Archaic and Classical Times, Miscellanea Graeca* I, Herman Mussche, Paule Spitaels and F. Goemaere-De Poerck, eds, Ghent.

—— 1984/85, "Laurion: Agrileza, 1977–83: Excavations at a Silver-mine Site," *Archaeological Reports* 31: 106–23.

Jones, J. Ellis, L. Hugh Sackett and A.J. Graham, 1962, "The Dema House in Attica," *Annual of the British School at Athens* 57: 75–114.

Jones, J. Ellis, A.J. Graham, and L. Hugh Sackett, 1973, "An Attic Country House Below the Cave of Pan at Vari" *Annual of the British School at Athens* 68: 355–452.

Joplin, Patricia Klindienst, 1991, "The Voice of the Shuttle is Ours," in *Rape and Representation*, Lynn A. Higgins and Brenda R. Silver, eds, New York.

Joseph, Gloria and Jill Lewis, eds, 1981, *Common Differences: Conflicts in Black and White Feminist Perspectives*, New York.

Joshel, Sandra R., 1986, "Nursing the Master's Child: Slavery and the Roman Child-Nurse," *Signs* 12: 3–22.

—— 1992a, *Work, Identity and Legal Status at Rome*, Norman, Okla.

—— 1992b, "The Body Female and the Body Politic: Livy's Lucretia and Virginia," in *Pornography and Representation in Greece and Rome*, Amy Richlin, ed., New York and Oxford.

Just, R., 1985, "Freedom, Slavery and the Female Psyche," in *Crux: Essays in Greek History presented to G.E.M. de Ste. Croix*, P.A. Cartledge and F.D. Harvey, eds, London.

—— 1989, *Women in Athenian Law and Life*, London and New York.

Kakavoyiannis, Evangelos, 1989, "Archaiologikes erevnes stin Lavreotiki yia tin anakalypsin metalleftikon ergon kai metallourgikon enkatastaseon ton proklasikon chronon," *Athens Annals of Archaeology* 22: 71–88.

Kampen, Natalie, ed., 1996, *Sexuality in Ancient Art*, Cambridge.

Kaplan, Michael, 1990, *Greeks and the Imperial Court, from Tiberius to Nero*, New York and London.

Kaser, Max, 1955, *Das römische Privatrecht*, vol.1: *Das altrömische, vorklassische und klassische Recht*, 2nd edn, Munich.

Kaster, Robert, 1995, *Suetonius: De Grammaticis et Rhetoribus*, London.

Katz, Marilyn A., 1991, *Penelope's Renown: Meaning and Indeterminacy in the Odyssey*, Princeton, NJ.

—— 1994, "Ideology and 'the Status of Women' in Ancient Greece," in *Feminists Revision History*, Ann-Louise Shapiro, ed., New Brunswick, NJ.

Keith, A.M., 1994, "*Corpus Eroticum*: Elegiac Poets and Elegiac *Puellae* in Ovid's *Amores*," *Classical World* 88: 27–40.

Kennedy, Duncan, 1993, *The Arts of Love*, Cambridge.

Kirk, G.S., J.E. Raven and M. Schofield, 1983, *The Presocratic Philosophers*, Cambridge.

Klapp, Orrin E., 1962, *Heroes, Villains and Fools: The Changing American Character*, Englewood Cliffs, NJ.

Kleinman, Arthur, 1980, *Patients and Healers in the Context of Culture*, Berkeley, Calif.

Klotz, A., 1909, "Zur Literatur der Exempla und zur Epitoma Livii," *Hermes* 44: 198–214.

—— 1942, *Studien zu Valerius Maximus und den Exempla* (Sitzungsberichte der Bayerischen Akadamie, Phil.-Hist. Klasse 1942, 5).

Knapp, C., 1979, "References in Plautus and Terence to Plays, Players and Playwrights," *Classical Philology* 14: 35–55.

Kock, Theodor, ed., 1884–88, *Comicorum Atticorum Fragmenta*, 3 vols, Leipzig.

Kojève, Alexandre, 1969, *Introduction to the Reading of Hegel*, Allan Bloom, ed. and James H. Nichols, trans., New York.

Kolendo, J., 1981, "L'esclavage et la vie sexuelle des hommes libres à Rome," *Index* 10: 288–97.

Koniaris, George L., 1980, "An Obscene Word in Aeschylus (I)," *American Journal of Philology* 101: 42–4.

Konishi, Haruo, 1989, "Agamemnon's Reasons for Yielding," *American Journal of Philology* 110: 210–22.

Konstan, David, 1977, "The Social Theme in Plautus' *Aulularia*," *Arethusa* 10: 307–20.

—— 1978, "Plot and Theme in Plautus' *Asinaria*," *Classical Journal* 73: 215–21.

—— 1983, *Roman Comedy*, Ithaca, NY.

—— 1993, "The Young Concubine in Menandrian Comedy," in *Theater and Society in the Classical World*, Ruth Scodel, ed., Ann Arbor, Mich.

—— 1994a, "The Classics and Class Conflict," *Rethinking the Classical Canon*, *Arethusa* 27.1: 47–70.

—— 1994b, *Sexual Symmetry: Love in the Ancient Novel and Related Genres*, Princeton, NJ.

Kopytoff, Igor, 1986, "The Cultural Biography of Things: Commoditization As A Process," in *The Social Life of Things: Commodities in Cultural Perspective*, Arjun Appadurai, ed., Cambridge.

Körte, A., ed., 1938–59, *Menandri quae supersunt*, revised and augmented by A. Thierfelder, vol. I: *Reliquiae in papyris et membranis vetustissimis servatae*, 3rd edn, 1938, repr. with addenda 1955, 1957; vol. II: *Reliquiae apud veteres scriptores servatae*, 2nd edn, 1959, Leipzig.

Kovacs, David, 1987, "The Way of a God with a Maid in Aeschylus' *Agamemnon*," *Classical Philology* 82: 326–34.

Kudlien, Fridolf, 1968, "Platon als Zeuge medizinischer Praxis und das Problem der 'Sklavenärzte' in klassischer Zeit," *Die Sklaven in der griechischen Medizin der klassischen und hellenistischen Zeit*, part 3, Wiesbaden.

Labate, Mario, 1984, "L'arte di farsi amare: Modelli culturali e progetto didascalico nell'elegia ovidiana," *Biblioteca di Materiali e Discussioni* 2, Pisa.

Lacan, Jacques, 1966, "La signification du phallus," *Écrits* vol. 1, Paris.

Lain Entralgo, Pedro, 1970, *The Therapy of the Word in Classical Antiquity*, L. J. Rather and John M. Sharp, eds and trans, New Haven, Conn.

Lane, Eugene N., ed., 1996, *Cybele, Attis and Related Cults: Essays in Memory of J. J. Vermaseren*, Leider.

Lanham, Richard A., 1988, "The 'Q' question," *South Atlantic Quarterly* 87.4: 653–700.

Lattimore, Richmond, 1942, *Themes in Greek and Latin Epitaphs*, Urbana, Ind.

—— 1972, "Introduction to the *Oresteia*," in *Aeschylus: A Collection of Critical Essays*, Marsh H. McCall, Jr, ed., Englewood Cliffs, NJ. First published in 1953, *The Complete Greek Tragedies: Volume 1, Aeschylus*, David Grene and Richmond Lattimore, eds.

Lauffer, Siegfried, 1979, *Die Bergwerkssklaven von Laureion*, 2nd edn, Wiesbaden.

Law, John, 1994, *Organizing Modernity*, Oxford.

Lefkowitz, Mary R. and Maureen B. Fant, eds, 1992, *Women's Life in Greece and Rome*, 2nd edn, Baltimore, Md.

Leo, Friedrich, 1912, *Plautinische Forschungen*, 2nd edn, Berlin.

Leppin, Hartmut, 1992, *Histrionen. Untersuchungen zur sozialen Stellung von Bühnenkünstlern im Westen des römischen Reiches zur Zeit der Republik und des Prinzipats*, Bonn.

Lerner, Gerda, 1986, *The Creation of Patriarchy*, Oxford.

Lévi-Strauss, Claude, 1969, *The Elementary Structures of Kinship*, London.

Levine, Lawrence, 1977, *Black Culture and Black Consciousness: Afro-American Folk Thought from Slavery to Freedom*, New York.

Lévy, Edmond, 1989, "La théorie aristotélicienne de l'esclavage et ses contradictions," in *Mélanges Pierre Lévêque* 82, Marie Madeleine and Evelyne Geny, eds, Paris.

Lewis, Diane K., 1977, "A Response to Inequality: Black Women, Racism, and Sexism," *Signs* 3: 339–61.

Littré, E., 1839, *Hippocrates. Opera Omnia*, 10 vols, Paris.

Ljubenova, Veneta, 1984, "Einige Charakterzüge der thrakischen Kultur während des ersten Jahrtausends v. u. Z. im Gebiet der oberen Struma," *Dritter internationaler thrakologischer Kongress* II: 150–63.

Lloyd, G.E.R., ed., 1978, *Hippocratic Writings*, Harmondsworth, Middx., UK.

—— 1983, *Science, Folklore and Ideology: Studies in the Life Sciences in Ancient Greece*, Cambridge.

Lodge, Gonzalez, 1926, *Lexicon Plautinum*, 2 vols, Leipzig.

Lohmann, Hans, 1993, *Atene: Forschungen zu Siedlungs- und Wirtschaftsstruktur des klassischen Attika*, 2 vols, Weimar and Vienna.

Lonie, Iain M., 1981, *The Hippocratic Treatises "On Generation," "On the Nature of the Child," "Diseases IV": A Commentary*, Berlin.

Loraux, Nicole, 1986. *The Invention of Athens: The Funeral Oration in the Classical City*, Alan Sheridan, trans, Cambridge, Mass.

Lorde, Audre, 1984, *Sister Outsider*, Trumansburg, NY.

Lutz, Cora E., 1947, "Musonius Rufus: 'The Roman Socrates,'" *Yale Classical Studies* 10: 32–147.

Lyne, R.O.A.M., 1979, "Servitium Amoris," *Classical Quarterly* 29: 117–30.

MacBain, Bruce, 1982, *Prodigy and Expiation: A Study in Religion and Politics in Republican Rome*, Brussels.

MacCary, W.T., 1975, "The Bacchae in Plautus' *Casina*," *Hermes* 103: 459–63.

—— 1981, "The Comic Significance of Transvestism in Plautus, Shakespeare, Beaumarchais," *Letterature comparate, problemi e metodo: Studio in onore di Ettore Paratore* 1: 293–308.

MacCary, W.T. and M.M. Willcock, eds, 1976, *Plautus: Casina*, Cambridge.

McClintock, Anne, 1995, *Imperial Leather: Race, Gender and Sexuality in the Colonial Context*, New York and London.

McDonnell, M., 1983, "Divorce Initiated by Women in Rome: The Evidence of Plautus," *American Journal of Ancient History* 8: 54–80.

MacDowell, Douglas, 1978, *The Law in Classical Athens*, Ithaca, NY.

—— 1989, "The *Oikos* in Athenian Law," *Classical Quarterly* 39: 10–21.

MacEwen, Sally, ed., 1990, *Views of Clytemnestra, Ancient and Modern*, Lewiston, NY.

Macherey, Pierre, 1978, *A Theory of Literary Production*, Geoffrey Wall, trans., London.

McKay, Nellie Y., 1993, "Acknowledging Differences: Can Women Find Unity Through Diversity?" in *Theorizing Black Feminisms: The Visionary Pragmatism of Black Women*, Stanlie M. James and Abena P. A. Busia, eds, London and New York.

MacMullen, Ramsay, 1966, *Enemies of the Roman Order*, Cambridge, Mass.

—— 1986, "Personal Power in the Roman Empire," *American Journal of Philology* 107: 512–24.

Marwick, Max, ed., 1970, *Witchcraft and Sorcery*, Harmondsworth, Middx., UK.

Maslakov, G., 1984, "Valerius Maximus and Roman Historiography: A Study in the *Exempla* Tradition," *Aufstieg und Niedergang der römischen Welt* II.32.1.

Mather, Lynn and Barbara Yngvesson, 1980–81, "Language, Audience, and the Transformation of Disputes," *Law and Society Review* 15: 775–821.

Maurizio, Lisa, (forthcoming), "The Panathenaic Procession: Participatory Democracy on Display?" in *Democracy, Empire, and the Arts*, Kurt Raaflaub and Deborah Boedecker, eds, Cambridge, Mass.

Meridor, Ra 'anana, 1987, "Aeschylus' *Agamemnon* 944–57: Why Does Agamemnon Give In?" *Classical Philology* 82: 38–43.

Merry, Sally Engle, 1990, *Getting Justice and Getting Even: Legal Consciousness among Working-Class Americans*, Chicago.

Michelini, Ann N., 1979, "Characters and Character Change in Aeschylus: Klytaimestra and the Furies," *Ramus* 8: 153–64.

Middleton, John and E. H. Winter, eds, 1963, *Witchcraft and Sorcery in East Africa*, London.

Milcev, Ath, 1980, "Thrakische Siedlungen und Festungen in Bulgarien während des 1. Jahrtausends v. u. Z.," *Actes du IIe congrès international de thracologie* I: 337–64, Radu Vulpe, ed., Bucharest.

Miller, Margaret C., 1997, *Athens and Persia in the Fifth Century BC: A Study in Cultural Receptivity*, Cambridge.

Millett, Paul, 1991, *Lending and Borrowing in Ancient Athens*, Cambridge.

Mommsen, Theodor and Paul Krueger, eds, 1985, *Digest of Justinian*, A. Watson, trans., 4 vols, Philadelphia, Pa.

Monaco, L., 1984, "*Veneficia matronarum*: Magia, Medizina e Repressione," *Sodalitas: Scritti in onore di Antonio Guarino*, Naples.

Moore, John Hammond, ed., 1993, *A Plantation Mistress on the Eve of the Civil War: The Diary of Keziah Goodwyn Hopkins Brevard, 1860–1861*, Columbia, SC.

Morgan, M. Gwyn, 1973, "Villa Publica and Magna Mater: Two Notes on Manubial Building at the Close of the Second Century BC," *Klio* 55: 213–45.

Morris, Ian, 1987, *Burial and Ancient Society: The Rise of the Greek City-State*, Cambridge.

—— 1992, *Death-Ritual and Social Structure in Classical Antiquity*, Cambridge.

—— (forthcoming), *Archaeology as Cultural History: Words and Things in Ancient Greece*, Oxford.

Münzer, Friedrich, 1920, *Römische Adelsparteien und Adelsfamilien*, Stuttgart.

Murgatroyd, Paul, 1981 "*Servitium Amoris* and the Roman Elegists," *Latomus* 49: 589–606.

Murnaghan, Sheila, 1987, *Disguise and Recognition in the Odyssey*, Princeton, NJ.

—— 1988, "How a Woman Can Be More Like a Man: The Dialogue Between Ischomachus and His Wife in Xenophon's *Oeconomicus*," *Helios* 15: 9–22.

Murray, Stephen O., 1983, "Fuzzy Sets and Abominations," *Man* 18: 396–9.

Mussche, Herman, 1965, "Le quartier industriel," *Thorikos I, 1963*: 87–104, Brussels.

—— 1967, "Le quartier industriel," *Thorikos III, 1965*: 57–71, Brussels.

—— 1969, "Le quartier industriel," *Thorikos IV, 1966/1967*: 121–30, Brussels.

—— 1975, "Thorikos in Archaic and Classical times," in *Thorikos and the Laurion in Archaic and Classical Times, Miscellanea Graeca*, 1, Herman Mussche, Paule Spitaels, and F. Goemaere-De Poerk, eds, Ghent.

—— 1990, "Insula 3," *Thorikos IX, 1977/1982*: 12–62, Brussels.

Mussche, Herman, and Constantin Conophagos, 1973, "Ore-washing Establishments and Furnaces at Megala Pefka and Demoliaki," *Thorikos VI, 1969*: 60–72, Brussels.

Mussche, Herman, Paule Spitaels and F. Goemaere-De Poerck, eds, 1975, *Thorikos and the Laurion in Archaic and Classical Times, Miscellanea Graeca* 1, Ghent.

Myerowitz, Molly, 1985, *Ovid's Games of Love*, Detroit, Mich.

Nagler, Michael N., 1974, *Spontaneity and Tradition: A Study in the Oral Art of Homer*, Berkeley, Calif.

Neiiendam, K., 1992, *The Art of Acting: Iconographic Studies in Classical, Hellenistic and Byzantine Drama*, Copenhagen.

Nevett, Lisa, 1994, "Separation or Seclusion? Towards an Archaeological Approach to Investigating Women in the Greek Household in the Fifth to Third Centuries BC," in *Architecture and Order: Approaches to Social Space*, Michael Parker Pearson and Colin Richards, eds, London 98–112.

—— 1995, "Gender relations in the Classical Greek Household: The Archaeological Evidence," *Annual of the British School at Athens* 90: 363–81.

Nims, John Frederick, trans., 1959, *Andromache*, in *The Complete Greek Tragedies*, David Grene and Richmond Lattimore, eds, Chicago.

Nitzch K.W., 1873, *Die römische Annalistik von ihren ersten Anfängen bis auf Valerius Antias: Kritische Untersuchungen zur Geschichte der alteren Republik*, Berlin.

Noël Hume, Ivor, 1962, "An Indian Ware of the Colonial Period," *Quarterly Bulletin of the Archaeological Society of Virginia* 17: 2–14.

Nowicka, Maria, 1975, *Les maisons à tour dans le monde grec*, Bibliotheca Antiqua 15, Wroclaw.

Noy, D., 1991, "Wicked Stepmothers in Roman Society and Imagination," *Journal of Family History* 16: 345–63.

Ober, Josiah, 1989, Mass and Elite in Democratic Athens, Princeton, NJ.

—— 1996, *The Athenian Revolution*, Princeton, NJ.

—— (forthcoming), *The Athenian Critics of Popular Rule*, Princeton, NJ.

O'Brihym, Shawn, 1980, "The Originality of Plautus' *Casina*," *American Journal of Philology* 110: 81–103.

O'Donnell, James J., ed., 1992, *Augustine. Confessions*, 3 vols, Oxford.

Oliensis, Ellen, 1995, "Life After Publication: Horace *Epistles* I.20," *Arethusa* 28: 209–24.

Olstein, Katherine, 1975, "*Amores* I.3 and Duplicity as a Way of Love," *Transactions of the American Philological Association* 105: 241–57.

Orr, D.G., 1978, "Roman Domestic Religion: The Evidence of the Household Shrines," *Aufstieg und Niedergang der römischen Welt* II.16.2, Berlin.

Orser, Charles, 1996, *A Historical Archaeology of the Modern World*, New York.

Osborne, Robin G., 1985, *Demos: The Discovery of Classical Attika*, Cambridge.

—— 1987, *Classical Landscape with Figures*, London.

Osten, Hans H. von der, 1937, *The Alishar Hüyük: Seasons of 1930–32. Part 3*, Chicago.

Painter, Nell Irvin, 1994, "Three Southern Women and Freud: A Non-Exceptionalist Approach to Race, Class, and Gender in the Slave South," in *Feminists Revision History*, Ann-Louise Shapiro, ed., New Brunswick, NJ.

Parker, Holt, 1989, "Crucially Funny or Tranio on the Couch: The *Servus Callidus* and Jokes about Torture," *Transactions of the American Philological Association* 119: 235–48.

—— 1992, "Love's Body Anatomized: The Ancient Erotic Manuals and the Rhetoric of Sexuality," in *Pornography and Representation in Greece and Rome*, Amy Richlin, ed., New York and Oxford.

—— 1994, "Violent Femmes: The Figure of the Adulteress in The Roman Popular Imagination," Paper delivered at the Annual Meeting of the American Philological Association, Atlanta, Ga., December 1994.

—— 1997, "The Teratogenic Grid," in *Roman Sexualities*, Judith P. Hallett and Marilyn B. Skinner, eds, Princeton, NJ.

Parker Pearson, Michael, and Colin Richards, 1994a, "Ordering the World: Perceptions of Architecture, Space and Time," in Parker Pearson and Richards 1994c.

—— 1994b, "Architecture and Order: Spatial Representation and Archaeology," in Parker Pearson and Richards 1994c.

—— eds, 1994c, *Architecture and Order: Approaches to Social Space*, London.

Parry, Adam, 1969, "The Language of Thucydides' Description of the Plague," *Bulletin of the Institute of Classical Studies* 16: 106–18.

Patterson, Cynthia, 1991, "Marriage and the Married Woman in Athenian Law," in *Women's History and Ancient History*, Sarah B. Pomeroy, ed., Chapel Hill, NC.

Patterson, Orlando, 1982, *Slavery and Social Death*, Cambridge, Mass.

—— 1991, *Freedom in the Making of Western Culture*, New York.

Pearce, T., 1974, "The Role of the Wife as *Custos* in Ancient Rome," *Eranos* 72: 16–33.

Peristiany, J.G., ed., 1965, *Honour and Shame: The Values of Mediterranean Society*, London.

Pheterson, Gail, 1986, "Alliances Between Women: Overcoming Internalized Oppression and Internalized Domination," *Signs* 12: 146–60.

Pine-Coffin, R.S., trans., 1961, *Saint Augustine Confessions*, Harmondsworth, Middx., UK.

Pitt-Rivers, Julian, 1977, *The Fate of Shechem or The Politics of Sex: Essays in the Anthropology of the Mediterranean*, Cambridge.

Pomeroy, Sarah B., 1975, *Goddesses, Whores, Wives, and Slaves*, New York.

—— 1976, "The Relationship of the Married Woman to Her Blood Relatives in Rome," *Ancient Society* 7: 215–27.

—— 1994, *Xenophon: Oeconomicus*, Oxford.

—— ed., 1992, *Women's History and Ancient History*, Chapel Hill, NC.

Prag, A.J.N.W., 1985, *The Oresteia: Iconographic and Narrative Tradition*, Chicago.

—— 1991, "Clytemnestra's Weapon Yet Once More," *Classical Quarterly* 41: 242–6.

Prince, Mary, 1987, *History of Mary Prince: A West Indian Slave*, in *The Classic Slave Narratives*, Henry Louis Gates, Jr, ed., New York.

Pritchett, W. Kendrick, 1956, "The Attic Stelai, part II," *Hesperia* 25: 178–328.

—— 1961, "Five New Fragments of the Attic Stelai," *Hesperia* 30: 23–9.

Purcell, N., 1986, "Livia and the Womanhood of Rome," *Proceedings of the Cambridge Philological Society* 32: 78–105.

Questa, Cesare, 1982, "Maschere e funzioni nelle commedie di Plauto," *Materiali e discussioni per l'analisi dei testi classici* 8: 9–64.

Rabinowitz, Nancy Sonkin, 1981, "From Force to Persuasion: Aeschylus' *Oresteia* as Cosmogonic Myth," *Ramus* 10: 159–91.

Raboteau, Albert J., 1978, *Slave Religion: The "Invisible Institution" in the Antebellum South*, New York.

Ramming, Gerhard, 1973, "Die Dienerschaft in der Odyssee," dissertation, Erlangen.

Rawick, George P., 1972, *From Sundown to Sunup: the Making of the Black Community*, Westport, Conn.

Rawson, Beryl, ed., 1986, *The Family in Ancient Rome: New Perspectives*, Ithaca, NY.

—— ed., 1991, *Marriage, Divorce and Children in Ancient Rome*, Oxford.

Rawson, Elizabeth, 1971, "Prodigy Lists and the Use of the *Annales Maximi*," *Classical Quarterly*. 21: 158–69.

—— 1985, "Theatrical Life in Republican Rome and Italy," *Papers of the British School in Rome* 53: 97–113.

Reardon, B.P., ed., 1989, *Collected Ancient Greek Novels*, Berkeley, Calif.

Redman, Charles L., 1986, *Qsar es-Seghir: An Archaeological View of Medieval Life*, New York.

Rhodes, P.J., 1981, *A Commentary on the Aristotelian "Athenaion Politeia,"* Oxford.

Ribbeck, Otto, ed., 1873–97, *Scaenicae Romanorum Poesis Fragmenta*, 2 vols, 2nd edn, repr. 1962, Hildesheim.

Riccobono, S. *et al.*, eds., 1968–9, *Fontes Iuris Romani AnteIustiniani*, 3 vols, 2nd edn, Florence.

Richlin, Amy, 1992, *The Garden of Priapus: Sexuality and Aggression in Roman Humor*, rev. edn, New York.

—— 1993, "Not Before Homosexuality: The Materiality of the *Cinaedus* and the Roman Law against Love between Men," *Journal of the History of Sexuality* 3: 523–73.

—— 1997a, "Foucault's *History of Sexuality*: A Useful Theory for Women?" in *Foucault, Sexuality, and Classics*, David Larmour, Paul Allen Miller and Charles Platter, eds, Princeton, NJ.

—— 1997b, "Gender and Rhetoric: Producing Manhood in the Schools," in *Roman Eloquence*, William J. Dominik, ed., London.

Riddle, John, 1992, *Contraception and Abortion from the Ancient World to the Renaissance*, Cambridge, Mass.

Riedweg, C., 1993, "Menander in Rom. Beobachtungen zu Caecilius Statius, *Plocium* fr. I (136–53 Guardì)," in *Intertextualität in der griechisch-römischen Komödie*, N. W. Slater and B. Zimmermann, eds, Stuttgart.

Ritschl, F., 1845, *Parerga zu Plautus und Terenz*, Leipzig.

Robinson, David M. and J.W. Graham, 1938, *Excavations at Olynthus VIII: The Hellenic House*, Baltimore, Md.

Roman, Leslie G., 1993, "White is a Color! White Defensiveness, Postmodernism, and Anti-Racist Pedagogy," in *Race, Identity, and Representation in Education*, Cameron McCarthy and Warren Crichlow, eds, New York.

Romero, Mary, 1995, "Life as the Maid's Daughter: An Exploration of the Everyday Boundaries of Race, Class and Gender," in *Feminisms in the Academy*, Domna C. Stanton and Abigail J. Stewart, eds, Ann Arbor, Mich.

Rosaldo, Michelle Zimbalist, 1974, "A Theoretical Overview," in *Woman, Culture, and Society*, Michelle Zimbalist Rosaldo and Louise Lamphere, eds, Stanford, Calif.

Rose, Peter W., 1992, *Sons of the Gods, Children of Earth: Ideology and Literary Form in Ancient Greece*, Ithaca, NY and London.

Rubin, Gayle, 1975, "The Traffic in Women: Notes on the 'Political Economy' of Sex," in *Toward an Anthropology of Women*, R. R. Reiter, ed., New York.

Rutter, Jeremy, 1990, "Some Comments on Interpreting the Dark-Surfaced Handmade Burnished Pottery of the Thirteenth- and Twelfth-century BC Aegean," *Journal of Mediterranean Archaeology* 3: 29–49.

Saïd, Suzanne, 1984, "Grecs et barbares dans les tragédies d'Euripide: la fin des différences?" *Kléma* 9: 27–53.

Ste Croix, G.E.M., de, 1981, *The Class Struggle in the Ancient Greek World: from the Archaic Age to the Arab Conquests*, Ithaca, NY.

Saller, Richard P., 1984, "*Familia, Domus* and the Roman Concept of Family," *Phoenix* 38: 336–55.

—— 1986, "*Patria potestas* and the Stereotype of the Roman Family," *Continuity and Change* 1: 7–22.

—— 1987, "Slavery and the Roman Family," in *Classical Slavery*, M. I. Finley, ed., London.

—— 1988, "*Pietas*, Obligation and Authority in the Roman Family," in *Alte Geschichte und Wissenschaftsgeschichte. Festschrift für Karl Christ zum 65. Geburtstag*, P. Von Kneissel, ed., Darmstadt.

—— 1991, "Corporal Punishment, Authority and Obedience in the Roman Household," *Marriage, Divorce and Children in Ancient Rome*, Beryl Rawson, ed., Oxford.

—— 1994, *Patriarchy, Property and Death in the Roman Family*, Cambridge.

Sams, G. Kenneth, 1977, "Beer in the City of Midas," *Archaeology* 30: 108–15.

—— 1994, *The Gordion Excavations, 1950–1973: Final Reports IV. The Early Phrygian Pottery*, Philadelphia, Pa.

Samson, Ross, ed., 1990, *The Social Archaeology of Houses*, Edinburgh.

Sandbach, F.H., ed., 1990, *Menandri Reliquiae Selectae*, Oxford.

Santini, Carlo, 1988, "Letteratura Prodigiale e 'Sermo Prodigialis' in Giulio Ossequente," *Philologus*, 132: 210–26.

Santoro L'Hoir, F. S., 1992, *The Rhetoric of Gender Terms: 'Man', 'Woman', and the Portrayal of Character in Latin Prose*, Mnemosyne Suppl. 120, Leiden.

Schaps, David M., 1981, *Economic Rights of Women in Ancient Greece*, 2nd edn, Edinburgh.

Schenkkan, Robert, 1993, *The Kentucky Cycle*, New York.

Schenker, David J., 1991, "A Study in Choral Character: Aeschylus, *Agamemnon* 489–502," *Transactions of the American Philological Association*, 121: 63–73.

Schilling, Robert, 1982, *La religion Romaine de Venus depuis les origines jusqu'au temps d'Auguste*, 2nd edn, Paris.

Schlaifer, Robert, 1968, "Greek Theories of Slavery From Homer to Aristotle," in *Slavery in Classical Antiquity: Views and Controversies*, M. I. Finley, ed., New York.

Schmidt, Erich F., 1933, *The Alishar Hüyük. Seasons of 1928 and 1929. Part 2*, Chicago.

Schmidt, Peter Lebrecht, 1968, *Iulius Obsequens und das Problem der Livius-Epitome: Ein Beitrag zur Geschichte der lateinischen Prodigienliteratur* (=*Akademie der Wissenschaften und der Literatur, Abhandlungen der Geistes- und Sozialwissenschaftlichen Klasse*, Jahrgang 1968, NR. 5), Wiesbaden.

Schneider, J., 1971, "Of Vigilance and Virgins," *Ethnology* 10: 1–24.

Schuhmann, Elisabeth, 1976, "Ehescheidungen in den Komödien des Plautus," *Zeitschrift für Römische Geschichte* 93: 19–32.

—— 1977, "Der Typ der *uxor dotata* in den Komödien des Plautus," *Philologus* 112: 45–65.

—— 1978, "Zur sozialen Stellung der Frau in den Komödien des Plautus," *Altertum* 24: 97–105.

—— 1984, "Zur unterschiedlichen Characteristik von *uxores* und *meretrices* in den Komödien des Plautus," *Actes du VII Congrès Internationale des Associations d'Etudes Classiques*, 2 vols, J. Harmatta, ed., Budapest.

Schultz, Elizabeth, 1985, "Out of the Woods and into the World: A Study of Interracial Friendships between Women in American Novels," in *Conjuring: Black Women, Fiction, and Literary Tradition*, Marjorie Pryse and Hortense J. Spillers, eds, Bloomington, Ind.

Scott, Eleanor, 1997, "Introduction: On the Incompleteness of Archaeological Narratives," in *Invisible People and Processes: Writing Gender and Childhood into European Archaeology*, Jenny Moore and Eleanor Scott, eds, London.

Scott, James C., 1990, *Domination and the Arts of Resistance*, New Haven, Conn.

Scott, Joan W., 1988, *Gender and the Politics of History*, New York.

—— 1991, "The Evidence of Experience," *Critical Inquiry* 17: 773–97.

Scott, John A., 1918, "Eurynome and Eurycleia in the *Odyssey*," *Classical Quarterly* 12: 75–9.

Scullard, H.H., 1981, *Festivals and Ceremonies of the Roman Republic*. Ithaca, NY.

Sebesta, Judith Lynn, 1994, "Symbolism in the Costume of the Roman Woman," in *The World of Roman Costume*, Judith Lynn Sebesta and Larissa Bonfante, eds, Madison, Wisc.

Second Ephoreia, 1991, "Thorikos," *Archaiologikon Deltion* 46.2: 66–9.

Sedgwick, Eve Kosofsky, 1985, *Between Men: English Literature and Male Homosocial Desire*, New York.

Segal, Erich, 1987, *Roman Laughter: The Comedy of Plautus*, 2nd edn, New York.

Shackleton Bailey, D.R., 1956, *Propertiana*, Cambridge.

—— 1989, *Quintilianus: Declamationes Minores*, Stuttgart.

Sharrock, Alison, 1991, "Womanufacture," *Journal of Roman Studies* 81: 36–49.

Sharpe, Jenny, 1993, *Allegories of Empire: The Figure of Woman in the Colonial Text*, Minneapolis and London.

Shaw, Brent D., 1987, "The Family in Late Antiquity: The Experience of Augustine," *Past and Present* 115: 3–51.

Silverman, Kaja, 1984, "Dis-Embodying the Female Voice" in *Re-Vision: Essays in Feminist Film Criticism*, Mary Ann Doane, Patricia Mellencamp and Linda Williams, eds, Frederick, Md.

Singleton, Tessa, 1996, "The Archaeology of Slave Life," in *Images of the Recent Past: Readings in Historical Archaeology*, Charles E. Orser, ed., Walnut Creek, Calif.: 141–65.

Skinner, Marilyn B., 1989, "*Ut Decuit Cinaediorem*: Power, Gender and Urbanity in Catullus 10," *Helios* 16: 7–23.

—— 1993, *"Ego Mulier*: The Construction of Male Sexuality in Catullus," *Helios* 20: 107–30.

Slater, Niall W., 1985, *Plautus in Performance: The Theater of the Mind*, Princeton, NJ.

Slenes, Robert W., 1996, "Black Homes, White Homilies: Perceptions of the Slave Family and of Slave Women in Nineteenth-Century Brazil," in *More Than Chattel: Black Women and Slavery in the Americas*, David Barry Gaspar and Darlene Clark Hine, eds, Bloomington, Ind.

Smith, Jonathan Z., 1985, "What a Difference a Difference Makes," in *"To See Ourselves As Others See Us": Christians, Jews, "Others" in Late Antiquity*, Jacob Neusner and Ernest S. Frerichs, eds, Chico, Calif.

Smith, Valerie, 1989, "Black Feminist Theory and the Representation of the 'Other,'" in *Changing Our Own Words: Essays on Criticism, Theory, and Writing by Black Women*, Cheryl A. Wall, ed., New Brunswick, NJ.

Smith-Rosenberg, Carroll, 1986, "Writing History: Language, Class, and Gender," in *Feminist Studies/Critical Studies*, Teresa de Lauretis, ed., Bloomington, Ind.

Solomon, Jon, 1985, "Thucydides and the Recognition of Contagion," *Maia* 37: 121–3.

Sommerstein, A.H., 1989, "Again Klytaimestra's Weapon," *Classical Quarterly* 39: 296–301.

Spelman, Elizabeth V., 1988, *The Inessential Woman: Problems of Exclusion in Feminist Thought*, Boston, Mass.

Spitaels, Paul, 1978, "Insula 3. Tower Compound 1," *Thorikos VII, 1970/1971*: 39–110, Brussels.

Spivak, Gayatri, 1988, "Can the Subaltern Speak?" in *Marxism and the Interpretation of Culture*, Cary Nelson and Lawrence Grossberg, eds, Urbana and Chicago.

—— 1989, "Three Women's Texts and a Critque of Imperialism," in *The Feminist Reader: Essays in the Gender and the Politics of Literary Criticism*, Catherine Belsey and Jane Moore, eds, New York.

Spranger, P., 1984, "Historische Untersuchungen zu den Sklavenfiguren des Plautus und Terenz," *Forschungen zur antiken Sklaverei* 17, Stuttgart.

Stahl, Hans-Peter, 1985, *Propertius: 'Love' and 'War'*, Berkeley, Calif.

Stallybrass, Peter and Allon White, 1986, *The Politics and Poetics of Transgression*, Ithaca, NY and London.

Stärk, Ekkehardt, 1989, *Die Menaechmi des Plautus und sein griechisches Original*, Tübingen.

—— 1990, "Plautus' *uxores dotatae* im Spannungsfeld literarischer Fiktion und gesellschaftlicher Realität," in *Theater und Gesellschaft im Imperium Romanum*, J. Blänsdorf, ed., Tübingen.

Starr, Chester G., 1977, *The Economic and Social Growth of Early Greece: 800–500 BC*, New York.

Stavropoullos, Ph., 1938, "Ieratiki oikia en Zotiri tis Attikis," *Archaiologiki Ephemeris* 1938: 1–31.

Stehle, Eva, 1989, "Venus, Cybele, and the Sabine Women: The Roman Construction of Female Sexuality," *Helios* 16: 143–64.

Stetson, Erlene, 1982, "Studying Slavery: Some Literary and Pedagogical Considerations on the Black Female Slave," in *All the Women Are White, All the Blacks Are Men, But Some of Us Are Brave*, Gloria T. Hull, Patricia Bell Scott and Barbara Smith, eds, Old Westbury, NY.

Stevenson, Brenda E., 1996, "Gender Convention, Ideals, and Identity among Antebellum Virginia Slave Women," in *More Than Chattel: Black Women and Slavery in the Americas*, David Barry Gaspar and Darlene Clark Hine, eds, Bloomington, Ind.

Strathern, Marilyn, 1988, *The Gender of the Gift*. Berkeley, Calif.

Summers, Kirk, 1996, "Lucretius' Roman Cybele," in *Cybele, Attis and Related Cults: Essays in Honor of M. J. Vermaseren*, Eugene N. Lane, ed., Leiden.

Sussman, Lewis A., 1987, *The Major Declamations Ascribed to Quintilian*, Frankfurt am Main.

—— 1994, *The Declamations of Calpurnius Flaccus*, Leiden.

Syme, Ronald, 1939, *The Roman Revolution*, Oxford.

Temkin, O., 1953, "Greek Medicine as Science and Craft," *Isis* 44: 213–25.

Thalmann, William G., 1985a, "Speech and Silence in the *Oresteia* 1: *Agamemnon* 1025–1029," *Phoenix* 39: 99–118.

—— 1985b, "Speech and Silence in the *Oresteia* 2," *Phoenix* 39: 221–37.

Thomas, Garth, 1984, "Magna Mater and Attis," *Aufstieg und Niedergang der Römischen Welt*, 17.3, Berlin.

Todd, S. C., 1990, "The Purpose of Evidence in Athenian Courts," in *NOMOS: Essays in Athenian Law, Politics, and Society*, Paul Cartledge, Paul Millett and Stephen Todd, eds, Cambridge.

—— 1993, *The Shape of Athenian Law*, Oxford.

Treggiari, Susan, 1973, "Domestic Staff in the Julio-Claudian Period," *Histoire sociale* 6: 241–55.

—— 1979, "Questions of Women Domestics in the Roman West," *Schiavitù, manomissione e classi dipendenti nel mondo antico* (Università degli studi di Padova. Pubblicazioni dell'Istituto di storia antica 13: 185–201), Rome.

—— 1991, *Roman Marriage: Iusti Coniuges from the Time of Cicero to the Time of Ulpian*, Oxford.

Turner, Victor, 1974, *Dramas, Fields, and Metaphors*. Ithaca, NY.

Tyrrell, Wm Blake, 1980, "An Obscene Word in Aeschylus (II)," *American Journal of Philology* 101: 44–6.

—— 1984, *Amazons: A Study in Athenian Mythmaking*, Baltimore, Md.

Velkov, V., 1964, "Zur Frage der Sklaverei auf der Balkanhalbinsel während der Antike," *Études balkaniques* 1: 125–38.

Vermaseren, M. J., 1977a, *Corpus Cultus Cybelae Attidisque (CCCA): III. Italia-Latium*, Leiden.

—— 1977b, *Cybele and Attis: The Myth and the Cult*, A.M.H. Lemmers, trans., London.

Vernant, Jean-Pierre, 1965, "Hestia-Hermès: Sur l'expression religieuse de l'espace et du mouvement chez les Grecs," in *Mythe et pensée chez les Grecs*, Paris.

Vernon, R., 1988, "17th-century Apalachee Colono-ware as a Reflection of Demography, Economics, and Acculturation," *Historical Archaeology* 22: 76–82.

Vernon, R., and A. S. Cordell, 1993, "A Distributional and Technological Study of Apalachee Colono-ware from San Luis de Talimali," in *The Spanish Missions of La Florida*, B. G. McEwan, ed., Gainesville, Fla.

Versnel, H. S., 1987, "Wife and Helpmate: Women of Ancient Athens in Anthropological Perspective," in *Sexual Asymmetry*, Josine Blok and Peter Mason, eds, Amsterdam.

Veyne, Paul, 1988, *Roman Erotic Elegy*, David Pellauer, trans., Chicago.

Vickers, Brian, 1988, *In Defence of Rhetoric*, Oxford.

Vickery, Amanda, 1993, "Women and the World of Goods: a Lancashire Consumer and Her Possessions, 1751–81," in *Consumption and the World of Goods*, John Brewer and Roy Porter, eds, London.

Vidal-Naquet, Pierre, 1986, *The Black Hunter: Forms of Thought and Forms of Society in the Greek World*, Andrew Szegedy-Maszak, trans., Baltimore, Md.

—— 1986, "Slavery and the Rule of Women in Tradition, Myth and Utopia," in *Myth, Religion, and Society*, R.L. Gordon, ed., Cambridge and Paris.

Vilatte, Sylvie, 1986, "La femme, l'esclave, le cheval, et le chien: les emblèmes du *kalòs kagathós* Ischomaque," *Dialogues d'Histoire Ancienne* 12: 271–94.

Vogt, Joseph, 1975, *Ancient Slavery and the Ideal of Man*, Thomas Wiedemann, trans., Cambridge, Mass.

Walbank, F.W., 1959–79, *A Historical Commentary on Polybius*, Oxford.

Walker, Susan, 1983, "Women and Housing in Classical Greece: The Archaeological Evidence," in *Images of Women in Classical Antiquity*, Averil Cameron and Amélie Kuhrt, eds, London.

Wallace-Hadrill, Andrew, 1985, "Propaganda and Dissent? Augustan Moral Legislation and the Love-Poets," *Klio* 67: 180–4.

Walters, K.R., 1993, "Women and Power in Classical Athens," in *Women's Power, Man's Game: Essays on Classical Antiquity in Honor of Joy K. King*, Mary DeForest, ed., Wauconda, Ill.

Ware, Vron, 1994, "Moments of Danger: Race, Gender, and Memories of Empire," in *Feminists Revision History*, Ann-Louise Shapiro, ed., New Brunswick, NJ.

Watson, Alan, 1965, "The Divorce of Carvilius Ruga," *Tijdschrift voor Rechtsgeschiedenis* 33: 38–50.

—— 1967, *The Law of Persons in the Later Roman Republic*, Oxford.

—— 1971, *Roman Private Law Around 200 BC*, Oxford.

—— 1975, *Rome of the XII Tables*, Princeton, NJ.

Watson, Patricia A., 1995, *Ancient Stepmothers: Myth, Misogyny and Reality*, Leiden.

Weber, Max, 1946, "The Sociology of Charismatic Power," and "The Social Psychology of the World Religions," in *From Max Weber: Essays in Sociology*, H.H. Gerth and C. Wright, eds and trans, Oxford.

Webster, T.B.L., 1960, *Studies in Menander*, 2nd edn, Manchester.

Wessner, P., ed., 1902, *Aeli Donati quod fertur Commentum Terenti*, 2 vols, Leipzig.

Westermann, William Linn, 1968, "Slavery and the Elements of Freedom in Ancient Greece," in *Slavery in Classical Antiquity: Views and Controversies*, M.I. Finley, ed., New York.

Whallon, William, 1980, *Problem and Spectacle: Studies in the Oresteia*, Heidelberg.

White, Peter, 1993, *Promised Verse: Poets in the Society of Augustan Rome*, Cambridge Mass.

Wickert-Micknat, Gisela, 1983, "Unfreiheit im Zeitalter der homerischen Epen," *Forschungen zur antiken Sklaverei* 16, Wiesbaden.

Wiedemann, Thomas, 1981, *Greek and Roman Slavery*, London.

—— 1987, *Slavery: Greece and Rome, New Surveys in the Classics* 19, Oxford.

Wiles, David, 1989, "Marriage and Prostitution in Classical New Comedy," in *Themes in Drama* 11 (*Women in Theater*): 31–48.

Wills, Gary, 1996, "John Wayne's Body," *The New Yorker*, August 19, 38–49.

Williams, Gordon, 1958, "Some Aspects of Roman Marriage Ceremonies and Ideals," *Journal of Roman Studies* 48: 16–29.

Winkler, John J., 1990, *The Constraints of Desire*, New York.

Winnington-Ingram, R. P., 1948, "Clytemnestra and the Vote of Athena," *Journal of Hellenic Studies* 68: 130–47.

Winterbottom, Michael, 1964, "Quintilian and the *Vir Bonus*," *Journal of Roman Studies* 54: 90–7.

Wistrand, Erik, 1976, *The So-Called Laudatio Turiae*, Goteborg.

Wood, Ellen Meiksins, 1988, *Peasant-Citizen and Slave: The Foundations of Athenian Democracy*, London.

Wood, Peter H., 1974, *Black Majority*, New York.

Wright, James, 1974, "Dancing in Chains: The Stylistic Unity of the Comoedia Palliata," *Papers and Monographs of the American Academy in Rome* 25.

Wright, Michelle Diane, 1991, "African American Sisterhood: The Impact of the Female Slave Population on American Political Movements," *The Western Journal of Black Studies* 15: 32–45.

Wyke, Maria, 1987 "Written Women: Propertius' *Scripta Puella*," *Journal of Roman Studies* 77: 47–61.

—— 1989, "Mistress and Metaphor in Augustan Elegy," *Helios* 16: 25–47.

—— 1994a, "Taking the Woman's Part: Engendering Roman Love Elegy," *Ramus* 23: 110–28.

—— 1994b, "Woman in the Mirror: The Rhetoric of Adornment in the Roman World," in *Women in Ancient Societies: An Illusion of the Night*, Léonie J. Archer, Susan Fischler and Maria Wyke, eds, New York.

Yaron, R., 1962, "Minutiae on Roman Divorce," *Tijdschrift voor Rechtsgeschiedenis* 30: 243–51.

Yentsch, Anne E., 1994, *A Chesapeake Family and Their Slaves. A Study in Historical Archaeology*, Cambridge.

Yngvesson, Barbara and Lynn Mather, 1983, "Courts, Moots, and the Disputing Process," in *Empirical Theories about Courts*, Keith O. Boyum and Lynn Mather, eds, New York.

Young, John H., 1956, "Studies in South Attica: Country Estates at Sounion," *Hesperia* 25: 122–46.

Young, Rodney S., 1951, "An Industrial District of Ancient Athens," *Hesperia* 20: 135–288.

Zagagi, Netta, 1980, *Tradition and Originality in Plautus: Studies of the Amatory Motifs in Plautine Comedy*, Göttingen.

Zeitlin, Froma, 1981, "Travesties of Gender and Genre in Aristophanes' *Thesmophoriazeusae*," *Critical Inquiry* 8: 301–28.

—— 1984, "The Dynamics of Misogyny: Myth and Mythmaking in the *Oresteia*," in *Women in the Ancient World: The Arethusa Papers*, John Peradotto and J. P. Sullivan, eds, Albany, New York.

—— 1996, *Playing the Other: Gender and Society in Classical Greek Literature*, Chicago.

INDEX

Absalom, Absalom! (Faulkner) 47
Achilles: quarrel with Agamemnon 30;
    sacrificed slave for honor 61
Achilles Tatius: *Leucippe and Clitophon* 35
Acilius 164, 168
actors 95, 140–2
Adelphasium 95
Aegisthus 41
Aemilius Lepidus, Marcus 166
Aemilius Scaurus, Mamercus 166
Aeschylus: Greek nationalism 44; *Oresteia*
    39–47, 51; *Women of Aetna* 44
Agamemnon: Clytemnestra's jealousy
    45–6; Hecuba sees as enslaved to mob
    62; honor permanently damaged 30;
    quarrel with Achilles 30
Agamemnon (Aeschylus) 6, 39–47;
    Cassandra's language 40–5;
    Clytemnestra and Cassandra 6, 36,
    39–47; Clytemnestra's expected
    acceptance 51; foreignness in
    Clytemnestra's speech 46; history and
    plot 39
age: alters relations 18–19, 110–13, 124;
    determines form of slavery 61
Agrippina the Elder 121
Airs, Waters, Places (Hippocratic Corpus)
    77
Aldus Manutius 236, 242, 250
Amasia Sentia 168
Amores (Ovid) 175–6, 182–4
Anatolia 203–4
Anderson, William 94
Andromache: and Hermione 63–6
Andromache (Euripides) 59, 62–6
Annaeus Cornutus, Lucius 158

Antipater, Coelius 153
Antistia Pollitta 167, 168
Antistius 166
Antius Restio 157, 159
Antonius, Marcus 159
Apollodorus 233–4
Appian: loyal wives 164, 165, 166, 168;
    on slaves and social breakdown 155–6;
    tales of loyal slaves 158–60, 162
Appius Claudius 100
Apuleius: bad-tempered women 123;
    Metamorphoses 119, 122
Aquilius, Manius 240
Arausio, battle of 241
archaeology: gender in domestic space
    195–6; housing 205–8; information on
    women and slaves 19–20, 193–7;
    invisibility of women and slaves
    219–20; male and female space
    214–18; material culture 208–10;
    pottery 197–8, 203–5
Aristogiton 17, 18
Ariston 229
Aristophanes: *Ecclesiazousae* 131
Aristotle 69; barbarians 17; dangers to
    young mothers 80; gender as a
    privilege of the free 231; on Greek
    advance in view of women 211–12;
    personal nature of slaves 3; rational
    ability of male slaves 71; *Rhetoric* 131,
    133; slave as animate property 14;
    slavery as natural and conventional 3,
    57–9; on women and slaves 1, 38;
    women inferior to men 70
Arria 164–5, 165–6
Arria the Younger 167